——— NARRATIVES OF GREATER MEXICO ———

NARRATIVES OF GREATER MEXICO

Essays on Chicano Literary History, Genre, and Borders

HÉCTOR CALDERÓN

UNIVERSITY OF TEXAS PRESS

AUSTIN

Permissions acknowledgments can be found on page 270.

Requests for permission to reproduce material from this work should be sent to
Permissions, University of Texas Press, P.O. Box 7819, Austin, TX 78713–7819.

⊚The paper used in this book meets the minimum requirements of ANSI/NISO
Z39.48–1992 (R1997) (Permanence of Paper).

LIBRARY OF CONGRESS CATALOGING-IN-PUBLICATION DATA

Calderón, Héctor.
Narratives of Greater Mexico : essays on Chicano literary history,
genre, and borders / Héctor Calderón.

p.   cm. — (CMAS history, culture, & society series)
Includes bibliographical references and index.

ISBN 978-0-292-70582-1

1. American literature—Mexican American authors—History and criticism.
2. American literature—20th century—History and criticism. 3. American
literature—Mexican influences. 4. Literary form—History—20th century.
5. Mexican Americans—Intellectual life. 6. Mexican Americans in literature.
7. Narration (Rhetoric) I. Title. II. Series.
PS153.M4C248 2004
810.9'86872—dc22
2004008744

Map on page ii is from Alvaro del Portillo y Diez Solano, *Descubrimientos y
exploraciones en las costas de California*, Serie 2.a: Monografías, Num. 7 (Madrid:
Publicaciones de la Escuela de Estudios Hispano-Americanos de Sevilla, 1947).

A la memoria de Amada Triana (1888–1962),
quien mantuvo vivos sus recuerdos de Zacatecas en su nieto,
Emir Rodríguez Monegal (1921–1984), quien me abrió un mundo
nuevo de literatura, y Américo Paredes (1915–1999), who gave
me the knowledge of Greater Mexico/América Mexicana.
Storytellers all.

CONTENTS

ACKNOWLEDGMENTS

Many friends and students have assisted me in making this book possible. For over twenty-five years, Ramón and José David Saldívar have been colleagues (more like brothers, actually) whose work and encouragement have inspired me to continue my own projects. Other colleagues of my generation—Norma Alarcón, Gloria Anzaldúa, Erlinda Gonzales-Berry, José E. Limón, Genaro Padilla, Sonia Saldívar-Hull, and Rosaura Sánchez—will find explicit and implicit references to their work in this book. I have also found valuable to the argument of this book the writings of my students, Bridget Kevane, Juanita Heredia, and Sandra Pérez-Linggi.

Through the years, I have relied on the diligence of a group of student research assistants at the University of California, Los Angeles (UCLA): Pete Barraza, Marisol Castillo, Juanita Heredia, Eleuteria Hernández, Molly Hoff, Bridget Kevane, Jeff Lamb, José Rósbel López-Morín, Marisol Pérez, Sandra Pérez-Linggi, and Melissa Strong Carrillo. To them goes my gratitude for their persistence in always returning to my office with that item requested by their professor.

The research for this book has taken me to institutions near and far from my home. The letters and manuscripts in the Tomás Rivera Archives at the Tomás Rivera Library, University of California, Riverside, were indispensable for understanding the genesis of ". . . y no se lo tragó la tierra." It was, indeed, a great stroke of luck (or destiny) when one of my former students, Joel Simon from Amherst, led me in 1987 to Marco Acosta. I gained a great deal of insight into the life and works of Oscar Zeta Acosta through conversations with his son, Marco. The photocopied material that Marco gave me in San Francisco was later enhanced by documents from the Oscar Zeta Acosta Collection at the University of California, Santa Barbara.

New Mexico has become a place to which I have returned numerous times both for research and to renew friendships. At the University of New Mexico in Alburquerque, I used collections in the Zimmerman Library. Teresa and Tony Márquez and Erlinda Gonzales-Berry were wonderful hosts during my visits. And my heartfelt thanks especially to Rudy and Patricia Anaya for offering me their Jémez Springs Casita during the final stages of this book. In Santa Fe, I came away with materials from the State Historical Archives and the Fray Angélico Chávez Santa Fe History Library. Orlando Romero, the Chávez Librarian, saved me a great deal of time by leading me to Mrs. Anita Gonzales Thomas, the eldest member of Santa Fe's La Sociedad Folklórica founded by Cleofas M. Jaramillo. Mrs. Thomas was kind enough to grant me a lengthy interview as well as to send me copies of the Sociedad's founding documents.

On two occasions, I traveled to Austin, Texas, where Américo Paredes and Rolando Hinojosa granted me interviews. Through the years, Rolando has never failed to respond—via letters and e-mail—to my requests for assistance. On my second research visit to the Austin campus of the University of Texas in 1996, Gilberto Cárdenas, Director of the Center for Mexican-American Studies, provided me with both a technician and equipment to videotape Américo Paredes. Although in failing health, Américo was more than cooperative and sat before the camera at his home for a two-and-a-half-hour interview. Laura Gutiérrez, Librarian at the Bentsen Collection, allowed me to photocopy her collection of Paredes news clippings. At the Castañeda Library, I discovered Paredes's dissertation, the original version of *"With His Pistol in His Hand."*

Since 1986 when we first met at Yale, Sandra Cisneros has given me manuscript copies of her work-in-progress as well as crucial information concerning her life and work. In the final stages of this book, she was always accommodating to my requests through mail and, most recently, e-mail. Thanks also to la Sandra for the emergency tortillas while I was at Yale.

Trips to northern Zacatecas—especially Sombrerete and Chalchihuites—and to Querétaro have greatly enhanced my understanding of the colonial settlements of Nuevo México and Nuevo Santander. La Licenciada María del Socorro Correa-M., Cronista de la Ciudad de

Sombrerete, and her mother were kind enough to open el portón to their patio interior and sit with me one Sunday afternoon in their sala de espera and confirm my grandmother's tales of Revolutionary Mexico and answer my questions on the settlement of la Nueva México.

Over the years, I have had the support of my parents and my six sisters. Some very dear friends have listened to me across the table, on the telephone, and through e-mail as I tried to explain the progress of the book. Ellas y ellos know who they are and I thank them. Melissa, Bridget, and José, thanks for reading the manuscript. You were my guides. My daughters Catherine's and Christine's sense of social justice has been inspirational.

Uclatlán, Califas

INTRODUCTION

Lt was a dark and stormy night in New Haven, Connecticut, when I informed Ramón Saldívar in Austin, Texas, that I was thinking of writing a book on Chicano literature. "Great," he said. Little did I know what a difficult task that would be. The world has changed since that phone conversation of long ago. We no longer inhabit the twentieth century and the field of Chicana and Chicano literary studies is no longer an endeavor relegated solely to regional or marginal status. This literature and its criticism are in many ways links between dissimilar cultural traditions on both sides of the international divide. Scholars in comparative American (in the broadest sense of the term) literary and cultural studies are now following the lead of their Chicana and Chicano colleagues in seeing the necessity of linking American ethnic, American, and Latin American literatures. At the beginning of the twenty-first century, we are aware of our basic nepantilismo, that in-between state where cultures converge. Because of rapidly changing demographics, market penetration, an international media based largely in the United States, and the Internet, we will see more interaction in cultural and artistic spheres across the borders of the Américas.

My project is less ambitious than some of the recent studies of the literatures of the Américas; mine is more local and historical. This is a study of major Mexican American narrative forms from 1958 through 2001 through the works of Américo Paredes, Rudolfo A. Anaya, Tomás Rivera, Oscar Zeta Acosta, Cherríe L. Moraga, Rolando Hinojosa-Smith, and Sandra Cisneros. I present this book knowing full well that I am crossing academic borders. Early on in the history of the field, the

Modern Language Association bestowed on this new literature American status. Although I am a scholar of Chicano literature, an Americanist, I have always belonged to departments of Spanish and Portuguese because of my training, teaching, and research in Latin American literature. With this book, I hope to add to the growing body of work published recently by my colleagues in English, ethnic studies, and American studies. However, from the other side of the disciplinary divide, I would offer this book as a revisionary endeavor, altering traditional Mexican studies. We can no longer continue to think of Mexican people and culture in the United States as if they were completely dislocated from the nation of Mexico, its culture and artistic traditions. Indeed, the reader will find as the book progresses toward an ending, that the interrelatedness of Mexicans on both sides of the border is inescapable.

For the better part of my career, many of my readings of Chicana and Chicano writers have been filtered through the concept of genre. I have continued in that direction; however, genres are now more "thickly" described, set against their historical and cultural milieux. Genres, invoking Fredric Jameson as a guide, are useful insofar as they relate to the social worlds that give rise to them. Though this study is based on a limited number of writers, these writers have chosen a wide variety of narrative forms. Through autobiography, novel, chronicle, satire, romance, the narrative of the Mexican Revolution, telenovelas, folktales, and corridos, I explore the consequences derived from the choices that writers themselves have made regarding a specific narrative form.

In some chapters, I have made use of secondary sources—my own travel diaries, conversations, interviews, writers' personal papers, correspondence, and e-mail exchanges—as well as the more traditional critical studies. I hope that this personal and critical strategy will shed new light on the interrelations between writer and work. I see this strategy contributing not only to literary history but also to the wider text of history linking Mexico and the United States.

Readers of Chicano literary studies may be surprised at the title of this book. "Greater Mexico" is a term most associated with the work of Américo Paredes and José E. Limón. Though linked with cultural studies of Texas, and especially cultural conflict along the Lower Río Grande Valley, it is a term that is for me broadly embracive. Over the course of my years in teaching, I have gravitated to the term. Though Paredes coined the term in his 1958 landmark study, *"With His Pistol in His Hand,"* what I consider its Spanish equivalent, América Mexicana, made its appearance centuries before. In a seventeenth-century map, Nicolás de Cardona, who sailed the interior of the Baja California peninsula in 1615, names the area from the Isthmus of Tehuantepec to what is now Oregon across to the Mississippi América Mexicana. A smaller section of a misshapen North America is represented as Nova Francia; there is no Nova Inglaterra on the map. The cultural diaspora that began with the Spanish conquest of Mexico in Veracruz in 1519, that spread to northern Mexico in Zacatecas, Querétaro, and Nuevo León in the 1540s–1570s, to la Nueva México in the 1590s, to Texas and California in the 1740s–1780s, and is still spreading today across the southern and eastern United States offers the best understanding of Mexican American or Chicano literature at the juncture of two centuries.

I do not intend to displace the term "Chicano." It is part of a historical moment that many of my generation lived through. History will record the Chicano Movement as a brief period of Mexican American social and cultural history. And its brevity does not diminish its full impact in all spheres of public life. The Movement changed the way Mexican Americans viewed themselves, the way mexicanos viewed their brethren across the border. It is part of a larger process of history that goes back to the nineteenth century. The Chicanos of the 1960s and 1970s were not the first to be concerned with issues of identity and cultural conflict. Someone like Paredes writing in isolation as early as the 1930s was fully aware of this fact.

I was a Mexican before I became a Chicano. Mexican—culture, language, religion—was the way I viewed myself growing up on the Alta and Baja California border in Calexico-Mexicali. Mexican is the way that Anglo-American society of that time (and still today) viewed me. The Chicano Movement gave historical credence and cultural dignity to my basic Mexicanness—Spanish-speaking, working-class, and mestizo. I am not alone in reasserting cultural ties with Mexican culture. In recent works, older and younger Mexican American writers are affirming their diversity within their Mexicanness. This is one of the great lessons learned in writing this book—the diversity of political views, geographic settings, and cultural traditions of Mexican culture in the United States. In the past century, studies by U.S. Mexicanista scholars have stressed "lo mexicano" and "mexicanidad," relying essentially on cultural identities from south of the border and, indeed, defined and promoted by intellectuals from the center, Mexico City. In the year 2003, I think that we can no longer ignore the many manifestations of Mexican culture both within and outside the political borders of the Mexican nation-state. The writers in this study lived through important U.S. historical moments of the twentieth century—the Great Depression, World War II, the Korean War, the civil rights movement, the Chicano Movement, the feminist movement, gay and lesbian liberation. The traditional notions of "lo mexicano," "mexicanidad," and the Mexican patria have been transformed, at times radically altered, by the writers in this study. We are in many ways, taking from a term coined by Sandra Cisneros, American Mexicans. There are more than twenty million American Mexicans traveling back and forth across political and cultural borders. The writers in this study have contributed to the history of these border crossings.

Américo Paredes was born in 1915 on the border in Brownsville, Texas, and learned to sing and play Mexican corridos at an early age in Tamaulipas, México. That early childhood education was transformed into scholarly studies of what Paredes termed "Greater Mexico," Mexico in a cultural sense. Paredes was drafted and served his country in World War II as a journalist in Asia. After covering the war crimes trials in Japan, the mature Paredes returned to Texas through Matamoros, México, to put on trial the history of Texas in his doctoral dissertation, which was published as *"With His Pistol in His Hand."* "Redefining the Borderlands" traces a century of Southwest studies from Charles F. Lummis, through Nina Otero de Warren, Cleofas M. Jaramillo, and Aurelio M. Espinosa to the emergence of Paredes as a public intellectual, as one of the founders of Mexican American studies.

In the sixteenth century, la Nueva México was the first mestizo settlement of what was to become the United States. Antonio de Espejo named this territory with the hope of finding another México, another fabled Tenochtitlán. As a result of U.S. cultural domination, New Mexicans have been caught since the late nineteenth century in a struggle for identity between Old Spain and Nueva España, Old Mexico and la Nueva México. Rudolfo A. Anaya was born in 1937 in the Spanish-speaking village of Pastura in Guadalupe County, New Mexico. He is the son of Martín Anaya and Rafaelita Mares who were born in the U.S.-controlled Territory of New Mexico. The Anaya surname appears on the list of colonists who arrived in la Nueva México in 1693. Anaya, however, was raised in the Mexican American barrio of Barelas in Alburquerque. After attending the University of New Mexico and traveling to Mexico, Anaya began writing what was to become his vast historical romance of New Mexico. "Writing the Dreams of la Nueva México," is a study of Rudolfo A. Anaya's seven novels from the 1972 classic *Bless Me, Ultima* through the

1999 *Shaman Winter* as he puts to rest the fantasy of the Spanish Southwest and affirms the Mexican-mestizo origins of la Nueva México.

Tomás Rivera's ". . . *y no se lo tragó la tierra*" was a milestone in the literatures of the Américas when it was awarded the first Premio Quinto Sol for a novel in 1970. It was an American novel by a Mexican American written in colloquial Mexican Spanish. Rivera's *Tierra* (1971) was also a Mexican novel that crossed the border. Tomás Rivera was born of Mexican immigrant parents in Crystal City, Texas, in 1935 during the Great Depression. Rivera was raised as a farmworker child in labor camps throughout the Midwest. As elders gathered round after the day's work to tell tales, the child Rivera saw and listened. Rivera graduated from Crystal City High School and earned a bachelor's degree in English at Southwest Texas State University in 1958. In 1962 Rivera traveled south to study Mexican literature in Guadalajara under the guidance of mexicanista scholar Luis Leal. Rivera also learned much from Mexican writer Juan Rulfo's concise but complex storytelling. Assuming the stance of the folk poet in *Tierra*, Rivera gathered around him a new community of readers. Like no other writer before him, Rivera had transformed the Mexican-mestizo cultural world of Greater Mexico into the beginning of the Chicano narrative tradition.

Oscar Thomas Acosta was born in 1935 in El Paso, Texas, and raised, in his own words, in the Mexican sector of Riverbank, California. Acosta, as is well known, became a legendary attorney-activist-writer of the Chicano Movement. The writer Oscar Zeta Acosta related in *The Autobiography of a Brown Buffalo* his ill-fated journey to American selfhood within U.S. society of the forties and fifties. Through the Chicano Movement, all the racism that Acosta had internalized exploded in his unique brand of sixties counterculture fiction-journalism, an in-your-face, drug-induced, cranked-up, rock 'n' roll–like style. As is well known, Hunter S. Thompson and Acosta were road buddies: the fictional Raoul Duke and his Samoan (Chicano) attorney sidekick, Doctor Gonzo, of *Fear and Loathing in Las Vegas* (1971). Thompson is credited, deservedly so, with the Gonzo style of writing. However, Acosta is also an original practitioner of Gonzo writing, with the crucial difference that his writing was meaningful with regard to his ethnicity: Acosta lived his life like his writing. The former Boy Scout transformed himself into the Zorro-like outlaw hero, the Chicano militant attorney Oscar Zeta Acosta. Toward the end of his crazy life, México became a place of refuge for writing. He completed the 1972 *Autobiography of a Brown Buffalo* in Michoacán. Acosta had plans for "The Rise and Fall of General Zeta" when he disappeared somewhere near Mazatlán, México, in 1974.

In the last paragraphs of her 2000 edition of *Loving in the War Years*, Cherríe L. Moraga sees herself reflected in an eighteenth-century Mexican casta family portrait by Miguel Cabrera. Moraga describes the mestizo child sitting on the lap of his Spanish father as the child looks longingly at his Indian mother. Moraga's autobiographical writings are both self- and family portraits. Moraga, born in Los Angeles in 1952, is the daughter of a white father and a Mexican mother; she grew up white in the suburbs of Los Angeles in the San Gabriel Valley. In the tortuous journey to finding her identity, Moraga too has looked pa'trás—at la línea de las mujeres, at her mother, Elvira, with straight black and gray hair, at Malintzín/doña Marina, at Coyolxauhqui, at La Llorona, at Dolores the grandmother, Dolores the daughter, Dolores the daughter's daughter. Through her writings from 1981 to 2000, the lesbian-feminist-activist has maintained a critical dialogue with Mexican literature and culture on the secondary status of women. Moraga is, at the end of the twentieth century, the Mexican lesbian mother who has been "making familia from scratch."

Rolando Hinojosa-Smith was born in 1929 in Mercedes in the Río Grande Valley of Texas. At a formative age, Hinojosa spent summers in Arteaga, Coahuila, where he wrote his first story in Spanish. He also learned to sing two national anthems in escuelitas established by men and women exiled in the United States during one phase or another of the Mexican Revolution. "Mexicanos al Grito de Guerra," is both a song of cultural identity and a call to arms. Indeed, in Hinojosa's multivolume *Cronicón del condado de Belken/Klail City Death Trip*, his Korean War experience is crucial for the reconstruction of Texas as the Land of Our Fathers, the land defended by Mexican revolucionarios. In 1859 don Juan Nepomuceno Cortina was the first to rise up and defend his rights against Anglo-Texan authority. At his family's Rancho del Carmen, Cortina fought the Brownsville Rifles and Tobin's Rangers. The fictional don Jesús Buenrostro, the axial figure of Hinojosa's vast cronicón, also defended his land at his own Rancho del Carmen. From Hinojosa's 1973 *Estampas del valle* to his 1998 *Ask a Policeman*, the site of Mexican resistance maintains its rich symbolism as the locus of identity for the Buenrostro lineage.

Sandra Cisneros is a second-generation American Mexican born in Chicago in 1954; however, she was also raised in Mexico City, in the colonia Tepeyac, on calle Fortuna 12, within walking distance of the Basílica to the Virgen de Guadalupe. Cisneros's American Mexican mother, Elvira Cordero

Anguiano, handed down to her daughter the fierce language, the voice of an urban immigrant child, working-class, anti-Catholic, free-thinking, and smart-mouthed. Cisneros's Mexican-born father, Alfredo Cisneros del Moral, gave her the Spanish language, el lenguaje de la ternura. Cisneros has combined her two cultures in her feminist stories of the late-twentieth-century Méxicos that exist beyond borders. Through her strong, resilient female characters, Cisneros critically confronts a folkloric, legendary, romantic, and utopian Mexico to which working-class mexicanas and mexicanos on both sides of the border have turned for cultural identity—La Llorona, Tonantzín, the legend of Popocatépetl and Ixtaccíhuatl, la Virgen de Guadalupe, religious ex-votos and milagritos, Mexican movies, boleros and rancheras, telenovelas and fotonovelas, popular magazines, José de Helguera's Aztec Indian kitsch calendars, the Mexican Revolution, the legend of Emiliano Zapata, and el Grito de Independencia. However, the love and respeto that Cisneros has for her Mexican culture are also evident in her border tales from the 1991 *Woman Hollering Creek and Other Stories.*

These writers, like other Mexican American writers, give evidence to a cross-border solidarity that is finally being acknowledged by Mexican writers and artists. In his novel *La frontera de cristal* (1995), Carlos Fuentes gives Chicano literature (he cites el cuento de Cisneros) a role in shattering la frontera de cristal, the lack of communication that divides Mexicans on both sides of the border. In early studies by Mexican scholars of the Chicano Movement, Chicanos were labeled "los chicanos, la otra cara de México." At the current moment, as this book's epilogue, América Mexicana 2001, argues, we should begin to think of Mexico as "México, la otra cara de los chicanos." Mexico in the era of globalization is beginning to look very much like us. We, in fact, as the writers in this study teach us, underwent the changes of economic imperialism and cultural domination now transforming Mexico. Carlos Monsiváis, a frank Mexican cultural critic, has written that Mexico is witnessing the first generation of americanos born in Mexico. Redefined Mexican cultural symbols boldly taken up by the Chicano Movement of the sixties have returned to the center of Mexican identity. Mexico City's pioneering rock en español band, Maldita Vecindad, has written on cross-border artistic inspiration:

El movimiento chicano siempre nos llamó la atención.

En 1985, cuando comenzamos, muchos grupos en México tocaban en inglés o tenían nombres en ese idioma. Había una influencia musical muy fuerte del rock inglés o americano, se reproducían géneros como el blues, el punk o el heavy metal.

En la cultura chicana había una redefinición de idea de mexicanidad y eso se reflejaba en la música de fusión, la pintura callejera con el graffiti, los íconos populares: Zapata, la Virgen de Guadalupe, la bandera, el teatro campesino, los pachucos o la presencia popular de la cultura prehispánica, por ejemplo.

Nuestro trabajo en Maldita siempre ha tenido muchos puntos de contacto con esa búsqueda de la cultura chicana. (Maldita Vecindad, *Gira pata de perro* 93)

In the last decade of the twentieth century, this Mexican rock banda de pueblo, like Chicano writers before, seized upon the migration of people and culture in its politically engaged, working-class music. In its concerts throughout Mexican United States, Maldita Vecindad has become a borderless cultural institution influencing a generation of post–Chicano Movement young people on both sides of the border.

I hope that this book on the bilingual, bicultural U.S. mexicano writers will add to this already-evolving history of la Nueva México, el México diverso as well as profundo, that is emerging on both sides of the border.

Unless otherwise noted, translations are mine. Spanish is not a foreign language to me or to millions of citizens of the United States; for that reason, I have not italicized Spanish in my text. I have, however, maintained the crucial distinction between the English term "romance" and the Spanish ballad form *romance*.

NARRATIVES OF GREATER MEXICO

REDEFINING THE BORDERLANDS

From the Spanish Southwest to Greater Mexico, from Charles F. Lummis to Américo Paredes

Mexican-Americans have been awake to their problems since the time of Cortina. They have also been quite preoccupied with questions of self-analysis and identity, ever since the Treaty of Guadalupe. The Chicano "awakening" of the 1960s is the culmination of a long and continuous struggle, spanning more than a century.

— AMÉRICO PAREDES, *A TEXAS-MEXICAN "CANCIONERO"*

The creators of borders are great pretenders. They post their projects in the world with the sturdiest available signs and hope that conventions . . . will keep them in place. But even as the first stakes are driven, the earth itself, in all its intractable shiftiness, moves toward displacement. Amused, "unamerican" spectators— who may not even know how to read—recognize immediately that they, too, have a stake in displacement.

— HOUSTON A. BAKER JR., "LIMITS OF THE BORDER"

I

For the first seventeen years of my life, la línea was a daily presence. From the north end of the Imperial Valley in Brawley, Highway 86 winds down past agricultural fields and several cities—Imperial, El Centro, and Heber—to eventually arrive as

Highway 111 at the very limits of the American Southwest at the border, at Calexico, California. I who grew up on Imperial Avenue, also Highway 111, and Sixth Street in Calexico, five blocks from la línea, would rather think of the border not as a limit but as la encrucijada de culturas e historias; for Calexico, like no other border town, has a mirror held up to it in Mexicali, Baja California. Both cities have been historical and cultural reflections of each other; both the same, yet quite different.

Calexico began in the last decade of the nineteenth century as an encampment for laborers in a water diversion project that transformed an area of the Sonoran Desert into one of the most productive agricultural regions of both the United States and Mexico. The valley was named by developers of the California Land Company. On the other side of the border, el Valle de Mexicali was controlled by the Colorado River Land Company led by Harry Chandler, publisher of the *Los Angeles Times*. In 1903 Calexico and Mexicali were among the first towns incorporated in the valley. El Ayuntamiento de Mexicali, which had been an early extension of Calexico, rapidly outgrew its sister city. By the fifties, during my childhood, Calexico remained a dusty border town of eleven thousand; Mexicali, la capital de Baja California Frontera Norte since 1915, was a thriving (as only Mexican cities can thrive), tumultuous city of one hundred thousand. Nowadays, Calexico boasts a population of twenty-two thousand; I would wager that the population of Mexicali and its surrounding valley is close to one million, both its economy and population boosted by assembly plants, maquiladoras, built by U.S. companies on the Mexican side under the Border Industrial Program initiated in 1968.

Both cities, ingeniously named by a Mr. L. M. Holt, who also gave the valley its name, are in fact a single economic entity separated by a fence constructed in the twentieth century. Commercial traffic has flowed more or less freely across the line. Many Mexican families from Calexico, including mine, would spend three to four days of the week in Mexicali, whether to visit relatives, to shop or dine, or seek any number of professional or medical services. The Mexicali upper crust would frequent our Calexico stores, while the lower class would compete with us for jobs as clerks, domestics, and, most important of all, agricultural workers. At 4:00 A.M., the sleeping border town would awaken, and the Calexico downtown, the four blocks on Second Street, would be busier than at any time of the day with both foot and auto traffic on the way to El Hoyo, "The Hole," near the New River (one of North America's most polluted rivers). Here labor contractors and their hawkers awaited men, women, and

2

children to take them in summer as far north as Indio to harvest Thompson seedless grapes or in winter as near as the outskirts of Holtville or El Centro to pick carrots or lettuce. The Imperial Valley, you see, has a year-round growing season; it is where "the sun spends the winter"; it was also where groups of families would return from northern California, from as far as Napa and the Central Valley, to work in winter crops.

In the forties and fifties in this poor, working-class city, we were reminded of both what we were and what we were not. To the Euro-American minority of ranchers, shopkeepers, clerks, and government officials, we were not real Americans, we were foreigners, Mexicans. To our brothers and sisters on the other side of the line, we were pochos, inauthentic, Americanized Mexicans, identifiable by our mutilated Spanish and our dress, "con lisas y tramados y calcos siempre bien shiniados."[1]

Crecí mestizo y rascuachi en Calecia y Chikis. Recuerdo escuchando por las tardes con mi familia el noticiero de la XEW, "sirviendo a la comunidad mexicana de ambos valles." En nuestra casa se oían los ritmos afro-cubanos del mambo y el chachachá; las orquestas de Luis Alcaraz o Pérez Prado; los boleros del puertorriqueño Daniel Santos; la Banda de Sinaloa; las polkas y corridos norteños cantados por los Alegres de Terán; la canción ranchera cantada por los ídolos Jorge Negrete, Lola Beltrán, José Alfredo Jiménez, Amalia Mendoza; y la canción romántica de Agustín Lara interpretada por Pedro Vargas o Toña la negra, o Libertad Lamarque. Los viernes estaban reservados para las vistas, "el mono," en el Aztec Theater donde llorábamos con las películas melodramáticas de los hermanos Soler, doña Sara García, Chachita Muñoz y Pedro Infante o nos reíamos con los cómicos Cantinflas, Resortes o Clavillazo. Mis lecturas en español se limitaban a las fotonovelas de mi héroe, el Santo, "el enmascarado de plata," o la serie de las vidas ilustradas. A estos medios de comunicación modernos debo añadir las creencias, cuentos, proverbios, dichos y refranes de la tradición oral almacenados en la memoria de mi abuela. Para nosotros, un murciélago era un ratón que de tan viejo le habían crecido alas; y todas las noches detrás del callejón vagaba La Llorona.[2]

Although many of our daily, seasonal, and religious activities were still dictated by Mexican oral and cultural traditions, our world was rapidly changing. The alternative to the Mexican radio station XEW was the appropriately named KROP of Brawley, on which we listened to R&B and rockabilly as they became rock 'n' roll. We danced to James Brown, Little Richard, Chuck Berry, LaVern Baker, Buddy Holly, and Ritchie Valens, the Platters, Doowop y el Elvis and even Hank Williams and Patsy

Cline on the "West Side of Your Hit Parade." We really hit the big time when the Ike and Tina Turner Revue came to the El Centro National Guard Armory and Little Richard played at the Gimnasio de Mexicali. And yes, the Cisco Kid was a friend of mine.

This multicultural lens through which we viewed the world certainly made us "Mexicans" different from Euro-American Calexicans. However, in schools we were told, assured, that we were white, Spanish, descendants of the conquistadors. Many years later, as I read my birth certificate, I think about how much our world has changed, for my race in 1945 was identified as white. And though we were legal citizens, we were not treated equally. When my parents were children they were barred from commercial establishments that bore the sign, White Trade Only.

I attended schools through the eighth grade in segregated classrooms, and punishment for speaking Spanish on school grounds was commonplace. Each year, as students enrolled in Calexico schools, one class was almost completely Anglo, composed of children of merchants and farmers; the rest of the classrooms were almost completely Mexican, with the exception of the few Asian American and African American students. Most of the students in my classroom, rumored to be one of the toughest and lowest academically, were the children of migrant farmworkers who lived in the oldest Mexican neighborhood, La Garra. "The Rag" was a shanty town with unpaved streets across the tracks from the main part of town. From the first grade, in 1951, through the eighth grade my class was kept pretty much intact. Out of some thirty-plus students, three of us graduated from high school on time, a few others had to repeat grades, and the rest were lost along the way.

We were still, after all, foreigners, the children of Mexicans who had arrived in large numbers in the first decades of the past century to play a significant role as laborers in a region that was undergoing a major economic transformation. These ethnic and class contradictions come back to me as I recall our most important festive occasion, the parade and pageant known as the Calexico Desert Cavalcade. Begun one night by a small group of organizers in the depression year of 1939 to boost the morale and the economy of the border community, the pageant was the invention of Herminia "Ma" Keller, who had the support of the editor of the local newspaper, the *Calexico Chronicle*, the president of the Chamber of Commerce, and representatives of the city's service clubs. The Desert Cavalcade was "the fulfillment of a little group of men and women in Calexico" (*Ninth Annual International Desert Cavalcade*). This reenactment of California's past began with the Spanish conquistadors, "those stout-hearted pioneers who brought God and civilization to the Southwest."

My fourth-grade experience is especially memorable: dressed, like all my classmates, as an Indian in painted face, feathers, and buckskin, I fell in behind the gallant Juan Bautista de Anza and kindly black-robed padres as we paraded past our two important architectural landmarks, the Spanish colonial revival Hotel de Anza and the missionlike church Nuestra Señora de Guadalupe on our way to Monterrey in Alta California. That the Spaniard (the term used in the published pageant guide) De Anza, a second-generation fronterizo on his mother's side, was born in 1735 in the Mexican border town of Fronteras, Sonora, not far from the present Arizona border, or that he did not establish a settlement in the area in 1775, was not important to pageant organizers.[3] Actually, De Anza had the important task of establishing an overland route from Tubac, Sonora, in what is now southern Arizona, to Alta California, a task made easier by existing Native American trails. For his efforts, De Anza was rewarded with the governorship of New Mexico in 1777. In the twentieth century, De Anza was rewarded with Calexico's architectural landmark, the Hotel De Anza. It also did not matter to Cavalcade organizers that their cultural activities made no sense given the cultural, historical, and economic realities of this overwhelmingly Mexican town. It probably did not make any sense either to Mrs. Yokum, Pete Emmett and Lucille, our African American neighbors, or Mar Chan, who owned the Sanitary Food Market on the corner of Imperial and Seventh Street.

We were never so different from our relatives across the border as when we asserted this, our Spanish heritage, in "the great Imperial Valley of the Southwest" (*Ninth Annual International Desert Cavalcade*). Though we were biologically and culturally indistinct from one another, we were Mexican mestizos, we had different cultural heritages and ideologies imposed from above by educators, civic leaders, and government officials. Just a short distance across the border, streets, buildings, and monuments bore the names of Mexican revolutionary and political leaders. The wide Avenida Obregón led border crossers to a statue of Alvaro Obregón and Mexicali's Palacio de Gobierno. President Obregón's statue is in homage to the man who led Mexico's reconstruction after the Revolution of 1910. One of Obregón's important acts after being elected president in 1920 was to appoint José Vasconcelos to the post of secretary of education. It was Vasconcelos who commissioned artists, Diego Rivera, José Clemente Orozco, and David Alfaro Siqueiros, among others, to paint murals on the walls of Mexico City's government buildings. Given free intellectual and artistic rein, they produced scenes depicting the Mexican Revolution and Mexico's Indian past. Thus emerged Mexico's artistic renaissance in the twentieth century. Beginning in the twenties, Native American culture was purified by Mexican intellectuals and leaders into the norm of the classic. From José Vasconcelos's *La raza cósmica* (*The Cosmic Race*) of 1925 to Octavio Paz's *El laberinto de la soledad* (*The Labyrinth of Solitude*) of 1950, Native American culture was not only the historical base for the nation but also a possibility for the future. In the Mexican historical drama, Cuauhtémoc, Fallen Eagle, the last Aztec emperor, became the nation's hero and Cortés, the Spanish conquistador, became the archvillain. These different popular and intellectual traditions show us why until the mid-twentieth century one side of the border was "Spanish" and the other "Mexican," although we shared the same Mexican-mestizo culture.

It is now historically accurate to acknowledge that "Spanish" culture throughout the Americas was a mestizaje, a mixture of American and European elements. What traces of the Spanish heritage that were left after the wars of independence in Latin America were reinterpreted and, at times, severely criticized by liberal intellectuals as they sought to bring their emerging nations into the modern world. Two South American writers from opposite ends of the political spectrum, Domingo Faustino Sarmiento and Manuel González Prada, can stand as important examples of anti-Spanish sentiment. Before rising to the presidency of Argentina in 1868, Sarmiento had written in 1845 in *Facundo o Civilización y barbarie* (*Argentina in the Time of the Tyrants*) on the backwardness of Spanish American culture in the wake of the dissolution of the empire. An admirer of the United States and a proponent of easy polarities, the civilization and progress of the city versus the barbarism of the wilderness, Sarmiento declared Spanish colonial feudalism to be a primitive lifestyle incompatible with government, discipline, and civil justice; in the mixture of Spanish, Native American, and African American races he found only indolence and an incapacity for industry. Part of the solution to these national problems sought by Sarmiento called for European immigration, but not from Spain. At the beginning of the twentieth century, in 1906, the early leftist activist and symbolist poet, the Peruvian Manuel González Prada, in "El problema indígena" ("The Native American Problem") delivered a scathing attack on Spanish civilization:

No se necesita ser un águila sociológica para decir que desde el arribo de los blancos a las costas del Perú surgió una de las más graves cuestiones que agitan a la Humanidad, la cuestión étnica: dos razas se ponían en contacto, y una de ellas tenía que vencer, oprimir y devorar a la otra. Dada la crueldad ingénita de los españoles, crueldad agravada con la codicia morbosa de los lanzados sobre la América del Sur, ya se comprende lo feroz de la conquista, lo rapaz de la dominación. (González Prada 1941, 155)

One does not need to have the sharp eye of a sociologist to declare that since the arrival of whites on the shores of Peru, one of the most serious problems that troubles Humanity emerged, the ethnic question: two races came in contact with each other, and one of them had to conquer, oppress and devour the other. Given the innate cruelty of the Spaniards, cruelty rendered intolerable by the morbid greed of those who rushed upon South America, one can understand the savagery of the conquest, the ferocity of domination.

The sharp distinctions of a conservative and reactionary romanticism, common in the Spanish Southwest, against the more oppositional Latin American perspective stem from the cultural domination that followed U.S. military conquest. The activities of our Anglo-American leaders in inventing a Spanish past for all of us was not unique to Calexico. It was a tradition that began in earnest in the last decades of the nineteenth century.

II

Sun, silence, and adobe—that is New Mexico in three words. . . .
It is the Great American Mystery—the National Rip Van
Winkle—the United States which is not United States. Here is
the land of poco tiempo—the home of "Pretty Soon." Why hurry
with the hurrying world? The "Pretty Soon" of New Spain is
better than the "Now! Now!" of the haggard States. The opiate
sun soothes to rest, the adobe is made to lean against, the hush of
day-long noon would not be broken. Let us not hasten—mañana
will do. Better still, pasado mañana.

—CHARLES F. LUMMIS, *THE LAND OF POCO TIEMPO*

Perhaps the single most influential agent of Euro-American cultural imperialism was Charles F. Lummis, whose lifelong activities and writings changed the image of a region, Mexican America/América Mexicana, that had been acquired through conquest some thirty-six years before his arrival in Santa Fe, New Mexico Territory, in 1884.[4] In 1925, three years before his death, in *Mesa, Cañon and Pueblo*, Lummis boasted that he had been the first to apply the generic name "Southwest" or more specifically "Spanish Southwest" to the million square miles that include New Mexico, Arizona, southern California, and parts of Colorado, Utah, and Texas (vii). In a span of nine years, from 1891 to 1900, Lummis published ten books, changing what was for writers and readers a "vast physical and cultural desert, repulsive and dangerous, totally without attraction other than its storied mineral wealth," into a land internationally known for its seductive natural and cultural attractions (see Lummis 1989, xvii). Though in truth an amateur inclined toward self-promotion and melodramatic and hyperbolic writing, he became the founder of the "Southwest genre," recognized by both professionals and the popular media as the undisputed authority on the history, anthropology, and folklore of the Southwest.

Born a preacher's son in Lynn, Massachusetts, on 1 March 1859 and educated at Harvard, Charles Fletcher Lummis arrived in January 1885 in El Pueblo de Nuestra Señora la Reina de Los Angeles, a mostly adobe city of some twelve thousand, where, according to Lummis, the Spanish-speaking population outnumbered "gringos" two or three to one (Lummis Fiske and Lummis 1975, 29). Lummis had traveled to California from Chillicothe, Ohio, at the behest of publisher Colonel Harrison Gray Otis (a Civil War veteran and later a general in the Spanish-American War) who had offered him a position as the first city editor of the *Los Angeles Daily Times*, recently founded in 1882.

The manner of Lummis's trek across the continent gives a good indication of his personality and his flair for the dramatic. He fancied himself a storyteller and a poet; his first publication had been a tiny book of poems, *Birch Bark Poems* (1879), printed on birch bark, copies of which he sent to Emerson, Longfellow, Lowell, and Whitman. It is obvious from this book of nature verse and all his subsequent publications on the Southwest that Lummis couched his arguments in the language of a transplanted European Romanticism that had already become a popular idiom in the East. It was partly the romantic artist-hero in Lummis that urged him to walk, in itself a romantic trope, from Cincinnati to Los Angeles. This tramp of 3,500 miles across the West earned him celebrity status upon his arrival in California, for he had sent weekly dispatches both to the *Chillicothe Leader* and the *Los Angeles Daily Times* that were published throughout the country and later collected in revised form in *A Tramp Across the Continent* (1892).[5]

What we glean from Lummis's early writings, *A New Mexico David and Other Stories and Sketches of the Southwest* (1891), *A Tramp Across the Continent* (1892), *Some Strange Corners of Our Country* (1892), *The Land of Poco Tiempo* (1893), and *The Spanish Pioneers* (1893), is the story of an Easterner who experiences an almost religious conversion on setting foot in Santa Fe in 1884:

> I loved New England in all its hardness and all its humanity. It was marvelous how human the hardest could be and how hard the most human! I have never known either finer or tenderer hearts than I knew in old New England. But I have seen many other temporary suspensions of the Attraction of Gravitation.
>
> Then I came to Santa Fe. And once I had reached Spanish America and the hearts of its people, I realized that this was where I belonged.
>
> Though my conscience was Puritan, my whole imagination and sympathy and feeling were Latin. That is, essentially Spanish. Apparently they always had been, for now I had gotten away from the repressive influence of my birthplace I began to see that the generous and bubbling boyish impulses which had been considerably frosted in New England were, after all, my birthright. (Cited in Lummis Fiske and Lummis 1975, 20–21)

However, this was not the same Lummis that appeared in letters to the *Chillicothe Leader* in Ohio.[6] His dispatches upon entering the New Mexican territory are, except for a few lines on good-looking, well-built Indians and the seductiveness of Spanish feminine beauty, devoid of the many romantic commonplaces that would characterize his later prose. Here is his first encounter with Mexicans in Alamosa, Colorado, in November 1884, published only in 1989:

> The Mexicans themselves are a snide-looking set, twice as dark as an Indian, with heavy lips and noses, long straight, black hair, sleepy eyes, and a general expression of ineffable laziness. Their language is a patois of Spanish and Mexican. These may be poor specimens along here. I hope so. Not even a coyote will touch a dead Greaser, the flesh is so seasoned with the red pepper they ram into their bellies in howling profusion. (Lummis 1989, 97)

On the term "greaser," Lummis explained to his Ohio readers that it was of the same coinage as "nigger," not much to take offense at. As for Santa Fe, it was a city of mostly Mexicans and Pueblos, composed of mud huts and a few modern buildings with unpaved streets full of burros. Some of the most astonishing reporting concerns the high prices of rents and real estate in Los Angeles.

In his letters to the *Los Angeles Daily Times*, Lummis deleted racist passages and elaborated more on sensational episodes and personal heroics. By the publication of *A Tramp Across the Continent* in 1892, his trip had been transformed into a polished book composed of chapters, much more discreet and more self-promoting. Moreover, Lummis added new incidents that had not been mentioned in his letters to the *Chillicothe Leader*, and which could not have taken place given his own chronology until returning to New Mexico at a later date (see Lummis 1989, xii–xiv). He also deceives his readers as to the motives for his trip to Los Angeles.

> I am an American and felt ashamed to know so little of my own country as I did, and as most Americans do. . . . Furthermore, I wished to relocate from Ohio to California. So here was a chance to kill several birds with one stone; to learn more of the country and its people than railroad transfer could ever teach; to have the physical joy which the confirmed pedestrian knows; to have the awakening of insights and experiences.
>
> These were motives which led me to undertake a walk of 3507 miles. . . . It was purely "for fun" in a good sense; and the most productive of a rather stirring life. There was no desire for notoriety. (Lummis 1892b, 2)

His arrangement with Colonel Otis of the *Los Angeles Daily Times* is never mentioned.

Unlike writers who traveled through the West before him, Lummis made this area his own domain foremost through his showmanship, his imaginative commercial instinct for making his travelogues available to a wide readership. The full title of a 1925 publication captures Lummis at his best, sounding like a sideshow hawker: *Mesa, Cañon and Pueblo— Our Wonderland of the Southwest—Its Marvels of Nature—Its Pageant of Earth Building—Its Strange Peoples—Its Centuried Romance*. Though never a serious writer, his prestige grew through the articles he published in Eastern journals, through his correspondence and association with the archaeologist Adolph Bandelier, President Theodore Roosevelt, who was his classmate at Harvard, Mexico's dictator Porfirio Díaz, and the Spanish king Alfonso XII. With the advent of the mass media, especially the films of Hollywood, the image of the Southwest invented by Lummis imprinted itself on the popular imagination.

In the West, Lummis discovered and invented for his readers a culture much like the fictional characters and settings of romantic literature. Unlike the East, the West had a folk culture of simple and picturesque, yet dignified, souls still existing in a pastoral or agricultural mode of production undisturbed by the modern world.

So taken was Lummis by the alien culture he encountered that he adopted it as his own, learned Spanish, took on the name Don Carlos, and was fond of posing for photographs in Spanish, Western, Apache, and Navajo attire. And until his death in 1928, Lummis worked actively for the preservation of his Southwest culture. He traveled throughout the Southwest and Latin America photographing natives, rituals, and archaeological sites and collecting Native American artifacts. He established both the Southwest Society to continue his work and the Southwest Museum in Los Angeles to house his collections. In addition to his numerous writings, he published two journals, *Land of Sunshine* and *Out West*, promoting California. He also participated in the revival of "Spanish" architecture in California through his efforts to reconstruct the California missions. Always bent on speaking his mind, he was critical of U.S. imperialism and racism. He wrote against U.S. intervention in the Spanish-American War and became a defender of Indian rights.

However, like other foreigners who make native culture their own, there was also a conservative and patronizing side to Lummis. He was intent on writing only about the most folkloric and romantic elements of Native American and Mexican mestizo culture. Thus we find Lummis attracted to courtly Dons, beautiful, dark-eyed Spanish señoritas, innocent Indian children, kind Mexican peons, real "live" witches, liturgical feast days, medieval penitents, haciendas, burros, carretas, and sunshine. Though he found Indians innocent, gracious, dignified, noble, and contented when domesticated, his descriptions of them sharply change when recalling the bloodthirsty savages, bucks, and squaws who fought against the Spaniards in the sixteenth century and General Crook in 1886.

So inclined was Lummis toward paternalism, to see the strong arm of heroic men as the vehicle for civilization rather than the welfare of all members of society, that in *Awakening of a Nation* (1898) he read Mexico under the dictator Porfirio Díaz as a modern and progressive nation (5). And charmed by the "child-hearted" Spanish he encountered in the

Southwest, Lummis became an apologist for the Spanish conquest of the Americas. *The Spanish Pioneers* (1893), a history of the heroic padres and gallant Spaniards who brought God and civilization to the Americas, is a culmination of ideas and attitudes to which Lummis had devoted passages in each of his previous books. In the Preface, he states that he has written this book for misinformed Anglo-American readers (a reference to the Black Legend) out of a sense of justice to finally tell the truth of the Spanish conquest. What follows is page after page of unparalleled heroism of the generous, brave, and gallant Spaniards; Lummis concludes by writing:

> I have wished only to give the reader some idea of what a Spanish conquest really was, in superlative heroism and hardship. Pizarro's was the greatest conquest; but there were many others which were not inferior in heroism and suffering, but only in genius; and the story of Perú was very much the story of two thirds of the Western Hemisphere. (Lummis 1893b, 292)

This strategy of glorifying the past ignored the real historical fact that the land upon which Lummis first set foot in 1884 was conquered Mexican territory.[7] In all the writings by Lummis, I have yet to see this fact recorded and thoroughly analyzed. It is as if Spain became the United States without centuries of racial and cultural mixture. And though he admired Native American culture, it could not match his glorification of the Spanish past. He also ignored the fencing of the free range, the elimination of the buffalo and other wildlife, and the usurpation of Spanish and Mexican land grants by Anglo-Americans. The years shortly after Lummis's arrival in the Southwest witnessed the end of the Indian Wars in Arizona and the elimination of free Native Americans from their ancestral lands, the first real estate booms in California, and the growth of major Western urban centers.

III

This is an interesting portrayal of the Spanish-speaking presence in the Southwest: first, toward the end of the sixteenth century, a wave of purebred Castilian clotheshorses in search of gold and silver; then, three centuries later, a second wave made up of

> *furtive, landless peons in search of bread and a job. And in*
> *between—presumably—nothing.*
>
> AMÉRICO PAREDES, *A TEXAS-MEXICAN "CANCIONERO"*

New Mexico Territory and its capital, Santa Fe, had always been central to Lummis's view of the Southwest. It was also a place to which he lured Eastern writers and artists, where his influence was widespread and profound, especially during the twenties and thirties when many Southwest genre classics were published.[8] Nowhere else have native inhabitants believed themselves to be so Spanish. Writers Nina Otero-Warren and Cleofas M. Jaramillo and scholar Aurelio M. Espinosa, whose lives span almost one hundred years, from 1878 to 1958, and who therefore witnessed firsthand enormous historical and social changes in New Mexico, illustrate the seductiveness of the Spanish myth.

Both Otero-Warren and Jaramillo were daughters of prominent Santa Fe area families and were schooled in English through college. Otero-Warren was active in Río Arriba politics and held important educational administrative positions. She was a suffragist; elected superintendent of public schools for Santa Fe County; a Republican nominee for the U.S. House of Representatives in 1921 when women were granted the vote; and served as inspector of Indian schools in Santa Fe County. Cleofas Martínez de Jaramillo, who went by the name Cleo, was the daughter of Taos area rancher and merchant Julián Antonio Martínez.[9] Jaramillo married her cousin Venceslao Jaramillo who later was elected state senator from Río Arriba County and was one of the original signatories to the Society for the Preservation of Spanish Antiquities in New Mexico. Jaramillo is herself well known for founding in 1935 in Santa Fe La Sociedad Folklórica dedicated to preserving Spanish culture.[10]

Otero-Warren's *Old Spain in Our Southwest* (1936) and Jaramillo's *Shadows of the Past/Sombras del Pasado* (1941) and *Romance of a Little Village Girl* (1955) are written in the Lummis English-language idiom of the romance of the Spanish Southwest: "the great Spanish families lived in haciendas" and "a Spaniard always had time for courtesy" in Otero-Warren; "wise Columbus," "intrepid Cortez," "brave De Vargas," "hardships only meant exciting adventure," "conquering savage Indian tribes" in Jaramillo. What collective history both can recall is reduced to a familiar gloss of history: we are descendants of heroic conquistadors who in this isolated region of the world fought the Indians, shed their blood, tamed the wilderness, and built a civilization that was a model of conduct.

Given this nostalgia for the past, both recall a harmonious world of aristocratic pretense where all behaved themselves in times of rejoicing and suffering with dignity, courtesy, and sympathy, the patrón with the peon and vice versa. Whatever realities Otero-Warren lived through in her political and administrative career in Santa Fe disappear in her fantasy memoir. She is especially guilty of concentrating on her childhood Spanish hacienda life and drawing easy and fictional parallels between Southwest families and the royal court in Spain. She provides no information on Mexican New Mexico. And although Jaramillo offers historical dates and events on the importance of Mexico in the nineteenth century, she identifies herself as white and Spanish. Out of fear of racism, both minimized the mixing of cultures and races, ignored caste and class antagonisms, and concentrated on witchcraft, the Brotherhood of the Penitents, and special occasions in the seasonal and liturgical calendars. As for the U.S.-Mexico War, New Spain passed into the hands of the United States, as Jaramillo records: "The royal and red flag of Spain over the *Palacio Real*, seat of Spanish rule and headquarters of this vast province, replaced by the red, green and white of Mexico, now gave way to the stars and stripes of the United States. The last phase of Spanish rule passed" (Jaramillo 1955, 6).

Although the Spanish Dons (Jaramillo's term) saw the need to send their children to Eastern schools to learn the English language so that they could deal with "this new energetic race," the newcomers had forced the old Spanish families to retreat to the seclusion of their culture: "Crushed at first with this hard change, but with their spirits still strong, with inherent courage and religious resignation, they bore their trials. In an effort to keep satisfied and cheerful, feast days, weddings, and other celebrations were kept up, with feasting, music and dancing" (ibid., 9). These women wrote out of a desire to protect their world from Anglo-American misinterpretations and to preserve their Spanish culture for succeeding generations. Yet one cannot but be amazed at this conservative strain of Mexican American thought, especially when one considers that it was expressed well into the twentieth century.

Aurelio M. Espinosa also followed in the footsteps of Lummis collecting Spanish songs, *romances*, and folktales in New Mexico.[11] Although Espinosa was born in southern Colorado in 1880 in the village of El Carnero, on the basis of family records and tradition he traced his paternal origins in New

Mexico to Captain Marcelo Espinosa, who in 1598 accompanied New Mexico's conqueror and first governor, Juan de Oñate, who was born in Mexico. Espinosa was also related to Cleofas Martínez de Jaramillo on his mother's side. He shared with Cleofas a great-grandfather, José Manuel Martínez, who received the Tierra Amarilla land grant from the Mexican government in 1835.

Espinosa began his teaching career at the University of New Mexico in 1902. An interest in the folklore and Spanish language of northern New Mexico led eventually to his doctoral dissertation, "Studies in New-Mexican Spanish," from the University of Chicago in 1909. In his dissertation, Espinosa demonstrated that the "Spanish spoken by residents of northern New Mexico and southern Colorado, who were isolated for over two centuries from the direct influence of the urban centers of Spanish America, developed from the language of Spain's Golden Age during the sixteenth and seventeenth centuries, with local traits that are also found in Spain, as well as other parts of Spanish America" (Espinosa 1985, 17).[12] In "The Spanish Language of Northern New Mexico and Southern Colorado," Espinosa wrote: "If Cervantes were to return to the Spanish world and speak with natives from Castile, Andalucía, or New Mexico, he would observe practically the same words, idioms, grammar, and syntax today that he himself used in the sixteenth century, but his pronunciation would be different from that of all of the above regions" (ibid., 234).

Espinosa rose to prominence as an internationally recognized scholar at the inception of Romance studies in the West; in 1917 he was one of the founders of the American Association of Teachers of Spanish; he was a highly regarded member of the American Folklore Society, its president in 1924 and 1925; he organized the graduate studies program in Spanish soon after his arrival at Stanford and chaired the Department of Romance Languages from 1932 until his retirement in 1947. Espinosa received the order of knighthood from King Alfonso XIII of Spain in 1922.

Espinosa's publications from his first in 1907 to his last in 1955 were of major consequence in establishing the prevailing interpretation of Southwest folklore. His goal in collecting folklore, which he repeated often, was to support the theory that the folklore of the Spanish Southwest was fundamentally and principally of peninsular Spanish origin. Espinosa conducted fieldwork mainly in three Spanish-speaking areas: southern Colorado and northern New Mexico, the California coastal area between San Francisco and Santa Barbara, and Spain. His publications were based mostly on materials that he had collected. Using positivistic methods,

Espinosa studied traditional New Mexican Spanish verse forms—*romances* tradicionales, corridos, décimas, coplas, and versos—and quantified parallel motifs of New Mexican tales with those of tales from different regions in Spain. The early twentieth century was a period of great pioneering folklore studies and collecting throughout the Spanish-speaking world: Ramón Menéndez-Pidal in Spain, Ramón A. Laval and Julio Vicuña Cifuentes in Chile, Robert Lehmann-Nitsche in Argentina, and Fernando Ortiz in Cuba. This great awakening to the Peninsular folk legacy in the Americas was probably fueled by the Spanish-American War of 1898 and the emergence of the United States as a world power. Espinosa, who met and corresponded with these scholars, played an important role in the new scholarly field of Hispanic American studies.

There is no doubt that much folklore of the Spanish American world is of Peninsular origin. As a student of Spanish and Latin American literature, I was able to disentangle the origins of much of the great wealth of oral and folk traditions—Genoveva de Brabante, Juan Oso, La Llorona, la danza de los Matachines, las cabañuelas, for example—bequeathed to me by my grandmother during my childhood in the Mexican world of Calexico. For me, this folk world demonstrated that I was Mexican as opposed to the Anglo-American minority of Calexico. In his "Spanish Tradition in America," Espinosa marveled during his first trip to Spain in 1920 at the similarities between New Mexican and Spanish proverbs, greetings, the guitarristas and cantadores, the luminarias, the custom of pedir la novia, the relationship between the padrino and the ahijado, belief in the mal de ojo, and the practice of placing a statue of San Antonio upside down (Espinosa 1985, 68–76). These similarities demonstrated that yes, indeed, Espinosa did have a cultural legacy—it was Spanish.

Had Espinosa ventured south and conducted his studies in a comparative fashion he would have found the same folkloric traditions on both sides of the border. However, given the temper of the times he chose to ignore Mexico. Even in his own New Mexico, it was evident that New Mexicans called their ballads not by the Spanish term *romance* but by the Mexican term "corrido" or "cuando." He admitted in "Modern Local Ballads" ("*Corridos*") that there are "probably hundreds and hundreds of them." "[T]he name for *romance* or ballad in New Mexico is *corrido* . . . also called *cuandos*, probably from the very common occurrence of the word *cuando*, 'when' at the beginning of the composition" (Espinosa 1985, 128). These ballads were identified by Espinosa as modern local ballads and should have provided him with relevant folk and cultural studies. However, he chose to ignore their value:

> Of modern local ballads—that is to say, ballads in octosyllabic meter and in assonance, the traditional Spanish ballad form, but composed in New Mexico— examples are numerous. In fact, they are still being created. Political campaigns, untimely deaths, and notorious crimes furnish the themes of most of them. Some of the versions of this class of ballads that one hears in New Mexico are of Mexican origin, such as the famous ballad of Macario Romero, which came from Mexico in the last years of the nineteenth century. Although most of these ballads lack the spirit of the traditional ballads and have little interest for comparative literature, they represent, nonetheless, an important aspect of popular local folk narrative. (Ibid., 126)

He offers one example of a local ballad, untitled in his text: "Widely known in the early decades of this century, it exemplifies the sentiments and feelings of a disgruntled New Mexican who in a few concise verses gives voice to his indignation in the year 1909 over new immigration of English-speaking Americans from Oklahoma into New Mexico" (ibid., 128). Nothing more is said about the historical context of the ballad. Here are the first verses with Espinosa's English prose translation:

> Año novecientos nueve,—pero con mucho cuidado,
> voy a componer un cuando—en nombre de este condado.
> Voy a cantar este cuando—Nuevo Méjico mentado,
> para que sepan los güeros—el nombre de este condado.
> Guadalupe es, el firmado—por la nación mejicana,
> madre de todo lo creado,—virgen, reina soberana.

> In the year nineteen hundred and nine, with very great care, I am going to compose a popular ballad, for the honor of this country. I am going to sing this ballad, Oh famous New Mexico!, so that the fair haired ones [Anglo-Americans] will know the name of this country. It is Guadalupe country, the name adopted by the Mexican nation, the name of the mother of all creation, the Virgin, the sovereign queen. (Ibid., 129–130)

Here then is a Mexican cantador using the Spanish *romance* verse form, adapting it to a new historical context. The poet identifies with his native land New Mexico as part of the Mexican nation. Espinosa translates *condado* as "country," which may be incorrect. The corrido or cuando may have been composed in New Mexico's Guadalupe County, in the eastern llano, the name given to that particular area in 1891 as part of the Territory of New Mexico in honor of the Virgen de Guadalupe. The composer also identifies with the mestizo-Indian Virgin, Guadalupe, la patrona de México. Why Espinosa chose this particular corrido is not clear, since it stands in sharp distinction to his Spanish New Mexico: it is in 1909 a statement on political and cultural strife in conquered Mexican land—the Territory of New Mexico under U.S. rule. What is clear, however, is the outline of Espinosa's work: to concentrate on pursuing Spanish origins and ignore altogether the social and historical contexts that made materials collected by him as much Spanish as Mexican.[13] What changes had occurred in New Spain's society that affected the transmission of the oral tradition in the intervening years between the conquest of Mexico in 1521 and the establishment of Santa Fe in 1610, or what changes had occurred by the time of collection in the twentieth century? These issues would come to the forefront in the next period of Southwest folklore studies, especially in the innovative work by scholar and public intellectual Américo Paredes on the Texas-Mexican borderlands.[14]

Like his New Mexican predecessors, Otero-Warren, Jaramillo, and Espinosa, Paredes saw enormous changes in a life that spanned almost the entire twentieth century. Although younger (Paredes was born in 1915), he was in many ways their contemporary. After a long and distinguished career as scholar and teacher at the University of Texas, Austin, Paredes died on 5 May 1999. Those of us who knew him as a friend and scholarly role model mourn his passing. He is best known for his pioneering work on the Texas-Mexican corrido, his doctoral dissertation, *"With His Pistol in His Hand,"* published in 1958 (incidentally, the year of Espinosa's death). This book anticipated in its political content and innovative form the literary movement that resulted from the Chicano Movement. During the sixties on the Austin campus, Paredes was a leader and joined with a new generation of Chicano students in establishing the Center for Mexican American Studies in 1971. However, his work before and after the Chicano Movement concentrated on the first half of the twentieth century. Historically, Paredes belonged to another world, quite different from the one enjoyed by his activist students.[15] Although Paredes continued writing through the decade of the eighties, his collecting and fieldwork which began early in his life ended for the most part in 1962–1963, just before the civil rights movement and the ethnic movements of the sixties (Paredes 1993, 12).[16] Like his New Mexican contemporaries from upriver, he was formed within the Spanish-speaking world that originated with the first Spanish colonies, towns, and ranches along the banks and valleys of the Río Grande. Although he conducted fieldwork as far south as Mexico City and as far north as East Chicago, it was his lifelong duty beginning with his 1942 "The Mexico-Texan Corrido" to study and chronicle the Mexican world of the Lower Río Grande Valley from the two Laredos in the north to Brownsville and Matamoros in the south.[17]

Born in the Texas border town of Brownsville, Paredes was raised on both sides of the Río Grande. His family dates back to the first settlers in Camargo and Mier along the river with the founding of the Spanish colony of Nuevo Santander by José de Escandón in 1749. His ancestors had arrived in 1583 in northern Mexico from Spain with the Portuguese Sephardic adelantado Luis de Carbajal in what is now Tampico, Tamaulipas.[18] Of his ancestors, Paredes explained to me: "They came directly to Tampico and then inland. They were a colony of *sefarditas*, supposedly converted Spanish Jews, who most of them still kept many of their ideas. They were very anticlerical" (Calderón and López-Morín 2000, 203). Paredes was raised within Spanish-language culture and through childhood and adolescence absorbed a great deal of knowledge of northern Mexican history. His great-grandfather had fought with the Mexican army at Palo Alto and Resaca de la Palma during the U.S.-Mexico War. He came from a literate family; his father would compose décimas, a popular Spanish poetic form. He learned to read and write in his first language, Spanish, and at an early age read the Spanish-language newspaper *La Prensa* of San Antonio.

As a Mexican American, Paredes attended Brownsville schools, graduating from Brownsville Junior College in 1935. His home environment was a combination of both Anglo and Mexican worlds. However, from a very young age he enjoyed summers in Tamaulipas on the south bank of the river, living in a rural Mexican environment on a ranch near Matamoros that belonged to one of his older brothers. In 1976 in *A Texas-Mexican "Cancionero"* Paredes wrote: "[I started] 'collecting' . . . songs around 1920, when I first became aware of them on the lips of *guitarreros* and other people of the ranchos and small towns. Few of those singers are alive today. Nacho Montelongo, who taught me the first chords on the guitar, and many of his songs, still farms on the Mexican side of the river" (xviii). *A Texas-Mexican "Cancionero"* contains sixty-six songs dating from Spanish colonial days through the 1950s; songs that Paredes learned from his mother, relatives, friends, and border singers; songs that Paredes knew as part of his musical repertory. His studies of the oral tradition, in the form of musical compositions, which would later serve him well, were not purely academic; he learned and lived the musical culture of the border before becoming a professor.

"With His Pistol His Hand" was a bold reinterpretation of the reigning theories of the origin and dissemination of Spanish folklore in the Southwest.[19] Instead of reading the folklore of border Mexicans as a museum piece, as a remnant of Spanish colonization, Paredes chose to place his study of the rise and decline of the border corrido tradition in situ, within the history and culture of the Spanish colony of Nuevo Santander described in Part One of his book. "The Border people," writes Paredes in Part Two, "made and sang their ballads in response to an inner need, whose sources have been fully discussed in the first part of this book" (Paredes 1958, 182). And he chose one particular corrido, "El Corrido de Gregorio Cortez," to demonstrate that Mexican American folklore was a result of cultural conflict between Anglo Texans and Border Mexicans. He did not dismiss Spanish colonization. The establishment of the province of Nuevo Santander in 1749 marked the beginning of what would be the Mexican-mestizo ranching culture later appropriated by Anglo Texans. The Spanish *romance* ballad, argued Paredes, had been adapted in the mid-nineteenth century by Mexican guitarreros who followed *romance* conventions: a simplicity of versification that led to strength of expression (ibid., 206); a bare bones narrative keeping adjectives and figures of speech to a minimum (216); observance of Spanish meter devices in keeping with the traditional alternating octosyllabic assonant structure (211). To complete his innovative dissertation, Paredes had to pursue interdisciplinary studies and make his own categories. He wrote his dissertation in the English Department and was required to take History of the English Language and courses in the English and American classics. And, of course, he had to take a greater number of graduate courses in Spanish—History of the Spanish Language, El Cid, El Siglo de Oro, and the Spanish ballad tradition. As a performer of corridos, Paredes enriched his study with references to the interrelations between, on the one hand, Spanish verse and meter and, on the other, pitch, tone, and vocalization (215–216).

Through the centuries, the Spanish *romance* was transformed into the border corrido that would express the ideals of the borderers in their struggle against domination. For Aurelio M. Espinosa, the corrido lacked the spirit of the traditional Spanish ballads and was of little value for comparative literature; for Paredes, the corrido, like all folk traditions, was responding to an inner cultural need.[20]

As is well known, Paredes's book has been crucial for the interpretation of Mexican American or Chicano folklore and literature as forms of cultural resistance, and in particular the figure of Gregorio Cortez has assumed almost epic proportions in criticism, a Mexican hero whose life was portrayed on the screen in *The Ballad of Gregorio Cortez* (1984).[21] The privileging of the male warrior hero as the paradigmatic form of Chicano resistance in literature has led to criticism (see Padilla 1993, 38–40).[22]

It would serve us well to recall that Cortez was a son of Mexico, born in 1875 on the south bank of the Río Grande, and that like others searching for work, he migrated north at the age of fourteen working as a vaquero and farmhand in south Texas. Years later, on his farm near Kenedy, Texas, Cortez became a victim of the all-too-familiar Texas justice—shoot first and ask questions later. In 1901 he was unjustly accused of horse theft, and after Sheriff W. T. Morris of Karnes County shot his brother, Romaldo, Cortez drew his gun in self-defense. Fearing being lynched, he ran for his life toward the border and was eventually captured, imprisoned without bond, and tried in a court of law more than once. He was finally convicted in 1905 and sentenced to life imprisonment for the murder of Gonzales County Sheriff Robert M. Glover (not Sheriff Morris), killed during a night shootout when a posse descended upon the house where Cortez had been hiding with a Mexican family. After many appeals, Cortez was eventually pardoned in 1913.[23]

This is hardly the biography of a great warrior hero; however, this is a man who retaliated in self-defense. The corridos and legends that sprang up around Cortez's celebrated ride toward the border emphasized the defiant hero, the one who utters "la defensa es permitida," a concept in the Hispanic world that dates to the conquest of the New World on the rationale concerning a just war of resistance. Paredes would agree with others including writers from his home state of Texas (see Chapter 6, on Rolando Hinojosa) that there are many forms of resistance—surviving, enduring, being resilient in the face of domination—and many kinds of cultural conflicts including those within academia. I am arguing that I am less interested in Gregorio Cortez and more in the individual Américo Paredes who emerged in 1958 as a public intellectual to take a stance in Southwest studies by uttering what was never or seldom admitted but quite obvious, that "[a] restless and acquisitive people, exercising the rights of conquest, disturbed the old ways" (Paredes 1958, 15).[24] In effect, Paredes's book was a redefinition of the borderlands, which is to say, not the "Old Spain in Our Southwest" of the New Mexican elite or the "Spanish Borderlands" of Anglo-American Southwest historiography but Greater Mexico, a historically determined geopolitical zone of military, cultural, and linguistic conflict.

Paredes came late to academia, but his was a meteoric rise to the level of respected scholar. After graduation from Brownsville Junior College in 1936, Paredes worked as a journalist for newspapers on both sides of the border. He was drafted into the army in 1941 and experienced firsthand the turmoil of World War II and the breakout of hostilities in Korea. He was a war correspondent for newspapers in Latin America; served as editor for the U.S. Armed Forces daily *Stars and Stripes*; encountered the devastation, poverty, and suffering in Japan, China, Manchuria, and Korea; and met Hideki Tojo while covering the war crimes trials in Japan. The World War II veteran returned to Texas in 1950 and, at the age of thirty-five, began his undergraduate and graduate studies at the University of Texas, culminating with his Ph.D. in 1956. His experiences with the history of imperialism in Asia would be of great importance for his study of border balladry. In Part One of his dissertation, the mature and wiser graduate student would place on trial the history of Texas, exposing an unjust war of conquest against Mexico and the world of white supremacy (defended by well-known Texas scholars) that ensued after military and cultural domination.[25] One could explain the two-part division of *"With His Pistol in His Hand"* in the following manner. Part Two is written by the university-trained scholar, whereas Part One is written and structured by the wandering point of view of the journalist-correspondent.

Gathering evidence on individuals and events to render judgment on behalf of Mexican borderers was the immediate context for Paredes's developing concept of Greater Mexico.[26] The term "Greater Mexico" implies that there is more than one Mexico beyond the Mexican Republic. And Paredes first defined it in the opening of Part Two of *"With His Pistol in His Hand"* in a parenthetical statement: "Greater Mexico (as we will call the area now comprising the Republic of Mexico, with the exception of the border regions)" (129–130). Born and raised on the Mexican border, Paredes knew that there existed another Mexico under U.S. rule, Mexico in a cultural sense. On the identification of the Texas border corrido composers with Gregorio Cortez, Paredes offers the following: "The point of view is local rather than national. There is no flag-waving, no generalizations about international relations or nationalities. Cortez is Cortez. . . . He refers to himself as a Mexican, but the word has no national connotations. Its meaning is cultural; it is a word that describes Cortez and his kind of people. . . . All people of Spanish culture are *mexicanos*" (ibid., 183). Given the marginality of Mexicans in all areas of U.S. culture and the perceived innate cultural inferiority of Mexicans during the fifties, Paredes's public acceptance of his Mexican identity was a bold statement. One of Paredes's major articles after his 1958 study was "El folklore de los grupos de origen mexicano en los Estados Unidos," published in 1966.[27] Paredes informed an international scholarly audience that there were two Mexicos (today we would say there are many Mexicos): one, the "real" one, was limited to the political boundaries of the Mexican nation; the second, México de Afuera as Mexicans called it, was composed of all the persons of Mexican origin in the United States. Paredes noted the mutual influences of Mexican American and Mexican cultures upon each other as he argued earlier in the study of the border corrido tradition that traveled south to influence the Corrido of the Mexican Revolution. Later, Paredes would collapse the inside/outside polarity into one cultural totality in his 1976 *A Texas-Mexican "Cancionero."* After conducting fieldwork from central Mexico through Chicago in 1962–1963 on the intercultural jest (published in 1993 in *Uncle Remus con chile*), Greater Mexico, now as Greater Mexican areas, would acquire new wider meaning away from the political boundaries of the Mexican republic and the Texas border region: "'Greater Mexico' refers to all the areas inhabited by people of Mexican culture—not only within the present limits of the Republic of Mexico but in the United States as well—in a cultural rather than a political sense" (Paredes 1976, xiv).

In "Old Songs from Colonial Days," the first section of *A Texas-Mexican "Cancionero,"* Paredes confronts directly the myth of the Spanish Southwest invented by Lummis and his followers. Historically, Paredes argues, Mexican culture in the so-called Spanish Southwest has existed since the late 1590s. Although Mexico as a political entity did not come into existence until 1821, culturally, Mexico had its beginnings soon after 1519 when Cortés landed in Veracruz. The regions of New Spain such as New Mexico, which were said to be isolated for centuries from central Mexico and therefore retained their "original" Spanish ancestry, continued to have contact with central Mexico. Immigration and settlement from Mexico continued unabated through the seventeenth and eighteenth centuries and on through the nineteenth century after the U.S. takeover of Mexico. To the New Mexican elite, Paredes responds: "Culturally speaking . . . the *braceros* who came from Mexico after 1890 were part of a continuous process that had begun in the 1590s" (Paredes 1976, 4). Genetically, Mexican culture is mestizo—Spanish and Indian (Mexican Indian as well as Yaqui, Apache, and Comanche), Jewish and black, with other non-Spanish Europeans adding to the mix. Culturally, these Mexican mestizos "are all one people, as far as any people may claim to be a single whole" (ibid.). There are of course regional differences; urban Chicanos from East L.A. and rural New Mexicans do not act exactly alike; these differences are "due more to the North American environment than to the culture they share with each other and the inhabitants of the Republic of Mexico" (ibid.). To deny or ignore this long-standing cultural history is to deceive oneself, argued Paredes against the Hispanophile view of culture in the Southwest.

A *Texas-Mexican "Cancionero"* appeared a few short years after the first important Chicano literary works were published: Rivera's ". . . *y no se lo tragó la tierra"* (1971), Anaya's *Bless Me, Ultima* (1972), and Rolando Hinojosa's *Estampas del valle y otras obras* (1973) and scholarly articles such as Luis Leal's "Mexican-American Literature: A Historical Perspective" (1973) and Juan Bruce-Novoa's "The Space of Chicano Literature" (1975). Paredes, a well-known scholar with an established career in Mexican and Mexican American folklore studies, also responded to the emerging Chicano community of activists, artists, and scholars. Although Paredes admired the Chicano Movement's renewed interest in Mexican culture, he had this to say about the Chicano awakening in the sixties: "Mexican-Americans have been awake to their problems since the time of Cortina [1859]. They have also been quite preoccupied with questions of self-analysis and identity, ever since the Treaty of Guadalupe. The Chicano 'awakening' of the 1960s is the culmination of a long and continuous struggle, spanning more than a century" (Paredes 1976, 27).

Struggle, as Paredes knew well personally and professionally, was indeed one of the defining features of Mexican culture in the United States. However, this Mexican cultural world is not a homogeneous one. Drawing on his experiences while collecting folklore in 1962–1963, Paredes began to analyze internal conflicts and restated his case in *Uncle Remus con chile*: "Since the publication of 'The Anglo-American in Mexican Folklore' in 1966, I have modified my views about cultural conflict as expressed in these texts. At that time I dealt with the conflict between

Anglos and Mexicans exclusively. I am now aware that the conflict is many layered: the Mexican anywhere in Greater Mexico against the *gringo*; the Mexican on both sides of the border against the *agringado*; the Texas-Mexican against the Mexican across the Rio Grande (*los del otro lado*); the Mexican on both sides of the river against the Mexican from the central plateau" (Paredes 1976, 14).[28]

In the last decade of the twentieth century, we discovered that before entering the world of academia Paredes had desired to be a writer. Manuscripts he had completed and abandoned (some of which had been awarded literary prizes) through the course of his scholarly career were finally published. *Between Two Worlds* (1991) is a collection of poetry in a variety of genres written in both Spanish and English during the early thirties, from Paredes's high school years to his participation in World War II. *George Washington Gómez: A Mexico-Texan Novel* (1990) re-counts Anglo-American cultural domination on the border and the emergence of the bilingual Mexican American cultural world during the thirties and forties.[29] *The Hammon and the Beans* (1994) is a collection of seventeen short stories written during the forties and fifties dealing with intercultural relations from the world of south Texas to wartime Japan.[30] And *The Shadow*, a short novel completed around 1955, was published in 1998, not long before his death. In this book, Paredes turns his creative energies toward the south bank of the Río Grande to deal with Mexican class prejudice during the agrarian reform movement in the aftermath of the Mexican Revolution.[31] In 1993 Richard Bauman edited *Folklore and Culture on the Texas-Mexican Border*, a collection of Paredes's eleven major essays on folklore genres and the negotiation of identity. From 1934, the date of "The Rio Grande," the first poem of *Between Two Worlds*, to 1986, when he delivered his last public lecture at Stanford University, Paredes had a remarkable career as writer, journalist, scholar, professor, and mentor.

Here, then, was a writer working for the major part of his life in isolation without a publisher or reading public devoting his life both in the creative and scholarly realms to Mexican culture in the United States.[32] All his work from adolescence to maturity reflects a consistent artistic and political perspective. The 1936 "Alma pocha" from *Between Two Worlds* is a prideful poem of acceptance of a young man's marginalized cultural identity, caught between, on the one hand, the new conquerors, and, on the other, having to withstand the shame of being a pocho, an Anglicized Mexican. On both counts, the Mexican pocho is a foreigner in his native land. However, Paredes ends the poem with a sense of hope: "Alma pocha, / alma noble y duradera, / la que sufre, / la que espera" (Paredes 1991, 36). In the Spanish sonnet "A César Augusto Sandino" of 1939, Paredes, critical of his government's military intervention in Latin America, finds solidarity with the fallen leader of the Nicaraguan Revolution. In the introduction to *Between Two Worlds*, Paredes writes: "I am aware that if this volume finds favor with the reader it will be mostly as a historical document. It is thus that I offer it, as the scribblings of a 'proto-Chicano' of a half-century ago" (11). Even back in 1936 and 1939 Paredes was both intellectually and ideologically my contemporary.

I discovered *"With His Pistol in His Hand"* as an undergraduate at UCLA in 1965 while I was working as a bibliographer for the folklorist Wayland D. Hand, chair of the Program in Folklore and Mythology. In the small departmental library, my gaze came upon the spine of a book with a Spanish-surname author. This was the first book I read by a mexicano from the United States. In those days before the Chicano Movement, I had read several books on the Mexican presence in the United States, the most important of which were attorney-activist-writer Carey McWilliams's *North from Mexico: The Spanish-speaking People of the United States* (1949) and Mexican poet Octavio Paz's *El laberinto de la soledad* (1950). At midcentury, in some intellectual quarters, the Spanish presence in the Southwest had been questioned and rejected. Both McWilliams and Paz focused, though in different ways, on the Mexican mestizo identity of my adopted city, Los Angeles. McWilliams pointed out the multiracial Mexican character of Los Angeles's founding families (McWilliams 1968, 36).[33] Paz, who began his schooling in Los Angeles, returned in 1943 as an adult recognizing the Mexican ambience—people as well as structures—of Los Angeles in conflict with Anglo-American reality.[34] The city with its Mexican American pachucos was crucial, argued Paz, for understanding the extremes of Mexican identity. I had also perused in the departmental library books by J. Frank Dobie, founder of Southwest Studies at the University of Texas, Austin, and the acknowledged authority on Texas history and folklore.[35] However, Paredes's classic study of a border world that I knew well but was alien to books and documents was the molding influence for me: it was the answer to the silencing of our voices, the stereotyping of our culture, and the reification of our history. As others like myself discovered the book, Paredes developed into one of the pivotal figures in the emergence of Chicano literature and scholarship in the early seventies.

The following chapters are devoted to my contemporaries, Rudolfo A. Anaya, Tomás Rivera, Oscar Zeta Acosta, Cherríe L. Moraga, Rolando Hinojosa-Smith, and Sandra Cisneros, writers who at various historical junctures through innovations in form and perspective have contributed greatly to the literature that emerged out of the Chicano Movement.[36] Born between 1929 and 1954, these writers of the second half of the twentieth century have displaced the myth of the Spanish presence in the Southwest and continued on the north side of the Río Grande to both embrace and transform Mexican culture by offering in their work new versions of mujer y hombre, mestiza y mestizo, and mexicana y mexicano. Although from different regions of the United States—California, Illinois, New Mexico, Texas—culturally, they are part of the same diaspora begun in the late sixteenth century; quoting Paredes, they are "all part of a people, as far as any people may claim to be a single whole." However, no culture is without social fissures or immune to history. These writers have continued to bring to the forefront the continuing intra- and intercultural struggles—Spanish versus Indian, Spanish versus Mexican, Anglo versus Mexican, and Mexican versus Mexican. As I argued in the opening autobiographical section of this chapter, in many ways the international border never existed. In 2001, Mexican workers had taken their culture beyond the traditional limits of the Southwest to small towns and urban centers in the South and in the Northeast. However, this Mexican culture of some one hundred fifty plus years is now formed by the cultures and languages of Spain, Mexico, and the United States. This, then, is the literature of the bilingual, bicultural Mexican mestizos of the United States, another area of the cultural amalgam that is Greater Mexico.

WRITING THE DREAMS OF LA NUEVA MÉXICO

Rudolfo A. Anaya's Bless Me, Ultima *and the Southwest Literary Tradition*

Under the apparent deadness of our New Mexico villages there runs a romantic current invisible to the stranger and understood only by their inhabitants. This quiet romance I will try to describe in the following pages of my autobiography.

— CLEOFAS M. JARAMILLO, *ROMANCE OF A LITTLE VILLAGE GIRL*

Roberto owns and operates the small, run-down grocery store that lies off the dirt road in Arroyo Hondo. In the darkness of his dusty, cramped store, he welcomes me in a friendly yet perplexed manner because I am asking questions about the Martínez family that owned a hacienda in Arroyo Hondo as well as the land grant of Tierra Amarilla, given to Manuel Martínez in 1835 by the recently formed Mexican government. I had traveled north of Santa Fe along the foothills of the Sangre de Cristo Mountains on the Camino Alto visiting Nambé, the Santuario del Santo Niño de Atocha at Chimayó, the talladores de Córdova, and the old church at Las Trampas, driving beyond Rancho de don Fernando de Taos and Taos Pueblo to Arroyo Hondo. This far northern area seems to me isolated now, as it was during the seventeenth through nineteenth centuries when the province of la Nueva México was described in official documents and reports by Spaniards and Mexicans alike as a place of subsistence farming, backward and lacking civilization (see Pérez-Linggi 2001, 55–65). Even today, New Mexico, the fifth largest state in the Union, has a population of less than two million. Yet the annual calendar of Southwest cultural festivities has continued to lure many tourists to Charles F. Lummis's Land of Enchantment. I too had come to see for myself a land and people that had been caught in the twentieth century in the politics of identity, between Old Spain and Nueva España, Old Mexico and la Nueva México.

Roberto recalls that across State Highway 522 once was located a large house owned by a powerful sheep ranching family. Nothing remains of that house or the original hacienda or the harmonious world of Spanish Dons and señoritas, kind Mexican servants, and Inditas described by Cleofas Martínez de Jaramillo in her *Shadows of the Past/Sombras del Pasado* (1941) and *Romance of a Little Village Girl* (1955). Roberto continues talking and asking me about my home state, California. Like other young male New Mexicans in the forties, Roberto left his native land to serve in the Pacific in World War II. After the war he worked in an aircraft factory in California for a while but eventually returned to his isolated village of Arroyo Hondo north of Taos. He repeats some well-known historical facts about the Spanish in New Mexico and is pleased to show me some relics from the past that he has collected. I see dusty agricultural tools and an old stove.

In the September afternoon sun, he walks with me outside and shows me the very large pile of wood he has collected for the severe winter to come. On bidding farewell, he encourages me to come back and is emphatic, motioning with his finger, about taking the dirt road away from the village so that I may walk down to the ojo caliente, the hot springs, at the Río Hondo, one of the tributaries of the northern Río Grande. After miles of dirt road and an isolated footpath, I approach and wonder about Alvar Núñez Cabeza de Vaca as he walked through the First Nations in the first decades of the sixteenth century. "Romance and adventure," Jaramillo wrote in *Romance of a Little Village Girl*, "have always ridden hand in hand with the Spanish race" (1). However, I am reminded that I am at the edge of the wilderness when a small rattlesnake to which I yield the right of way crosses my path. However, I am more astonished by my later discovery. Standing overlooking the ojo caliente, my gaze comes upon a nude couple, two Anglo escapees from the postsixties world, I imagine, who have found redemption in an embrace in the warm waters of New Mexico.

The following day is a sunny but cool afternoon, perfect weather for the 280th celebration of the Santa Fe Fiesta. In 1918, Santa Fe's Anglo-American artists persuaded community leaders to reinvent an old tradition, a fiesta that would be authentically Spanish. Amidst tourists and Santa Feans—Chicanos, Native Americans, Anglo-Americans—I, the outsider from California, make my way along the Santa Fe Trail with its trendy, expensive shops and their faux Southwest fronts to the central plaza. Festivities for the Fiesta include the burning of Zozobra, the effigy of gloom; a dance at which the Fiesta queen is chosen; a parade; and in front of the Governor's Palace the reenactment of the reconquest of Santa Fe by Diego de Vargas. This commemoration takes the form of a peaceful meeting between Spanish padres and conquistadores and Pueblo Native Americans. Pageant guides with scripts in hand call out for actors, who are neither Spaniards nor Native Americans, to take their positions. As the actors gesture to each other, others at the plaza stage read their dialogue in English into a microphone for all in attendance to hear. I cannot help but notice across the street the faces of indifferent Native Americans who sell their wares—silver jewelry, beads, and ceramics—under the portal of the Governor's Palace. As I leave the plaza, I hear over the loudspeaker that a direct descendant of Diego de Vargas has been brought from Old Spain as a guest of the 1992 Fiesta organizers.

II

The present is a husk—the past was a romance and a glory.

— CHARLES F. LUMMIS, *THE LAND OF POCO TIEMPO*

Like the other border states of Texas, California, and Arizona, New Mexico has a history of exploration and settlement from northern Mexico, with one notable exception, Alvar Núñez Cabeza de Vaca.[1] He left Spain in 1527 as a member of an expedition to conquer Florida. After wandering for eight years through what is now Texas, southern New Mexico, and Mexico, he returned to northern Mexico in Culiacán, Sinaloa, in 1536. It was from the northern outpost of Culiacán that the exploration of New Mexico began with Fray Marcos de Niza in 1539 and Francisco Vázquez de Coronado in 1540–1542.[2] In 1582, this northern territory received its name from wealthy Antonio de Espejo who both commanded and financed an exploration through central and northern New Mexico. The hope of finding another Mexico, la Nueva México, another Tenochtitlán with its great natural and cultural wealth, was possibly the reason for this American name used by Espejo.

With provisions gathered around the Ciudad de Nuestra Señora de los Zacatecas and traveling from the outpost of Santa Bárbara in what is now the state of Chihuahua, Juan de Oñate took possession of this northern land in 1598, establishing El Paso del Norte and, as capital of la Nueva México, San Juan de los Caballeros, north of present-day Santa Fe. Oñate, born in 1552 in Zacatecas, was the son of Cristóbal who had fought alongside Cortés in the conquest of Mexico and Zacatecas. Oñate was a "natural de provincia," an American of European blood, and his wife, Isabel Tolosa Cortés Moctezuma, was a mestiza, granddaughter of Cortés and great-granddaughter of Moctezuma; they had a son and a daughter (Chipman 1957, 299). Oñate's group included officers' wives, children, and servants; nearly half of the men had been born in Mexico (R. Gutiérrez 1991, 47). After the Pueblo Revolt of 1680, Diego de Vargas followed Oñate with at least three recorded waves of settlers from central Mexico and Zacatecas in the 1690s. This northern Mexican cultural diaspora probably explains why syncretic Spanish-Mexican-Zacatecan traditions such as the cults to the Virgen de Guadalupe and the Santo Niño de Atocha and the danza of the Matachines took root in la Nueva México.

These first settlers and those that followed are indicative of the cultural and racial mixture that was taking place in northern Mexico. By 1680, 90 percent of the New Mexican population was native born and had "undoubtedly become *mestizos*" (ibid., 104). At the end of the eighteenth century, it is calculated that a third of the Spanish-speaking population of New Mexico was composed of genízaros, Christianized children of Apache, Navajo, Ute, or Comanche nomads who lived in Spanish settlements and constituted one of three Spanish-speaking groups along with the Spanish and mestizos (Schroeder 1972, 62). Approximately 10 percent of all persons living in Spanish towns during the eighteenth century were "children of the church," mestizo babies left at the church doorstep by their raped Indian mothers. Of the 13,204 persons who were married legally in New Mexico between 1693 and 1846, only 76 individuals said that their parents were from places other than New Mexico, and of these only 10 said they were from Spain (R. Gutiérrez 1991, 149). In 1789, a church to the Mexican Virgin of Guadalupe was constructed in the capital, Santa Fe, at the end of the Camino Real connecting la Nueva

México with la Ciudad de México. The 1783 altarpiece of the Virgen brought from Mexico City was painted by well-known practitioner of the Mexican school of painting, José de Alcíbar.[3] The church, still standing today, is a clear indication that this mestizo cult to the Virgen, who had already been confirmed by Rome as the official patroness of Nueva España, was already widespread throughout the Catholic faithful. Indeed, a century earlier after the reconquest of Santa Fe in 1692, Tewa leader Don Luis Tupatú was carrying an image of Nuestra Señora de Guadalupe when he surrendered to Don Diego de Vargas and his Nuestra Señora de los Remedios, la Conquistadora (ibid., 144).

Despite this complex legacy, a product of conquest, appropriation, accommodation, and resistance evident in language, dress, cuisine, customs, architecture, and religion, the New Mexican literary tradition in English that surfaced in the late nineteenth century remained obsessed with the Spanish past. Following the conservative romantic tradition established by Charles F. Lummis that I described in Chapter 1, in 1936, Nina Otero-Warren, was promoting the culture of "the Spaniard" and "the Spanish" in New Mexico in her *Old Spain in Our Southwest*.[4] Cleofas Jaramillo is well known for her books on Spanish culture, *Cuentos del Hogar/Spanish Fairy Stories* (1939), *Shadows of the Past/Sombras del Pasado*, *The Genuine New Mexico Tasty Recipes/Potajes Sabrosos* (1942), and *Romance of a Little Village Girl*.[5] Equally telling of Jaramillo's love for things Spanish is the cultural society that she founded in Santa Fe. In 1935, Jaramillo convened meetings to establish La Sociedad Folklórica initially as a response to an incorrect tortilla recipe in *Holland's Magazine*. The bylaws established by the founders called for La Sociedad Folklórica to be composed of "thirty members of Spanish descent and that the meetings were to be conducted in Spanish" for the purpose of "raising more enthusiasm among our native people in participating in large numbers in the celebration of the Fiesta" (Jaramillo 1954).[6] La Sociedad Folklórica still participates in the Anglo-inspired Santa Fe Fiesta by staging La Merienda—An Old Fashioned Style Show, an afternoon fashion show of Spanish heirloom dresses, shawls, mantillas, and jewelry and serving bizcochos and hot "Spanish" chocolate as refreshments.

Based on the history of la Nueva México, the term "español" was not so much a sign of racial purity as a distinction from being tribal indio (R. Gutiérrez 1991, 104). In the Anglo-American period, español still has this distinction for Native Americans. However, for Anglos and New Mexicans, the terms "Spanish" and "español" had the added semantic dimension of racial purity, meaning essentially white. Miguel Otero, the first native New Mexican to serve as governor during the territorial period, used the Spanish translation of greaser, "ceboso," to distance himself from other New Mexicans (see Pérez-Linggi 2001, 143). While visiting the festival of the Corn Dance at Santo Domingo Pueblo, Jaramillo makes the distinction between white people and Indians. Indians pray to their sun god as well as to the white man's God, writes Jaramillo (Jaramillo 1955, 55). This was New Mexico's Hispano upper-class response to the fear of being labeled Mexican, mestizo, or greaser. In her 1932 *Earth Horizon*, Mary Austin writes: "The colonists who came here originally came direct from Spain; they had not much tarrying in Mexico. They brought with them what they remembered, and as soon as they began to create, they made things in the likeness of old Spain" (cited in Padilla 1991, 54). For Austin, some New Mexicans "are white like us." In the Anglo-American conquest of Mexico, as the writings of Lummis and his progeny illustrate, Mexican and mestizo cultural traditions were ignored. New Spain had become the United States without centuries of mixture, without being culturally Mexican.

In the first half of the twentieth century native scholars and compilers of folk collections would label their materials Spanish, although these materials betrayed Mexican origins. To the well-known Coloradan Aurelio M. Espinosa, who made it his life's work to establish the folk links between the Southwest and Spain (see Chapter 1), we should add New Mexicans Otero-Warren and Aurora Lucero-White and Arizonan Luisa Espinel.[7] As the state supervisor for education projects of the Work Projects Administration, Otero-Warren would title her 1942 compilation *Folk Songs of the Spanish Southwest*, although she included well-known Mexican songs such as "La Cucaracha" and "Adelita." In her "*Romances* and *Corridos* of New Mexico" (1936), done under the auspices of the Federal Writers' Project of New Mexico, Lucero-White writes: "New Mexico . . . continued to be an important and prosperous colony of New Spain and as Spanish as Spain itself. To this day she retains almost intact her Hispanic culture including traditional ballads" (1). Luisa Espinel's (Linda Ronstadt's aunt) *Canciones de Mi Padre* of 1946, collected for the *Arizona Quarterly*, carries the subtitle *Spanish Folksongs from Southern Arizona*. Espinel writes in her Introduction: "The songs in this collection are the songs of my father's people. They were descendants of a group of Spaniards who settled during the late eighteenth century in the little valley of Altar in Sonora, Mexico" (5). The awareness in the Chicano period of Mexican culture throughout the former Territory of New Mexico can easily be seen in the Mexican songs of Arizonan Linda Ronstadt's 1987 album, *Canciones de Mi Padre*.[8]

Before the contemporary Chicano period, a regional New Mexican literary tradition developed out of Anglo-American cultural hegemony and, in some instances, out of the complicitous relations of older Hispanic elites with newly arrived Easterners. After New Mexico achieved statehood in 1912, a set of discursive and cultural practices were set in motion by native writers and scholars which were marked by an emphasis on a beautiful, empty landscape, folkloric customs and religious rituals, aristocratic pretense, and an idyllic "Old Spain in Our Southwest" to the exclusion of the real historical and social conditions of the majority of New Mexicans.

III

We leave a lifetime behind . . . but that past has been like a dream. Now we move into the future.

— RUDOLFO A. ANAYA, *HEART OF AZTLÁN*

Since its publication in 1972 as the second book to receive the Premio Quinto Sol, Rudolfo Anaya's *Bless Me, Ultima* has gone on to achieve the status of a best-seller and a Chicano literary classic. Now it is clear that Anaya's book has its origins within the history and literature of the Southwest. We should situate Anaya's *Bless Me, Ultima* as the link between this earlier tradition in English and the emergent Chicano narrative.[9] Although some critics have aligned Anaya with Latin American magic realism, it is clear that his writings were inspired by and responded to one of the most dominant and powerful of Anglo-American artistic discourses called upon to reimagine recently conquered land and sentimentalize its Native American and Mexican inhabitants. If we consider what preordained narrative elements Anaya chooses for his book, such as the admiration for the heroic Spanish past, characters of noble bearing, the romantic landscape, witchcraft in the form of a curandera, and the liturgical and seasonal calendars, then we can also begin to understand the new interpretive focus—the Mexican American search for la Nueva México—that he will bring to the Southwest romance tradition in the seventies and more recently in his novels of the nineties, *Alburquerque* (1992), *Zia Summer* (1995), *Rio Grande Fall* (1996), and *Shaman Winter* (1999).

Perhaps the single most important new element is time. Unlike the older native writers, Otero-Warren and Jaramillo, *Bless Me, Ultima* is future oriented and looks back from an undetermined present at a moment that no longer exists. As the Chicano canon emerges, this emphasis on historical change will unite all regional tendencies. The Chicano Movement was also a call to recognize Mexican mestizo, working-class roots. Drawing on his ancestral roots, Anaya stages his story in the mythical town of Guadalupe, situated in the New Mexican llano east of Alburquerque in the actual county of Guadalupe with its towns, Pastura and Puerto de Luna. Beginning with *Bless Me, Ultima*, Anaya's stories will draw on the history of Río Abajo, New Mexico, not the traditional "Spanish" strongholds—the Santa Fe and Taos areas—of the northern Río Grande Valley.[10] The two central characters—Ultima, the peasant curandera, and Antonio, the child of working-class parents—are Anaya's answers to the Spanish aristocratic pretense of earlier nuevomexicanos from Río Arriba and the Anglo political-aesthetic re-creations of New Mexican history in literature and festivals. Ultima and Antonio are part of the territory's centuries-old historical and cultural reality judged too Mexican, Genaro Padilla argues, to be considered part of the United States (Padilla 1993, 51). Indeed, other areas of the Republic of Mexico, California and Texas, were granted statehood following the U.S.-Mexico War. This was largely due to the influx of Anglo settlers, which created a white majority. The isolated territory of New Mexico had to wait some sixty-four years to be accepted into the Union.

In Aztec myth, Aztlán, the land of the cranes, is the point of origin in the north for the Aztecs as they wandered on their journey to the central valley of Mexico, finally settling on the islands and lakes that were to become Tenochtitlán. At the height of the Chicano Movement's nationalist period, the Southwest, in particular New Mexico, was reclaimed as Aztlán. During the early seventies, Anaya, like other Chicanos, traveled to Mexico visiting archaeological sites such as Cholula in Puebla and Monte Albán in Oaxaca. And like other Chicanos, Anaya discovered an association with Indian Mexico (Anaya 1990, 382). In his second book, *Heart of Aztlán*, published in 1976 in the year of the U.S. bicentennial celebrations, Anaya chooses to focus his interest away from the innocent Spanish Southwest to the Indigenous Chicano Homeland. This novel, the sequel to *Bless Me, Ultima*, is situated in the city of Alburquerque as the Chávez family leaves its rural home of Guadalupe to be caught in the turmoil of fifties New Mexico in the Mexican Barelas barrio. It is saturated with gritty realism—the hopelessness of pachuco gangs, drugs, and poverty is countered by union organizing and the possibility of change. While the narrative still draws on myth and prophecy, as in *Bless Me, Ultima*, it is the Mexican myth of Aztlán that is central; Anaya avoids any mention of the heroic Spanish past that was crucial to the narrative framework of his first work. It was, therefore, for artistic and historical reasons that Anaya wrote his first book as an elegiac romance to capture New Mexico as it was about to be shaken by world events in the twentieth century. Thus through his first books, the Chicano writer Anaya brings closure to a period in New Mexican history.

To claim that Anaya's *Bless Me, Ultima* is a romance, however, implies more than just situating it in a literary tradition; it also involves explaining under what recent institutional conditions it is possible to reconceive this literary form. As bilinguals, Chicano writers have a variety of discourses at their disposal, and the language of literary expression is telling of influences. Through English, Anaya discovered the lyric talent to be used in fiction: the oral tradition could lend rhythm to the narrative, plot techniques learned in Saturday afternoon movies and comic books could help as much as the grand design of the classics he had read (Anaya 1990, 378). Anaya was an instructor of English and holds a master's degree in English from the University of New Mexico. Thus he knows the classics of Western literature and the English tradition, both British and American, as a writer of the late sixties. And although Anaya uses Native American and Chicano cultural motifs, English literary traditions by way of the Romantics, Gerard Manley Hopkins, T. S. Eliot, and James Joyce have played a significant role in shaping his book.[11] But also Northrop Frye—who has done so much to establish the legitimacy of romance as a critical concept—is an unquestionable dominant influence. From Frye, Anaya derives his plot structures of romance and key terms in his literary vocabulary, such as archetype, mythos, inscape, and epiphany.[12]

Historically, romance is possible, using Frye's often-repeated phrase, during periods of cultural transformation when myth is displaced toward the aesthetic realm.[13] As a written form, romance follows in the wake of the dissolution of a world conceived through mythic or, with reference to Lévi-Strauss, magical consciousness and whose dominant form of discourse is oral and formulaic. Displacement means that beliefs in foundation myths are depragmatized, removed from their original collective context, deprived of their truth effect and transformed into the metaphors and archetypes of imaginative literature. Most Mexican American residents of the Southwest belong to a literate, mass-media culture. However, because of the uneven evolution of the area, many Mexican Americans (like Latin Americans and other members of the Third World) still live in a world whose consciousness is still highly influenced by myths, folk beliefs, and superstitions, the remnants of pre-Columbian life together with Hispanic folk traditions. This discourse with its worldview and lively imagination is available to Chicana and Chicano writers, and in large measure accounts for similarities with contemporary Latin American fiction.[14] Although the displaced formulaic units of myths and folk beliefs stand out in *Bless Me, Ultima*, the book is not a folklore collection, nor is its style of presentation oral as is the case with novels written in Spanish (". . . *y no se lo tragó la tierra*," for example); this is a deliberately crafted fiction, written in lofty, often poetic style, treating of heroism and fabulous things. It approaches the level of narrative fantasy and should be interpreted accordingly.

The folk motif of La Llorona, for example, has a special function in the book and is related to the theme of misdirected responses to a calling or vocation. The "Wailing Woman" is transformed into an evil spirit who wanders along riverbanks seeking to drink the blood of men and boys, and is, therefore, a negative feminine archetype, along with the siren of the Hidden Lakes and the prostitutes of Rosie's house. As in *The Odyssey* and Joyce's *Ulysses*, these three figures act as blocking agents and beckon men to their haunts to seduce and turn them away from their heroic destinies. Along similar lines of argument, I cannot totally agree with David Carrasco, who reads *Bless Me, Ultima* as a religious text because of what he terms non-Christian, authentic Chicano religious experience depicted in the scene of curanderismo or folk healing (206–208). This most important scene occurs in Chapter 10, near the center of the book, and is contrived to reflect mythic patterns of both Native American and Christian traditions. The young (about eight years old) Antonio and Ultima must struggle against the sorcery of the three evil daughters of Tenorio Trementina. The blood of the youngest Márez is tested to resurrect his youngest uncle, Lucas Luna, from certain death at the hands of the Trementina sisters. For three days the innocent Antonio, the son of María and Gabriel, suffers in a semiconscious state and eventually through magical sympathy heals the bewitched Lucas. These events of the hero as donor, scapegoat, and savior show up for the reader not as an undisplaced religious belief but as a semantic component intrinsic to the romance when Ultima tells Antonio that life is never beyond hope because good is always stronger than evil (91).

This reading of *Bless Me, Ultima* within the history of New Mexico and the evolution of literary forms will benefit from two elements in the above scene of curanderismo: one is the semantic opposition between good and evil, and the other is the messianic structure of the plot. These elements in Anaya's narrative will lead, on the one hand, to the representation of subjectivity and, on the other, to the reconstruction of historical events in the romance form.[15]

We can approach the theoretical question of the representation of subjectivity in Anaya's romance through the high level of abstraction that runs through the stylized characters, both attractive and evil, settings, scenes, and almost any aspect of the physical landscape. These aspects of the narrative can be meaningfully good or evil, which is to say that through the filtering mind of the characters they can be given the categories of subjectivity and agency. Anaya portrays more than the physical landscape of eastern New Mexico, for a romantic sense of place unfolds for the reader in the opening paragraph of the book as Antonio's consciousness is awakened by Ultima's guidance to the spirit and beauty of the llano in summer. In the area surrounding the small town of Guadalupe even the dark River of the Carp has a soul, can experience feelings, rising and falling emotions. For Antonio, his friends, and Ultima, the river can be at times an evil presence that watches over people. The darkness of the river is counterbalanced by the sense of sanctity that pervades the clear pond where the golden carp, the image of a pre-Columbian god, surfaces every summer. There is a flow of agency among human, animal, and vegetable worlds. The town drunk Narciso can make his garden grow into abundance by ritual magic, by singing, dancing, and planting by moonlight. Anaya's commitment to the plots of myths and fairy tales is emphasized by the role given to Ultima's owl, which carries her soul within its body. It is her bond to time and the harmony of the universe, and when her protective spirit dies at the hands of Tenorio Trementina so does Ultima. In terms of the history of the evolution of consciousness, we are clearly in an animistic landscape where transformations can occur at any moment and events are the products of cyclical patterns or magical causality, spells, and curses. In sum, it is a preindividualistic world of higher and lower realms for which the magical and later religious categories of spirit and soul, not character, have served Anaya well.

Unlike the more secular plots of realism, a sense of messianic vocation governs the overall structure of *Bless Me, Ultima*. As in religion, at a privileged moment in history and in a forsaken world, there is a need for a providential hero capable of resolving the contradictions between past and future, good and evil. The hero of romance is analogous to the mythical Messiah, and such is the case with Antonio, whose destiny is prophesied by dream visions and epiphanies. The events crucial to the hero's maturation are structured around a harmonious past belonging to his forefathers and Ultima and a chaotic present symbolized by the dissolution of communal existence. Here Frye's notion of the romance as an expression of desire or nostalgia for an imaginative Golden Age is foregrounded for the reader (Frye 1957, 186).

Anaya's book can be described as an elegiac romance, a beautiful vision of a Hispanic Southwest that is passing out of existence set against the background of world-historical events whose repercussions are felt throughout the region surrounding Guadalupe. These events are dramatically significant because Anaya has felt the need to recall them: they are the end of World War II that disrupts the unity of the Márez family, turning sons against father and older ways of life, and the advent of the nuclear age that can signal the destruction of both humankind and nature.

The narrative fantasy of the Golden Age establishes on biological and historical levels an ancestral homeland for Antonio. The young protagonist is the son of Gabriel Márez and María Luna, members of patriarchal clans who have settled in Spanish New Mexico. These colonists are emblematic of two Spanish archetypes of male leadership, the conquistador and the priest. The Márez are rough men who derive their symbolic name from seafaring conquistadors turned sheepherders and vaqueros who ride the virgin llano (actually the western edge of the Llano Estacado, or Great Plains, explored by Coronado in 1542). The Lunas derive their patronymic from a priest who founded a farming community in the valley of the moon. Two antithetical but nonetheless similar principles are operative in these bloodlines. The Márez are people of the sun and lead a life of freedom on the unspoiled sea plain near the village of Las Pasturas; the Lunas are stable, more civilized, tied to the soil in the community of El Puerto de los Luna, and lead their life under the aegis of the moon. Though both settlements have historical antecedents in New Mexican towns with similar names, in the transformation of the area from Native American nomadic life to Spanish pastoral and agricultural stages, they represent idealized worlds better than the city life of

Guadalupe. These families belong to a romantic pastoral, a village life when men lived unalienated from nature and in harmony among themselves. Visions of extreme toil and hardship have been replaced by freedom, idleness, and happiness. Los Márez and Lunas enjoy a communal existence of a limited number of individuals, uncorrupted by the outside world, and are reminiscent of the Golden Age and the Earthly Paradise, two motifs that have continually molded the vision of the New World as witnessed in Columbus's first accounts of Native Americans.[16]

In "The Gospel According to Mark," Borges writes: "[G]enerations of men, throughout recorded time, have always told and retold two stories—that of a lost ship which searches the Mediterranean seas for a dearly loved island, and that of a god who is crucified on Golgotha" (310). These plot summaries of two collective epics have structured many of the plots of romance including Borges's fiction. The epics tell of departure and return, a rupture with an original unity and a quest for a lost homeland by way of suffering, endurance, and a perilous voyage. "Borges," writes Frye of these two plots, "is clearly suggesting that romance, as a whole, provides a parallel epic in which the themes of shipwreck, pirates, enchanted islands, magic, recognition, the loss and regaining of identity, occur constantly" (Frye 1976, 15). Similarly for Anaya, a patriarchal foundation myth, the ancestral homeland, provides a context for individual adventure, for what will be Antonio's difficult voyage to manhood and fulfillment of his destiny within the postlapsarian world of the twentieth century. Antonio wanders, as his restless, seafaring blood determines, through the world of romance. He crosses bodies of water, encounters evil groves, comes upon Narciso's enchanted garden in the wasteland of Guadalupe and witnesses the golden carp in its sacred pool. Along the riverbanks he meets with sinister feminine figures, La Llorona, the siren or mermaid, and the Circe-like Rosie, the madam of the brothel. At El Puerto he faces the one-eyed (Cyclops) Tenorio Trementina and his three evil daughters. And at the Agua Negra Ranch on the sea plain he is bewildered by the mystery of the "wandering rocks" that fall from the sky. He will suffer for three days in order to revive his uncle from certain death. In the end he will make the trip back to his spiritual homeland, to peace and contentment of mind.

Following the hero's adventure in romance, which is the individual equivalent of the cyclical patterns of collective myth, Antonio will be a figure of renewal. He is destined, as Ultima prophesies and his dream visions indicate, to continue the positive elements of two bloodlines that have fallen from their historic greatness. Las Pasturas is fast disappearing, and El Puerto is without the leadership of a man of learning, the priest. Having to relocate near the city of Guadalupe, the Márez father has lost the freedom of the range and is ineffectual as the patriarch of the family. No longer a vaquero, he now works on a highway gang and spends most of his idle time drinking. The three Márez brothers who have returned from the war in the Pacific no longer want to follow their father's dreams to go west to California as a family, nor do they want to farm like the Lunas. The shattering of the foundation myth as the context of heroic adventure is evident in the ironic gap between the brothers' actions and their names. León, the eldest, is symbolic of primogeniture, courage, and leadership, and also recalls the genealogical link of the Márez family with the Spanish Empire. The second son, Andrew, derives his name from the Greek *Andreas* and *andros*, signifying male or masculine. And the youngest, Eugene, is a reference to the Greek *Eugenios* and *eugenés*, meaning wellborn. Antonio's brothers should be strong male leaders of good breeding; yet they are self-interested, alienated men, corrupted by the outside world, and succumb to the pleasures and vices that money can buy, especially to the allure of Rosie's girls. Thus, the blood of the Márez men, formerly the exuberant freedom of the vaqueros, is turned into aimless wandering, and the peaceful, sedentary life of the Lunas turns into inaction.

Given these historical circumstances, Antonio's destiny is to seek a reconciliation between the two bloodlines. His role as mediator between past and future is demonstrated in his first of ten dreams that recalls both the Feast of the Nativity and the Feast of Epiphany. At his moment of birth, the two clans converge to greet María's son, offering gifts symbolic of both lifestyles from which Antonio must choose one. In the wake of the loss of paternal authority, like other wellborn heroes of romance—warriors, founding fathers, kings, and divine beings—Antonio must live up to his good breeding and forge a new image of manhood. As is foreseen, he will be a man of learning and choose the pen and paper. In a new historical configuration and as an intellectual, Antonio will be restless in his search for new understanding but tied to the traditions of his people and the land of his birth.

Since this problematic moment in the life of the Márez family is rendered in classic Romantic fashion—the dissolution of both Hispanic lifestyles and communal organization, and the consequent, sad transition to the free but alienated workers of capitalism, the disappearance of pastoral and agricultural modes of production with the concomitant estrangement from the cyclical world of nature—Anaya will follow through with his argument and seek a resolution to these historical transformations not through the hero of epic and conquest or the priest of institutionalized religion but through the Romantic artist-hero, here the child-man of sympathy and feeling. Only the visionary Antonio, who in his dreams dons the priestly robes as poet and prophet, is capable of articulating the teachings of nature.

Just as the father-centered myth of the Messiah through the archetypes of the Golden Age and the Earthly Paradise provides the background for the historical progression of events, a parallel matriarchal mythology through Ultima provides a vast panorama for the prehistory of the Southwest. Ultima is, thus, superior to any realistic portrayal of a curandera. Her vision animates the landscape for Antonio; through her prophecy his future is determined. She is, following Geoffrey Hartman's terminology, the Romantic genius loci of the llano with whose guidance the future writer Antonio (and Anaya) is blessed (Hartman 1970, 314). She possesses the collective memory of the mestizo race. In her role as shaman and midwife, she knows the secret healing power of plants. She instills in Antonio a respect for the spirit of all living things and a faith in the eventual goodness of nature. As Antonio states, her protective owl is the spirit of the llano, night and moon, and Ultima as night sorceress is, therefore, related to lunar fertility cults and the figurative representation of the natural world as an earth goddess renewing her vitality every year. Although the events in Guadalupe (another matriarchal cult) have their historical referents in the twentieth century, they are generated out of an immemorial past through the seasonal cycle: from the harvest of the fall, to the sterility of winter, followed by the eventual rebirth in spring and summer. Ultima as genius loci is the alternative to the other places symbolic of New Mexico—Taos, Santa Fe, and Spanish festivals.

Ultima is also a homogeneous figuration of woman taken in part from the storehouse of images of Jung's archetypal unconscious. It is significant to recall that Antonio's first meeting with Ultima occurs in his first dream, when he returns to the wilderness, to the land of his birth in Las Pasturas. Her name can be interpreted as an allusion to the anima spirit symbolizing those "feminine" tendencies in the male psyche such as intuitions, prophetic hunches, capacity for love, and, above all, feelings for nature.[17] These characteristics through Ultima's teachings set off Antonio from the rest of his "crude," male friends, especially Horse and

Bones, who usually assume the self-assured and aggressive behavior of machismo. Antonio's scene of heroic action will be not one of physical prowess but, thanks to his teacher, the chivalric knight's nobility of character, civility, courtesy, and sympathy for others. In terms of a psychological fantasy, Anaya's romance evokes from the lost past the secure world of mother-infant relationships before the Oedipal phase and the fixing of the male ego.

Antonio's symbolic relationship to Ultima is dramatically presented in the opening lines of the book through an unmediated perception of nature which Anaya terms the "epiphany in landscape" or the "writer's inscape." According to Joyce's classic definition of the concept, epiphany is a sudden spiritual manifestation when the artist instantaneously and irrationally gains new knowledge out of proportion with the commonplace object or event which produces it.[18] The wide currency of the term, though applied to certain modern fantastic narratives, is most significantly associated with the British Romantics' use of nature imagery.[19] For Frye, as is well known, the point of epiphany describes a turn in the plot of romance, a moment of illumination when the undisplaced apocalyptic world and the cyclical world of nature come into alignment (Frye 1957, 203). Anaya has a similar interpretation:

> In speaking about landscape, I would prefer to use the Spanish word *la tierra*, simply because it conveys a deeper relationship between man and his place, and it is this kinship to the environment which creates the metaphor and the epiphany in landscape. On one pole of the metaphor stands man, on the other is the raw, majestic and awe-inspiring landscape of the southwest; the epiphany is the natural response to that landscape, a coming together of these two forces. And because I feel a close kinship with my environment I feel constantly in touch with that epiphany which opens me up to receive the power in my landscape. (Anaya 1977, 98–99)

Although Anaya uses "la tierra," which refers more to raw nature, the land, he interprets his moment of epiphany as a vision or recognition of the timeless spiritual forces of the Southwest. His interpretation is wholly consistent with the structures of feeling that emerged out of the Romantic movement. Thus his use of nature is not geographic but aesthetic; it is a landscape which can inspire awe and feeling in the observer; it is a sense of place where the individual finds solace and comfort.[20] "I do not merely mean the awe and sense of good feeling which we experience in the face of grandeur and beauty," explains Anaya, "it means that there is an actual healing power which the epiphany of place provides" (ibid., 101). It is this sense of place that distinguishes Anaya's hero from his alienated brothers. Here Antonio describes Ultima's first touch:

> She took my hand and I felt the power of whirlwind sweep around me. Her eyes swept the surrounding hills and through them I saw for the first time the world beauty of our hills and the magic of the green river. My nostrils quivered as I felt the song of the mockingbirds and the drone of the grasshoppers mingle with the pulse of the earth. The four directions of the llano met in me, and the white sun shone on my soul. The granules of sand at my feet and the sun and sky above me seemed to dissolve into one strange, complete being. (Anaya 1972, 10–11)

And while the content of the epiphany is a spiritual return to one's ultimate origins, its representation in Romantic literature is that of inscape, a term that Anaya used and borrowed from Hopkins and which Frye associates with the concept of epiphany.[21] Inscape, as Antonio expresses above, is the underlying unity of all things, best exemplified through landscape imagery. In inscape, nature as an object of knowledge absorbs the subject, and the variety and individuality of all things become aspects of a higher cosmic unity beyond the normal functioning of the rational faculties.

The inspirational moments in Anaya's book are heightened and contrasted by imminent manifestations that are not produced by the two structures of learning that dominate the cityscape: the massive brown building that holds the Christian cross and the yellow schoolhouse with the promise of a new language. Although these institutions are for Antonio sacred in their own right, one for the mysteries of catechism, and the other for the magic in the letters, they can not equal Ultima's knowledge. Unlike the landscape, these lifeless structures offer no sense of harmony, nor do they hide beneath their surface a spiritual quality that will give rise to an epiphany. As many times as Anaya forces the reader to gaze along with Antonio from the hilltop on the edge of the llano at the church tower and the top of the schoolhouse across the river in Guadalupe, no new spiritual understanding is forthcoming. This fact is dramatically emphasized in the Christmas play at school which is not a Nativity scene but the Feast of Epiphany. Because of a blizzard, the girls, who had conceived along with Miss Violet the play of the wise men, are unable to attend school and participate in the performance. An important moment in Christian myth that assures all faithful the salvation of their souls turns into a satiric, topsy-turvy world because of the boys' inability to feel the traditional intensity and solemnity of the play in their newly assigned roles. Someone tips over and decapitates the Christ-child; Florence, who portrays one of the wise men, questions the idea of a virgin birth; Abel urinates during the performance; Horse, Mary in the play, rebels at being called a virgin; Bones sails down from the rafters landing on Horse; a free-for-all ensues, and in the tumult stage props are destroyed.

Another similar children's drama in which Florence plays a central role leads to the culminating point of non-Epiphany at Easter. On Holy Saturday, Antonio is forced into the role of religious leader and acts as priest for Horse and Bones, who are preparing for their first confession. This role is a realization of his mother's wishes and one which Antonio had performed before when he recited the Act of Contrition for Lupito when he was killed in the River of the Carp and when he heard Narciso's confession prior to his death at the hands of Tenorio Trementina. Unlike these earlier solitary and fatal moments, this public gathering of children is a beginning, a rite of passage from innocence to the knowledge of sin; it is an opportunity for Horse and Bones to boast about their sins which are sexual in nature. However, what had started out as a mischievous game turns into a deadly serious ritual when the heretic Florence is chosen to go third. He is someone who seeks the same understanding as Antonio but who has rejected the teachings of the Church. As an outsider to the Christian community, he forms a vivid symbolic triad with Ultima and the golden carp; all are bathed in light and serve as intellectual guides for Antonio. For example, as opposed to the red lightbulb outside Rosie's which serves as a "beacon of warmth inviting weary travelers," a religious aura radiates from Florence, giving him the appearance of an angel. During the school play, "Tall angelic Florence moved under the light bulb that was the star of the east. When the rest of the lights were turned off the light bulb behind Florence would be the only light" (148). In church, "[t]he afternoon sun poured through one of the stained glass windows that lined the walls and the golden hue made Florence look like an angel" (190–191). Although Florence is a nonbeliever and accuses God of sinning against him, he admits to no wrong. Knowing of Florence's unfortunate life—he is an orphan and his sisters are prostitutes at Rosie's—Antonio goes against the children's evil desires, now a mob seeking death as punishment, and absolves Florence without penance. For this act of compassion, Antonio becomes the object of vengeance and the boys "engulf him like a wave." The pitiless beating and torture that Antonio receives becomes a turning point in the plot when the angel (or Apollonian messenger) tells the would-be leader that he could never be their priest.

These dramatic moments are consistent with the salvational plot and the voyage of the romance hero, for they represent the fulfillment of the man of learning and sympathy. The ritual which propels the children into the world of adults through sexual and death drives is a repetition of the two earlier fatal moments, recalling that Lupito's blood was shed because of a call for vengeance from a mob of armed men and that Narciso's death was in part due to Andrew who had fallen under the spell of Rosie's girls and was unable to help. At this point in the plot, however, Antonio is not a bystander; he takes the opportunity to exercise his judgment as leader and to display, according to Ultima's teachings, the courage and the sacrifice of commitment to one less fortunate. Moreover, the burden of being a priest is, in a sense, lifted from his shoulders.

On the following day after receiving the Eucharist for the first time, Antonio gains no new understanding to compete with Ultima's magic or the Native American myth of the golden carp. He recalls:

> I had just swallowed Him, He must be in there! For a moment, on the altar railing, I thought I had felt His warmth, but then everything moved so fast. There wasn't time just to sit and discover Him, like I could do when I sat on the creek bank and watched the golden carp swim in the sun-filtered waters. . . .
>
> A thousand questions pushed through my mind, but the Voice within me did not answer. There was only silence. . . . On the altar the priest was cleaning the chalice and the platters. The mass was ending, the fleeting mystery was already vanishing. (210–211)

This high moment in the mass is not foreign to the quest-plot of romance, remembering the identification in chivalric literature of the pagan graal legend with the chalice of the Last Supper containing Christ's blood. However, this is not a traditional religious romance in which the Christian soul moves toward the illumination provided by God's grace. For Antonio, unlike the Christian knight, finds no answer to the evil and chaos that besets the countryside: the alienation in his family, the deaths of Lupito and Narciso, the ill fortune of Florence and his family. The church has ceased to be a house of wonders symbolized by the absence of the traditional magic and mystery of the mass. Antonio's experience in church is almost a nonevent compared to the high and expressive style with which the spiritual forces in the landscape, the healing power of Ultima, the beauty of the golden carp, even the frightful presence of Tenorio are described. If, as Lévi-Strauss asserts, "there is no religion without magic any more than there is magic without a trace of religion," then this scene can be read as a rejection of the Christian-quest plot together with its ideological content for the magic of a prior mythical world (221). According to the rhetoric of Anaya's argument, the Church and its ritual will now appear foreign and superimposed on a New World landscape with its new symbolic astral deities, Ultima who is associated with the moon goddess and the solar myth of the golden carp.

The weakened faith in the authority of the winter and spring rites of the liturgical calendar is counterbalanced by the knowledge that the seasonal cycle provides, and the religious book of revelations is replaced by the book of nature. As Antonio matures, he repeats similar patterns from the darkness of confusion to the clarity of vision. After he witnesses the death of Lupito—the soldier who returned sick and crazed from the war—Antonio is troubled by the evil *presence* that surrounds the River of the Carp. As Ultima hints, the "throbbing, secret message" hidden beneath the surface of the water is not yet ready to reveal itself. Unlike the barren, hard masculine structures of the church and the schoolhouse, the river is a more animated feminine symbol with a life-supporting rhythm of its own. Although it flows south to water the fertile valley of the Lunas, during summer it can be a torrent of churning water. At the appropriate cyclical time after the summer floods have washed away all life downstream, leaving only small pools of water, the hero beholds the beautiful and fatal struggle of the carp to regain their homeland in the north. Peace and tranquillity may be shattered by death and struggle, yet hope remains. Like Lupito, many fish will die along the river, but others will succeed and return to their origins and assure the continuity of future generations.

"I felt I sat on the banks of an undiscovered river," narrates Antonio of the River of the Carp in summer, "whose churning, muddied waters carried many secrets" (73). These hidden messages surface to consciousness from the past of collective memory through the tale of the golden carp. This Native American myth of origins explaining the yearly struggle of the carp is told to Antonio by Samuel, a fellow fisherman and schoolmate, whose father learned it from the only Indian in Guadalupe. It tells of a tribe's search for the promised land, the rewards of faith, and the necessity of punishment because of a broken promise. The beginning and ending of a vast human cycle are evident in the transformation of the tribe into carp. There remains, however, the existence of a god so overcome by sympathy and love for his people that he chose to be a carp and rule among them as the lord of the waters. As in the chronicles of discovery whose protagonists are pressed on by strange and wondrous tales, the descendant of conquistadors follows his barefoot, Indian-like guide, Cico, across the dark waters of the river in quest of his own El Dorado. Through Narciso's magic garden, the modern version of the promised land, along the banks of El Rito Creek, whose waters flow from the Hidden Lakes where mermaids dwell, Antonio and Cico finally arrive at the sacred pond where every summer the lord of the waters surfaces as a scenic register for a prior magical world. Under the clarity of the sun, in a pleasant environment, and as if in church, where one communicates only in whispers, Antonio experiences an epiphanic moment:

> Then the golden carp swam by Cico and disappeared into the darkness of the pond. I felt my body trembling as I saw the bright golden form disappear. I knew I had witnessed a miraculous thing, the appearance of a pagan god, a thing as miraculous as the curing of my uncle Lucas. And I thought, the power of God failed where Ultima's worked; and then a sudden illumination of beauty and understanding flashed through my mind. This is what I expected God to do at my first holy communion! (105)

This scene represents the fulfillment of the hero's search, given that Antonio witnesses in the golden carp the Romantic affirmation of beauty and love. This is certainly the message of goodness articulated over and over by the plot, which, in fact, closes the book with Ultima's death when Antonio understands that the tragic consequences of life can be overcome by the magical strength in the heart.

However, the initiation into the secrets of the past (shared by Antonio, Samuel, Cico, Narciso, and Ultima) brings with it not only understanding but responsibility and conscience as well; for the hero's plot converges with a providential master plot. As in other instances in the narrative where objects are coded in binaries of good and evil, love and hate, the beautiful moment is shattered when the "waters of the pond explode" with the arrival of the killer bass, the one who is capable of destroying his own kind:

> I turned in time to see Cico hurl his spear at the monstrous black bass that
> had broken the surface of the waters. The evil mouth of the black bass was
> open and red. Its eyes were glazed with hate as it hung in the air surrounded
> by churning water and a million diamond droplets of water. . . . The huge
> tail swished and contemptuously flipped it aside. Then the black form
> dropped into the foaming waters. (105)

And to underscore the unavoidable presence of evil and the sense of
impending doom, the golden carp has issued forth an apocalyptic prophecy to haunt the fallen world of the twentieth century. As proof of the
continued moral degeneration of Guadalupe, the sins of the people will
weigh so heavy upon the land that the city will be destroyed by the forces
in nature. Antonio learns that the bodies of water encircling Guadalupe
are united underground in a hidden lake (whose spring waters Narciso's
garden), which, like a nightmare breaking through from the unconscious,
will engulf the city and its people. Following a turn from the beautiful to
the sublime, the pleasure in feeling the radiance of a natural god is
converted to the terror of the future day of reckoning.

What is important at this point is not so much the confrontation of
mind and nature mediated through the Romantic imagination but the
curious parallels among the messages in the landscape, the incidents in
the magical world of the llano, the valley, and Guadalupe, and the historical events chosen by Anaya as a frame of reference. The personification
of the bass as hatred and contempt, together with event after event
reporting injury or death, can be interpreted as commentaries on war. All
these events lead back specifically to the world of men, their egos and
their aggressive instincts. They are related in earlier stages of development to the excitement aroused by fighting and bloodshed among the
boys. Florence's day of judgment, when the mob seeking vengeance asks
for his death, serves to confirm Cico's observation that people seem to
want to hurt each other, especially when they act in groups (102). In the
conflictive world of adults, Antonio is unable to account for the deaths of
Lupito, Narciso, and Ultima, except as the result of evil and revenge. The
killer bass from the world of nature certainly has his equal in the
unremorseful villain, Tenorio. That fighting can lead to disorder is portrayed in the ending of the school drama when all stage props are destroyed. The annihilation of the scenic world of the play is echoed by (1)
the rumors around Guadalupe that the world is going to end (69–70) and
(2) the feelings among the residents that the new bomb manufactured to

end the war has disturbed the seasons to such an extent that its knowledge will eventually destroy them all (184–185). Thus, it is not surprising that the providential master plot having the sins of the people against each other as a motive force should end in the complete destruction of a city.

The interpretation of a momentous historical shift that, as I have argued, accounts for the solace in nature and the passing of an innocent, paradisiacal world (Antonio writes many years after Ultima's death) allows us to say the following about the priority of a mythical code over secular history in romance. Those events which in an empirical narrative or a realistic novel could have been worked out and charged to the forces of history—ideologies, political conflicts, science and technology—are narrated along with events conceived as products of cyclical time, ritual, magic, prophecy, and sin portrayed through the myth of the hero in climactic moments as immanent moral or spiritual messages in nature.

This reading of *Bless Me, Ultima* was facilitated by a methodology which, beginning early in the twentieth century, has been not only a critical method but also one of the dominant aesthetics of our time, one which accounts in large measure for the book's international popularity. The reader's easy access into the Chicano world of Antonio is made possible by the archetypal or mythical method for which Eliot's *The Waste Land* and Joyce's *Ulysses* have been molding influences. In his review of *Ulysses* in 1923, Eliot took note that Joyce's book did not conform to the handling of events in the novel. And he added that while *A Portrait of the Artist* was a novel, he doubted if Joyce would ever write one again. In pursuing a parallel between *The Odyssey* and his own work through myths and archetypes, Joyce had discovered a method for others to follow. Eliot writes:

In using myth, in manipulating a continuous parallel between contemporaneity and antiquity, Mr. Joyce is pursuing a method which others must pursue after him. . . . It is simply a way of controlling, of ordering, of giving a shape and a significance to the immense panorama of futility and anarchy which is contemporary history. It is a method already adumbrated by Mr. Yeats, and of the need for which I believe Mr. Yeats to have been the first contemporary to be conscious. It is a method for which the horoscope is auspicious. Psychology (such as it is, and whether our reaction to it be comic or serious), ethnology, and *The Golden Bough* have concurred to make what was impossible even a few years ago. Instead of narrative method, we may now use the mythical method. It is, I seriously believe, a step toward making the modern world possible for art. (Eliot 1975, 177–178)

In the light of the years since the publication of Eliot's "Ulysses, Order, and Myth," his statements have proved prophetic. Modern psychology, Freudian but mostly Jungian, the Cambridge School of Comparative Anthropology through Frazer, Weston, and others, and the general interest in "primitive" art and culture were fruitful for some aspects of abstract art as well as for a modernist tradition of nonmimetic narrative. When we consider the enormous impact of modern psychology and anthropology on the traditions with which I am most familiar, the Latin American and the Chicano, then family resemblances can be perceived among *The Waste Land*, *Ulysses*, Borges's *El jardín de senderos que se bifurcan* (*The Garden of the Forking Paths*, 1941), Alejo Carpentier's *Los pasos perdidos* (*The Lost Steps*, 1953), Juan Rulfo's *Pedro Páramo* (1955), García Márquez's *Cien años de soledad* (*One Hundred Years of Solitude*, 1967), Fuentes's *Terra nostra* (1975), and *Bless Me, Ultima*.

Eliot's comments, written in a postwar decade, are not as significant for establishing a literary tradition for *Bless Me, Ultima* as they are for suggesting the usefulness of mythical structures for controlling, ordering, and giving shape to the "immense panorama and futility" of history. We are now in a better position to return to Anaya's romance and read its symbolic characterization, narrative sequences, and supernatural landscape not so much as positive fulfillments of generic specifications, but, as I have tried to suggest with the man of learning and sympathy, as an occasion to express symbolic solutions to the problems posed by the uncontrollable events of history (Jameson 1981, 79–80). Anaya's narrative strategies can be pressed for meaning in a wider cultural context and interpreted as a flight from history. The actual events of the discovery and conquest of the New World and the Southwest (the ground zero of interpretation for all Chicano narratives) are repressed and reconceptualized as a nostalgia for the heroic ideals of an earlier colonial society or as a return to the adventure and magic of the romance. The agents of imperialism, the conquistador and the priest, are legitimated and viewed as better alternatives to the fallen men of Guadalupe. And finally, the authority of a romantic rhetoric is called upon to produce an aesthetically effective and tightly knit structure of good and evil which is then superimposed on a region and modes of production properly belonging to Third World agrarian societies or peasant cultures, yet without any worthwhile analysis or attention to the contradictions of race, class, and gender which were the results of conquest.

Special attention is due the binary structure of good and evil. It is repeated throughout the narrative by pairings and oppositions beginning with the overall pattern of twenty-two chapters and ten dreams, conscious life versus semiconscious nightmares. As for characterizations, there are the abstract, phallocentric entities of male and female, María Luna versus Rosie, Ultima against Tenorio, the three sinful Márez brothers, the three Trementinas, the innocent bachelors that die, Lupito, Narciso, and Florence. Rural life is contrasted with city life, Las Pasturas with El Puerto, Narciso's garden with the evil grove of the Trementinas, the dark waters of the River of the Carp with the clear water of the sacred pond, and the golden carp with its rival the black bass. The writer uses a method of classification in which every narrative element appears to have its logical opposite. In addition, these binaries repeat the prophecy of redemption (Ultima's teaching that good will always triumph over evil) which functions as an alternative to history.

We should not think of this system of classification as naive or superstitious; it is one that is clear, lucid, and rigorous and shares much as an ideology with another structure of thought for which a term has already been invented, Lévi-Strauss's *pensée sauvage*.[22] Although many elements of myth are present in Anaya's book, such as the ancestors in the landscape, the case of magical sympathy, I am referring instead to a very purposeful system of thought that posits an all-embracing structure and leaves nothing to chance. This system does not care for natural events, for it builds inexhaustible structures of binary oppositions out of the debris of events and then proceeds to produce events out of these structures. For Lévi-Strauss, echoing Eliot, magical thought is a way of reordering events by not permitting contingency and necessity to interfere with the human world. Myths and rituals are, therefore, by necessity of a recurrent nature allowing for the priority of synchrony over diachrony. Anaya pursues a similar course. No effort is made to focus on the psychological distance between the adult narrator and the hero Antonio. Instead, the writer constructs a plot in which the traces of history are reorganized through abstract structures, folk motifs, romance archetypes, and a series of binary oppositions repeating the message of good and evil, and then a narrative is generated out of these structures. Given the nature of the oppositions and the repetition of the redemptive promise, the system is inexhaustible. Thus, what can be called the ideology of romance in *Bless*

Me, Ultima is a determined effort in form and content to portray a timeless or synchronic world despite the overriding presence of history.

And yet there remains a positive element in Anaya's Chicano romance of the Southwest. The choice of the historical moment for *Bless Me, Ultima* should earn it a place in American literature. Unlike the primitive artist who internalizes timeless myths and tales and externalizes purpose and objects, the modern writer, who dwells within and is determined by history, internalizes technique and craft and externalizes myth as an aesthetic (Lévi-Strauss 1966, 29). Regardless of how the writer may want to daydream and fantasize, the events of history will loom over the horizon like an ominous dark cloud. In a crucial scene, Ultima tells Antonio that the worst evil is to tamper with someone's destiny. Perhaps this is why the real incident of the black cloud and the falling rocks that bombard the house at the Agua Negra ranch that cannot be explained by magical causality is strategically placed near the end to mark the passing of an innocent age with Ultima's death and the coming nuclear age. The incident bears a resemblance to the mysterious evil (the residents of Guadalupe are aware of it) that visited the remote Mexican village of Carrizozo, New Mexico, on 16 July 1945 when its inhabitants were awakened by a roar to witness a pillar of fire six miles high just thirty miles away at point Trinity in what is now the White Sands Missile Range. Although Ultima constructs a platform to burn the three spirits which she conceives to be the cause of the wandering rocks, the reader should be aware that her magic is no match for the destructive forces that were released from a tower in the middle of the New Mexican desert in the same general vicinity as the Agua Negra ranch. The choice of this major historical turning point that is so much like sublime and apocalyptic visions in myth can be interpreted as the ultimate tampering with the destiny of the world. Now the book can be understood as a yearning for an innocent time as a response to a moment in which the future of humankind is at stake: there is no turning back from the nuclear age except through the fantasy of a Golden Age.

IV

*The city was an intricately patterned
blanket, each color representing
different heritages, traditions,*

languages, folkways, and each
struggling to remain distinct, full of
pride, history, honor, and family roots.
At the center they were all
struggling for identity.

RUDOLFO A. ANAYA, *ZIA SUMMER*

Some one hundred years after Charles F. Lummis published his first book on the Southwest, *A New Mexico David and Other Stories and Sketches of the Southwest* (1891), Rudolfo Anaya published the first book, *Alburquerque* (1992), of what would be a sprawling novel of Alburquerque and New Mexico in four installments. After *Alburquerque*, Anaya followed with *Zia Summer* (1995), *Rio Grande Fall* (1996), and *Shaman Winter* (1999). Anaya's seven novels span his own lifetime, from the beginning of the nuclear age in 1945 to the end of the twentieth century. They are his unique view of la Nueva México, his vast historical romance rendered in a variety of narrative forms. Like his first three novels, the nineties quartet emphasizes the role of feminine sensibility crucial for the male's maturation, the landscape and seasons rendered through states of feeling, and the incorporation of Mexican and Native American myths through dreams and visions. Now we can understand the crucial importance of *Bless Me, Ultima* in 1972, not only a classic of Chicano literature, but also the end of the "fantasy heritage" and the beginning of Anaya's fictional project emphasizing his Mexican mestizo heritage.

After the young Antonio of Guadalupe, Anaya followed with the adolescents of the Chávez family, Jason and Benjie, in *Heart of Aztlán* and *Tortuga*. From a new historical vantage point, Anaya in the nineties quartet will imagine the next generation of interrelated characters who have emerged from their Mexican barrio communities to take up their roles as cultural and political leaders of New Mexico in a post–Cold War, post–Chicano Movement world. From the romantic and Jungian-inspired llano of *Bless Me, Ultima* and the Barelas barrio of *Heart of Aztlán*, Anaya in his next four novels traverses almost the entire state of New Mexico. Each locale serves as a statement on the history of la Nueva México from the first Indian settlements to the present: Bandelier National Monument, home to the Anasazi, the ancestors of the Pueblo Indians; the Hispano village of Córdova in the Sangre de Cristo Mountains; Las Vegas on the eastern edge of the llano where in 1846 General

Kearny took possession of Mexican territory for the United States; Taos where in 1847 nuevomexicanos revolted and killed U.S. Governor Bent; the Los Alamos National Laboratories in the Jémez Mountains where the first atomic bomb was assembled in 1945; the art galleries along Santa Fe's Canyon Road representing Southwest chic; Alburquerque, New Mexico's major city with some half a million inhabitants, serving as a historical and commercial crossroads between north and south, east and west. "You have been a nation unto yourselves for so long," offers Japanese high-tech entrepreneur Akira Morino in describing New Mexico in *Zia Summer* (Anaya 1995, 270). This is an apt description of the world that Anaya and others have chronicled, now on the verge of another inevitable movement in history.

In 1992, *Alburquerque* was a clear statement by a native New Mexican to finally and honestly redefine New Mexico's racial and historical identity as Mexican and mestizo against the fantasy heritage and racial purity invented by Anglo rulers and Hispano elites. The title itself is a correction, restoring the city's name to the original Spanish spelling.[23] In 1706, the city was founded and named by Governor Francisco Cuervo after the Viceroy of Nueva España, Francisco Fernández de la Cueva who was the Duke of Alburquerque. Legend has it, Anaya writes in his epigraph to the book, that when the railroad reached la Villa de Alburquerque in spring 1880, the Anglo stationmaster could not pronounce the first *r* in "Albur" so he dropped it as he painted the station sign for the city. Anaya has the following to say in *Rio Grande Fall* on the less glorious but more political reasons for the founding of Alburquerque: "In 1706 Francisco Cuervo y Valdés, the governor of New Mexico, had the gall to proclaim the farming community that clustered around the church a villa: la villa de Alburquerque. The good governor thought the miserable kingdom of New Mexico deserved another villa. He looked south at the farms and adobe huts peopled by Mexicans, mestizos, and Indians, and decided that the families clustered around the farm of doña Luisa were the perfect foundations for a villa. . . . Ah, but he had to play politics. One way to get a small village of mud huts designated a villa was to please the Viceroy. . . . So he named the villa after the Viceroy" (280).

The plot of *Alburquerque* hinges on a young mexicano from the Barelas barrio who searches for his origins. Abrán González, a former Golden Gloves boxer now attending the university, discovers that he is a product of a Mexican father, the writer and university professor Ben Chávez, and an Anglo mother, the well-known artist Cynthia Johnson.

Ben and Cynthia are the adolescents Benjie and Cindy of *Heart of Aztlán*. Racism was the cause for Abrán being orphaned from his true identity; the Johnson patriarch refused to acknowledge the child and gave it to a mexicano couple. Cynthia herself is a product of a family who had to renounce its heritage in order to stay alive. Cynthia, through her mother Elvira, Abrán learns, is a descendant of the crypto-Jews who settled in Taos during Oñate's entrada. Walter Johnson arrived from Chicago penniless and sick from tuberculosis in Alburquerque during the Great Depression. He married New Mexican Vera, the former Elvira, who was raised by merchant don Manuel Armijo and his wife Eufemia, who, although of Mexican heritage, had to feign Spanish origins to be welcomed in Anglo circles. Benjie and Cindy were united by more than love: "These New Town Anglos don't like Jews, and they sure as hell don't like Mexicans" (221).

Abrán's best friend, Joe Calabasas, is a mixed-race Native American from Santo Domingo Pueblo. His father, Encarnación, married a Mexican woman, Flor Montoya, who, according to long-standing tradition, is labeled Spanish by Pueblo Indians. Joe is also orphaned from his culture by his tribal brethren because he has become white, a university student. These two young men, Abrán and Joe, are both coyotes, outsiders of mixed race linked by their common Mexican heritage. These two characters in the late twentieth century represent New Mexico's history of conquest and mestizaje. Now they must move out of their respective barrios to live and deal with the new rulers of an Alburquerque that has become central to the changing fortunes of New Mexico.

Against these private lives stands the public world of big money and politics in the spring mayoral race among three candidates. Marisa Martínez, the incumbent, was elected through a coalition of mexicanos and Anglo Democrats; she represents the interests of the mexicano communities. Walter Johnson is backed by the old conservative guard. Frank Dominic is supported by mexicanos and the new professionals—yuppies from the North Valley who have appropriated and transformed the Alburquerque adobe and Mexican rural lifestyle into an enclave of wealthy estates.

Dominic's plans for Alburquerque represent the renewal of the old dream of El Dorado. He wants to transform the city into a series of canals and gaming casinos all within an indoor weather-controlled mall under a huge dome. Dominic will be the embodiment of the old Spanish viceroy, he will be the Duke of Alburquerque. "The Spanish legacy," muses

Anaya's alter ego Ben Chávez, "was a vision that many grasped for, and many a nut in New Mexico had spent his life's earnings trying to find his link to a family crest" (70). If elected mayor, Dominic, relying on his wife Gloria's Hispanic lineage, would be the new Duke of Alburquerque looking down from his office building on his dream vision—a tourist mecca that would be both a Disneyland and a Las Vegas–Venice on the Río. This distorted Alburquerque, Anaya strongly suggests, would be another version of Lummis's Land of Enchantment as well as la Nueva México, the new Tenochtitlán, which wealthy Antonio de Espejo hoped to find in the New Mexico desert in 1582.

A countervision of New Mexico is inserted into *Alburquerque* by Ben Chávez in the form of a poem. Chávez as Benjie in *Heart of Aztlán* and *Tortuga* was a homeboy who suffered the violence of the Barelas barrio. Now he is a respected writer and university professor who lives on the West Mesa. The first piece of literature in Spanish from New Mexico is the Renaissance epic poem *Historia de la Nueva México* (1610) by Gaspar Pérez de Villagrá that begins with the formulaic invocation "Las armas y el varón heroico canto" ("Of arms and the heroic male, I sing"). Villagrá's poem narrates the 1599 war against the Indians of Acoma, one of the bloodier and more tragic events of the conquest for which Oñate and his captains were punished by the Spanish Crown.[24] Following Villagrá's example, Anaya published in 1985 a mock epic poem, *The Adventures of Juan Chicaspatas*, with two homeboys, Juan Chicaspatas and Al Penco, as the epic heroes who set out in search of the mythic Aztlán. Poem and characters make an appearance in *Alburquerque* through Chávez who reads from his own work beginning with the opening verse: "Arms of the women, I sing" (206). The moment of the reading is of no consequence for Alburquerque considering the media attention and hoopla surrounding the new Alburquerque proposed by Dominic, Chávez's Alburquerque High School friend. At Jack's Cantina, after pulling the plug on Julio Iglesias on the jukebox, the lonely writer recites his poem to a small group that includes his own creations, his son, Abrán, and his characters, Juan and Al, his homeboys who are also penitentes from Chimayó. Through the reading, listeners lose interest and leave. Only the three creations remain at the end of the poem.

The poem is a product of the Chicano Movement which now, like the writer himself, is marginalized by late-twentieth-century Alburquerque capitalism, big money, and politics. Unlike Villagrá's epic of conquest, Chávez's (and Anaya's) poem of hope is an exhortation to Chicanos to take up the sword of life and return to the barrios of Aztlán, for "[t]here is much work to do" (48). The reading in the bar allows for a reconciliation for the father-teacher and son within the cultures of New Mexico. Cynthia Johnson is dead, but she left Abrán a legacy of understanding mexicanos and their culture. She is the artist who captured the end of an era in Santa Fe, mexicanos as outcasts in their own land giving way to the museum city, Santa Fantasy. "Abrán," the narrator Chávez offers, "born of a Mexican father and a gringa mother, was the new Chicano, and he could create his own image, drawing the two worlds together, not letting them tear him apart. Abrán the new mestizo" (206). Indeed, Abrán has learned his lesson well; after winning the boxing match promoted by Frank Dominic, Abrán will retreat with his pregnant compañera, Lucinda, to the mountain village of Córdova.

The grisly ritual murder of Frank Dominic's beautiful wife, Gloria Domínguez, in *Zia Summer* plunges Sonny Baca into a world of international political intrigue in Anaya's next three novels. A minor character in *Alburquerque*, Joe Calabasas's primo, Baca, surfaces as the Chicano private investigator in a series of murders and adventures probing the not so enchanting side of New Mexico. The three novels, while rich in concrete detail of New Mexico, are broadly symbolic, a combination of noir detective fiction and historical allegory. The connected chain of events of the detective genre followed by Baca lead eventually in *Shaman Winter* to Baca's reconstruction of his own genealogy in crucial moments in New Mexican history.

Zia Summer establishes the importance of the Pueblo sun symbol for solving Gloria Dominic's murder. The Zia sun symbol—a circle with four rays extending from the center—which was etched on Gloria's navel is also New Mexico's state symbol. The discovery of a small lunatic fringe cult responsible for Gloria's death presents Sonny with his archenemy, Raven, also known publicly as Anthony Pájaro, who poses as an antinuclear activist. In *Zia Summer* Raven is the leader of a secret postsixties commune of women living by a strange blend of mystical beliefs, a misinterpretation of the Pueblo Indian way of life where sacrifice is necessary.

According to Native American myths, Coyote is the giver of life and light, as well as the trickster, the survivor, who lives by his strength and cunning (see *American Indian Trickster Tales* 1998, 1–15). Raven is another character in trickster tales and is a scavenger and a thief (ibid., 244–250). In tales, Coyote and Raven can shift shapes and appear in human form. In New Mexico, both creatures share the river bosque surrounding the upper Río

Grande. Drawing on both Native New Mexican beliefs and the area surrounding Alburquerque, Anaya pits Sonny the Coyote against Raven. Though they are different characters, they are in effect related. (Throughout these four seasonal novels, Anaya is drawing on the New Mexican belief that because of intermarriage through the centuries, nuevomexicanos consider themselves primos.) According to Anaya's mythical reenactment, Coyote and Raven are mirror images of each other, positive and negative forces. Sonny, like the heroic Native American Coyote, will fight the good fight against violence in the form of Raven's terrorist act against a truck carrying radioactive waste. At the end of *Zia Summer*, during the summer solstice, Sonny is able to avert a nuclear disaster and wrest from Raven the Zia sun medallion, the symbol of light and life.

Sonny is tied to the history of New Mexico through his namesake and great-grandfather, New Mexican lawman, activist, and attorney Elfego Baca. However, Sonny is anything but respected like his legendary relative. He is known for solving petty cases. Now the thirty-year-old, divorced ladies' man, confident in his masculinity, will be forced by the murder of Gloria, his cousin and first love, to discard his macho identity and grow into his Indian spirit guide, his nagual, the Coyote. Through the assistance of his compañera Rita López, neighbor don Eliseo, whose Romero family has lived in the valley since before 1680, and Mexican curandera Lorenza Villa, Sonny will learn to trust his dreams and his unconscious and become a Coyote on the hunt. Possession of the sun medallion has given Sonny clarity of vision in his struggle with Raven. However, the responsibility which the medallion represents is both a shield and a curse and renders him vulnerable.

Rio Grande Fall, set during Alburquerque's October Hot Air Balloon Fiesta, contrasts the Anglo-dominated tourist economy with the less noteworthy city, regional, and hemispheric problems. Sonny, for example, encounters the problems of the homeless families who live along the river bosque. Taking his plot from political events in a post–Cold War world and the realm of possibility, Anaya has Sonny uncovering and thwarting a conspiracy involving former CIA agents, the Colombian Cali cartel, a Ukrainian nuclear physicist, and the Avengers, a white supremacist group. An enormous shipment of cocaine brought across the border in El Paso-Juárez will be used by ex-CIA Central American operatives to pay off a scientist to build a nuclear bomb for terrorists afraid of the brown hordes coming from south of the border. The threat of a race war and nuclear catastrophe is led by Raven.

The 1999 *Shaman Winter* opens with a dream of origins. Sonny sees his ancestral parents, the Spaniard Andrés Vaca and the Indian Owl Woman, during Oñate's 1598 entrada. To confirm his visions, actually his identity, Sonny becomes a genealogist and historian by borrowing books— Villagrá's *Historia de la Nueva México*, Fray Angélico Chávez's *New Mexico Families*, and others—from the library at the University of New Mexico. Each of Sonny's dreams leads to a realistic reinterpretation of New Mexican history. In his book of dreams, Sonny reads and writes his origins in la Nueva México set within the tyranny of the Spanish encomienda and repartimiento system, the destruction of the Pueblos, and the European diseases that decimated the Indian population. He realizes in the present that "he wasn't Spanish, he was Nuevo Mexicano, a mestizo from the earth and blood of the Hispano homeland, which was also the Pueblo homeland. He was a coyote" (Anaya 1999, 146). Sonny understands spiritually and historically that he is a mestizo, a survivor, where each succeeding period of history has left its imprint on him.

In each dream, Sonny discovers an ancestral relative from four different regions of New Mexico. However, in every case, Sonny's dreams are left truncated, unfulfilled because of the work of Raven in his different manifestations as violence and chaos. Raven has meddled with history; he captures Sonny's four historical grandmothers, rendering the good dream of la Nueva México—mestizaje, harmony, and peace—impossible. Each dream with its symbolic direction and related historical event brings Sonny closer to the present, to his final destined meeting with Raven. In the final dream reconstruction during the winter solstice, the sun warrior will enter combat armed with a Native American dream catcher provided by don Eliseo and the Zia medallion blessed by Lorenza. In Anaya's Native American trickster allegory, the Coyote will outwit the sword-wielding Raven, making him pass through the dream catcher like a bad nightmare. At the Sandía Labs outside of Alburquerque, Anthony Pájaro is discovered dead near the plutonium core he wanted to steal; he had walked into a fusion machine, an accidental victim of a laser experiment. And Sonny, who has learned commitment and trust in the beliefs of the old ways, will return from his dream a man transformed.

The twentieth century began with New Mexicans stressing the purity of their Spanish heritage. Aurelio M. Espinosa, Nina Otero-Warren, and Cleofas Martínez de Jaramillo felt it necessary to identify with a foreign land. Commenting on a 1920 research trip to Spain sponsored by the American Folklore Society, Espinosa marveled at the similarity of

Spanish folklore—tales, ballads, proverbs—to his own in New Mexico, and asked: "Was this New Mexico or was it Spain?" (Espinosa 1985, 68).[25] In 1935, Otero-Warren described older residents of Santa Fe as "people who might have just arrived from the Mother Country—Spain" (Otero-Warren 1936, 89). Even as late as 1955, Jaramillo wrote of her uncle Don Felipe as a "true type of fine Spanish gentleman [with] . . . fair complexion . . . almost as white as his hair and his long white beard" (Jaramillo 1955, 50). New Mexico was as Spanish as Spain itself. Such was the extent of cultural domination and the fear imbued by white supremacy.

Beginning with *Bless Me, Ultima*, Rudolfo Anaya has taken the Southwest tradition in new formal, stylistic, and cultural directions. From his 1972 elegiac romance to his contemporary thriller *Shaman Winter* of 1999, Anaya has affirmed with pride and growing historical conviction that the origins of New Mexico are in the New World, in the Mexican world that emerged out of Spanish conquest and colonization. This history has been traced in Anaya's seven major novels in the movement from rural to urban worlds while at the same time continually emphasizing the mutual influences of New Mexico's cultures on each other. The twenty-first century will provide Anaya with new events; how these events will be fictionalized in his continuing narrative project may depend on Anaya's new cast of characters, the Indian-Mexicano-Jewish-Anglo-Asian mestizos of his Alburquerque novels.

V

On Labor Day, Angelenos also celebrated the 219th birthday of the city of Los Angeles by retracing the 9-mile walk from Mission San Gabriel to Olvera Street, taken by 44 Spanish settlers in 1781.

LOS ANGELES TIMES, 5 SEPTEMBER 2000

It is 30 August 2000 and I am driving slowly down from the Jémez Mountains through Jémez Pueblo, the last remaining Towa-language pueblo, on my way to Alburquerque and a flight back to the Los Angeles area. On Highway 44 at the edge of the Zia Indian reservation, home to only seven hundred residents, I stop in Bernalillo at the Coronado State Monument. Here the Museum of New Mexico has excavated and restored an archaeological site, the Tiwa Pueblo of Kuaua situated on a bluff just overlooking the nearby meandering Río Grande. Kuaua, meaning "evergreen," like other Indian settlements, was made possible by the arrival of corn from central Mexico sometime around 1500 B.C. One entire room of the exhibit contains an impressive array of excavated murals, some of them depicting rain deities and natural phenomena. The fertile area is also a historical site. In 1540, Coronado, with 300 soldiers and some 800 Indian allies originally from Tlaxcala in Mexico, camped near the river not far from the village. As I pass Bernalillo on Interstate 25, I envision another conquest: Bernalillo, which had been a mexicano village on the road to Santa Fe, is now the beginning of Alburquerque's northern middle-class suburb Rio Rancho.

I tune to Spanish-language KZRY-FM 105.9 Radio Romántica to listen to the new generation of Mexican music stars, Alejandro Fernández, Pepe Aguilar, and Alejandra Guzmán, as well as Latino pop and rock artists from throughout the Americas such as Shakira and Carlos Vives, Christina Aguilera, and Enrique Iglesias. I had been clued to this contemporary Spanish music format station by the Mexican waiters and busboys from neighboring Chihuahua who work at Santa Fe's Plaza Restaurant. These young men and this music, indications of yet another migration into la Nueva México, stand in sharp contrast to what I had seen earlier in the week on the University of New Mexico campus. I had dropped by Zimmerman Library to escape the noonday heat and to read some materials at the Southwest Hispanic Research Institute. The new school year had just begun, and many students were sizing up the different offerings of groups and clubs on the central campus mall. In the center of student activity was a group of young women in Spanish dress dancing sevillanas. Yes, some traditions die hard. After all, last night on the Mexican Univisión affiliate KLUZ Channel 41, newscaster Bonita Ulibarrí had signed off with "buenas noches a la tierra del encanto."

Through the generosity of Rudolfo and Patricia Anaya, I had been enjoying a ten-day stay in the New Mexico mountains at their Jémez Springs writers' residence, la Casita. I had accepted Rudy's gracious offer in California, "come and see us," and traveled once again to la Nueva México hoping to find solitude and inspiration amidst the cobalt blue skies and ochre canyons of the Jémez Mountains. However, on this trip, I had the good fortune to finally meet Rudy and Pat. The retired university professor is a slight man of almost sixty-three years, deeply tanned, with thick gray hair. Our lively informal conversations over food and tequila in Alburquerque, Santa Fe, and Jémez Springs began to flesh out whatever biographical information I had come across in print.

Anaya identifies himself personally as husband, father, and grandfather, as well as nuevomexicano, manito, Chicano, indio, and mexicano. Although retired, he still maintains an active presence on the University of New Mexico campus. He and his wife, Patricia Lawless, sponsor the Premio Aztlán Literature Award and the Crítica Nueva, Critical Literary Series. He was born in 1937 in the Spanish-speaking village of Pastura in Guadalupe County to Martín Anaya and Rafaelita Mares, both from Puerto de Luna. Anaya is one of the pioneer family names: the Anayas arrived in New Mexico during the recolonization in 1693. After childhood in Santa Rosa on the Pecos River (the inspiration for the fictional Guadalupe), the Anaya family moved to Alburquerque and settled in the Barelas barrio. "I, like others of my generation," he explains over dinner, "was forced to assimilate." After graduation from Alburquerque High School in 1956, he enrolled and completed the accounting curriculum in the Browning Business School. His love for literature, nurtured by his rural childhood experiences and traditional storytelling, finally led him to the University of New Mexico, which, although in close proximity to his home in Barelas, he tells me, was in many ways a great distance. "Nobody from Barelas ever went up the hill to the university," laughs one of the characters in *Heart of Aztlán*. In 1963, after graduation from the University of New Mexico, he began teaching in Alburquerque public schools. In the following years, Anaya actively participated against the Vietnam War and came to an awareness of the Chicano Movement. It was during these turbulent sixties that Anaya struggled to learn the intricacies of writing fiction. After seven years of writing, *Bless Me, Ultima* emerged.

The drive to the Anaya home is complicated by freeway construction of Interstates 25 and 40, which cross each other in the heart of Alburquerque. Santa Fe, with its storied past, is the state capital, but Alburquerque, with about half a million residents, is the commercial and physical center of the state with the two major arteries crisscrossing each other on a north-south, east-west axis like the Zia sun symbol. Like its regional neighbors, Phoenix, Denver, and El Paso, Alburquerque has experienced tremendous growth in the second half of the twentieth century. Now "Surviving 'The Big I,'" the constant story on local television newscasts, takes on a greater reality for me. Forced to drive around through both interstates, I will arrive from I-40 at the Anaya home situated on the West Mesa near Petroglyph Hill overlooking the Río

Grande Valley, the river bosque, the city, and the Sandía Mountains beyond in the east. The entire Alburquerque landscape spreads out before my eyes under quickly moving clouds promising rain from México to a land that has suffered a very harsh summer.

I will return the keys to la Casita in the Jémez Mountains and express my gratitude to the Anayas for their generosity. My appreciation extends well beyond these past two weeks. *Bless Me, Ultima* opened up a new world to me both personally and professionally. Anaya's first book led to my first entrada into Chicano literary criticism, at the same time returning me to my childhood in Calexico, to my grandmother's Zacatecas cuentos, and the Calexico Desert Cavalcade, the local celebration of the Spanish heritage of the Southwest. My initial inquiry into la Nueva México mellowed by age has led to learning and understanding. New Mexico is still the Spanish Southwest. Lummis and his followers took care of that. However, New Mexico is much more. It is the Hispano Homeland. According to the Chicano Movement, it is also Aztlán. It is a unique fusion of Native American, Spanish, Mexican, and Anglo-American cultures, the first manifestation of Greater Mexico in what would be the United States.

THE EMERGENCE OF THE
CHICANO NOVEL

Tomás Rivera's "... y no se lo tragó la tierra"
and the Community of Readers

Hanse de casar las fábulas mentirosas con el
entendimiento de los que las leyeren.

—CERVANTES, *DON QUIJOTE* I

Perhaps the single most important element of Chicano
literature is that it was able to capture from the beginning
of the decade this very wisdom of a very disparate and
amorphous nation or kindred group. It was able to do that
because there was a hunger not only in the community but
in the Chicano writer to create a community.

—TOMÁS RIVERA, "CHICANO LITERATURE"

I

In 1967, during the first years of the
Chicano Movement, Quinto Sol began publishing *El Grito: A Journal of*
Contemporary Mexican-American Thought, founded by a group of stu-
dents at the University of California, Berkeley, and Professor Octavio I.
Romano-V. of the Department of Behavioral Sciences, with student Nick
Vaca as editor.[1] Two years later, in 1969, the Quinto Sol group published

El Espejo/The Mirror, the first anthology of Mexican American literature. Named after the fifth sun, the present age in Mesoamerican culture, Quinto Sol would be decisive not only in the way that Chicano literature would develop in themes and forms but also in establishing a canon. Moreover, unlike any other prior historical moment, these two publications indicated the possibility of a scholarly Mexican American community and a literate community of bilingual readers.

In 1969, Quinto Sol, now headed by Romano and Professor Herminio Ríos-C. of the Department of Comparative Literature and Ethnic Studies, announced the First Annual Premio Quinto Sol literary award. Of the manuscripts received in 1970, the editors elected to award first place to *". . . y no se lo tragó la tierra"/". . . and the earth did not part,"* a unique combination of tales, vignettes, fragments, monologues, and dialogues written in Spanish by Tomás Rivera, from Crystal City, Texas, who in 1969 had received a Ph.D. in Spanish literature with a minor in Latin American literature from the University of Oklahoma.[2] Although Rivera had written his dissertation, "La ideología del hombre en la obra poética de León Felipe," on a twentieth-century Spanish poet, it was obvious that he was a good reader of Juan Rulfo's Mexican fiction *El llano en llamas* (*The Burning Plain*, 1953) and *Pedro Páramo* (1955) and Américo Paredes's *"With His Pistol in His Hand."*[3] Rivera had read the Paredes book the year it was published, in 1958. And he had been introduced to Mexican literature when he attended the University of Arizona summer school in 1962 in Guadalajara, where he took courses from Hispanists Joseph Silverman and Carlos Blanco Aquinaga and Mexicanists Luis Leal and Seymour Menton, both of the latter well-known Rulfo scholars. Rivera, then a high school teacher, attended the Leal Mexican literature seminar where Rulfo's *El llano en llamas* was read (see García 2000, 118).[4]

After the publication of five thousand copies of *Tierra* in August 1971 in a bilingual edition, translated by Herminio Ríos, and the subsequent publication of Rudolfo A. Anaya's *Bless Me, Ultima* (1972) and Rolando Hinojosa's *Estampas del valle y otras obras* (1973), one could no longer question the existence of Mexican American/Chicano literature. In 1974, after awarding the Fourth Quinto Sol Prize to Estela Portillo-Trambley's short story collection, *Rain of Scorpions*, Romano and Ríos dissolved their relationship and Quinto Sol separated into two publishers, Editorial Justa and Tonatiuh International.

II

The inside history of this early prize may never be known. However, taking into account the ideological perspective of *El Grito*, one can begin to understand why Rivera's collection was selected as the first national Chicano literary publication. Both Romano and Ríos had received their doctorates in the early sixties and had emerged as leaders in the field of Chicano Studies. Quinto Sol was founded certainly to publish unknown Chicano writers but also to combat through *El Grito* the institutionally sanctioned representation in social science discourse of Mexican Americans as fatalistic, underachievers, and non–goal-oriented, as stated in the 1967 "Editorial" and the essay "Minorities, History, and the Cultural Mystique" by Romano.[5] Octavio Romano, leader of the Quinto Sol group, born in Mexico City but raised in the San Diego, California, area, had been trained as an anthropologist in the United States with a B.A. and an M.A. from the University of New Mexico and a Ph.D. from Berkeley in 1962. As a graduate student, Romano worked with anthropologist William Madsen, who studied Mexicanos of Hidalgo County in Texas from 1957 to 1962. Madsen's research was published in 1964 as *The Mexican-Americans of South Texas*. Madsen became a symbol of what early Chicano activists felt was wrong with the field of anthropology in the United States (see Paredes 1993a, 73). In its "Editorial" the Quinto Sol group addressed the following characterization of Mexican Americans found in social science discourse: "Mexican-Americans are simple-minded but lovable and colorful children who because of their rustic naïveté, limited mentality, and inferior, backward 'traditional culture,' choose poverty and isolation instead of assimilating into the American mainstream" (4). This characterization, which easily explained the poverty and discrimination suffered by Mexican Americans, was evident in Madsen's work.

In Rivera's book, the editors not only had a well-written, innovative piece of literature but also a characterization of farmworkers (who had become Chicano Movement icons) by a group insider that recast their stereotypical image. Rivera presented intellectual alternatives—that Mexicans from south Texas were not social vegetables, that they were participants in history, not totally resigned or fatalistic, and that they were rationally able to make choices. Rivera mirrored his culture by inventing characters in the process of self-reflection, questioning, and discovery.

The original manuscript that was to become *Tierra* underwent significant changes. In October 1970, Rivera sent Romano a manuscript collection of thirteen titled stories and twelve interpolated untitled fragments
totaling ninety-seven pages plus four other tales probably sent later, all
concerning the lives of Texas farmworkers in the forties and fifties.[6] The
collection was titled "Debajo de la casa y otros cuentos" after the ending
story. Rivera wrote Romano: "These are a total of 13 stories. Between each
there is a dialogue or situation which should be italicized. These are
cuadros which I placed between the stories to give the total work a
cohesiveness that I thought was needed. However, you may want to
exclude them."[7] Herminio Ríos played a crucial role in editing *Tierra* with
Rivera. It was obvious that Rivera desired through the cuadros to offer the
reader a participatory role and intended the work to be read as a whole, as
the experience of one year, framed by "El año perdido" and "Debajo de la
casa." However, the manuscript needed strong editing, especially in the
second half and at the ending. Four titled stories were eliminated from the
total of seventeen. From the correspondence between Rivera and Ríos, it
was Ríos who made the change to establish the structural unity of the work
around the twelve best stories representing one year.[8] Ríos also noticed the
sense of unity in the work, and decided to rearrange three tales to make an
implicit argument more explicit. In one table of contents, "La noche estaba
plateada" appears immediately after ". . . y no se lo tragó la tierra." "La
primera comunión" and "Cuando lleguemos . . .," which was probably the
last story composed by Rivera, appear as stories Nos. 5 and 6, not as Nos.
8 and 13 as in the published version.[9] Ríos wrote to Rivera:

> *El año perdido* y *Debajo de la casa* forman el marco artístico. *La noche estaba
> plateada, Y no se lo tragó la tierra, La primera comunión* temáticamente
> están relacionados y forman el núcleo central de la obra, *Y no se lo tragó la
> tierra* forma el núcleo de este terceto y de la colección entera.[10]

> *El año perdido* and *Debajo de la casa* form the artistic frame. *La noche
> estaba plateada, Y no se lo tragó la tierra, La primera comunión* are
> thematically related and form the central nucleus of the work, *Y no se lo
> tragó la tierra* forms the nucleus of this tercet and of the entire collection.

Rolando Hinojosa, a close friend of Rivera, in his 1987 English rendition
of *Tierra*, retitled *This Migrant Earth*, published the manuscript, according to Hinojosa, in its original three-part form with all untitled cuadros[11]

and tales placed at the center, dividing in half the titled tales.[12] After an initial reading, one may be disoriented by this version. On closer inspection, however, readers will discover the time frame of one year and a sense of plot developing from the interrelations of tales and cuadros. Taking advantage of the interesting interaction between form and content derived from realist and modernist influences, the editors of Quinto Sol chose to make the overall argument explicit for their readership and refashioned the work to emphasize the sense of cultural change. Tales were also rearranged to give readers a sense of both circular and linear plotting, the change through one calendar year. The editors must have been struck by the impression of unity that emerged from the twenty-seven short pieces. Although *Tierra* was first termed a collection of short stories by the Quinto Sol editors and some literary critics (see Menton 1972), the editors were also fully aware that the book seemed to be a Chicano version of a lengthier narrative form, that in its "creation in the thoughts, feelings, personality of the writer, in its structure and thematic presentation, [*Tierra*] reveals a unity that brings it close to the genre of the novel" (Rivera 1971, xv). Ten years later, Rivera writes: "*Tierra* germinated for several years. I had wanted to write a novel but I so liked the compacted dramatic elements of the short story that I finally decided to structure a work (novel) from which any element (chapter or short story) could be extracted, and stand, out of context, on its own."[13]

For me, this slim volume, less than one hundred pages in each language, performed an important mediatory function. *Tierra* was a Mexican novel that crossed borders: the reformulation of the Mexican mestizo cultural diaspora into the beginning of a Chicano narrative tradition.[14] Over the years, its influence has been felt throughout Chicana and Chicano creative and critical writings. Younger Chicana and Chicano writers continued the narrative mode of the short story cycle or novel-as-tales established by Rivera and Quinto Sol. The formal manipulations and transformations of the dominant literary tradition that were worked out in order to represent a working-class Chicano culture enables us to read *Tierra* as a reinvention of the formal and ideological possibilities of the novel.

III

Since its invention in Europe in the seventeenth and eighteenth centuries, the modern novel has been in the hands of writers a means of self-expression, and the genre's fluid narrative structure and psychological characterization have served novelists to dramatize the search for personal identity. With its emphasis on the individual self, its secularization of human experience, its critical rendering of popular beliefs, Rivera's *Tierra* is no exception to the form.

Like the progenitor of the genre, Cervantes's *Don Quijote*, Rivera's book begins with a scene of self-nomination: from an unknown source, a young anonymous protagonist is trying to answer to his name, only to discover that he had been calling himself. Readers, however, are not offered a fully realized character or place but rather a disembodied voice, an unmediated and unlocatable subjectivity trying to orient itself out of introspection toward identity. This division in the character between self and other could lead through traditional linear transformations in the plot to the affirmation of individual identity.

However, in a departure from the standard characterizations of this genre, the emergence of the protagonist's desire for completeness is artistically solved by Rivera through a nonindividualistic form of narration which culminates with an epiphanic moment, recognition of both personal and collective identity. In "Debajo de la casa," the final frame section of the novel, third-person omniscient and first-person, eyewitness narrators unite with the voices of many other characters through an impersonal, stream-of-consciousness technique that also recalls the relationship of oral storytellers to their audience. Despite the presentation of Mexican cultural norms held up for scrutiny and negation, the nameless protagonist finds his group identity through the memory of the people who have made his story. This solution is all the more rhetorically effective when we consider that readers must assist in reconstructing twenty-seven pieces—beginning and ending frames, twelve short titled tales, and thirteen untitled interpolated cuadros—into a unified plot.

A decade after the publication of *Tierra*, Rivera writes: "Perhaps the most important element of Chicano literature is that it was able to capture from the beginning of the decade this very wisdom of a very disparate and amorphous nation or kindred group. It was able to do that because there was a hunger not only in the community but in the Chicano writer to create a community. Up to the present time, one of the most positive things that the Chicano writer and Chicano literature have conveyed to our people is the development of such a community" (Rivera 1982, 17).[15] *Tierra* should hold special significance not just because in 1971 it was the first novel published by Quinto Sol Publications; more important, the book parallels the Chicano Movement of the late sixties through its reassessment of traditional culture, its historical self-consciousness, and, especially, through its developing sense of group solidarity.

From hindsight, contemporary readers may be deceived by the apparent transparency of Rivera's novel. We should realize that being in the vanguard of contemporary Chicano print media, Rivera was working under new political assumptions. Because of the exigencies of the moment, the need to maintain ethnic pride and cultural autonomy, Chicano literature was marked by a strong didactic and reformist character.[16] These elements were certainly evident in the first artistic success of the Chicano Movement, the group of actors, activists, and farmworkers who formed the Teatro Campesino in 1965. Closely allied with César Chávez's farmworkers' union at its inception, the Teatro Campesino under the guidance of Luis Valdez increasingly aspired to a national theater, a public forum where social issues relevant to Chicanos could be addressed. Indeed, from their first actos dealing with the farmworkers' strike, *Las Dos Caras del Patroncito* (*The Two Faces of the Boss*, 1965), the group took on the issues of Chicano identity, *Los Vendidos* (*The Sell-Outs*, 1967), and the Vietnam War, *Soldado Razo* (*Buck Private*, 1971). For anyone writing in the late sixties, the social function of art was, therefore, an important consideration, as was the representation of Chicano subjectivity. But the performance genre of drama is not the same as the novel. In fact, the *Actos* of the Teatro Campesino, which were not published until 1971, circulated freely by word of mouth and did not rely totally on the printed word.[17] Much of the artistic success of *Tierra*, therefore, depended upon how well the writer Rivera imagined his future Mexican American audience, on his ability to judge what kind of rhetorical strategies readers were able to accept. To his credit, Rivera was able to modify the literary strategies of the novel to meet the needs of his community.

I do not want to dismiss writers previous to the tradition established by Quinto Sol Publications. That Spanish and Mexican literary traditions existed in Spanish-language journals and newspapers of Greater Mexico is a historical fact that was documented by Luis Leal, Juan Rodríguez, and Nicolás Kanellos, among others.[18] Equally important was the English-language tradition described by Raymund Paredes, the one which, it seems to me, culminated with José Antonio Villarreal's *Pocho* in 1959.[19] My argument is simply that these writers did not have at their disposal the potential popular and academic readers that the movements of the sixties and the institutionalization of the Chicano experience had made available to Rivera and those who were to follow after him. Ramón Saldívar was correct in 1979 in pointing out the interesting relationship between *Pocho* and *Tierra*; there are some striking conceptual similarities that Saldívar described.[20] In terms of the Chicano literary tradition, Rivera's work can be read as an intertextual response to the negative attitudes toward social involvement of the omniscient narrator, Villarreal, and character, Richard Rubio, in *Pocho*. To be sure, the cultural ambiguities of not being an authentic Mexican or American that lead to the sudden Joycean ending of Villarreal's novel (recalling Stephen's escape in *A Portrait of the Artist*) are solved by Rivera at the end of the sixties precisely because of the ideology of the Chicano Movement.

Here, I am arguing against the view of Chicano narrative as a ready-made object to be defined, studied, and historicized in evolutionary terms as was the case with the first writings about this literature. Are the chronicles of the Southwest written by Spaniards of the sixteenth and seventeenth centuries part of Chicano/Mexican American literature? These questions are not easy to answer. My solution is to pose them in another form. If we are to radically historicize Chicano literature, should we not study, instead, how the forces of change have formed Chicanos and their literature in the twentieth century? *Tierra*'s narrative structure, it seems to me, allows us to see these historical transformations and the emergence of a new group identity.

Since it is my contention that *Tierra* is directed toward a particular group of readers that will be actively involved in the development of the plot, it will serve us well to interpret this novel stressing its dual dimensions. It is a structure of signs informed by ideological and historical contexts. As is well known, Rivera wanted to capture through their own voices, in northern Mexican Spanish vernacular, the experiences of Texas-Mexican farmworkers in the forties and fifties in their travels throughout the Southwest and Midwest.[21] But as I emphasize, the novel is more than a denotative or literal representation of a period, for through the fragmentary plot, readers are forced into reconstructing a historical logic and producing for themselves situations in which choices and judgments have to be made about traditional Mexican culture. The performative working out of possibilities and alternatives makes this novel both exemplary with reference to the individual reader and utopian in relation to the historical moment.

Although the many plots of the book are proffered by a combination of third-person and first-person narrators in fragmentary installments with each section complete in itself, the book has a clear formal design.

Two pieces dealing with the young male protagonist, "El año perdido" ("The Lost Year") and "Debajo de la casa" ("Under the House"), frame the twelve tales and thirteen interpolated cuadros. The tales concerning the many anonymous characters have an impression of formal unity and development among them emphasized by the first story, "Los niños no se aguantaron" ("The Children Could Wait No Longer"), followed by the central story, literally and figuratively, ". . . y no se lo tragó la tierra" (". . . and the Earth Did Not Part"), and concluding with "Cuando lleguemos . . ." ("When We Arrive"). All three focus specifically on the plight of farmworkers in their work-associated settings. The opening murder of a farmworker child in the fields who could no longer tolerate thirst and went against the patrón's command must be read against the rebellious consciousness of the adolescent farmworker in the central piece. In turn, this individual act of rebellion should be interpreted in relation to the concluding tale, in which a truckload of farmworkers on their way north to work express, through a series of interior monologues, their desire to break out of the cycle of migrant work.

In addition, the inner core of the plot, the three tales "La noche estaba plateada" ("It Was a Silvery Night"), ". . . y no se lo tragó la tierra," and "Primera comunión" ("First Communion"), recounts crucial moments of individual rebellion and cultural transgression in the life of a young boy of varying ages. With their theme of personal identity, these radiate back to the initial frame tale and forward to the concluding section of the novel when all characters, tales, and cuadros are united in a vast narrative moment. Moreover, as if to circumscribe the novel, the beginning and ending frame pieces can be read as a complete ironic statement, "El año perdido debajo de la casa," which is the case because the young protagonist had been recalling the incidents within the cycle of a year that he thought had been lost to him; from hindsight, however, he discovers that he had gained the experience of one year.

In sum, this novel-in-pieces encourages the reader to conceive of it as a legible whole through an intertwined plot that is both linear and circular, static yet changing. And just as the concept of the frame in communication theory gives instructions or aids in understanding the message within the frame, the readers of *Tierra* should discern the overall frame of reference, which is to say, the concern for individual identity within group collectivity that structures the beginning and ending pieces as well as the reader's participation. And because all twelve tales are framed for analysis by a pair of interpolated cuadros, the role of the reader emerges from the gaps that must be filled in order to ensure structural and thematic continuity.[22] Thus, the developing plot is explicitly based on a series of changing relationships. That Rivera supplies instructions for this process of understanding can be grasped from the last interpolated cuadro and the final collective moment in which he delivers his views on the social function of art as these inform the private act of reading.

In the last interpolated cuadro (163), Rivera describes the artist's responsibility to his public as one of binding together. A first-person narrator recalls the folk poet Bartolo who would come around in December when the farmworkers had arrived from migrant work in northern states.[23] His poems would sell quickly because they contained the townspeople, la gente del pueblo, and affected the audience in a way that was both emotional and serious, emocionante y serio. Moreover, Bartolo tells his audience, using the inclusive and ethnically conscious la raza, to read his poems out loud because the voice was the seed of love in the dark. Rivera's portrait of the artist contains the social function of storytelling, which is to bind the culture—la gente, la raza—together by representing human experience and providing both pleasure and instruction during times of leisure. And the suggestion to read out loud is Rivera's reference to an oral-aural context in which the human voice memorializes the culture. There are obvious interesting points of coincidence between early Chicano Movement print culture and sixteenth- and seventeenth-century Spain, in which the emergence of writing and print media existed within a culture that was largely oral. Renaissance chapbooks, the pliegos sueltos, the romancero, even the "reading performances" of the chivalric romances (recalling the illiterate farmworker audience at Palomeque's inn in *Don Quijote* I), like Bartolo's poems, combine both traditions. Rivera, who draws his creative sustenance from the example of the folk poet, was a writer from a working-class culture only partially literate.[24] Rivera's Spanish patterns (what the unnamed narrator of the beginning and ending frames remembers seeing and hearing), which imitate the simple and direct, face-to-face oral style, are, therefore, a means of working out of individualistic writing/reading toward an emergent social whole or group in which a high degree of literacy is not crucial for communicating. This ending story in the novel is a strong self-referential moment through which the individual Chicano reader can be made aware of his or her own cultural experience represented through the voices of the many nameless characters. That this artistic and social context should also provide instructions for the interaction between text and reader is evident from the concluding narrative of the many voices delivered by the young anonymous protagonist from beneath the house. In his interior monologue he realizes,

> Aquí sí que está suave porque puedo pensar en lo que yo quiera. Apenas estando uno solo puede juntar a todos. Yo creo que es lo que necesitaba más que todo. Necesitaba esconderme para poder comprender muchas cosas. De aquí en adelante todo lo que tengo que hacer es venirme aquí, en lo oscuro, y pensar en ellos. (101–102)

> I like it here because I can think about anything I please. Only by being alone can you bring everybody together. That's what I needed to do, hide, so I could come to understand a lot of things. From now on, all I have to do is to come here, in the dark, and think about them. (205)

And as the boy emerges from the darkness to the clarity of thought, the third-person omniscient narrator offers a solution to the problem of identity as one of understanding his changing relationship to his people:

> Se fue sonriente por la calle llena de pozos que conducía a su casa. Se sintió contento de pronto porque, al pensar sobre lo que había dicho la señora, se dio cuenta de que en realidad no había perdido nada. Había encontrado. Encontrar y reencontrar y juntar. Relacionar esto con esto, eso con aquello, todo con todo. Eso era. Eso era todo. Y le dio más gusto. (102–103)

> Smiling, he walked down the chuckhole-ridden street leading to his house. He immediately felt happy because, as he thought over what the woman had said, he realized that in reality he hadn't lost anything. He had made a discovery. To discover and rediscover and piece things together. This to this, that to that, all with all. That was it. That was everything. He was thrilled. (206)

While most critics have correctly interpreted this conclusion as part of the process of maturation of the central character, this ending frame in which the voices of the characters reappear through the consciousness of the narrator also offers explicit instructions to readers, to mirror the character's sense of memory and discernment by relating the twelve tales and thirteen cuadros one to another and to bind together the many plots into a meaningful whole, un todo. Through its structure and with the assistance of the reader, Rivera's novel reinforces the thematic constant of the individual's relationship to her or his community. As evidence of the importance of this tale, it serves us well to recall that Rivera had originally titled his collection "Debajo de la casa y otros cuentos."

Given Rivera's performative strategies, given that crucial tales repeat the overall plot of discovery and understanding, *Tierra* should be placed within the tradition of realist exemplary fiction established by Cervantes with *Don Quijote* and the *Exemplary Novels*. Moreover, *Tierra* can return critics to that prenovelistic rural world of the novel, before the genre became the English-language bourgeois literary monument that it is today.[25] I have already mentioned similar cultural contexts faced by both professional writers Rivera and Cervantes living in social worlds that still relied largely on oral traditions. Though *Don Quijote* appeared at the dawn of European modernity, and although it incorporated the new emergent scientific discourses of psychology and linguistics, it also owed much to the didacticism of traditional storytelling, ballads, legends, popular tales, sayings, and proverbs. Indeed, one of the most crucial and famous scenes in *Don Quijote* I illustrating affective and intellectual responses to fiction involves farmworkers who gather after harvest time at Palomeque's inn to listen to the reading of chivalric romance. A similar case can be made for Rivera's cultural situation and the publication of his book, which appears as Chicano culture becomes an object of institutionalized knowledge.

We should also recall that *Don Quijote* I, like *Tierra*, was an experimental event with the short story form. In the first *Don Quijote*, Cervantes was reworking the epic principle of maintaining the reader's interest through the variety of incidents without sacrificing formal unity. Cervantes's first novel can be considered a string of interpolated exemplary tales unified by its fully psychologized characters. And such is the case, for the story of the insane hidalgo, rasquachi vato loco, must have begun as a short tale, its composition dated around the time Cervantes hit upon psychological realism with his first exemplary tales, such as the "Glass Licentiate" (see El Saffar 1974, 13–19). This realistic form, as yet unnamed, must have developed out of the shorter novela or short story. And when, in the words of the Canon of Toledo, Cervantes states that the reader's understanding should be wed to plot, he is saying, among other things, that formal unity is also the critical reader's duty.

Cervantes's observations on audience responses and reader's duties demonstrate that the act of reading was fast developing in a private situational context that reflected the unique talents of the writer and the individuality of the reader. Cervantes's personal concern for prose fiction allowed him to transform into an ideological precondition for the novel, in its first historical phase, the aesthetic norm which dictated that serious poetry should be both pleasing and instructional. Cervantes steered a middle course between these Horatian precepts, allowing readers to receive pleasure and profit from their own sense of discernment. His characters, like Rivera's, display a capacity for making judgments which are also indicative of the reader's own transformation during the reading process. By exemplary literature, therefore, I mean writing whose aims are epistemological rather than openly didactic, because readers are encouraged by literary strategies to make their own judgments, which then stimulate a process of learning.[26] And while both Cervantes and Rivera write in Spanish and, in a sense, invent or imagine a "nation" or "community" of readers, Rivera reminds the reader that she or he is part of a larger social whole by invoking la gente del pueblo, la raza, by structuring all his stories around the Mexican family.[27]

In Rivera's transactive approach to reading, anonymous characterization, widely acknowledged folk and religious beliefs, and typical cultural situations serve as mirrors for Chicano readers. In addition, the transformation of the unnamed central protagonist through the two frame pieces and the three central tales should be reflective of the reader's capacity for making judgments about his or her own Chicano/Mexican American experience. This participatory phenomenon is all the more evident in the design of the book. Although it is fragmentary, it is not, as I argue, a pastiche or chaotic or self-destructive as are other Western modernist and postmodernist texts. On the contrary, care is taken to involve readers in an orderly plot and encourage construction of meaning through interpolations, Rivera's cuadros. Cervantes used a somewhat similar technique with his interpolated tales, which transform the main plot into its very opposite in order to give the reader a clear view of what she or he is supposed to understand.[28] However, in the absence of an omniscient narrator aiding in the necessary connections, the reader of Tierra is called upon to take a more active role, to retrace the mapped-out strategies.

In general, the discerning reader of Tierra is challenged by Rivera's oppositional strategies to project alternative social possibilities. The reader is forced to evoke traditional norms and examine them critically. These strategies are also ideological in the sense that Chicano readers are made aware of the structural and conceptual limits of their own class and cultural situation. Through the first half, the novel's changing structure calls into question commonly held beliefs. And the direction of the plot is toward a rationalization of the landscape and a more worldly interpretation of the Chicano experience. This movement in the plot is well within the novel's secularization of thought, which is to say, the conception of a psychological subject no longer totally immersed in a natural world of spiritual forces or ruled over by myth, religion, and abstract notions of fortune. From the initial cuadro, readers should distinguish a series of contrasts between, on the one hand, ignorance, superstitions, and religious beliefs, and, on the other, the oppressive material conditions experienced by farmworkers. The interrelation of these two poles is that these beliefs blind Chicanos to the real causes and conditions of their existence. For example, the young boy of the first interpolated cuadro who drinks the glass of water that his mother placed underneath the bed for the spirits establishes an opposition between metaphysical agency and human action. The negation of this residual popular belief from Mexican culture should be compared and read against (1) the repressive conditions and the natural elements of sun and heat that weigh heavily upon the thirsty children of "Los niños no se aguantaron," (2) the exploitative and falsely reassuring spiritualist of the second cuadro, who communicates with the missing soldier, and (3) the mother of "Un rezo" ("A Prayer"), who relies on the will of God to return her son from Korea. Through the first cuadros and tales, the novel is punctuated with examples of racism, exploitation, and fatalism whose causes are not supernatural but social and historical.

Mexican or mestizo is the name for the dark world of these farmworkers who live in poverty, ignorance, and superstition and whose conduct is almost totally controlled by the institution of the Church. One cannot deny that the historical forces that gave rise to this social group were set in motion with the colonization of the New World. Although these people live in the twentieth century, in the fifties, their group consciousness has its origins in the feudal-like organization of life in which Native Americans, blacks, mestizos, and mulattos formed the bottom tier of a peonage and caste system. Rivera, who had been a farmworker, was not ignorant of the colonized mind, and he spoke to this fact in an essay on Richard Rodriguez.[29] Rivera's oral style has often been compared to Juan Rulfo's. This is a valid comparison; Rivera learned much from Rulfo.[30] But we should also understand that both were acutely aware of the forces of colonial feudalism and gave voice in their writings to a group—peasants, peones, and campesinos—whose discourse has always been marginal to power.[31] Rulfo knew rural Mexico well and worked for the Instituto Indigenista. In several interviews, he also commented that his tales of rural Jalisco owed much to a ruthless patriarchal structure established by encomenderos, caciques, and the Church.[32] Despite the changes brought about by the Mexican Revolution, Rulfo's literary characters, like Rivera's, live in a timeless world beset by sin and an unyielding fatalism. Within Chicano scholarship, on the question of colonization, Tomás Almaguer among others has adequately shown that migrant farmworkers as a seasonal labor force in the capitalist economy of the United States have their origins in another mode of production, the repartimientos, encomiendas, and cuadrillas of the Spanish colonial empire.[33] And we should add that structures of religious thought that Rivera foregrounds originated with the evangelizing zeal of the Church. Given this context, Rivera is formulating a version of the Chicano subject as socially situational and historical in opposition to subjectivity based on the religious soul.

This opposition is crucial to the understanding of the three central tales, in which a younger generation's questioning of religious orthodoxy points toward a major turning point in the world of farmworkers. In these tales Rivera is repeating an important moment which Spanish Americans had experienced in the nineteenth century when governments stripped, with a vengeance, all secular power from the Church. This seems to be the first major political move in postcolonial societies ruled almost totally by the Church. This is a juncture in the plot of *Tierra* to which Mexican Americans, especially young ones, cannot remain indifferent. In these tales, Rivera foregrounds the importance of traditional Catholic values for an older generation. Yet what gives hope and consolation to farmworker parents against the insecurities of existence becomes conservative, static, and unyielding for the young protagonist. This is a significant historical moment of change precisely because traditional values are emptied of their pragmatic content and, instead of confirming reality, express the limits of a repressive hegemony.[34] The tensions between metaphysical agency and the oppressive conditions of existence—the elements of sun, heat, and thirst of the first cuadro and tale—finally come to a climax in the central tale, ". . . y no se lo tragó la tierra," when the young protagonist violates his parents' ultimate cultural taboo and blasphemes against divine will. With this act of rebellion against fatalism, the central character simultaneously acknowledges the materiality of space (the earth does not part) and affirms his own reason and freedom. As an individual subject, he feels capable of doing whatever he desires:

Tenía una paz que nunca había sentido antes. Le parecía que se había separado de todo. Ya no le preocupaba ni su papá ni su hermano. Todo lo que esperaba era el nuevo día, la frescura de la mañana. . . . Salió para el trabajo y se encontró con la mañana bien fresca. Había nubes y por primera vez se sentía capaz de hacer y deshacer cualquier cosa que él quisiera. (46)

He felt at peace as never before. He felt as though he had become detached from everything. He no longer worried about his father nor his brother. All that he awaited was the new day, the freshness of the morning. . . . He left for work and encountered a very cool morning. There were clouds in the sky and for the first time he felt capable of doing and undoing anything he pleased. (150)

The emotional state of the character foreshadows the comic ending of the final frame. And the thematic direction of the plot toward personal responsibility and self-determination is previewed in various ways by the preceding cuadro, in which a group of farmworkers is left without hope of breaking its ties to the soil. Nothing was realized by the well-intentioned motives of the Protestant minister who wanted to teach them carpentry. For the reader, however, the adolescent farmworker's cool detachment from everything that results from his successful private act of rebellion must be weighed against the concern for the group.

This central tale is flanked by two others that examine from a secular perspective abstract or religious notions of good and evil. The inquisitive boy of "La noche estaba plateada," after calling forth the devil by his name, comes to the awareness that all remained the same, all was peaceful: "Todo estaba igual. Todo en paz." (37) / "Everything was the same. All peaceful" (141). Although evil is personified by the figure of the devil in a pastorela, it does not exist as a spiritual entity directly affecting human lives as Catholic doctrine teaches. On the contrary, evil can be all too human and social, as the boy, a victim of racism, in the preceding cuadro understands completely well after he is refused a haircut: "Entonces comprendió todo" (33) / "Then it all became clear" (137). The last story in the central triad, "La primera comunión," injects humor into these otherwise serious narratives. Rivera pokes fun at the institution of catechism, which forces children into manufacturing sins of the flesh although they have not committed such wrongdoing and do not fully understand the concept of the body as the temple of evil. On the way to confession, the young character witnesses a couple copulating, what he imagines in his own way to be a sin of the flesh. Like the other rebellious characters, he refuses to admit to his sin during confession and, in fact, imagines the pleasure one gains from such sins of the flesh to be like the good feeling one receives from God's grace. That humankind has an important physical nature that can be pleasurable is implied by the grandfather of the preceding cuadro who is paralyzed from the neck down. He realizes the foolishness of his grandson who wants to dismiss his youthful years and rush in an instant of time to his thirtieth birthday. Taking into account the development of the plot through the reinterpretation of these notions of good and evil, readers can detect an important historical conjuncture, a break with the past in the sense that an alternative mode of consciousness, inconceivable to an older generation, is emerging from the medievalism of traditional Mexican-Chicano working-class culture. These secretive acts of rebellion—the characters do not reveal their thoughts and actions to others—overturn deeply ingrained beliefs that date back to the early church fathers. While at the same time collapsing stages in the development of Western thought, Rivera leads the reader away from traditional Mexican culture to the understanding that spiritual entities do not directly affect human lives, that individuals have a role to play in determining their own actions, that the body, the materiality of one's identity, should be a source of pleasure.

Rivera is not unlike other Christian and especially Catholic writers in his urgent need for the negation of what he portrays as repressive ideologies. However, Rivera will turn in the second half of his novel from these isolated rebellious individuals to the more important affirmation of the whole. And as if to stand the religious opposition of spirit and matter on its head, Rivera effects a relocation of the spirit toward a communal cohesiveness, a desire for change arising out of the material conditions of existence.

Rivera's depiction of changes in Texas-Mexican farmworker culture of the fifties is not an idealistic one. Although the seeds of change are apparent in both men and women, young and old, some will not escape their historical circumstances. A case in point is the representation of male-female relationships in "La noche que se apagaron las luces" ("The Night of the Blackout") and "La noche buena" ("Christmas Eve"). These tales dealing with two generations of women are placed side by side to be compared by the reader. For doña María of "La noche buena," who aspires to change by liberating herself from her confinement to the home, the moment of courage will end in failure. On the other hand, the young

81

Juanita of the companion tale will stand up against the foolish phallocentric attitudes of her boyfriend, Ramón. Juanita's future will, perhaps, be different from doña María's. We should recall that Juanita's family wants her to finish her education before she marries.

Other examples of change include cuadro 11, in which a whole community of parishioners rise up against the priest who had exploited farmworkers by charging them for his blessings. With the money saved, the priest had visited his native Spain and returned with picture postcards to encourage more financial support for his church. This priest could not understand why his new pews and postcards were disfigured by his angry parishioners. The tale that follows, "El retrato" ("The Portrait"), concerns a father who does not accept exploitation and eventually, after searching in San Antonio, finds the wrongdoer.

These exemplary tales that readers have been reconstructing into a legible whole reach a utopian conclusion in the final tale, titled in the Spanish subjunctive mood of future uncertainty, "Cuando lleguemos . . .,"[35] in which different voices echo the desire to break out of the cycle of migrant work, and in the ending frame in which the narrator completes his search for identity through the characters of his tales.[36] The locus of hope for the older generation, the celestial paradise, is displaced by a desire for a yet unrealized transformation of the present.[37] This concluding utopian vision of the future is due as much to the expression of collective hope as to the decentering of individualism. Admittedly, Rivera's literary context is the individualistic one of print capital. He writes for the individual reader. And certainly the triumphant moment of struggle that gives the title to his narrative is a private one which leads the protagonist to feel happy and detached from everything, "todo." This thematization of individualism, however, is structurally counterbalanced by the tales and cuadros with their many nameless characters, the Mexican families, and the ending frame.

Rivera's novel, therefore, offers readers a collective vision in which the narrator (ultimately the writer) tries to harmonize individualistic tendencies with society as a whole. Rivera's desire for community is all the more evident when we read him against other early Chicano narratives in which the male subject is represented or characterized through generational conflicts or sexual rivalries. The absence of a proper name, a patronymic, for the central narrator and protagonist indicates Rivera's perspective on egocentrism and Mexican machismo and the Hispanic version of the Oedipal triangle of father, mother, and son. Rivera does not dwell on these elements of individualistic writings. And while Rivera's protagonist is an exemplary figure guiding the reader through a process of learning or maturation, he is not a preordained hero in any romantic way. The kind of unity between the narrator-character as singular subject and his community that Rivera was striving for is realized by the impersonal epic moment of the ending frame, when the novel form yields up its individualistic conceptualization. In the final moment of epiphany, the narrator momentarily disappears, not to withdraw from his culture, but to take a stance like the prenovelistic oral poet; he surrenders his consciousness and allows the collective voices of his people to speak through him.[38] This last frame, therefore, is emblematic of the book just completed.

IV

Given the historical and social conditioning of Mexican mestizo culture, the possibility of a Chicano readership in the late sixties and early seventies was itself a revolutionary idea. Early Chicano writers were thus able to seize upon utopian currents already present in the Chicano Movement and give expression to them. As Rivera imagined his community of readers in *Tierra*, he was also contributing in a unique way to the history of the novel in Spanish in the Americas. And while Mexican and Mexican American readers will be able to identify with the world depicted in *Tierra*, many other readers will find Rivera's culture of poverty (migrants living in chicken coops) and oppression (patrón, boyfriend, husband, father, and church) remote and alien. This is so because in his novel Rivera was mediating between a First World modernist aesthetic and what should be judged a Third World experience. In this sense, unlike José Antonio Villarreal's *Pocho*, Rivera's novel-as-tales shares much with other emerging national literatures of the second half of the twentieth century. In these literatures of emancipation, native writers, through traditional storytelling or oral consciousness, address problems of a natural, rural, or agricultural world as it is being transformed by new economic and superstructural realities. Thus, Rivera looks back to his childhood and adolescence in south Texas from the thirties through the fifties when this region was being transformed into the Winter Garden area as earlier Mexicano ranching culture was being replaced first by cotton farming and then by large-scale farming. A similar phenomenon occurred in California's San Joaquin and Imperial Valleys as the increasing population of Mexican workers supplied the seasonal labor force. From the point of view of 2001, this emergence from a colonial mentality can now be reconceived as a form of Third World postmodernism. I am constructing a master narrative for Chicano literature because one is already implicit in the work of Rivera, and also because it is a necessary critical task to understand the emergence of Chicano consciousness from economic and ideological structures that were set in place with the conquest and colonization of the Americas. And the salient features of this new consciousness are the rejection of the metaphysical and the acceptance of the social, the decentering of the autonomous subject and the reconciliation of individual desire within a wider social movement.

"A RECORDER OF EVENTS WITH A SOUR STOMACH"

Oscar Zeta Acosta and
The Autobiography of a Brown Buffalo

*On nights like this when one can do nothing
but gasp for fowl [sic] air—the ripples of blood inside my brain
pound bonk, bonk, bonk—and I sit on the edge of squeeky [sic]
springs and wonder—why not?*

— OSCAR ZETA ACOSTA, "ON NIGHTS LIKE THIS"

I

San Francisco has occupied an important place in the American imagination. Recalling Tony Bennett's 1962 signature song, it is "the city by the bay" where like no other architectural structure on the West Coast the Golden Gate Bridge marks the end of the continental United States. The only structure similar to it is, of course, New York's Statue of Liberty. Like the Statue of Liberty, California's Golden Gate has been the point of entry for waves of immigrants from Asia, Latin America, and Europe. So many different ethnic groups called this seaport their home that in the fifties, several decades before the United States realized that its national character had many colors, San Francisco was billed for the tourist trade as one of America's most cosmopolitan cities.

The mid-sixties added a new imaginative and social dimension to the San Francisco urbanscape. In the formerly run-down, working-class Victorian neighborhoods of the Haight-Ashbury district, a new youth culture of mostly disaffected middle-class whites was living up to the old ideals of the Beat Generation (but without the jazz) and paying heed to the words of their intellectual guru Timothy Leary, "tune in, turn on, drop out." By spring 1967, San Francisco was bracing itself for the up to two hundred thousand young people who would descend upon the Haight-Ashbury district for a summer of revelry. Drugs, sex, and rock 'n' roll were never more in evidence than in that summer of 1967, to be remembered, with the Monterey Pop Festival, the Beatles' album *Sgt. Pepper's Lonely Hearts Club Band*, Jefferson Airplane's "White Rabbit" and "Somebody to Love" from the album *Surrealistic Pillow*, Procol Harum's "Whiter Shade of Pale," and the "love-ins" in Golden Gate Park, as the "summer of love," the summer when the Rock Generation found its libido. Many who were living in California during that summer, as I was in UCLA's Westwood, remember the multitudes of long-haired youths who journeyed from throughout the United States, hitchhiking their way to deliverance in San Francisco.

Deliverance did not come. The assassinations of Martin Luther King Jr. and Robert Kennedy, the war in Vietnam, the increasing militancy of the civil rights movement, the rise of Black Power, the American Indian Movement, and the Chicano Movement followed by the paranoia of the Nixon administration showed up the social fissures that separated Americans from each other. The "American melting pot," the American ideological solution to issues of race and class, no longer held for Lyndon Johnson's Great Society of the sixties or for Nixon's law and order. Oscar Zeta Acosta's *The Autobiography of a Brown Buffalo* (1972, 1989) begins precisely in San Francisco on the first day of July 1967, as a response to some very romantic and ultimately escapist solutions to some very real social problems. "I speak as a historian, a recorder of events with a sour stomach," writes Acosta. ". . . I have no love for memories of the past" (18).[1] These words describe Acosta's bilious attitude as he escapes from San Francisco in his '65 Plymouth in his Arrow shirt, jeans, and construction boots across the western American landscape—California, Nevada, Idaho, Colorado, New Mexico, Texas—on his way to the Mexican border, his birthplace, El Paso/Ciudad Juárez.[2]

II

Although Acosta's *Brown Buffalo* has been labeled a sixties drug trip, like other cultural manifestations of that decade its origins are in the fifties. The Beat Generation, with its celebration of the vernacular, sex, misogynism, drugs, speed, and marginality, was an important molding influence on Acosta, although he does not admit it. A Bay Area resident during the fifties, Acosta is aware of the presence of the Beats in the sixties: "Ginsberg and those coffee houses with hungry-looking guitar players never did mean shit to me. They never took their drinking seriously. And the fact of the matter is that they got what was coming to them. It's their tough luck if they ran out and got on the road with bums like Kerouac then came back a few years later with their hair longer and fucking marijuana up their asses, shouting Peace and Love and Pot. And still broke as ever" (18).

Like Kerouac's *On the Road*, Acosta's book is a road trip in search of salvation and paradise.³ According to Mark Feeny, Kerouac's Sal Paradise and Dean Moriarty would have a lasting influence on American culture as it emerged in the sixties, especially in the celebration of the machine on the road and the buddy framework, evident, for example, in television's *Route 66*, Hollywood's *Bonnie and Clyde* of 1967, *Bullitt* of 1968, and the big hits *Butch Cassidy and the Sundance Kid* and *Easy Rider* of 1969. All these buddies, whether in cars, on motorcycles, or on horseback in large measure owed their sense of loner outsiderness and nonconformity to Kerouac. Acosta, writing in the tradition of Kerouac, was following his partner in crime, Hunter S. Thompson, who had just published *Fear and Loathing in Las Vegas: A Savage Journey to the Heart of the American Dream*, which had appeared on 11 and 25 November 1971 in *Rolling Stone* magazine. This now well-known narrative featured Thompson as the writer Raoul Duke and Acosta as the Samoan attorney Doctor Gonzo.⁴ Acosta returned the favor by fictionalizing Thompson as Karl King in his own buddy narrative in *Brown Buffalo*.

Thompson has received much credit, and deservedly so, for the Gonzo style of journalism, a first-person account in a fast-paced vernacular produced under the influence of drugs and alcohol. The originator of the term, according to Paul Perry, Thompson's biographer, is Bill Cardoza, editor of the *Boston Globe Sunday Magazine*, who in a letter to Thompson described Thompson's piece on the Kentucky Derby (see "Kentucky

Derby Is Decadent and Depraved") as "pure Gonzo" (Perry 1992, 142). The relationship between Thompson and Acosta is well known, at least in Chicano circles. Two budding writers with similar sensibilities met, according to them, when Acosta left San Francisco in 1967. Acosta fictionalized two versions of this meeting, the lasting one in *Brown Buffalo*, and Thompson confirmed it in his now-famous requiem for Acosta in *Rolling Stone*, "The Banshee Screams for Buffalo Meat."[5] Thompson's use of the term first appears in his *Fear and Loathing in Las Vegas* to describe the character Doctor Gonzo, Oscar Zeta Acosta. Certainly, Thompson is the writer-as-eyewitness Raoul Duke, who is responsible for the book, and writes in Chapter 2, "Do it *now*. Pure Gonzo journalism" (12). However, it is also the crazy and outrageous character Doctor Gonzo who is emblematic for the style of this most famous of his books, made into a film of the same title.[6] Two years after the appearance of *Fear and Loathing*, the Gonzo style was officially attributed to Thompson in the November 1973 *Playboy* "On the Scene," titled "Hunter S. Thompson, Commando Journalist": "His method, known as Gonzo Journalism (his term), involves participating in the story, filling his notebooks with whatever comes up and printing all of it with few if any changes. It produces a very cranked-up style and he stays well cranked in order to maintain the pace: Guacamole, Dos Equis and MDA are the staples of his diet" (188).

Acosta responded privately to the fame and fortune that Thompson had earned. In an undated typed manuscript that I obtained from Acosta's son, Marco, that Acosta had corrected by hand, Acosta has this to say about their literary relationship: "[Ever since my arrival in East Aztlan in the winter of '67] I'd been teaching him all that I [found out] about Doctor Gonzo, the grand master of Mongolia. . . . But it had taken him three years to learn the basic facts of the universe. I finally had to show him the holes in my palms before he'd consent to be my official biographer" (9).[7] This document narrates, from Acosta's point of view, the situation just prior to *Fear and Loathing in Las Vegas*. According to Acosta, he had called Dwark (Thompson) to come to East L.A. to write an article examining the death of *Los Angeles Times* journalist Rubén Salazar when Dwark got the call to do a piece on an international, off-the-road motorcycle derby in Las Vegas.

In answer to the 1973 *Playboy* sketch on Thompson, Acosta drafted a letter to the *Playboy* Forum that may never have been sent; but what I do know is that it never appeared in *Playboy*. I am citing from an undated, corrected, signed typescript copy with a San Francisco address. Acosta writes:

Sir:

Your November issue, *On The Scene* section on Mr. Hunter S. Thompson as the creator of Gonzo Journalism [*sic*] which you say he both created and named. . . . Well, sir I beg to take issue with you. And with anyone else who says that. In point of fact Doctor Duke and I—the world-famous Doctor Gonzo—together we both hand in hand sought out the teachings and curative powers of the world-famous Savage Henry the ScagBaron [*sic*] of Las Vegas and in point of fact the term *and* methodology of reporting crucial events under fire and drugs which are of course essential to any good writing in this age of confusion—all this I say came from out of the mouth of our teacher who is also known by the name of Owl. . . . These matters I point out not as a threat of legalities or etcetera but simply to inform you and to invite serious discussion on the subject.[8]

Acosta signs the letter "Yours very truly, Oscar Zeta Acosta—Chicano Lawyer." And adds "P.S. The Guacamole and XX he got from me" (Acosta n.d., Letter to *Playboy* Forum).

Savage Henry, the Scag Baron, is mentioned in both the book and the film version of *Fear and Loathing in Las Vegas*. Savage Henry was actually Robert Henry, a good friend of Acosta. How Hunter Thompson came to know Henry is uncertain. In Thompson's biography Paul Perry identifies Henry as a San Francisco drug dealer who lived with his schoolteacher wife in the Castro district. Perry relates a meeting between Henry and Thompson in the mid-sixties in which Henry dispenses hash, opium, and cocaine to Thompson (109–110). Henry, as Acosta writes in his letter to the *Playboy* Forum, was also known as the Owl, the fictional character of the fat Irish seaman Ted Casey, the Owl, in *Brown Buffalo*.[9] There is a videotape of a 1972 home movie that I saw with Marco Acosta in August 1987 at the San Francisco home of Ann Henry, Henry's widow, in which Henry and Acosta plus a young Marco celebrate the publication of *Brown Buffalo*. Both adults are under the influence of fire and drugs. True to his personality, Acosta narrates the section of the sexual fantasy with Alice, Ted Casey's wife, who of course was Ann, Henry's spouse.[10] Both Ann and Robert Henry were Acosta's dearest friends; after his disappearance in 1974, they cared for Marco as if they were his parents.

Acosta was born in 1935 and Thompson in 1939. These contemporaries responded intellectually to forties and fifties American culture by buying into the Beat Generation's myth of the road, drifting and breaking away, searching and writing. "It was a time," writes Thompson on his days in San Francisco, "for breaking loose from old codes, for digging new sounds and ideas, and for doing everything possible to unnerve the Establishment" (Thompson 1979c, 460). Both lived significant stages of their life in Latin America, Acosta in the armed forces and Thompson as a journalist. In the sixties, both found their way to San Francisco. Both aspired to writing novels.[11] In the early sixties, Acosta worked for the *San Francisco Examiner* as a copy boy, attended San Francisco State majoring in creative writing and mathematics, and was halfway through a novel when he dropped out of college to complete it.[12] In 1962, he wrote to Vanguard Press selling a novel, "My Cart for My Casket," and to Macmillan and Alfred A. Knopf seeking publication for the short novel, "Perla Is a Pig."[13] Though Acosta was unsuccessful in his solicitations, these letters confirm his claim in *Brown Buffalo* that he had completed the novel, "My Cart for My Casket." From 1962 to 1964, Thompson wrote journalistic pieces from South America. Both were influenced by journalist-writer Ernest Hemingway and intrigued by his suicide. Thompson wrote "What Lured Hemingway to Ketchum?" for the *National Observer* in 1964. Acosta too devotes important scenes in his *Brown Buffalo* to Hemingway's suicide in Ketchum. In an early version of *Brown Buffalo* published in *Con Safos*, Acosta wrote: "I had not read any fiction after *The Old Man and the Sea*, which an editor for Doubleday had accused me of plagiarizing in my then-unpublished short novel, *Perla Is a Pig*" (Acosta 1971, 37). It was out of this American cultural experience that they developed similar sensibilities. Like Kerouac, both took to the road. However, unlike Kerouac's gentle characters, Acosta's Brown Buffalo and Thompson's Raoul Duke and Doctor Gonzo were full of resentment and anger.

Reading the letters and postcards that Acosta wrote to family and friends reveals the literary personality that will arrive fully matured as Brown Buffalo, Oscar Zeta Acosta, and Doctor Gonzo in the early seventies. This correspondence is written with the same energy, urgency, and edginess as *Brown Buffalo* and the companion piece, *The Revolt of the Cockroach People* (Acosta 1973 and 1989b). Acosta and Thompson thrived on each other and for a brief moment in time articulated the madness and paranoia of the late sixties and early seventies through a mixture of journalism and personal history. *Fear and Loathing* is Thompson's most enduring and popular work, his great American novel. According to William Mckeen, "*Fear and Loathing in Las Vegas* was Thompson's first sustained and conscious attempt to write Gonzo journalism" (Mckeen 1991, 49). Thompson has not repeated that stylistic success, much of it owed to Acosta, as is evident in Thompson's Gonzo profiles of Acosta in "Strange Rumblings in Aztlan," "The Banshee Screams for Buffalo Meat," and the Introduction to the 1989 Vintage editions of Acosta's *Brown Buffalo* and *The Revolt of the Cockroach People*. With hindsight, Acosta should also be considered an innovator in American literature, one of the early practitioners of Gonzo writing.

The striking difference between the two writers is that Thompson, according to Acosta, was a hillbilly from Tennessee and Acosta was a Mexican from Riverbank, California. In a central and crucial chapter in *Fear and Loathing*, within the hallucinatory madness of Las Vegas, Thompson looks back on the mid-sixties in San Francisco as a very special time and place to be a part of: "So now, less than five years later, you can go up on a steep hill in Vegas and look West, and with the right kind of eyes you can almost *see* the high-water mark—that place where the wave finally broke and rolled back" (68). Acosta, on the other hand, leaves San Francisco to begin his journey toward identity precisely at the moment that would be recalled as the summer of love.

Two other well-known twentieth-century writers, both associated with the Hispanic culture, play a prominent role in *Brown Buffalo*. Federico García Lorca is the Spanish poet who passionately portrayed the repression of the gypsies of Andalucía and the blacks of Harlem and converted it into myth and art through his *Romancero gitano* (*Gypsy Ballads*, 1928) and *Poeta en Nueva York* (*Poet in New York*, 1940). "Verde que te quiero verde" ("Green that I want you green"), the initial verse line of Lorca's "Romance sonámbulo," or "Sonambulesque Ballad," from *Romancero gitano*, lends symbolic color to Acosta's hallucinatory book. Like Lorca in his ballads, Acosta expresses a sense of an advancing, inevitable death. Just before Acosta decides to leave San Francisco on his road trip in search of himself, he writes: "Five years of madness in this hideout. No wonder I'm cracking up. I take the green death into my hands and see my reflection in waves on the mirror behind the bar. I am the son of Lorca, I remind myself. The only poet of this century worth reading. Did he suffer with those black eyes? That long, smooth greaser hair; did it make him hurt?" (66–67). The surrealism of Lorca's "Verde que te quiero verde" translates into the green tonality of death throughout the book.[14]

With regard to a suicidal tendency in his central protagonist, Acosta invokes Ernest Hemingway, the writer of the Lost Generation, who made male bravado—hunting—and Hispanic obsession with death—bullfighting—into a code of life and a theme in literature. And yet, after a life of heavy drinking and shock treatment for paranoia and depression and further treatment for physical illness at the Mayo Clinic, Hemingway committed suicide in Ketchum, Idaho, on 2 July 1961. Acosta will leave San Francisco on 1 July 1967, eventually arriving on the Fourth of July at the grave of Hemingway in Ketchum: "A simple slab of stone with his name chiseled into the rock is all that holds Papa down under. I took a bunch of yellow chrysanthemums from a neighboring grave and placed them over his head. Careful not to step on him, I sat beside his bed and waited for his message on this sunny, warm afternoon." (104). After the Fourth of July night of revelry—beer, corn chips, guacamole mixed with peyote—with the wealthy of Sun Valley, Idaho, Acosta again finds himself in the presence of Hemingway waiting for the message: "I stared at the stars and thought of old Ernie and his corny stories about the Left Bank and all the fine wines and wonderful meals he guzzled with his lesbian friends. I couldn't understand why he had to go all the way to Paris to look for companionship. Maybe he just couldn't take it, I thought to myself as I fell asleep" (126). After this encounter with the ghost of Hemingway, Acosta would go in search of the man, Karl King, who would show him the way to salvation (136).

III

Oscar Acosta the public figure appeared on the scene in Los Angeles in 1968. Those of us who remember the beginning of radicalization of Chicano youth in Los Angeles know that he participated in spring 1968 in the East L.A. "blow-outs," the demonstrations when students walked out of East L.A. high schools protesting the inequalities of the Los Angeles Unified School District. Acosta began to fashion a public persona as a Chicano activist lawyer, Chicano being more important than lawyer with regard to his lack of respect for the racism of the court system. He appeared in the *Los Angeles Times* defending four Mexican American activists who allegedly had set nine fires in the Biltmore Hotel while Governor Ronald Reagan was giving a speech on the evening of 24 April 1969 ("4 Activists Surrender," 28). The four activists were indicted on charges of "conspiracy, arson, burglary, burning personal property and malicious destruction of electrical lines" (ibid.). Acosta maintained that the fires had been set by a Los Angeles Police Department infiltrator and informant, Fernando Sumaya. Sumaya, a rookie policeman, had infiltrated the Brown Berets and was on the scene the night of 24 April 1969. Acosta also charged that the grand jury that voted in favor of the indictment 16 to 4 was illegally constituted. In arguing his case, Acosta subpoenaed every Superior Court judge in Los Angeles County to examine them under oath about their racism, to find out how many Mexican Americans were appointed to grand juries. The survey revealed that Mexican Americans were indeed excluded from participation in the legal system through the grand jury system.[15] During the trial proceedings, presiding judge Arthur L. Alarcon jailed Acosta along with fellow attorneys Beth Livesey and Joan Andersson for contempt of court after a verbal encounter with him ("Contempt in Arson Case," 1971, 1). When the jury deadlocked and failed to reach a verdict, Judge Alarcon declared a mistrial.

In July 1970, Acosta, now calling himself Oscar Zeta Acosta, began a campaign for sheriff of Los Angeles County to unseat Peter Pitchess.[16] His "Declaration of Candidacy for Office of Sheriff" called for the dissolution of the Sheriff's Department and the establishment of "The New People's Protection Department." His seven-point platform included "(1) the ultimate dissolution of the Sheriff's Department; (2) the immediate demilitarization of the office; (3) the immediate withdrawal of sheriffs from the barrios and ghettos; (4) investigations by the 'People's Protection Department' into misconduct; (5) the establishment of community review boards; (6) the community review boards would recommend personnel in programs which are useful for the entire community; and (7) equality and justice for all members of the community must always precede claims for 'law and order.'"[17] I saw him campaigning under the banner of the Raza Unida Party at one of the first celebrations for Mexican American unity in Los Angeles at the Los Angeles Sports Arena, a celebrity-studded event. Among those in attendance onstage were Anthony Quinn and Vicki Carr.[18] The movement for new ethnic pride that had begun on college campuses was finally being felt throughout the Mexican American community. Quinn introduced Acosta with other Mexican American candidates for office in the Los Angeles area. Acosta failed in his candidacy for sheriff, but he received more than 108,000 votes.[19]

Because of his activities within and outside the law, Acosta was under surveillance by federal as well as local agencies. The FBI had a file on him which authorities only recently declassified.[20] However, the file does not include anything noteworthy. For example, one entry of 28 May 1970 describes Acosta as one of the speakers, along with Reverend Jesse L. Jackson, at a Southern Christian Leadership Conference rally at the Los Angeles City Hall where, according to the report, "he set forth what he termed the oppressive conditions of the Mexican-American in the United States and specifically condemned the United States government for being historically responsible for these conditions" (U.S. Department of Justice 1970, 2).[21] His run for sheriff on his radical platform and his association with the Brown Berets must have led to his being tailed by the Los Angeles County Sheriff's Department. In 1972, Acosta was acquitted of illegal possession of forty-seven benzedrine tablets. On 28 August 1971, he had been arrested by undercover sheriff's deputies who claimed that he had tossed away a package of cigarettes containing the tablets. After the arrest, according to the *Los Angeles Times*, "Acosta announced that he was leaving the practice of law to move to Modesto, where reportedly he has been living the life of a farmer while preparing a book" ("Ex-Attorney Acquitted," 1972, 5).

Throughout his life, Acosta wrote often to his family, his parents, his wife, and Marco, and to his friends Robert "the Owl" Henry and Hunter Thompson. He wrote to explain his new experiences and changes and to ask for money. These writings are a rich repository of private thoughts and feelings with which to understand the troubled personality of the public figure and the writer. He had attempted suicide in the fifties shortly after his stint in the air force and had been under psychiatric care. In an undated, typed letter to his first wife, Betty Acosta, shortly after the birth of their son, Marco, Acosta confesses coming through a difficult emotional period: "Don't misunderstand me, I am not bubbling over with joy or any of that jazz, but it seems to me that I can contemplate the world and suffering and cruelty and sexuality and etcetera almost from a distance without having it cause me to become depressed or morbid or frustrated" (Acosta n.d., letter to Betty Acosta, 1). Personal conflicts did not cease, and in a compelling letter dated 12 July 1967 from Aspen, Colorado, Acosta writes to his parents: "As you well know I have been at war with myself and the universe, with mankind and God, with the whole of society and all it has to offer. I have been in this conflict for so many years I can't even remember when was the last time I felt at peace" (Acosta 1967, 1). In this letter to his parents, he explains that he had left San Francisco and his work as a Legal Aid lawyer to find peace and himself in Colorado.

During his first years in San Francisco, while working for the *San Francisco Examiner* and attending San Francisco Law School, Acosta became increasingly politicized with regard to ethnicity. He had joined Willie Brown's campaign for state assemblyman but, in an undated, typed letter on *San Francisco Examiner* letterhead to "Dear Willie," Acosta criticizes the campaign for focusing on African American, Chinese, and white constituencies to the exclusion of Mexican Americans (Acosta n.d., letter to Willie Brown).[22] In the first months of 1968, he would find an outlet for both his resentment and his creativity in the Chicano Movement. In a March 1968 letter from Los Angeles to a young Marco with the salutation "Dear Cholo," Acosta proclaims his radical transformation from Legal Aid lawyer to Chicano activist:

> I have a new job. The man from the old job didn't like me because I tell everybody what I think. . . . He thinks all Mexicans are dumb, and no good. But he is wrong and stupid. . . .
>
> My new job is working with Mexicans. Down here we call Mexicans Chicanos. That is what I am. I am a Chicano. You are a Chicano too if you want to be. But you have to learn to speak Spanish. This summer I will teach you. I want you to come down here and learn how to be a Chicano.
>
> This weekend I went to Delano and talked with a man who is a friend of Robert Kennedy. Robert Kennedy is President Kennedy's brother. He was there to tell everybody what a great man Cesar is. Cesar is a Chicano. He is not afraid of anybody. He wants me to help him put the cops in jail because the cops are bad, stupid pigs. (Acosta 1968)

Thus by the late sixties, Acosta had found his political cause by joining the struggle for justice begun by César Chávez.

After failed attempts to publish in the early sixties, Acosta now had material for literature. To the "Romeo and Juliet story of Oakies [*sic*] and Chicanos in the valley" (Acosta n.d., "Oscar Acosta," 4) that no one wanted to publish, he would add the adventures of the militant Chicano lawyer. Acosta had come to Los Angeles, certainly to join the movement but also to find literary material. In the autobiographical document titled "Oscar Acosta," Acosta writes: "I arrived here in L.A. in February [1968] intending to stay for a few months, write an article about it and then get out" (5). But then he agreed to take cases on behalf of Chicano activists. There was no doubt that Acosta took his activism and militancy seriously, but he also was in search of material for his writing. After all, after his acquittal on drug charges in 1972, he had announced to the *Los Angeles Times* that he was retiring to prepare a book. Acosta's desire for fame went beyond literature. He yearned for the status of popular culture hero, as he wrote in a letter from Mazatlán, México, to Alan Rinzler, his editor at Straight Arrow Books: "I think you have to be bold enough to accept the idea that the story of Zeta and the Brown Buffalo are king-sized movie material . . . I swear, I *see* it. I know we can do something on film" (Acosta 1972b, 3).

Along with his activism came increased drug use, which began to play a large role in his various identities. By his own admission in his typed manuscript "Oscar Acosta," he had begun to drop acid during his trip to Aspen in summer 1967 (5). This reliance on drugs continued during his activist period: "I think psychedelic drugs have been important to the development of my consciousness. I don't think I'd have gotten to where I am without the use of these drugs. They've put me into a level of awareness where I can see myself and see what I'm really doing. Most of the big ideas I've gotten for my lawyer work have usually come when I am stoned. Like the Grand Jury challenge was the result of an acid experience. . . . A lot of the tactics I emply [*sic*] I get the ideas for when I am stoned which is not to say that I wouldn't get them if I wasn't stoned. A lot of my creativity has sprung from my use of these psychedelic drugs" (ibid., 14). Acosta was a freak who lived his life as wild and on the edge as possible.

All these experiences coalesced into a new persona. During his campaign for sheriff, he had begun to use Zeta in his name. "My name is Zeta," he announces in an undated single-page typed document, because it has "numerous strange meanings, derivitives [*sic*] from ancient gods and inscribed in stone tablets rising skyward into foggy mists. It is also the sixth letter of the Greek alphabet and the last of the Spanish" (Acosta n.d., "My Name Is Zeta"). He continues, admitting to having seen the now-classic Costa Gavras film Z in which the letter meant "He shall return." "And of course," Acosta ends, "we musn't [*sic*] forget our old friend: Zoro [*sic*]." During his campaign, he began to sign his documents with a Z, with the mark of Zorro. This marks a transformation from Oscar Thomas Acosta to Oscar Zeta Acosta, Chicano lawyer, from English to the Spanish language, from Legal Aid lawyer to outlaw hero. Militancy, ethnicity, drugs, and literature were all coming together for Acosta, as he fashioned a persona that would be the subject of his work.

Actually, this Oscar Zeta Acosta was also known as General Zeta, the militant, often violent personality, one of three names (and personalities) that he used when referring to himself or writing to his family and friends. This side of his personality is the subject of *Cockroach People*. In January

1974, Acosta produced for Helen Brann of Random House a plot summary of fourteen handwritten pages, a chapter-by-chapter account of a planned third book that was titled "The Rise and Fall of General Zeta" (Acosta n.d., letter to Helen Brann). The plot summary begins with his last day as a trial lawyer in Los Angeles, followed by his relationship with Raoul Duke, how they meet up to write *Fear and Loathing*, the Biltmore case, his relationship with *Rolling Stone*, and ending with the possible death of General Zeta from overdose. Had it been written and published, it would have been a bitter, angry tell-all book by someone who, at that point in 1974, was very ill. Another side of his personality is Doctor Gonzo, the crazy, paranoid, hallucinatory writer and literary character. This personality is most clearly represented in Thompson's *Fear and Loathing in Las Vegas*. Yet there was also another dimension of his personality that was hidden from the public. He referred to himself as Brown Buffalo or Buffy, his gentler side. A former managing editor of *Rolling Stone*, Harriet Fier, describes Acosta as "a real sweetheart. . . . He had a very soft, whispery voice and he had a very feminine side. He loved women and his kids. When he got filled up with a bunch of stuff he acted very tough. But he always came back to being very gentle" (cited in Perry 1992, 156). This side of his personality is also evident in his correspondence—he was a family man, caring son, brother, and loving father.

By 1974, the sixties decade was a thing of the past and the Chicano Movement's initial militant rebellious phase was over. By 1974, Acosta had retreated from Chicano activist law, tired of the internal conflicts of the Chicano Movement, especially with his Brown Beret companions. He was angry with *Rolling Stone* and editor Alan Rinzler for not making good on promotional promises and bitter that he was unable to secure the fame and money that he believed he deserved. In the letter to Helen Brann that includes the plot summary of "The Rise and Fall of General Zeta," the admittedly embittered Acosta writes: "I know full well that I am a good writer and a unique storyteller. A lot of the credit that has gone to the so-called 'Gonzo Journalism' is rightfully mine" (19). He was alone and sick. His state of mind must have been complicated by recurring depression and physical illness. He was hospitalized at the John Wesley Hospital in Los Angeles and "just in case" decided to handwrite to Marco the "Last Will and Testament of Oscar Acosta" dated 13 January 1974, a document that revoked all former wills and left his entire estate to Marco (Acosta 1974).[23] It might have been that Acosta saw his own end coming. The plot summary of his third book is a reflexive and chaotic chronicle of the violence and madness that he lived during and after *Brown Buffalo* and *The Revolt of the Cockroach People*. It marks the end of a riotous, crazy period and of one man who lived it. The end of "The Rise and Fall of General Zeta" comes when Zeta "receives notice from the State Bar of his impending disbarment and notice from the Internal Revenue Service for failure to pay taxes for ten years. Perhaps he dies of an overdose?" (17). During Acosta's Los Angeles period, México had become a place of refuge. He spent time in Mazatlán, Sinaloa, and Morelia, Michoacán, writing or seeking a respite from political struggles. After his release from John Wesley Hospital, Acosta headed for México. Marco was one of the last to receive a postcard from Acosta. Somewhere in Sinaloa in June 1974, Acosta disappeared.

IV

In the absence of a Chicano literary tradition, the writer Acosta drew on Anglo-American literary influences for *Brown Buffalo*. I have already noted the importance of the Beat Generation and Kerouac's *On the Road*. Other literary forms were to emerge out of the sixties, a bold, in-your-face, subjective, activist form of writing, such as the alternative, underground, and ethnic presses, and rock journalism, as well as the more canonical, New Journalistic writing produced by such varied literary personalities as Truman Capote, Norman Mailer, Tom Wolfe, and, of course, Hunter Thompson. Acosta's affiliations with Jann Wenner and Alan Rinzler of *Rolling Stone* magazine and Straight Arrow Books, his personal and literary relationship with Hunter S. Thompson, and his publications in the East L.A. *Con Safos* magazine, show *Brown Buffalo* to be a part of this new writing.[24] Acosta was fully aware of his place within this genre and referred to his writing as a combination of "journalism and personal history" (Acosta 1972b, 2). What distinguished Acosta in this new genre was that his writing meant something different, something more: he was personally political with regard to his Mexican identity. The former activist had held up a mirror to himself to painfully address social issues in his own version of Gonzo journalism and fiction.[25]

Judging from its title, *The Autobiography of a Brown Buffalo* is an empirical narrative, a self-portrait in which the writer has selected those events and experiences in his life that build an integrated pattern. Like others before him, Acosta has drawn on the easily recognizable Christian narrative of guilt, confession, and redemption. Acosta superimposes on his autobiographical narrative the story of the Christian Messiah. In his thirty-third year (he was actually thirty-two), Acosta will symbolically die in San Francisco to be reborn, resurrected in El Paso as a Chicano and as a leader of his people.

In the opening paragraph of the book, the reader finds Acosta on the Monday morning of 1 July 1967 shamelessly naked before the mirror in the midst of a spiritual crisis to which he will not admit. As he tells his imaginary psychiatrist Dr. Serbin: "Can't you see? It's a Goddamned physical thing" (13). It is a physical thing in the sense that he is bothered by ulcers. In a narrative that will shuttle between the past and the present events of 1967 and 1968, we discover what has led to his present condition. He is a man for whom masculinity is connected to ethnicity, his Mexicanness. Although he is careful to describe his naked body in terms of his ethnicity, "my brown belly, two large chunks of brown tit, my peasant hands, my sunbaked face, my brown ass," he will not admit fully to his Mexican identity until Chapter 6 when he begins recounting his childhood: "Although I was born in El Paso, Texas, I am actually a small town kid. A hick from the sticks, a Mexican boy from the other side of the tracks. I grew up in Riverbank, California; post office box 303; population 3,969" (71).

Acosta's childhood is one of seeking a common ground between two cultures. The Acosta household was ruled by a father, an ex-GI who had served in the Pacific in World War II and upon returning to Riverbank imposed the rules of the *Seabee's Manual* on his two sons. "It seemed," writes Acosta, "that the sole purpose of childhood was to train boys to be men" (75). The child Acosta was supposed to take life seriously, accept any challenge like *un hombre*, and never back off from a fight. There were plenty of opportunities for fighting in Riverbank: "We had to fight the Okies because we were Mexicans!" (78). All might have been fine for the man-in-the-making except for his body and his color—he was a fat, dark Mexican, a Brown Buffalo. The first woman in his life, his mother, had him convinced that he "was obese, ugly as a pig and without any redeeming qualities whatsoever" (82). As he leaves his home culture to join the Boy Scouts, the first of many rites of passage into American culture, Acosta declares that to all his Okie buddies he was a Jigaboo, a nigger. "The name was not meant as an insult," writes Acosta tongue-in-cheek. "It was simply a means of classification. The tone of one's pigmentation is the fastest and surest way of determining exactly who one is" (86).

Friends and enemies called him nigger until the day he whipped his archenemy Junior Ellis on the school playground. After that fight no "Okie sonofabitch" ever called him nigger to his face.

The victory, however, was a hollow one, and the roar of playground approval gives way to classroom laughter and ridicule because of his blue-eyed *Miss It*, Jane Addison, who complains to the teacher Joan Anderson: "Will you please ask Oscar to put on his shirt? . . . He stinks" (94). A dark fat Mexican, he was the nigger, after all: "My mother was right. I am nothing but an Indian with sweating body and faltering tits that sag at the sight of a young girl's blue eyes. I shall never be able to undress in front of a woman's stare" (94–95).

This 1942 event will give rise to the first of several death fantasies: "Even as Miss Anderson continues the story of Perry Mason I leave my dead head in my arms and cast myself into the iron jaws of her father's saw . . . dressed up in fine linen, my hands folded over my chest, a rosary in the delicate fingers, I await my maker in a golden, finely carved casket which shall be my resting place throughout eternity. There they sit, all of them: my folks, her folks, Bob, Hector, all my cousins, my grandmother . . ." (95). The lack of value attached to his identity by his family and society lead to the feelings of meaninglessness and to visualizing himself dead while his family and friends mourn his passing. In *Brown Buffalo*, Acosta claims, confirmed by letters to publishers, to have written a novel of his youth and adolescence in forties and fifties Riverbank titled "My Cart for My Casket." As the title suggests, only in death does his life have meaning. This death fantasy will give way to suicidal tendencies in both *Brown Buffalo* and Acosta's life. The flight from San Francisco to Ketchum to the site of Ernest Hemingway's grave and the evocation of García Lorca's green death poem are the literary manifestations of a deeply rooted personal problem. We now know that as an adult, Acosta was treated for depression after the attempted suicide. His letters to family and friends speak of depression, conflict, and death. In our conversations, Marco told me that his father spoke often about death. In Marco's Afterword to the 1989 Vintage edition of *Brown Buffalo*, Marco writes about his father: "My father used to ask me rhetorically, especially when we were on top of a beautiful mountain in Colorado or by the sea in Mexico, 'Today would be a great day to die, wouldn't it?'" (202). Even his eventual escape to and mysterious disappearance in Mexico bear witness to the importance of these childhood memories whether real or imagined that Acosta has chosen to record for his readers.

Another all-informing moment that leads back to the morning of 1 July 1967 concerns his high school romance with Alice Brown. Acosta was in his senior year in high school, 1951–1952. He had quit hanging around with his Mexican grade school friends because they constantly talked about the gringos, Okies, and Americans "and all kinds of things that I could not accept as true since for me all was going king ass" (112). He never dated Mexican girls because they refused to participate in school activities, and "also they were square and homely" (112). He had avoided girls since Jane Addison told him he stunk until he was once again struck by love, this time by the green-hazel eyes and braces of Alice Brown. All would have been fine for these two teenagers except that racism and the law prevented their love. Alice's stepfather was a fervent racist who had the chief of police intervene. With the assistance of Acosta, Alice had been crowned queen of the winter dance. In the spotlight and with the crowd roaring with delight, Acosta danced with his queen. When the waltz was over, young Acosta decided: "'Tonight's the night. We'll just have to face it'" (118). While both were holding hands in front of Alice's house, the chief of police drove up with Acosta's parents in the back seat. Chief of Police Lauren explains that Alice's parents had filed a complaint: "'Mr. and Mrs. Brown here. They already done signed a *complaint* so it ain't exactly *private* no more . . . if I catch you two together again . . . I'll just have to take you both into juvenile . . . it's already been done . . . now, I known you for . . . since you was just a tyke . . . but under the law, if I catch you two together again, I'll take you in . . . Savvy?' He tried to smile" (119). That is the night when, while laughing uncontrollably and drinking a beer with his father, the stomach convulsions that were to plague him throughout his life first began: "The convulsions down under began that night. The wretched vomit, the gas laden belly formed within my pit when the chief of police asked me if I understood. Savvy?" (119–120). This recollection is framed while Acosta is sitting by Ernest Hemingway's grave on 4 July 1967. Just prior to recalling this important moment in his life Acosta "sat beside his [Hemingway's] bed and waited for his message, on this warm sunny afternoon . . ." (104).

These childhood and adolescent events are crucial for understanding the lonely and alienated Acosta on 1 July 1967, still struggling with both his Mexican and his masculine identities:

> Every morning of my life I have seen that brown belly from every angle. It has not changed that I can remember. I was always a fat kid. I suck it in and

expand an enormous chest of two large chunks of brown tit. But look, if I suck it in just a wee bit more, push the bellybutton up against the back; can you see what will surely come to pass if you but rid yourself of this extra flesh? Just think of all the broads you'll get if you trim down to a comfortable 200. (11)

Holding his breath too long leads to grumbling and convulsions in his stomach. With his hands around the toilet he waits for the green bile which does not come. He sits on the bowl and looks into the mirror at an "outrageously angry" face staring him down to which Acosta responds with laughter at the sight of a Brown Buffalo sitting on his throne.

Acosta stares into the mirror searching for answers to his physical dilemma from three well-known outlaws and tough guys of the American cinema, Humphrey Bogart, James Cagney, and George Raft, who offer constipation as the answer. His problem is a physical thing! After he relieves himself he enters the shower, his favorite room, accompanied by his fantasies and Bogart. Acosta clenches his fists and tightens his body as the steam burns his chest. "Hang tough," encourages Bogart. When the Japanese see that he will die before he talks, they turn off the hot steam and immediately turn on the freezing cold water. Having survived this torture, Acosta awaits his reward. Bogart pats him on the back. "Okay kid. You did a good job. Now finish her off" (15). With the hot and cold water equalized to pleasantly warm, Acosta masturbates first to a fantasy of undressing his mother followed by the orgasm as he makes love to another Alice, his friend Ted Casey's girl.

These fantasies of self-inflicted torture, heroism, and sexual prowess stand in sharp contrast to his past and to the present in San Francisco. This is a man who is at odds with himself and with his world. For one year he has worked within the justice system fighting for a cause through his position as a Legal Aid lawyer in President Lyndon Johnson's War on Poverty. On this day, however, he will realize that the struggle within the system is beyond his efforts. This has been shown to him at his office in the slums of East Oakland by the black, Latino, and Okie women with a look of desperation who present themselves to him. Poor women with hungry children. Women who are beaten by their husbands. Women who have to sit in front of him and stare at his $567 IBM typewriter on his mahogany desk. This has caused him numerous sleepless nights:

Am I really supposed to believe they actually live on $268 a month for a family of four in the year the Beatles made a million? Doesn't LBJ know that Watts burned in '65? That Detroit rioted in '66? That the Panthers started carrying guns in '67? Am I to prevent all this with a carbon copy of a court order that compels a Negro janitor to pay child support for his nine kids? Does anyone seriously believe I can battle Governor Reagan and his Welfare Department even with my fancy $567 IBM? Do you think our Xerox machine will save Sammy from the draft? Or that our new Witkin law books will really help turn the tide in our battle against poverty, powdered milk and overdrawn checks? (28)

After a year of winning more than one hundred uncontested divorce cases that will give his female clients welfare assistance and securing temporary restraining orders against their husbands or boyfriends, Acosta has learned to lie and play the game. "When I first passed the Bar I *tried* to obey the law. But that was twelve months ago. Now I simply ask a few questions and my secretary does the rest" (20). Pauline, the secretary with female problems, is the sweetest and most understanding woman he has known, except for his grandmother. Since he first walked into the Legal Aid Society in Oakland, she had coddled him, protected him, and preserved him for the serious work, the heavy research he never got around to. It is learning on that Monday morning of the death of Pauline from cancer that will finally set him off to begin his odyssey in search of his past. He is orphaned at thirty-three years of age, "the same age as when Jesus died," and the green bile that would not come that morning, does finally come at his work. "The designs of curdled milk and scrambled eggs with ketchup are a sight, a work of genius. I ponder the fluid patterns of my rejections and consider the potential for art. Dali could do something with this, I'm sure." He goes on, "But wait. 'Good God, I didn't use any ketchup. . . . It's blood, God damn it! *Blood*, do you hear?'" (25). He yells this to his shrink, Dr. Serbin, who has accompanied him into the green-walled toilet. At the end of the harrowing day, to which Procol Harum's "Whiter Shade of Pale" lends a spiritual feeling, after an orgiastic night of food, alcohol, and drugs, "[d]eath is welcome after the events of this day, the first of July, 1967" (70).

Thus begins the trip back to his origins, reversing the traditional westward-symbolic-mythical American quest.[26] Acosta's story is one of trying to belong, of the young Oscar Thomas Acosta entering American boyhood and adolescence—Boy Scouts and learning to masturbate; football and playing dirty without getting caught—to the exclusion of his Mexican buddies from his neighborhood. However, as he recalls for his readers, since childhood he had come across obstacles—racism, name-calling, the law. He had come up against white supremacy, an obstacle that neither he nor his father nor the *Seabee's Manual* could overcome. As a Legal Aid lawyer he tried to work within the system. Now, as he begins his trip, he has surpassed his "puppy love-trip" with the law. Acosta on the lam is the Acosta who will surface later in Los Angeles as the mad Doctor Gonzo, as the Brown Buffalo, as the reincarnation of Zorro in his old California haunts, the often-violent Chicano lawyer Oscar Zeta Acosta who has no respect for the criminal justice system. How he comes to be Chicano is, of course, the point of his self-portrait.

After escaping San Francisco, Acosta travels to Hemingway's grave in Ketchum, cavorts with the wealthy in Sun Valley, Idaho, on the Fourth of July, strikes up a friendship with Karl King (Hunter S. Thompson) in Alpine, Colorado, and works at a variety of jobs in Colorado and New Mexico. No longer forestalling the inevitable, the divided Acosta arrives at the dividing line for national and cultural identities, the El Paso/Juárez border: "I decided to go to El Paso, the place of my birth, to see if I could find the object of my quest. I still wanted to find out just who in the hell I really was" (184). Crossing the border into Juárez, Acosta experiences a sense of belonging in the Mexican people that mirrors his own ethnicity: "All the faces are brown, tinged with brown, lightly brown, the feeling of brown" (185). Listening to Spanish, he recalls the prohibitions against speaking his first language. His father told him he would not learn English if he didn't stop speaking Spanish. He finally gave up Spanish the day Mr. Wilkie, an American, explained to him that in order to stay in the *American* school he had to speak only English on the school ground. While playing football, Acosta and his playmates had used Spanish and had been accused by the Okies of using secret messages. Since that event of 1947, Acosta had not spoken Spanish until he crossed the border some twenty years later.

Finally on his way to Mexican male selfhood, Acosta arrived at the ultimate resolution to his problem of identity—a Mexican woman would have an answer to his pain. His romantic illusion is foreclosed when he walks into an Americanized topless bar where Jefferson Airplane's "White Rabbit" is blaring. He is approached by two women, Sylvia, a redhead with peach skin, and Teresa, a tall blond. Sylvia asks for a drink: "*Me compra una copa?"* (189). He can reply only in English since he assumes that Sylvia is American. Sylvia calls to Teresa, *"Qué dice este indio?"'* "What is this Indian saying?" The blond Teresa interprets in English. Sylvia taunts in Spanish, questioning his Mexicanness: *"Y este, no me digas que no es Mexicano?"'* The years of jokes, lies, and refusal to answer to his ethnicity with *Americanos* no longer works in Juárez. The woman had a legitimate question. She knew he was *mexicano* but he couldn't even offer her a drink in Spanish. Sex with these women leads Acosta to accept that he is finally his *indio* father's son.

However, these women do not have an answer to his pain; it is an educated, bilingual, gray-haired Mexican woman, a judge, who does not conform to the image of a woman as an object of sexual pleasure or as a coddling, protective mother. The day of judgment for the attorney comes after he has been arrested for disorderly conduct with a hotel clerk. Acosta, in demanding a heater for his cold room, resorted to foul language and insults. Standing before the judge he must answer simply *sí o no* to the charges. He has no recourse but to confess publicly that he is guilty: *"Sí, soy culpable,"* he confesses in Spanish. The first moment of humility for Acosta in *Brown Buffalo* happens before a woman. In the first chapter, he would not admit to anything to his Jewish shrink, Dr. Serbin. He would not come to terms with his impotence, his lack of sexual prowess, and his false male bravado. But at the end he confesses to this Mexican woman that he is guilty of nasty things, vile language, gringo arrogance, and *americano* impatience with lazy *mexicanos*. He is not mexicano after all. The judge offers a solution: *"Why don't you go home and learn your father's language?"* (194). However, upon crossing back into El Paso, the border guard questions his citizenship: *"You americano? . . . You don't look like an American, you know?"* (195).

Brown Buffalo, however, also begs to be read as more than just the empirical narrative of the coming-to-consciousness of an individual. The book is, in fact, a palimpsest of genres, facts coupled with the force of fiction. No doubt, Acosta has drawn on his personal biography and historical events to tell the story of the Brown Buffalo. Many of the historical details and facts in *Brown Buffalo* are true, such as place of birth, parents, siblings, education, military service, and profession. As Acosta drives to his work in Oakland on 1 July 1967, he is surprised by Procol Harum's "Whiter Shade of Pale." This song did have its U.S. release on that day. However, personal events from childhood and adulthood have been imaginatively manipulated in *Brown Buffalo* for effect on the reader. In the letter to his parents of 12 July 1967, Acosta explains, that after a year with the Legal Aid Society, he left San Francisco to search for himself, landing in Aspen where he had found a job as a cook in a Mexican restaurant. He is living with a couple that he met in Aspen, he explains to his parents, and a fellow that left with him, Tim, is still with him. He ends the letter by asking for money and stating that he can be reached via telegram at the Daisy Duck bar. There is no mention of meeting or knowing Hunter Thompson. Moreover, while some characters and scenes in the book are fictionalized from Acosta's friends in San Francisco and Los Angeles, other important personal details are excluded. Character Ted Casey, the Owl, and his wife, Alice, for example, are drawn from Acosta's friends Robert and Ann Henry. His grade school teacher Joan Andersson is also the name of a fellow attorney who worked with Acosta on the Biltmore fire case. In creating the character of the alienated loner, the Brown Buffalo, Acosta chose to leave out his family, his wife, Betty, and son, Marco.

Taking to the road is a time-honored literary device and *Brown Buffalo* shares much with the kind of narrative genre in which the road trip serves as pretext for looking at society through a critical, often distorted, lens. As Acosta looks outward from himself in *Brown Buffalo*, we recognize family resemblances with Rabelais's *Gargantua and Pantagruel*, the picaresque *Lazarillo de Tormes*, Voltaire's *Candide*, Swift's *Gulliver's Travels*, Woolf's *Orlando*, and Thompson's *Fear and Loathing in Las Vegas*. In all we find the imaginative corrective impulse of the satirist.

In *Brown Buffalo* the reporting of drug-induced surreal events, the cunning and mental agility of the narrator, the in-your-face confrontation with the reader outside the normal rules of decorum and good taste, all characteristics of Gonzo writing, are also consonant with the satirist's display of intellectual wit and fancy, of humor and the grotesque. The first chapter of *Brown Buffalo* can stand as one of the great examples of recent satire, as the character, the alienated attorney Oscar Zeta Acosta, full of anger and resentment toward himself, his family, and his culture, intellectualizes his bodily functions for the reader: belching, vomiting, farting, defecating, urinating, and masturbating. Two of the solemn scenes in the plot of the Christ figure—the last supper and the suffering of the Madonna—are invoked through the grotesque lens of satire. The dinner scene in North Beach's well-known Italian restaurant La Fior d'Italia is the culmination of a night of drinking, LSD, and cocaine in celebration of Acosta's dropping out from straight society on 1 July 1967. It is a repugnant affair where we find Acosta passed out, stretched out on the dining table as the Owl carves a hole in his chest with a golden sword followed by his Armenian nurse girlfriend who holds his head like a Madonna and sucks out mucous from his nose after too much cocaine (63).

The apparently anarchic plot, self-indulgent and digressive, is crucial to the transformation of Acosta's character. Depending upon scene and episode, Acosta is an athlete, musician, writer, religious man, lawyer, or laborer. He is a high school football player in Riverbank; a clarinet player in the Air Force Band; a Southern Baptist missionary who finds Jesus and salvation in the jungles of Panama converting natives to Christianity; an author of a novel, *My Cart for My Casket*; a physical therapist in a mental hospital for the rich in St. Louis; a lawyer in San Francisco; Henry Hawk, a Samoan, in Nevada; a Blackfoot Indian Chief, Brown Buffalo, in Idaho, who had also been a driver for Ernest Hemingway in Cuba; a dishwasher, plumber, and construction worker in Colorado; and finally a pimp in Juárez. And depending upon Acosta's whim, the improbable or unexpected events are either blown up to the level of a scene or relegated to summary narration in a sentence. As we have seen, Acosta's plot is the search for a Chicano identity. However, in reference to the social character of satire, the plot of *Brown Buffalo* should also be construed as an occasion to reject the limitations of novelistic discourse and capture a broad sequential representation of social and cultural life in the United States.

In his travels through his life both before and during the summer of 1967, Acosta forces the reader to look at society as divided between American and "un-American" worlds, which is to say, to look at those that have been marginalized by middle-class American society. In telling his life through a wide variety of social spaces, Acosta offers from the Chicano point of view a powerful critique of America's ideological solution to ethnicity and class conflict, the melting pot.

Disaffected white youth in San Francisco had one solution to authority, to the conformity and normalcy of the culture of their elders: "tune in, turn on, drop out," "make love, not war," "peace and love." On several occasions in *Brown Buffalo*, Acosta chooses to distance himself from the leaders and participants of the hippie movement. Through friends Dick Dettering, Van Tilburg Clark, Mark Harris, and Herb Gold at San Francisco State, Acosta had met Timothy Leary before he became the guru for the movement, when he "was into rats and monkeys . . . sticking little electrical jabs in their brains to find out what was in the human head" (100). Seven years later, when he greets Leary at the first round of love-ins at Golden Gate Park in spring 1967, Acosta writes: "Tim floated down to us through the eucalyptus wearing a white gown. . . . He was so fucked up I doubt he knew of his own existence. I walked up to him and said, 'Hey, Tim! You old bastard, how are you doing?' He stared right past and showed me a mouthful of white teeth. I knew right then and there that religion and hard drugs just don't mix. So I couldn't take his message to heart" (101).

On his pilgrimage to Hemingway's grave in Idaho, Acosta joins a Fourth of July celebration in Sun Valley. He had been invited to the Independence party by the Peace and Love–invoking Karin Wilmington, a young, blue-eyed hitchhiker he had picked up in Nevada, who at her home drives a Porsche. Acosta finds himself completely out of place, among the upper-class, long-hair types who find pleasure with such Indian/Mexican things as peyote, corn chips, and guacamole.

In the last chapters of *Brown Buffalo* in the fictional town of Alpine (Aspen), Acosta meets up with Karl King, the character based on Hunter Thompson. This is Acosta's own buddy narrative, the "prequel" to the 1970 events in *Fear and Loathing in Las Vegas*. After drowning down a case of beer, Acosta and King enter a love-in near the summer home of Robert McNamara, Johnson's secretary of defense. Those at the demonstration stand out against Acosta's class and ethnicity: "Blond teenyboppers with tight bellbottoms" and "blue-eyed boys with tanned muscles and frizzy curls laced their heads with headbands of many colors" (174). Both Acosta and King are dressed as masked outlaw-heroes described by Acosta as the Lone Ranger and Tonto. High on alcohol, sarcastic and irreverent, both characters express a disdain for those present at the love-in. Of his new friend's similar lifestyle, Acosta remarks, "a good boozer is hard to come by when everyone wants to wear flowers and fade into little puffs of white smoke" (172). The futility of the demonstration is criticized by Acosta when he asks one of the love-in's leaders, "You didn't negotiate a fucking peace treaty with McNamara?" (175).

Acosta aligns himself with another representation of society. Before the summer of love, Acosta had found his way to Trader JJ's, "a rumrunners' hideout before the fire of '06, the oldest bar in the city of sin with cells for Shanghai affairs" (44). At Trader JJ's, Acosta had found laughter and sarcasm as well as comfort and community among a group of alienated drunks of diverse ethnicities, genders, and sexualities: "hard-core intellectuals, funky artists, tough-minded engineers, humble poets, un-published writers, drunken lawyers and dropouts of all description, who had managed somehow to keep the joint free of all foreign ideology" (43). Trader JJ's serves as a base of operations as Acosta drives through the neighborhoods of San Francisco and Oakland. Through Acosta's eyes the San Francisco cityscape is not rendered solely through well-known build-ings, areas, and streets. Acosta is also always careful to describe the social landscape of the city in terms of conflict. We are witnesses to the sharp racial, class, and group divisions: "Grant Avenue is a block away. Here the yellow horde is cut off. From chow mein to pizza pies in one block. From slant-eyed, yellow people to black-eyed olive oils all spliced by a single stop light at Grant & Broadway" (59) and "[t]he Fillmore District where all the niggers lived until they drove them out to make room for white people, the Catholic Church and some rich Japs" (32). Almost every character in *Brown Buffalo* is identified by ethnicity and nationality, some seventeen types composed of Mexicans, Native Americans, African Americans, Europeans, Latin Americans, and Asian Americans. These divisions in sixties San Francisco are repetitions of his forties and fifties own small rural community, Riverbank, where the city is sharply divided, sectioned off: "Riverbank is divided into three parts. And in my corner of the world there were only three kinds of people. Mexicans, Okies and Americans. Catholics, Holy Rollers and Protestants. Peach pickers, can-nery workers and clerks" (78).

In *Brown Buffalo*, Acosta forces the reader to note the decidedly ethnic character of U.S. society in the sixties, as he discovered as a child. In Riverbank, Acosta learned to be a nigger, forced to respect territorial and ethnic limits. As a young boy on a fateful Halloween night, on crossing into Okie territory he is ambushed and caught by Junior Ellis and his group and called a "fuckin' nigger." Many years later as an adult, he is called a nigger. "Puke, you sonofabitch," Acosta exhorts himself on 1 July 1967. "Aren't you the world's champion pukerupper?" (12). The illness that had festered inside him for so many years in his sour stomach now clearly articulated in the summer of 1967 comes across loud and clear in Acosta's use of racial and sexual slurs—spic, greaser, okie, nigger, jap, chinks, hillbillies, and fags—to map out ethnic and group boundaries. These terms certainly do exist in the English language. Like the word "nigger" that Acosta internalized, these words now explode out from inside him. Although not in good taste, these terms refer not so much to racist language but to the obscenity of racism that Acosta had endured throughout his life until he arrived at his new ethnic identity in his place of birth, El Paso: "What I see now, on this rainy day in January, 1968, what is clear to me after this sojourn is that I am neither a Mexican nor an American. I am neither Catholic nor a Protestant. I am a Chicano by ancestry and a Brown Buffalo by choice. Is that so hard for you to understand? Or is it that you choose not to understand for fear that I'll get even with you?" (199).

V

The sixties decade has had a clichéd existence in the United States. Mainstream media has focused particularly on hippies, drugs, and rock music. However, the sixties were also the decade when long-standing racial inequality could no longer be ignored. The first years of the decade marked the beginning of the black-inspired civil rights movement: in 1960, the first sit-ins in the South take place, in Greensboro, North Carolina; in 1961, the first Freedom Ride buses are burned in Alabama; in 1963, Martin Luther King delivers his famous "I Have a Dream" speech; in 1965, the Chicano Movement begins with César Chávez leading the farmworker strike in Delano, California. Outside the borders of the United States, the sixties began in the previous decade in the decolonization of British and French Africa and Latin America. The Battle of Algiers and the independence of Ghana in 1957 were followed by the Cuban Revolution in 1959.[27] The sixties decade was, then, the period in which "natives," minorities, marginals became human beings with the right to speak in a collective voice. Acosta's tortured life and writings are, personally, an interrogation of Chicano/Mexicano masculinity as well as, historically, the development of an ethnic consciousness out of the cultural confusion and racism of the forties and fifties. In this sense, Acosta should be understood not just as part of a Chicano or American experience but also as one of the many voices of an international sixties period.

"MAKING FAMILIA FROM SCRATCH"
Cherríe L. Moraga's Self-Portraits

I come from a long line of Vendidas. *I am a Chicana lesbian. My being a sexual person and a radical stands in direct contradiction to, and in violation of, the women I was raised to be.*

— CHERRÍE MORAGA, *LOVING IN THE WAR YEARS*

My family is beginning to feel its disintegration. Our Mexican grandmother of ninety-six has been dead two years now and la familia is beginning to go. . . . My line of family stops with me. There will be no one calling me, Mami, Mamá, Abuelita. *. . . . I am the last generation put on this planet to remember and record.*

— CHERRÍE MORAGA, *THE LAST GENERATION*

The pages that follow are my own queer story of pregnancy, birth, and the first years of mothering. It is a story of one small human being's—my son's—struggle for life in the age of death/the age of AIDS.

— CHERRÍE MORAGA, *WAITING IN THE WINGS*

An image stays in my mind: a Casta painting by Miguel Cabrera of 18th century New Spain. It is a portrait of miscegenation. In

> *the painting, the mixed-blood child sits on the lap of*
> *his Spanish father. . . . His mestiza-india mother stands next*
> *to the pair. This child is looking back, back at her, to his Indian*
> *antecedents. To his past and his future he will choose. This is*
> *my own face looking back.*

— CHERRÍE L. MORAGA, *LOVING IN THE WAR YEARS*

The year 1983 looms large as we look back on Cherríe Moraga's emergence as a voice in Chicana feminism.[1] That year the second edition of *This Bridge Called My Back: Writings by Radical Women of Color*, coedited with Gloria Anzaldúa, *Cuentos: Stories by Latinas*, coedited with Alma Gómez and Mariana Romo-Carmona, and Moraga's own *Loving in the War Years: Lo que nunca pasó por sus labios* were published. The three works were a timely and bold affirmation of a new subjectivity linking sexuality, feminism, race, and class. A wide variety of themes were associated with Moraga as coeditor and author. The first book, the coedited anthology, was a woman-of-color critique of the American left and white feminism as well as a response to the emerging political right of the eighties. In *Cuentos*, the editors laid claim to a bilingual Latina literary tradition emphasizing both the oral testimonio and the printed word. In response to the male Latin American boom, the editors hoped for a feminist connection with women writers in Latin America.[2] Finally, *Loving in the War Years* was the mixed-blood Chicana lesbian's personal response to the secondary status of women in Mexican culture.

With *This Bridge Called My Back*, first published in 1981, Cherríe Moraga and Gloria Anzaldúa creatively and critically revitalized Chicana and Chicano literature in the decade of the eighties. Moraga and Anzaldúa gained prominence outside of the traditional politics of the Chicano Movement in feminist-lesbian groups headquartered in Boston, New York, and San Francisco. Both should be credited with the advancement of a Third World or radical feminist perspective through *Bridge*. The anthology was first conceived by Anzaldúa in 1979 as a reaction to being the token outsider at a San Francisco Bay area women's conference. What had begun as a reaction by two Chicanas to "the racism of white feminists soon became a positive affirmation of the commitment of women of color to our *own* feminism" (Moraga and Anzaldúa 1983, xxiii). The anthology eventually grew to include works by Asian American, African American,

Chicana, Latin American, Native American, and Puerto Rican women. "We envision the book," write Moraga and Anzaldúa in their Introduction, "being used as a *required* text in most women's studies courses" (xxvi). *Bridge* did indeed meet the goal established by its editors. Since the 1983 publication of the second edition of *Bridge* by Kitchen Table: Women of Color Press, the anthology has become a standard text of women's studies courses and bibliographies across the nation.[3] In 1981, Moraga and Anzaldúa also hoped for a wider distribution of a translated *Bridge* so as to "mak[e] a tangible link between Third World women in the U.S. and throughout the world" (xxvi). In 1988, the Spanish translation, *Esta puente, mi espalda: Voces de mujeres tercermundistas en los Estados Unidos,* coedited by Moraga and Ana Castillo, was published by Ism Press of San Francisco.

Although the first edition of *Bridge* challenged both the American left and Anglo-American feminism, Moraga acknowledged in 1983 in her Foreword to the second edition, which she titled "Refugees of a World on Fire," that in a changing political climate *Bridge* could be read in an international context as a response to the wars in Central America, the U.S. invasion of Grenada, the political repression in Chile, the assassination of Aquino in the Philippines, and apartheid in South Africa, and in the United States as a response to the conservative groundswell during the early years of the Reagan Revolution. Indeed, Moraga and Anzaldúa had taken the lead within the progressive politics of the Chicana and Chicano Movement in a dialogue against the moral majority and the religious right, the resurgence of the university core curriculum, and the attacks on ethnic and women's studies. Gregory Jay, in his *American Literature and the Culture Wars* (1997), credits *Bridge* with widening the horizons of American literary studies. According to Jay, *Bridge* was a foundational text "in opening the canon, in linking the study of race and gender, and in connecting the social change movements of the 1960s to the campus reforms of the subsequent decades" (4).

The struggle for individual and collective representation in the publications associated with the editorial and creative work of Moraga and Anzaldúa was as important for the eighties as the Berkeley Quinto Sol group was for the early seventies.[4]

In the Foreword to the second edition of *Bridge*, Moraga elaborated on her projects: a *Bridge* conceived in 1983, not 1979, would "speak much more directly now to the relations between women and men of color, both gay and heterosexual" (n.p.). *Loving in the War Years* is

Moraga's intellectual autobiography, a self-analysis, as well as a critique of male and female relations within Mexican culture. As such, it marked an important juncture in Moraga's continuing intention of speaking honestly and directly to the relations between women and men of color, both gay and heterosexual. It was also a book written by a "movement writer" with the authority and power of a leader, an unprecedented event in the male-dominated Chicano literature.

Moraga tells her story through a variety of literary forms: narrative, poetry, dreams and fantasies, journal entries, and an ending academic essay complete with endnotes and a glossary for Spanish terms. In writing autobiographies, in seeing one's life as a story, writers have cultural stories to tell their own personal life. Moraga explores her life through a social and cultural pattern that originated in the history of Spanish conquest of the Americas, in sixteenth-century Indian Mexico. Moraga's life is a well-known Mexican story of betrayal, exile, and return.

Beginnings and endings are the frame of reference for a plot. In recognition of this fact, Moraga chose to emphasize the endpoints of the book of her life by choosing the bilingual title *Loving in the War Years: Lo que nunca pasó por sus labios.* My reading of Moraga's autobiography is framed and focused by her *Introducción* titled "Amar en los años de guerra" and the ending coming-out section *"Lo que nunca pasó por sus labios"* with the extensive academic essay "A Long Line of Vendidas." This closing essay, dated March 1983, was the last section to be written and chronicles Moraga's return to her mother's and grandmother's culture.[5]

"Amar en los años de guerra" opens with the following dream. The dreamer is in a prison camp with her lover: *"We are in love in wartime"* (i). Both lovers are almost certain to die. The male prison guard who refuses to help them has informed them of this truth. There is a slim chance of escape to freedom but only for one. The dreamer thinks of leaving her lover imprisoned while she might be free. She chooses to stay with her lover, even unto death. She will not betray her lover; being together is what makes the suffering, even their dying, human.

This is an allegory of life, not the marriage of till death do us part, but the acknowledgment of life as a battleground: "I was born into this world with complications" (ii). Life forces one to take positions in a struggle that is both personal and political: "I had been chosen, marked to *prove* my salvation" (ii). One is never totally free, one acts out life from a situation or position involving race, class, and gender. For Moraga, the defining

114

position is sexuality. She chooses desire over the possibility of individual freedom. This is the situation from which she speaks in her autobiography of coming to consciousness as a Chicana lesbian intellectual: "This is my politics. This is my writing" (ii). This intellectual and political positioning is symbolically and literally reenacted in the closing subsection, "Epilogue: La Mujer que Viene de la Boca" to "A Long Line of Vendidas."[6]

In the Introducción, following a literary tradition addressing the problem of intended audience, Moraga divides herself into the writer and a friend. The reader finds the following situation in *Journal Entry*: 2 de julio 1982. She is riding in a commuter train with a friend. In completing her book, she wonders what her readers might think about her being a "representative" writer: "You don't speak for me! For the community!" (vi). Her friend consoles her: "Ah, Chavalita. . . . The only way to write for la comunidad is to write so completely from your heart what is your own personal truth. This is what touches people" (vi). Moraga is stating that she does not necessarily speak for, or on behalf of, but speaks from her own situation. Through her own personal truth, she hopes she may touch the reader, someone who would understand her situation. And who is the intended readership: "La procesión de mujeres, sufriendo. Dolores my grandmother, Dolores her daughter, Dolores her daughter's daughter. Free the daughter to love her own daughter. It is the daughters who are my audience" (vii). The date is 1983, and this is an acknowledgment that the Chicana intellectual community has undergone a dramatic change and that the Chicano Movement must make room for other voices. From a hard-won position in which she was forced to escape from her own culture, yet fighting for a position in the other, she now brings her own concerns to her own community: "To speak two tongues. I must. But I will not double-talk and I refuse to let *anybody's* movement determine what is safe and fair to say" (vi).[7]

Who Cherríe Moraga is and how she came to be a Chicana lesbian feminist is, of course, the plot of her autobiography. She was born in Los Angeles on 25 September 1952 and was reared in American suburbs, in the San Gabriel Valley of California. Moraga has written that she was "blessed to be born into a huge extended Mexican family" that was presided over authoritatively by her grandmother Dolores (Moraga 1997, 17). However, Moraga was born Cecilia Lawrence, the child of a white father and a Mexican mother. She was born a fair-skinned woman and was encouraged by her mother to take advantage of her color and pass for white. She also realized that passing for white was a way of liberating herself from the constraints of her culture. In public, with her name and her light skin, she could pass for white; in her mother's home, however, she was the Mexican daughter. She attended Catholic schools through high school and college, Immaculate Heart College in Los Angeles. Her education further separated her from her mother and family. "[I]t is my education, my 'consciousness' that separated me from them [her family]" (Moraga 1983, ii–iii). "I grew white. Fought to free myself from my culture's claim on me" (ii).

As a profession, Moraga chose teaching. She could have become a middle-class American woman, falling away nameless into the mainstream of this country, except for her sexuality. That desire brought her back to the culture, through her mother. As she stated in her Introducción, she has committed herself to radical feminism because of the suffering of her mother and the daughters. And in returning to her mother, she has rejected patriarchy, the law of the father. She does not carry the name of the father, the patronymic that defines subjects within patriarchal society. She consciously chose to rename herself in the name of the mother. She returns to the home culture as Cherríe Moraga.

The road from the Catholic school child to the activist is a difficult one indeed. Moraga recounts crucial private moments in her life. At the age of eight, she realized that there was ultimately no protection in life. Moraga recalls visiting her mother, Elvira, in the hospital. With her mother at the point of death, Moraga first encountered her lifelong identification with women. At age twelve, sexual feelings emerged—kissing and masturbation—and she had her first dream of lesbian desire from which, given her strict Catholic Mexican world, she retreated for the major part of her young life. At nineteen, she lost her virginity to a man. In her twenties, she finally came out. However, though she was out in the world, she was still estranged from her feelings. Clarity finally arrived finding other women like herself in Third World feminism.

Moraga's personal story is informed by one of Mexico's strongest cultural symbols, the Indian woman who is considered both traitor and mother by Mexicans: Malinalli/Marina/Malintzín/Malinche. The maligned Malintzín is the Indian woman whom she envisioned in her own sick mother as a child: *"I hear my tía say to an older woman—skin and bones. An Indian, I think, straight black and grey hair pulled back. I hear my tia say, 'Elvira'"* (94). In her self-analysis, Moraga refers to this scene, the eight-year-old child fearful of losing her mother, as the defining moment in her life: "I vowed never to forget—the smell of a woman who is life and home to me at once. The woman in whose arms I am uplifted, sustained. Since then, it is as if I have spent the rest of my years driven by this scent toward la mujer" (94). Moraga, like other Chicana writers, writes a matriarchal story, reclaiming the mother as well as redefining the cultural images of women. In returning to her mother's culture, Moraga will also redefine Malinalli/Marina/Malintzín/Malinche from a lesbian feminist perspective. In Malinche's voice she will critique patriarchy in both the Mexican and the Chicano cultural world. It is as she says, "I am Malinche but I refuse to be 'La Chingada.'"

Although scant historical references are available for the cultural symbol of the traitor Malinche, she has had a prominent and complex existence within Mexico's cultural, artistic, and political imagination. Moraga cites the following sources for her own re-creation: Norma Alarcón's "Chicana's Feminist Literature: A Re-Vision through Malinzin/ or Malintzin: Putting Flesh Back on the Object"; an untitled, unpublished work-in-progress by Gloria Anzaldúa; Aleida del Castillo's "Malintzin Tenepal: A Preliminary Look into a New Perspective"; and the English translation of *The Bernal Díaz Chronicles*, the acknowledged historical source for Malinche's biography. Moraga's sources, except for Bernal Díaz, are taken from Chicanas seeking to reimagine Malinche from a feminist perspective. Moraga writes: "The sexual legacy passed down to the Mexicana/Chicana is the legacy of betrayal, pivoting around the historical/mythical female figure of Malintzin Tenepal. As translator and strategic advisor and mistress to the Spanish conqueror of Mexico Hernan Cortez, Malintzin is considered the mother of the mestizo people. But unlike La Virgen de Guadalupe, she is slandered as La Chingada, meaning the 'fucked one,' or La Vendida, sell-out to the white race" (99). Moraga's "A Long Line of Vendidas" is one of the first major statements in a cross-border alliance that would come to the forefront in the eighties decade.

How this young Indian woman Malinalli/Marina, a victim of war and conquest, slavery and rape, came to be La Chingada, the "fucked one," covers the period from 1519 to 1950.[8] In Hernán Cortés's *Cartas de relación*, his five dispatches to King Charles I, he refers to the Christian Indian Marina only on two occasions. He mentions her in his second letter, 1520, describing her as "la lengua que yo tengo, que es una india desta tierra que hobe en Putunchan" (192) ["the translator that I have, who is an Indian from this land of Putunchan"], and in the fifth and last letter, in 1526, "para que creyese ser verdad, que se informase de aquella

lengua que con él hablaba—que es Marina, la que yo conmigo siempre
he traído—porque allí me la habían dado con otras veinte mujeres" (574–
575) ["so that he should understand the truth, he should gather information from that translator that was speaking to him, who is Marina, whom
I always had in my company and who was given to me there along with
twenty other women"]. What modern readers understand from these two
brief references, the first 1519 and the second 1524, is that this young
Indian woman, his translator, his "lengua," was constantly at his side
before and after the fall of Tenochtitlán. Indeed, Marina bore Cortés a
son, Martín, in 1522. The Marina that emerges from the historical record,
a very minor figure in the male-dominated historiography of the conquest, was a young woman not yet out of her adolescence who was a slave
and sexual servant to the most powerful man in Mexico.

We are indebted to Bernal Díaz del Castillo's *Historia verdadera de la
conquista de la Nueva España* for the biographical material on Malinalli/
Marina. According to Bernal Díaz, she was one of twenty young Indian
women slaves given to Cortés in 1519 by the Indians of Tabasco. The
young woman of probably fourteen or seventeen years of age was christened Marina after her Indian name, Malinalli. Malinalli came to be
Malintzín, the suffix *-tzin* meaning someone of high standing, a lady.
Malinche, by which she was also known to both Indians and Spaniards,
was a Spanish corruption of Malintzín. Malintzín was also the name given
to Cortés by the Indians because of his close relationship to his translator.[9]

According to Bernal Díaz, Marina belonged to a privileged, educated
class. She was probably the firstborn of a cacique and due to inherit his
position: "quiero decir de doña Marina que desde su niñez fue gran señora
y cacica de pueblos y vasallos (91) ["I want to say about doña Marina that
since childhood she was a lady of great standing, ruler of cities and subjects"]. She was a child when her father died. Her mother remarried
another, younger cacique with whom she had a son. Her stepfather and
mother "dieron de noche a la niña doña Marina a unos indios de Xicalango,
porque no fuese vista, y echaron fama que se había muerto, y en aquella
sazón murió una hija de una india esclava suya, y publicaron que era la
heredera" (91) ["gave the child lady Marina at night to some Indians from
Xicalango, so as not to be seen, and proclaimed that she had died, and at that
time a daughter of one of her Indian slaves died and they announced that
she was the heiress"]. Malinalli's stepfather and mother sold her into slavery
in order to safeguard the new child and his right to rule. She was sold to
Indian traders, who in turn sold her to the Indians from Tabasco.

Moraga repeats the Bernal Díaz story, finding that he gives birth to a new version of the "inherent unreliability of women, our natural propensity for treachery which has been carved into the very bone of Mexican/ Chicano collective psychology. *Traitor begets traitor*" (Moraga 1983, 101). Here, Moraga is stating a not-too-dissimilar characterization of Malinche expressed earlier in Mexican writer Rosario Castellanos's well-known 1972 poem, "Malinche."[10] Castellanos, using the first person, retells the child Malinalli tale presented by Bernal. The adult Malinche looks back at her childhood and speaks through her mother revealing the tears of the self-hatred and betrayal among women because of the rivalry over men, of putting the man first. In this version, the feminist Castellanos presents a sympathetic portrayal of Malinche, not the woman who betrayed Mexico, but a child who because of patriarchy was betrayed by her mother and sold into bondage. Moraga is repeating in the Chicana/ Mexicana context a similar feminist Malinche tale.

Bernal Díaz ends his brief biographical account by describing the reunion in 1524 of Marina and her mother and stepbrother, who were now both rulers of Marina's Guazacualco home.[11] Mother and brother, christened Marta and Lázaro, were fearful of what might happen with Marina's triumphant return at the side of Cortés. Marina, according to Bernal Díaz, consoled them, sympathizing and forgiving them, understanding that they didn't know what they were doing when she was given to traders. God had taken mercy on her, liberating her from worshiping idols. She was a Christian with a son from her amo y señor, "master and lord," Cortés and now married to a Spaniard, the hidalgo Juan Jaramillo (Díaz del Castillo 1989, 92).

While Cortés mentions Marina only twice, Bernal Díaz is very clear in granting her a prominent role in the conquest: "doña Marina en todas las guerras de la Nueva España y Tlascala y México fue tan excelente mujer y buena lengua. . . . [A] esta causa la traía Cortés siempre consigo" (92) ["doña Marina in all of the wars for New Spain and Tlascala and Mexico was a courageous woman and good translator. . . . For this reason Cortés always had her at his side"]. A lady among Spaniards after her marriage to Jaramillo, doña Marina was also a lady, Malintzín or Malinche, among the Indians: "la doña Marina tenía mucho ser y mandaba absolutamente entre los indios en toda la Nueva España" (92) ["doña Marina was a lady of great standing and ruled absolutely among the Indians in all of New Spain"].

The negative image of doña Marina emerges after the wars of independence in the nationalist period in the anonymous novel published in

Philadelphia in 1826, *Jicotencatl*.[12] The novel's title is taken from its central character, the Tlaxcalan prince who resists the evil and tyrannical Cortés. In the novel, Marina's fate is sealed as "la Malinche," traitor to her people. The conquest is seen as an allegory of the newly born patria, the Republic of Mexico, trying to rid itself of Spanish influences. Marina is characterized as an accomplice to evil, foreign influences that can corrupt and divide the nation. She uses her feminine guile to bring down the Indian nations. She becomes the Mexican Eve and her original sin is betrayal. However, she repents of her sinful ways at the birth of her son, Martín Cortés. Only as a mother of a mestizo is she portrayed in a positive light.

It is not until the mid-twentieth century that Malintzín is transformed into La Chingada. As is well known in Mexican literary and cultural studies, it is Octavio Paz in his *El laberinto de la soledad* (*The Labyrinth of Solitude*, 1950) who sees in Cortés and Malinche the symbols for what ails modern Mexico.[13]

Paz's broadly symbolic study of Mexican culture and history was greatly influenced by post–World War II existentialism. The book is Paz's assessment of Mexico some forty years after the outbreak of the Mexican Revolution. The forces unleashed by the Revolution—a state with a new constitution, an ever-powerful ruling political party, and a bourgeoisie whose interests directed the future of Mexico—had all contributed to the making of a modern Mexico. Paz's closing statement in his book affirmed that Mexicans were finally at the point of entering world history: "Somos, por primera vez en nuestra historia contemporáneos de todos los hombres" (Paz 1959, 174) ["For the first time in our history, we are contemporaries of all mankind"; Paz 1961, 194]. With progress and stability, though attained through the misfortune of many, Paz argued, Mexico found itself with the possibility of making choices, whether to continue with old cultural habits or seek new ones open to change: "Si nos arrancamos las máscaras, si nos abrimos, si, en fin, nos afrontamos, empezaremos a vivir y pensar de verdad" (Paz 1959, 174) ["If we tear off these masks, if we open ourselves up, if—in brief—we face our own selves, then we can truly begin to live and to think"; Paz 1961, 194].

The rhetoric of the old and new, closed and open that permeates Paz's book is based in large measure on the powerful country to the north, the United States, the country with which Mexico was entering into a new political and cultural relationship. The values and social forms of Europe—most notably Spain and France—which Mexico had exhausted in a brief historical period now had to be reinterpreted given the progress and technology of the north. La Malinche and the term "malinchista" Paz took not only from Mexico's previous history of colonialism; Paz refers to the "éxito del adjetivo despectivo 'malinchista', recientemente puesto en circulación por los periódicos para denunciar a todos los contagiados por tendencias extranjerizantes" (Paz 1959, 78) ["the success of the contemptuous adjective *malinchista* recently put into circulation by the newspapers to denounce all those who have been corrupted by foreign influences"; Paz 1961, 86]. We should also recall that Paz's book began with "El pachuco y otros extremos" ("The Pachuco and Other Extremes"), with traditional Mexican values in conflict with Anglo-American culture in the pochos, the Anglicized Mexicans of Los Angeles.[14]

Two chapters from Paz's book, "Máscaras mexicanas" ("Mexican Masks") and "Los Hijos de la Malinche" ("The Children of the Malinche"), address unethical Mexican attitudes and habits first in love relationships and second in social relations in general.[15] In both cases the Mexican woman served a central but subservient role. It is Paz's broadly sweeping polarity, contrasting male and female, that has given rise to an intellectual dialogue with feminist readers. With her autobiographical "A Long Line of Vendidas," Cherríe Moraga also entered this profoundly Mexican dialogue on Mexican identity.

Paz begins "Máscaras mexicanas" with the following statements on Mexican alienation: "El mexicano siempre está lejos, lejos del mundo y de los demás. Lejos, también de sí mismo" (Paz 1959, 26) ["The Mexican is always remote, from the world and from other people. And also from himself"; Paz 1961, 29]. Reserve and hermeticism are strategies learned to cope, given the history of Mexico, with a difficult and hostile environment. The relations between male and female, writes Paz, reveal the extent to which Mexicans assume a defensive posture. The ideal of Mexican manhood is "no rajarse," "not to open up, to crack"; those who open, "se abren," are considered cowards. Unlike other cultures, Mexicans do not value openness: it is a weakness, a betrayal. Therefore, the ideal of the man, the macho, is to be closed within himself. Manhood "se mide por la invulnerabilidad ante las armas enemigas o ante los impactos del mundo exterior" (Paz 1959, 28) ["is judged according to one's invulnerability to enemy arms or the impacts of the outside world"; Paz 1961, 31].

Mexican history is replete with phrases and episodes, argues Paz, of indifference and resignation in the face of danger and suffering. Indeed, readers of Mexican literature find this estrangement, impassiveness, and resignation in the face of suffering in the literature of this period, in the classic twentieth-century works by Juan Rulfo and Carlos Fuentes. Women, Indians, peasants, and servants in Rulfo's *El llano en llamas* (*The Burning Plain*, 1953) and *Pedro Páramo* (*Pedro Paramo*, 1955), and in Fuentes's *La muerte de Artemio Cruz* (*The Death of Artemio Cruz*, 1962), respond to circumstances with fatalism; and those who hold power, like the political bosses Pedro Páramo and Artemio Cruz, never openly display vulnerability. Some thirty years after Paz, Moraga responds to these male writers with her own long-standing resignation and suffering: "La procesión de mujeres, sufriendo. Dolores my grandmother, Dolores her daughter, Dolores her daughter's daughter. Free the daughter to love her own daughter. It is the daughters who are my audience" (Moraga 1983, vii).

In a world made in the image of men, the woman is only a reflection of masculine will or desire. She is the repository of values—virgin, goddess, mother, martyr. Woman is a passive being, she attracts, and the center of her attraction is her sexuality. As Paz says, a woman is a sleeping goddess until her body is awakened by the man. In another rendition, she is decent, modest, and long-suffering. The long-suffering woman, writes Paz, is a defensive gesture. In the face of a natural and social vulnerability, the woman makes a virtue and strength of her weakness: "[Ella] se transforma en víctima, pero en víctima endurecida e insensible al sufrimiento, encallecida a fuerza de sufrir" (Paz 1959, 34) ["She becomes a victim, but a victim hardened and insensible to suffering, bearing her tribulations in silence"; Paz 1961, 38–39]. Thus is born the myth of the long-suffering woman or "la mujer abnegada" who ironically achieves the same characteristics of the man—invulnerable, impassive, and stoical.

Paz was describing at midcentury Mexican attitudes defining men and women that are still displayed even now in the nightly soap operas of Mexican television. Paz argues clearly that these attitudes undermine Mexican personal relations. Ideally, one would want to conceive of love relationships as mutual penetration, opening ourselves to each other and revealing intimacy:

> Cuando nos enamoramos nos "abrimos," mostramos nuestra intimidad, ya que una vieja tradición quiere que el que sufre de amor exhiba sus heridas ante la que ama. Pero al descubrir sus llagas de amor, el enamorado transforma su ser en una imagen, en un objeto que entrega a la contemplación de la mujer—y de sí mismo—. Al mostrarse, invita a que lo contemplen con los mismos ojos piadosos con que él se contempla. La mirada ajena ya no lo desnuda; lo recubre de piedad. (Paz 1959, 36–37)

> When we fall in love we open ourselves up and reveal our intimate feelings, because an ancient tradition requires that the man suffering from love display his wounds to the loved one. But in displaying them the lover transforms himself into an image, an object he presents for the loved one's—and his own—contemplation. He asks her to regard him with the same worshipful eyes with which he regards himself. And now the looks of others do not strip him naked; instead, they clothe him in piety. (Paz 1961, 41)

However, Mexicans, argues Paz, conceive of love relationships not so much as a mirroring of each other but as struggle and conquest. For the Mexican patriarchal couple, love relations are circumscribed by the penetration and violation of the female body. In response, the woman, resigned to her fate, will cope, accepting penetration but not conquest—love without intimacy.

The fatality of the patriarchal couple—struggle between the closed, aggressive masculinity and the open vulnerability of the woman—is best exemplified in Mexican literature of this period in Carlos Fuentes's historical novel *La muerte de Artemio Cruz*. The two central characters, Artemio Cruz and Catalina Bernal, cannot escape their historical, cultural, and gendered fatality. Cruz rises from the Mexican Revolution (1910–1919), manipulating all in his path to become first a member of the Mexican Chamber of Deputies (1924), then a political ally of President Plutarco Elías Calles (1927), and eventually a powerful industrialist, when he sells Mexican interests to U.S. investors (1941). Cruz met the young provincial woman Catalina from Puebla in the aftermath of the Revolution (1919). Catalina became Cruz's wife when her ailing father, Don Gamaliel, a member of the defeated landed aristocracy, gave his daughter and property to Cruz in exchange for a life of ease. Given their relationship, they humiliate and hurt each other. Fuentes makes it clear that they cannot come out of their own pride to express mutual compassion and love. Catalina, especially, expresses her unwillingness to choose based on weakness as a woman. She is, here in a conversation with Artemio, resigned to her fate as a woman who allows her body to be taken at night but who hides her feelings by day:

> —Déjame. Estoy en tus manos para siempre. Ya tienes lo que querías. Conténtate y no pidas imposibles. . . .
> —Déjame. No me toques. No me eches en cara mi debilidad. Te juro que no volveré a dejarme ir . . . con eso. . . .

—No te acerques. No te faltaré. Esto te pertenece. . . . Es parte de tus
triunfos. . . .
—Ahora ya sé cómo consolarme. Con Dios de mi lado, con mis hijos, nunca
me faltará alivio. (Fuentes 1962, 111)

"Leave me alone. I will be in your hands forever. You've got what you
wanted. Take what you've got and don't ask for the impossible." . . .
"Leave me alone. Don't touch me. Don't throw my weakness in my face.
I swear to you I'll never let myself go with you again." . . .
"Don't come closer. I won't deprive you. After all, that belongs to you.
It's part of your winnings." . . .
"I know what my consolation is. With God on my side, with my children,
I'll never lack for solace." (Fuentes 1991, 104)

Fuentes takes up many of Paz's central themes expressed in *El laberinto de
la soledad*, among them Mexican identity and alienation; conquest and love.
Moreover, Artemio and Catalina serve as historical reference points for the
positions of a male and female within Mexican society harkening back to the
time of conquest. Cruz has entered Mexico City by way of Veracruz. His
ancestral origins are in Cuba. Cruz is an ex-slave, a mulatto, a product of a
white master and an African slave. His mother, Isabel Cruz, belongs to the
history of the Caribbean-Mexico slave trade necessary for the sugarcane
economy. Artemio Cruz is also the strong willful man (à la Cortés) who takes
advantage of the situations presented to him by history. At the end of his life,
Cruz resides in a colonial mansion in Coyoacán, Cortés's colonial neighborhood, after the conquest of the island capital city—Tenochtitlán. In his
dealing with U.S. economic and political interests, Cruz is a "malinchista."
Catalina, the sexual pawn used by both Cruz and her father in his political
relations with Cruz, is a twentieth-century embodiment of Malinalli/
Marina, a victim of war and conquest, slavery and duty.

In *Loving in the War Years*, Moraga writes to find a place for herself
within the Mexican/Chicano family and society. In confronting her gender's
history of oppression, Moraga has written a Mexican book rehearsing the
same themes of her Mexican predecessors of midcentury. Her book also
focuses on love relations, on the couple in the time of war, within the
broader frames of values, culture, and history. For Moraga, the historical
moment is the postfeminist, post–Chicano Movement period. She too
feels the need to speak honestly to a culture at the moment of choice, to
"stop the chain of events" (vii): whether to remain static and conservative

or open to new gender and sexual identities. Should the Chicano Movement want to move forward it must look critically at traditional Mexican values—the male as strong man, the passivity of women, women as sexual objects. As a woman, Moraga must not only cite but also confront Octavio Paz and his version of the patriarchal couple—el chingón and la chingada.

Paz's central chapter, "Los hijos de la Malinche," is a famous disquisition on Mexico's word, *chingar*. Paz finds at the beginning of Mexican culture, in the conquest, the Mexican view of life as struggle, divisions in society between the haves and the have-nots, between the strong and the weak, between chingones and chingados. Always be a chingón, never side with the chingados is a rule for Mexican politicians and bureaucrats. *Chingar*, according to Paz, means to do violence to another. The verb is masculine, active, cruel. It humiliates. The person who suffers the action is passive, inert, open.

Paz's 1950 essay on Mexico's word found creative expression in *La muerte de Artemio Cruz*. In the crucial central chapter, Fuentes presents a litany of the word, twenty-four phrases in which the word *chingar* is used ending, echoing Paz, with "Viva México, jijos de su rechingada" (144). These uses of the word, ending with the "Viva Mexico, children of the fucked mother," are a summary of Mexico's history, writes Fuentes. However, Fuentes ends calling on his Mexican readers to rethink the fatality of the word: "Déjala en el camino, asesínala con armas que no sean las suyas: matémosla: matemos esa palabra que nos separa, que nos petrifica, nos pudre con su doble veneno de ídolo y cruz: que no sea nuestra respuesta ni nuestra fatalidad" (Fuentes 1962, 146). ["Abandon her on the road, murder her with weapons that aren't her own. Let's kill her; let's kill that word that separates us, that petrifies us, rots us with its double venom of idol and cross. Let it not be our answer or our fatality"; Fuentes 1991, 138.] Moraga will also use the forbidden but much-used Mexican word and pose this urgent question to the daughters: should we continue with chingón and chingada, or transform Mexican gender relations?

The historical pattern of violation, Paz writes, is found in the conquest, in Cortés and Marina/Malinche, el chingón and la chingada. Doña Marina converted into La Malinche, the symbol of violation, is the woman who gives herself willingly and, when no longer useful, is discarded. Malinche can stand for all the Indian women, fascinated or violated or seduced by the Spaniards. And just as the small boy does not forgive the mother for abandoning him to go in search of the father, Mexicans will not forgive Malinche for her betrayal. Malinche is the living symbol of lo abierto, lo chingado, "what is open, what is fucked." In the face of repeated conquests, Mexico's (male) Indians remain stoical, impassive, and closed. This blaming the victim is what has earned Paz, and rightly so, the ire of Mexican and Chicana feminists. Elena Garro, Paz's first wife, answers Paz by titling her 1964 story, "La culpa es de los tlaxcaltecas," "The fault lies with the Tlaxcaltecas," the Indians who marched into Tenochtitlán allied with Cortés and the Spanish army. Indeed, the alliance between Cortés and the Tlaxcala chiefs was crucial for the conquest of northern Mexico; Spanish conquest after conquest, in Zacatecas in the 1540s and New Mexico in the 1590s, was aided by the Tlaxcaltecas.

"Even if a Chicana knew no Mexican history," Moraga writes, "the concept of betraying one's race through sex and sexual politics is as common as corn. As cultural myths reflect the economics, mores, and social structures of a society, every Chicana suffers from their effects" (Moraga 1983, 103). Thus, to develop her own autonomous consciousness, Moraga had to work through la mujer mexicana, uncover the sources of women's oppression to find her own salvation. Paz's *Laberinto de la soledad*, as an expression of the Mexican myth of betrayal, seen in this chapter in Mexican history and literature, is central to Moraga's "A Long Line of Vendidas." Although Moraga will take the term "malinchista" as a positive affirmation of her sexuality, she will never accept the historical and cultural baggage of La Chingada—passive, inert, open.

Moraga explores from the woman's point of view problems of dominance and subservience in the Mexican family. "Traitor begets traitor," proclaims Moraga in one of the opening sections of "A Long Line of Vendidas." Her mother betrayed her culture by marrying an Anglo. Her mother forced her to betray her race by placing the father's culture first; a light-skinned Mexican, she grew up white, educated, middle class. In school she was tracked based on her light skin, eventually college prep in Catholic high school (96). And as an adult, she could indeed choose to use her light skin and good English to her advantage (97). Moraga thus writes candidly to expose Mexican racism: the value attached to light skin color. Her mother also betrayed her by putting her brother first. For any Chicana mother, Moraga emphasizes, *"The boys are different"* (102). As a child Moraga was always the servant for the mother, the son always was first. "To this day," confesses Moraga, "in my mother's home, my brother and father are waited on, including by me" (90). Thus in her own family Moraga lived the many layerings of the Malinalli/Marina/Malintzín/Malinche legacy.

What Moraga had wanted from her mother, equality among the sexes, "was impossible" (103). It meant going against Mexicano/Chicano tradition: you are a traitor to your race if you do not put the man first. Now, in the midst of a conservative Chicano politics and an emerging Chicana feminist consciousness, there are choices to be made. From the section examining Marina's roles during the conquest, "Traitor Begets Traitor," Moraga will follow with the section "We Fight Back with Our Families" to redefine the Mexicano/Chicano family. "Chicanos' refusal to look at our weaknesses as a people and a movement is in the most profound sense, an act of self-betrayal" (112). Like her mother within her home, Chicanas in the Movement betray their gender by putting the male first, by fighting back with the family. The family has always been cited as a source of strength against oppression. Out of loyalty to the cause, Moraga writes, Chicanas betray each other. The struggle against white supremacy should also be the struggle against male supremacy. Moraga offers a new definition of familia: "Family is *not* by definition the man in a dominant position over women and children. Familia is cross-generational bonding, deep emotional ties between opposite sexes, and within our sex. It is sexuality, which involves, but is not limited to, intercourse or orgasm. It springs forth from touch, constant and daily. The ritual of kissing and the sign of the cross with every coming and going from the home. It is finding familia among friends where blood ties are formed through suffering and celebration shared. . . . The strength of our families never came from domination. It has only endured in spite of it—like our women" (111).[16]

In "La Malinchista," Moraga too admits betraying her culture, corrupted by foreign influences. She is a feminist who defies her role as subservient to the male, and as a lesbian she chooses a sexuality that excludes all men and therefore most dangerously, Chicano men. As she writes, "*I come from a long line of Vendidas.* I am a Chicana lesbian. My own particular relationship to being a sexual person; and a radical stand in direct contradiction to, and in violation of, the women I was raised to be" (117).[17] Here then malinchista, vendida, sellout are not negative renditions; they are positive affirmations of the woman she is and of her fidelity to women.

One of the more intimate sections of "A Long Line of Vendidas" concerns Moraga's coming to terms with her emerging sexuality. In "Inocencia Meant Dying Rather Than Being Fucked," Moraga takes aim at Paz's appropriation of the Malinalli/Marina/Malintzín/Malinche figure as La Chingada, the fucked one. Moraga uncovers the origins of her negative view of feminine sexuality. While coming from society at large, her view of sex as rape and duty comes more specifically from Mexicano/ Chicano culture, from the myth of "La Chingada, Malinche" (118). She cites Paz on the chingón/chingada patriarchal couple: "Chingar then is to do violence to another, i.e., rape. . . . The chingón is the macho, the male; he rips open the chingada, the female, who is pure passivity, defenseless against the exterior world" (119). In this violation, the woman, the victim, is seen as responsible for her sexual victimization. "Slavery and slander," writes Moraga, echoing the Mexican history of struggle and conquest, "is the price she must pay for the pleasure the culture imagined she enjoyed" (118). Little wonder, Moraga concludes, that women divorce themselves from the conscious recognition of their own feelings, from essentially their own sexuality.

She recalls a dream she had at twelve years in which she saw herself with breasts and a menstruating penis. As a child she could not cope with such a dream, being in the position of male as well as female, which is to say, having feelings for other females. As an adult, she sees the dream reflecting a desire for wholeness, integration, of trying to come to terms with both her biology and her sexuality. At that age, she retreated from her body's messages. She developed a coping mechanism to deal with her sexuality. In order not to embody the chingada, or the femalized and therefore perverse version of the chingón, she became pure spirit—bodiless. "For what indeed," Moraga asks, "must my body look like if it were both the chingada and the chingón?" (120–121). She had internalized the Mexican patriarchal couple within herself, which meant living distanced, doubly estranged from her own feelings as a lesbian.

The breakthrough and breakdown came when she saw in her lover, a woman, the chingón that she so feared recognizing in herself, "the active, aggressive, and closed person." She was finally forced to confront how, in resisting feeling the chingada, meaning resisting fully feeling sex at all, she had become the chingón. "In the effort not to feel fucked," she says "I became the fucker even with women. In an effort not to feel pain or desire, I grew a callus around my heart and imagined I felt nothing at all" (125). This was what being a Chicana/Mexicana lesbian had meant. After the breakdown, Moraga asserts her sexuality and refutes Mexican culture's notion of sex as rape, sex as duty. She could, indeed, choose sex freely, as pleasure and intimacy, as well as assert her race and culture. The healing also came in the form of

community, not within the resistant Anglo-American feminist movement, but within the Latina woman-of-color or Third World feminism,
not just as a member but as a leader. Coming to the end of her essay and
the coming-out-book of her life, she is asserting her culture, she is a
Chicana lesbian.

This then is the overall argument to the book of her life. She knows she
was a vendida, a traitor to her culture. She was a light-skinned Mexican
who passed for white. She is also a lesbian who internalized the chingón-
chingada couple of patriarchy. She suffered through her sexuality. Now
she has recovered and returns to her culture as a leader of a movement,
and the Chicano Movement can no longer be resistant to change. It can
be progressive and accept her as a Chicana feminist and lesbian, or it can
remain conservative and reactionary and hold on to the traditional Mexican family and to homophobia. If those in the movement choose the
second option, they will be in the same position as the eighties Anglo-
American religious right. The young woman who left her culture returns
as an agent of change.

The last section, "Epilogue: La Mujer que Viene de la Boca," presents
the final parallel with Malinche and the Mexican patriarchal couple. After
betrayal and living a life of outsidedness and estrangement, Moraga
returns to her mother's Spanish language, her lengua, and to her mother's
culture as a Chicana lesbian feminist. This is her coming-out statement,
taking back her body and seeking acknowledgment: her radical
reconceptualization of the masculinist version of Mexican womanhood—
subservient, passive, vulnerable—inherited from Mexican history, culture, and literature. We find her in the most intimate of moments, in the
act of love, outside of Mexican patriarchy. She is nude, vulnerable and
open. However, she is displaying her feminist lesbian activism. She is on
her back, passive, and is allowing herself to be in touch with her feelings,
allowing for mutual penetration with her female lover. "I think," Moraga
offers to all her readers, *"soy mujer en español*. No macha. Pero mujer,
soy Chicana open to all kinds of attack" (142). This act of love has allowed
her to be out to the world, to give birth to herself. Moraga recounts one
final recurring dream: "my mouth is too big to close; that is, the *outside*
of my mouth, my lips cannot contain the inside—teeth, tongue, gums,
throat. I am coming out of my mouth, so to speak. The mouth is red like
blood and the teeth, like bones, white" (142). As a Mexicana reborn,
Moraga finally declares: "La boca spreads its legs open to talk, open to
attack. 'I am a lesbian. And I am a Chicana'" (142).

POSDATA

In 1985, after a five-year, self-imposed exile in the Northeast, Cherríe Moraga returned to her home state of California. She had accepted her lesbian identity at the age of twenty-two in 1975. Now the Chicana activist was returning home. In the 1993 *The Last Generation*, her book of prose and poetry after *Loving in the War Years*, Moraga writes: "I . . . witnessed the emergence of a national Chicana feminist consciousness and a litera-ture, art, and activism to support it. I've seen the growth of the lesbian-of-color movement, the founding of an independent national Latino/a lesbian and gay men's organization, and the flourishing of Indigenous people's international campaigns for human rights" (146–147). At the height of the Chicano movement during the 1968 student blow-outs in East L.A., the teenager Cecilia Lawrence watched from a distance in her San Gabriel home. Now a quarter century later, she has found a place within the Chicanada. Although it may not be a safe place, it is this familial place which compels her to write (147).

Shortly before a tragic accident ended her life in 1974, the Mexican intellectual Rosario Castellanos published her collected poetic works, *Poesía no eres tú* (1972). This collection included "Meditación en el umbral" ("Meditation at the Threshold"), a poem on the woman intellectual's personal life of imprisonment. Castellanos cites the per-sonal tragedies of the British Austens, the American Dickinson, the Spanish nun Santa Teresa de Jesús, and the Mexican Sor Juana Inés de la Cruz, and ends her poem hoping for change: "Debe haber otro modo . . . / Otro modo de ser humano y libre. / Otro modo de ser." (Castellanos 1998, 213) ["There must be another way . . . / Another way of being human and free. / Another way of being"]. Moraga begins *The Last Generation* with these three verses in homage to the founder of modern Mexican feminism. The epigraph also reflects Moraga's turn toward Mexican and Indian feminist cultural traditions.

The essays in *The Last Generation* were written within the first three years of the nineties, between the loss of the Sandinista election in 1990 and the Quincentenary in 1992. Noting the urgency of the times, Moraga responds to the following events: "the Gulf War, the collapse of the Soviet Union, Indigenous people's international campaigns for sovereignty, hundreds of thousands of deaths of gay people, women and people of color from AIDS and breast cancer, the Los Angeles Rebellion, and the blatant refusal by the United States to commit to environmental protection at the Earth Summit in Brazil . . ." (3). In "War Cry," Moraga bemoans the political timidity of Chicano literature during conservative times: the Bush administration, the end of the Nicaraguan Revolution, and the invasion of Panama. In "La Fuerza Femenina," Moraga turns toward a new model of Mexicana/Chicana womanhood in the Aztec moon goddess Coyolxauhqui. She, the rebellious sister of the sun god Huitzilopochtli, is "the Chicana writer's words, the Chicana painter's canvas, the Chicana dancer's step" (74). In "Queer Aztlán: The Reformation of Chicano Tribe," Moraga calls for the sixties dreams of a Chicano nation within a nation. Aztlán was, of course, for Chicano Movement activists a reminder of the Indian and Mexican roots of the U.S. Southwest. However, this time, Moraga hopes for a queer Aztlán that includes all, "a nation strong enough to embrace a full range of racial diversities, human sexualities, and expressions of gender" (164). This queer Aztlán moves beyond political and cultural borders. It is Moraga's global utopian views on the verge of a new millennium five hundred years after Columbus. Against globalization, market penetration, ethnic cleansing, and cultural nationalism, Moraga calls for a renewed reverence for mother earth and respect of Indigenous peoples' rights throughout the world.

The Last Generation, like her previous work, is both broadly political and deeply personal. As the title implies, the book is also written as a personal prayer out of a fear of loss and endings. In the introductory essay, "The Last Generation," Moraga recalls a gathering of her family to celebrate Christmas Eve 1986. Celebrating with the family of grandfather, children, and grandchildren, Moraga foresees the disappearance of those who nurtured her. As in *Loving in the War Years*, Moraga is caught between past and future. Despite the growth in numbers of her family, her aging family elders will take to their grave their Mexican culture and language: "Our Mexican grandmother of ninety-six years has been dead two years now and la familia is beginning to go. Ignoring this, it increases in number. I am the only one not contributing to the population. My line of family stops with me. There will be no one calling me, *Mami, Mamá, Abuelita* . . . I am the last generation put on this planet to remember and record" (9).[18]

On the Feast of Epiphany, 6 January 1993, Cherríe Moraga conceived a child at home "immaculately" through the intercession of artificial insemination. *Waiting in the Wings: Portrait of a Queer Motherhood* (1997) is Moraga's moving diary kept during the first three years of motherhood. Assisted by her lover, Ella, who handled the syringe, and her gay Chicano friend Pablo, who provided his sperm, Moraga fulfilled her dream of motherhood. For the woman who believed she would give birth to a little girl and planned her insemination accordingly, it was a shock to be notified on 2 marzo that the child she was carrying was a male. Moraga was thus thrust into the all-too-familiar but for her untraditional role of the long line of Mexican mothers, *the Mexican mother and her son*. From that revered place accorded to Mexican motherhood, Moraga is surprised by how much the biology of the female body changes with pregnancy. As nature and culture begin to take over, she notes the roundness of her body, the femininity of her longer hair, emotions welling up within her into visible tears, and the evolving family relationship between mother, co-mother Ella, and father Pablo.[19]

In her diary, Moraga records: On 3 julio 1993, Rafael Angel Moraga was born months premature in the City of Angels. From julio until Rafael Angel is released on 16 octubre from the hospital, Moraga describes the mother's suffering, fears, and hope as her son's life hangs in the balance due to complications and infections. Moraga begins her diary with an epigraph taken from Michel de Montainge's essay "To Philosophize Is to Learn to Die": "We do not know where death waits us: so let us wait for it everywhere. To practice death is to practice freedom. A man who has learned how to die has unlearned how to be a slave" (11). Carlos Fuentes chose the same epigraph, "La préméditacion de la mort est la préméditacion de la liberté," to begin his Mexican classic *La muerte de Artemio Cruz*. Both Fuentes and Moraga write about life hanging in the balance and found in the French Montaigne a profoundly Mexican attitude toward death. On 19 abril, Día del indio, 1997, Moraga ends her diary on the meaning of her son: "Rafael Angel is the messenger of death, not in the negative sense of the word, but in that he brings the news of the cruel and sudden miracle of our lives. I could write he is a messenger of life, but I know it is truer to acknowledge that my sometimes quiet sadness at the deepest moments of joy with my child had to do with the knowledge of impermanence. In the face of that knowledge, I visit my aging parents, bring my woman coffee in bed, and stroke the silk of my son's hair. This, too, will pass" (127).

"Growing up," writes Moraga, "the *we* of my life was always defined by blood relations. *We* meant family. We are my mother's children, my abuela's grandchildren, my tíos' nieces and nephews" (Moraga 1997, 17). And even though Moraga searched for a *we* that could embrace all the parts of herself "far beyond the confines of heterosexual family ties, . . . the need for familia, the knowledge of familia, the capacity to create familia remained and has always informed my relationships and my work as an artist, cultural activist, and teacher" (17–18). In the end and at the beginning, Moraga realizes blood matters. Thus her need to have her own child: "There is no denying that I had this baby that he might be a Mexican, for him to know and learn of mexicanismo, and for him to feel that fuego, that llama, that riqueza I call lo mexicano" (91).

In 2000, Cherríe L. Moraga published the second expanded edition of *Loving in the War Years*. To the first edition, she added a new lengthy final section, "A Flor de Labios," the latest flowering of her late nineties sensibility, and a new Foreword, "Looking Back," dated 8 de junio 2000, oakaztlán, califas. In 1978, workers in Mexico City discovered a stone monolith depicting the fragmented body of the moon goddess, Coyolxauhqui. According to Aztec myth, the sun god Huitzilopochtli had been conceived by the Sky within the womb of Coatlicue, Mother Earth. When the warriors of the night, the stars Centzonhuitznáhuah and the moon Coyolxauhqui, learned of this new rival, they conspired to kill both Coatlicue and her new warrior son. Huitzilopochtli, however, born fully formed as a warrior, defeated the deities of the night, decapitating his sister, breaking her into pieces down the hill of Coatépec. The beautifully carved, round Coyolxauhqui stone was clear evidence that near the central Zócalo, buried beneath a sixteenth-century colonial patio was quite possibly a great find, the Huey Teocalli, the great Aztec temple to Huitzilopochtli and Quetzalcóatl. Indeed, those late seventies excavations led to the reconstruction of the Templo Mayor—the symbolic Coatépec of myth. The museum next to the excavation site houses and exhibits recent findings. But the Coyolxauqhui stone is still the center-piece, a reminder of a world in rubble lying beneath the center of Mexico City. In 1977, when Moraga began to write the first works that were to become *Loving in the War Years*, she had not heard of "Coyolxauhqui, severed into pieces by her brother, but I knew of her brokenness" (Moraga 2000, iii). Moraga, like other Mexicans, did indeed discover Coyolxauhqui. Now modifying the Malinche-inspired writings of 1983, Moraga is taking up the figure of the fragmented body-in-pieces of the Aztec woman warrior. Moraga offers to the reader her own body-in-pieces, the further evolution of her life in her own words.

"A Flor de Labios" consists of four essays interpolated by single poems. "Looking for the Insatiable Woman," "Sour Grapes: The Art of Anger in

America," "Out of Revolutionary Minds: Toward a Pedagogy of Revolt," and "The Dying Road to a Nation: A Prayer for a Pueblo" are similar to "A Long of Line of Vendidas"; they are wide-ranging scholarly as well as personal essays, documented with endnotes. Dated between 1995 and 1999, these essays are Moraga's reflections as a feminist activist, now the Indígena woman warrior, acknowledged artist, teacher, and mother at the end of the twentieth century.

"Looking for the Insatiable Woman" is Moraga's rewriting of the Mexican-Indian myth of La Llorona. The traditional La Llorona tale that Moraga cites tells of a mother who kills her children in retaliation for her husband's infidelity. For her sin, the woman must forever wander crying for her children. Although Moraga never heard the story as a child, as an adult her investigation of the legend informs her meditation on feminist storytelling, in a sense, a manifesto of her life's work: looking for the insatiable woman. From Aztec myth Moraga reinterprets the story of the hungry woman, so hungry, her body was made of mouths. To comfort her "the [spirits] flew down and began to make grass and flowers out of her skin. From her hair they made forests, from her eyes, pools and springs, from her shoulders, mountains and from her nose, valleys" (146).[20] Not satisfied and still hungry, the woman wails at night. This hungry woman has been the topic of her work: "She is the story that has never been told truly, the story of that hungry Mexican woman who is called puta/bruja/jota/loca because she refuses to forget her half-life is not a natural-born fact" (147). The ancient myth, along with La Llorona and Coyolxauhqui, reminds Moraga that "culturally speaking, there is no mother-woman to manifest who is defined by us outside of patriarchy. We have never had the power to do the defining" (147). Women do not wander in search of their dead children as in the patriarchal tale of La Llorona. Like Castellanos's Malinche, who returns to the scene of her stolen childhood, Moraga must wander searching in her writing for her lost self, sexuality, spirituality, and sabiduría (147).

After *Loving in the War Years*, Moraga turned her artistic energies to theater. Through the decade of the nineties she was an active working playwright, writing *Giving Up the Ghost* (1986), *Shadow of a Man* (1990), *Heroes and Saints* (1992), *Watsonville: Some Place Not Here* (1996), and *The Hungry Woman: The Mexican Medea* (2000), as well as serving as teacher and mentor to a new group of writers through her residency at San Francisco's Brava theater workshop from 1990 to 1996.[21] "Sour Grapes" addresses the plight of the Chicana lesbian-feminist playwright in the face of continuing homophobia, the misunderstanding of critics, and the racism of the American theater establishment.

Moraga recounts the tale of producing *Watsonville* through the Brava Theater Center, having a very diverse audience through six weeks, eventually having to close because of negative reviewers still adhering to the biased requirements of the accepted formalist format of the "well-constructed play": Aristotle and the Western tradition. The play centering on a cannery workers' strike in Watsonville, California, drew in "the mainstream theatergoer, all the major press, the arts community, the politically active Chicano community, student groups, youth groups from the barrios of San Francisco and Watsonville, queers of all kinds, feminist activists, women's groups and a steady base of Mexican immigrant workers from the greater Bay Area" (Moraga 2000, 159–160). Here then was a play, epic in structure because of its many characters appealing to a wide range of groups, yet having to close because of bad reviews: "I wasn't moved, writes the critic" (159). Theater, like no other art form, requires the economic support of a wide set of money players. More often than not, support will disappear because of cultural bias and cultural tyranny. In the United States, Moraga affirms, some minorities are more equal than others: some get support, others do not; some receive positive reviews, others do not. Broadway's bias against U.S. Latino theater (Moraga cites the case of *Zoot Suit*'s short run on Broadway) is an important reminder of the marginality of Mexican, Chicano, or Latino culture within the theater establishment. This essay, really Moraga's own critical review of theater in America, ends with a call to Ethnic Studies programs to initiate their own writers-in-residence programs to nurture and support the next generation of artists.

Moraga has been a teacher for more than twenty years. She has labored in nontenured positions in a wide variety of settings in different areas of the United States: "I have taught high school, poets-in-the-schools, the Marxist school, myriad youth programs, so-called 'gang-prevention' and 'high-risk' programs, theater for queer youth and immigrant women. . . . I've served as an adjunct instructor (mostly) in Women's Studies, Ethnic Studies, Creative Writing, Drama, and in Spanish and English Departments from the 'country club' of Stanford University to the innercity campuses of community colleges and state universities on both coasts" (185–186). "Out of Revolutionary Minds," first presented as the keynote address for the "Chicano Cultural Production: The Third Wave" conference at the University of California, Irvine, on 15 April 1999, is an essay, following Paulo Freire's *Pedagogy of the Oppressed*, on education, self-empowerment, and social change. Like others who became writers as well as teachers, Moraga turned to books because "of a love for language and ideas and an innate sense of social responsibility that was, in part, inspired by books that responded in radical ways to the contradictions and inequities in their lives" (174). On the state of critical theory in the academy, Moraga takes a dim view of the recent rhetoric of postcolonialism and postmodernism as an "immoral waste of words" (176). Gloria Anzaldúa's concept of the borderlands has been appropriated by the academy, emptied of its social and historical significance, and transformed into a "postmodern homeland for all displaced peoples of mixed blood and mixed affinities[,] . . . a mythologized location" (177). The academy and especially the Ethnic Studies programs that emerged as a response to the social movements of the sixties should cultivate "moral, ethically responsible words." However, Moraga laments that Ethnic Studies and Women Studies programs have moved away from the political struggles out of which they emerged. Teaching by example, Moraga recalls her friend Ingrid, who against the warnings of the U.S. State Department, traveled to rural Colombia at the behest of the U'wa indigenous group. Ingrid was to develop an indigenous-based curriculum for the tribe. She went during a dangerous time of political struggle. Ingrid returned to the United States to her Menominee Nation in a black body bag. As Ingrid's life shows, teaching can be a most noble and valorous profession that asks the ultimate price of an Indigenista-activist-teacher. "Do we have to die to be teachers of revolt?" asks Moraga. She answers, "I want to think not" (190). In the meantime she is "trying to find the words . . . learning to spell *revolution*" (190).

In the closing section, "The Dying Road to a Nation: A Prayer Para un Pueblo," Moraga is caught contemplating the ultimate finality to her autobiographical writings. Death teaches that there is no protection: a powerlessness that Moraga had learned as a child when her mother was near death. When Moraga's only child was born three months premature with his life hanging in the balance, she was reminded that death is "the one word I understand for God" (197). From the mid-sixties through the early eighties, a new generation of U.S. Mexicans came of age. Now in 2000, nearing her fiftieth birthday, Moraga, like many of her Chicana and Chicano contemporaries (including this author), awaits the death of parents, a situation that forces Moraga to think about her own death as well. Through all of Moraga's autobiographical writings, salvation had always come in the form of family. And, as at the end of the first *Loving in the War Years*, Moraga has found solace once again in her culture— feminismo and indigenismo. Always painfully honest, Moraga confesses that she has ended a long-term relationship with a white woman to return to Mexicanismo in the form of "someone 'Indian.' Mexican Indian, yes. Indian via las montañas de México and Chicana-bred . . ." (202). At the end of the new book of her life, Moraga sees her self-portrait through the famous casta paintings of Mexican colonial artist Miguel Cabrera where a mestizo child looks away from his white Spanish father toward the Indian mother, toward the Mexican Indian past. "This is my own face looking back," writes Moraga (212).

Years have passed since Cherríe Moraga offered her first self-portrait, *Loving in the War Years*, to the daughters. The 2000 expanded second edition of *Loving in the War Years* is written by the public intellectual Cherríe L. Moraga, who now acknowledges the name of the father, Lawrence. Indeed, Moraga has undergone many changes. "Twenty years ago," writes Moraga, "I was not a mother, only a daughter. I can state, unequivocally, as I did in the first edition of *Loving*, 'It is the daughters who are my audience'" (vi). However, the biological and symbolic mother in Moraga adds: "And any son who will listen" (vi). She now has a son of seven who she hopes "*is* listening" and a "whole family of queer and blood relations" that she "couldn't have dreamed possible at twenty-seven" (vi). For almost twenty years, Moraga has been, through her theater, poetry, essays, teaching, and activism, a major artistic and political force in Chicana/Mexicana and Chicano/Mexicano culture of the second half of the twentieth century. For those years as a lesbian, activist, daughter, sister, and mother, Moraga has been revising, remaking herself and her familia. During those years, though she may not have known, her community of readers has grown. Along with the daughters, the son of María de la Luz Valle of Torreón, Coahuila, has been listening—reading and learning. In Moraga's Preface, "I Have Dreamed of a Bridge," to the first edition of *This Bridge Called My Back*, she ended with the following: "In the dream, I am always met at the river." I too have shared that dream.[22]

"MEXICANOS AL GRITO DE GUERRA"

Rolando Hinojosa's Cronicón del condado de Belken

*También tengo enfilado y ya harta parte de gente llegada para ir
a poblar el río de Palmas, que está en la costa del norte . . .
porque tengo información que es muy buena tierra y es puerto.*

— HERNÁN CORTÉS, "CARTAS DE RELACIÓN"

Aquí empieza lo nuestro, claven esas estacas.

— ANDRÉS BUENROSTRO RINCÓN (1729–1801),
FROM ROLANDO HINOJOSA'S *CLAROS VARONES DE BELKEN*

*La tierra, en parte, se la quitaron a los viejos; en parte, nosotros
mismos también la perdimos y otros más la vendieron. Eso ya
pasó . . . y, como quiera que sea, la tierra ni se muere ni se va a
ningún lado. A ver si mis hijos o los de ellos, cuando los
tengan . . . a ver si ellos mantienen o si recobran parte de ella.
Si también nos quitan o si perdemos o vendemos el idioma,
entonces no habrá remisión. El día que muera el español esto
dejará de ser el valle.*

— JESÚS BUENROSTRO (1887–1946),
FROM ROLANDO HINOJOSA'S *CLAROS VARONES DE BELKEN*

Some promises I made to myself in the lines I've kept. Others will be met and kept when I return home, home to Texas, that land described by my father, don Jesús Buenrostro, "Texas, our Texas, that slice of hell, heaven, purgatory and land of our Fathers."
Vale.

— RAFE BUENROSTRO, PORT OF PUSAN, KOREA, 1 SEPTEMBER 1951,

QUOTED IN ROLANDO HINOJOSA'S *THE USELESS SERVANTS*

I

Rolando Hinojosa's first book, *Estampas del valle y otras obras* (1973; *The Valley*, 1983), was interpreted by critics as an expression of Spanish American costumbrismo.[1] Mexican intellectual Julio Torri, writer of estampas, "sketches," was invoked in comparison to Hinojosa's first book.[2] Indeed, Herminio Ríos, the Quinto Sol editor, noted in the Introduction to the first edition of *Estampas*: "Fue Julio Torri quien introdujo la estampa como género literario en México. Es ahora Hinojosa quien continúa ese género literario aquí en EE.UU., encarnando el principio estético que señalara Julio Torri, pero, claro conservando su propia originalidad" (n.p.). ["It was Julio Torri who introduced the *Estampa* as a literary form in Mexico. It is now Hinojosa who continues this literary genre in the United States, incorporating Julio Torri's aesthetic principle, but of course maintaining his own originality."] There is some truth to Ríos's comparison with Torri; Hinojosa was writing estampas in Spanish with his own particular style, wit, and formal innovations. However, Torri's literary sensibility, notably expressed in two brief volumes, *Ensayos y poemas* (1917) and *De fusilamientos* (1940), can be described as aphoristic, brief expositions of ideas, and not wholly comparable to Hinojosa's more narrative style. With some ten published books, it is evident that the early costumbrista label—local color fiction, essentially static and flat—could not define an expanding fictional world composed of a variety of genres. Thus, in 1990, Ramón Saldívar called Hinojosa's seven-volume work "an ongoing, multivolume novel in the tradition of Trollope, Galsworthy, Proust, and Anthony Powell[,] . . . a dynamic, living chronicle of twentieth-century Chicano life" (Saldívar 1990, 132). Earlier, in 1985, I had stated the case for a multivolume work exploring the imaginative possibilities offered by the chronicle genre (Calderón 1985, 133).[3] Hinojosa's insistence on a sense of place, family genealogies, factual data, and historical events leads readers to interpret his fictions against the history of the Lower Río Grande Valley. Indeed, through his ten books, beginning with the 1973 *Estampas del valle* and through *Ask a Policeman* of 1998, Hinojosa has managed to invent with literally hundreds of characters the history of small-town life of the Mexican border region of Texas from the eighteenth century to the end of the twentieth century, a living reminder of the conquest and settlement of the Gulf of Mexico region that began in Cuba in 1519.

In his second book, published under two different titles—as *Klail City y sus alrededores* (1976; *Klail City*, 1987) in La Habana, Cuba, and as *Generaciones y semblanzas* (1977) in Berkeley, California—Hinojosa named the narrative form, the Spanish cronicón, that would allow him the freedom and range to narrate the day-to-day activities of the Mexicans of his fictional Belken County, Texas.[4] The cronicón is a fifteenth-century Peninsular form, the history of a kingdom told, following Plutarch's *Parallel Lives*, through a series of biographical sketches, estampas and semblanzas, of illustrious individuals. The terms "estampas" and "semblanzas" are still invoked in the Spanish-speaking world even now, in the news media, to briefly describe the achievements of well-known individuals who have just passed away. In the twentieth century, Hinojosa transforms the genre from classical antiquity to give expression through the Buenrostro male genealogy to the Mexicano ranching culture that grew out of the eighteenth-century Spanish province of Nuevo Santander. As well as selecting a Spanish narrative form, Hinojosa chose to write three of his first four books in Spanish, in colloquial northern Mexican Spanish, revealing both the cultural enmity between and fusion of Mexicanos and Texas Anglos.

However, Hinojosa is also the Texas writer who in his English works, *Korean Love Songs* (1978), *Rites and Witnesses* (1982), *Partners in Crime* (1985), *The Useless Servants* (1993), and *Ask a Policeman*, is equally adept at capturing the nuances of Texas English spoken by both his Anglo and his Mexican characters as they interact with each other. *Korean Love Songs*, his third book and the first in English, deserves brief but special notice for its interesting comingling of cultures and languages. It is a collection of poems of death and destruction caused by war—the Mexican calavera genre rendered in English but written under Spanish syllabic norms, twelve- to fourteen-syllable lines of arte mayor, popular in Spain before the Italianate revolution of the Renaissance (see Hinojosa 1985a, 27, 31).[5]

Like Hinojosa crossing the line between literary traditions in his Spanish and English books, Hinojosa's protagonist, writer, and narrator Rafa Buenrostro, will move within both Spanish- and English-speaking worlds. Throughout his life, both as a youngster and as a middle-aged man, Buenrostro will always be recalled by Mexicanos on both sides of the border and by Anglo-Texans as a member of the founding families that arrived in the eighteenth century with the first Spanish-Mexicano settlements. In *Generaciones y semblanzas*, among the Klail City old-timers Esteban Echevarría and don Aureliano Mora, young Rafa is the son of Jesús Buenrostro "El *del quieto*" (151; "The son of *the quiet one*," 152). In 1972, as lieutenant of the Belken County Homicide Section, thirty-seven-year-old Rafa will be referred to in English as Rafe, Young Buenrostro (Hinojosa 1985c, 75). In the nineties, after years on the force, Chief Inspector Buenrostro will be referred to as a great-great-grandson of a norteño family by María Luisa Cetina, directora del orden público for Barrones, Tamaulipas; "one of our illustrious Santa Anna's lost children," adds Mexican Judge Avila (Hinojosa 1998, 140).

This bilingual, bicultural fictional world is also captured through its titles. Character Jehú Malacara in *Generaciones y semblanzas* and el periodista y escritor P. Galindo in *Mi querido Rafa* (1981; *Dear Rafe*, 1985) and *Claros varones de Belken* (1986) refer to "el cronicón del condado de Belken y de su gente" ["the chronicle of Belken County and its people"]. In his third book, *Korean Love Songs: From Klail City Death Trip* (1978), another title is announced for the first time. The entire sequence of works has come to be known as the Klail City Death Trip Series.[6] In *Claros varones de Belken*, his fourth installment, the author officially introduces the book as a part of this ongoing American literary project: "Como se sabrá, *Claros varones de Belken* viene siendo la cuarta parte de 'Klail City Death Trip'" (13). ["As some of us know, *Fair Gentlemen of Belken* is the fourth part to 'Klail City Death Trip'"; 12.] Hinojosa borrowed his title from recent American historiography, from Michael Lesy's 1973 *Wisconsin Death Trip*, a noir biography-collage of bizarre deaths in Black River Falls, Jackson County, Wisconsin, in the 1890s told through vintage photographs and newspaper articles.[7] The author in *Claros varones de Belken* also identifies the work by its Spanish form: "En este cronicón se contarán, entre cosa varia, casos de las vidas de Rafa Buenrostro, Esteban Echevarría, Jehú Malacara y P. Galindo" (15). ["In the lengthy chronicle, among sundry things, events in the lives of Rafa Buenrostro, Esteban Echevarría, Jehú Malacara and P. Galindo will be related"; 14.] The figure of el escritor P. Galindo, the itinerant chronicler, is taken from the Mexican American journalist Pepe Díaz, who wrote in "El Lunes Literario" for *La Prensa* of San Antonio under the pseudonym P. Galindo, from the Spanish "Pega poco pero pega lindo." Thus Hinojosa's works can be from either side of the cultural divide, whether inside or outside, as either a Spanish or an English series. Hinojosa is, to be sure, the finest expression in Mexican American literature of how the languages and cultures of Spain, Mexico, and the United States have fused to form a Texas-Mexican culture of Greater Mexico.

II

"For me and mine," writes Hinojosa, "history began in 1749 when the first colonists began moving into the southern and northern banks of the Río Grande. That river was not yet a jurisdictional barrier and was not to be until almost one hundred years later; but by then, the border had its own history, its own culture, and its own sense of place: it was Nuevo Santander, named for old Santander in the Spanish Peninsula" (Hinojosa 1985d, 19). History on the Río Bravo/Río Grande begins for Texas-Mexicans with the colonization of the border area known in Viceregal Mexico as el Seno Mexicano.[8] To check the westward advance of French colonists to Texas from Louisiana, the Colonia de Nuevo Santander was established in 1748. It extended from the Pánuco River near the port of Tampico in the south to the San Antonio and Guadalupe Rivers at the Bahía del Espíritu Santo, now Corpus Christi, Texas, in the north, with the Sierra Madre Oriental, or Sierra Gorda, on the west and the Gulf of Mexico on the east as natural boundaries. To the north of Nuevo Santander lay la Jurisdicción de la Provincia de Texas, to the west la Jurisdicción de la Provincia de Coahuila and la Jurisdicción del Nuevo Reyno de León.

Although known and explored since the early sixteenth century, the regions of el Seno Mexicano and the Sierra Gorda had resisted conquest and settlement for over two centuries. Francisco Hernández de Córdoba, under orders from Cuba's Governor Diego Velázquez, had reached Mexican shores near the Pánuco River in 1517. In 1518, Juan de Grijalva left Matanzas, Cuba, to explore the coast of Mexico from Yucatán to Tabasco and Veracruz. In the same year of Grijalva's voyage, Hernán Cortés received capitulaciones from Diego Velázquez to captain yet another expedition to Mexico, to Yucatán, the result of which was the conquest and destruction of Indian Mexico and, eventually, the formation of the Viceroyalty of Nueva España. In 1526, in his last Carta de relación, his dispatch to King Charles, Cortés wrote of the possibility of expeditions to northern Mexico to settle the area from the Pánuco River to el Río de las Palmas to la Florida (Cortés 1993, 659). The Río Grande/ Río Bravo had been explored and named Río de las Palmas in 1519 by Alfonso Alvarez de Piñeda, who had sailed from Cuba. Fresh on the great success of Cortés's conquest of Mexico, Pánfilo de Narváez received a capitulación from Charles I in 1526 to conquer and pacify the area between the Río de las Palmas and la Florida. That expedition was a great failure. Alvar Núñez Cabeza de Vaca survived the Narváez expedition to write his widely known account of his eight years of wandering through what is now Texas and New Mexico. In 1580, Luis de Carbajal arrived from Spain at the port of Tampico with settlers, many of whom were Sephardic Jews, to establish el Nuevo Reyno de León. The descendants of these Spanish-Mexican Sephardic Jews were among the first wave of settlers into the Río Grande Valley in 1749.

Lieutenant don José de Escandón, in the service of the Querétaro militia since 1721, was selected in 1746 by the viceroy as leader of the conquest and pacification in northeastern Mexico. After first surveying the land between the Pánuco and San Antonio Rivers in 1746, Escandón set out from Querétaro on 1 December 1748 to settle the Provincia de Nuevo Santander. All told, there were seven entradas: three from the south to secure the Sierra Gorda, the Huasteca, and the coast north of Veracruz; three from the west into the Río Bravo Valley; and one from the presidio near the Guadalupe River in the province of Texas in the north. In the next years Escandón and his men established along both banks of the Río Bravo, also known as el Río Grande del Norte, a series of villas and rancherías: Camargo (1749), Reinosa (1749), Revilla (1750), Mier (1753), Laredo (1755), and San Juan de los Esteros Hermosos (1765), the present-day Gulf port of Matamoros. Laredo holds the distinction of being the first nonmissionary and nonmilitary Spanish settlement in the United States.

Escandón established the empresario system in the valley, creating settlements that were tax exempt and incurring few expenses from the royal treasury. Escandón offered land grants to individual colonists rather than create settlements entirely around the failing mission and presidio system. Like the Texas Anglo colonists of the nineteenth century, Escandón's settlers came lured by the promise of land. In the Escandón system, colonists provided for themselves and in exchange were given lands tax-free. Thus both the royal treasury and the individual rancher benefited. Like the settlers of New Mexico and California, the settlers of Nuevo Santander were in their majority Mexican mestizos from northern Mexico. From what are now the states of Coahuila, Guanajuato, Querétaro, Nuevo León, San Luis Potosí, and the Huastecas came farmhands, shepherds, and laborers composed of the different Mexican castes—españoles, criollos, mestizos, indios, pardos—to take part in the entradas into Nuevo Santander. With its capital Nuevo Santander in what is now the state of Tamaulipas, the colony of el Seno Mexicano thrived, becoming the origin of cattle ranching culture in the United States.

Rolando Hinojosa was born in the valley in Mercedes in 1929.[9] In 1883, Manuel Guzmán Hinojosa, Hinojosa's father, was born on the Campacuás Ranch three miles north of Mercedes, and his father was born on that ranch, as was his father's father. In his "Breve pesquisa del Valle del Río Grande," Hinojosa notes that the stability of the area from the eighteenth century to the present can be found in valley telephone books: "El primer censo se tomó en 1750, y muchos de los apellidos que aún se ven hoy día en las telefónicas, como Canales, García, Garza, Guerra, Hinojosa, Leal, Treviño, etc. forman parte de los apellidos que aparecieron en el censo original" (43). ["The first census was undertaken in 1750, and many surnames that even today are found in the telephone books, like Canales, García, Garza, Guerra, Hinojosa, Leal, Treviño, etc., form part of the surnames that appeared in the first census."] The gravestones in the Mercedes cemetery bear the names of the Hinojosa families. Like his valley relative Américo Paredes, Hinojosa was raised in a literate family. However, the history of the valley known to both men is also an oral one, a tradition kept alive through the stories and music of valley Mexicanos in their struggle with both Anglos and other Texas Mexicans. Juan Nepomuceno Cortina, from Brownsville, holds a special place in valley lore as the first in the nineteenth century to rise up against injustice—the Cortina war of 1859–1860. He was followed by Jacinto Treviño and Aniceto Pizaña and the Seditionists of 1915. Hinojosa recalls his father taking him to the place where los Sediciosos camped outside of Mercedes. For the special issue of the *Texas Monthly* published on the occasion of the sesquicentennial of the Texas Republic, well-known Texans were asked to contribute one page for each year that in sum would amount to the "150 Moments That Made Us the Way We Are." Hinojosa's contribution, "River of Blood," for 1916 recalls the racial strife and retaliatory bloodshed in the wake of the ill-conceived and ill-fated seditionist move-ment of 1915 that turned the border area into a war zone and caused hundreds of Mexicans to die. This insurrection was played out against the larger historical backdrop, Anglo commercial farming that was displacing Mexican ranching settlements (Montejano 1987, 117–128). According to Walter Prescott Webb in his *Texas Rangers*, "the number [of Mexicans] killed in the entire valley has been estimated at five hundred and at five thousand, but the actual number can never be known" (478). Hinojosa cites the *San Antonio Express* report that "finding the bodies of dead Mexicans had become so commonplace that it created little or no inter-est" (1916). Hinojosa ends his one page with an appropriate translated Spanish saying: "No pain lasts one hundred years, as we say in Spanish, but in South Texas it's been seventy years, and still counting" (1916).

However, Rolando Hinojosa-Smith is a product of two cultures, and as he has written, for him "the two cultures are inescapable" (Hinojosa 1985e, 12). His mother, Carrie Effie Smith, was born in Rockport, Texas, but arrived in the Río Grande Valley as an infant of six weeks in 1887 with the first wave of Anglo-American settlers enticed by early developer Jim Wells. "Texas Anglos were a minority at that time," Hinojosa informed me, "and my grandfather, Abraham Neumann Smith (a Union Civil War veteran), was named postmaster in the village of Progreso in the Valley. All of my mother's Anglo childhood friends (the Jeffords and others) were, like my mother, bicultural and bilingual and raised that way" (Hinojosa 2001a). Like other English-speaking settlers in close proximity to Mexican culture, the larger Smith clan, three aunts and four uncles, and Hinojosa's siblings, Roy Lee, Dora Mae, Clarissa Effie, and René Manuel, all spoke Spanish. Hinojosa gained an appreciation for his dual cultures as a young child through formal training and home experience. Hinojosa attended Mexican (both in the United States and in Mexico) and American schools. Moreover, both of his parents, who could read and write in Spanish, often read to each other, as well as individually (ibid.). Both parents fostered a respect for and acceptance of his two cultures: "I come from these two cultures, I'm a product—albeit not a finished one, yet—of them, I cannot be anything else, and I choose not to be anything else other than what I am" (Hinojosa 1985e, 14).

Hinojosa dedicates his 1998 *Ask a Policeman* to his parents, Manuel Guzmán Hinojosa, a policeman, and Carrie Effie Smith, the policeman's wife. These biographical references are rendered in fiction in this novel. Chief Inspector Rafe Buenrostro is married to an Anglo-Texan, Sammie

Jo Perkins, who, although from the ruling Anglo families, speaks Spanish and is "buena gente." Buenrostro's father-in-law, Noddy Perkins, a well-known Klail City banker now in failing health, requests a personal favor: "Son I want to be buried in the Old Families cemetery by the Carmen Ranch, on your brother's land" (19). Before the request, Perkins had confessed: "Straight off, Rafe, I want you to know I was never against your marrying Sammie Jo. And neither was Blanche. I want you to know that. I want you to get that straight from me.... I'm not a racist. I also want you to know that" (18). However, Perkins is a product of Texas class and race prejudice. He was not a member of the wealthy, "a fruit tramp for a father," but was able to enter the big house through marriage with Blanche Cooke, enhancing his stature through his banking and political deals. Although in an earlier book, Perkins hired and worked side by side with his chief loan officer Jehú Malacara, when he thought Jehú was having an affair with his daughter Sammie Jo, he exploded with, "You Mexican son-of-a-bitch" (Hinojosa 1981, 46). Late in the twentieth century old man Perkins, still the skillful operative, desires to be buried at the site of the origins of Texas-Mexican culture—at the Buenrostro Rancho del Carmen.

III

At a formative age, Hinojosa spent three summers—1943, 1944, and 1946—in Arteaga, a small Mexican village of twelve hundred, in the state of Coahuila.[10] Arteaga, situated high in the foothills of the Sierra Madre Oriental, looks down some fifteen kilometers away at Saltillo, the state capital. A young boy in his teens, Hinojosa had ventured for the first time out of the valley to stay with Manuel Guzmán Hinojosa's good friend don Eduardo Vela and his family. Young Hinojosa attended Mexican schools, lived his world entirely in Spanish, and generally enjoyed the adolescent experiences of unlimited freedom—swimming, horseback riding, movies. During his second summer in Arteaga, Hinojosa, with his imagination inspired by the Mexican environment surrounding him, wrote his first story in Spanish, a tale about two campesinos who tried to escape the levy during the Mexican Revolution. The ending of the story has one campesino die in an irrigation ditch, his blood spreading throughout Mexico.[11] This was during World War II. Hinojosa had brothers in the armed forces, one of whom, Roy Lee, had received a Bronze Medal and a Purple Heart while serving in New Guinea. Hinojosa had just graduated from high school in June 1946 before his last stay in Coahuila. Upon returning home to Texas from Arteaga in 1946, at the age of seventeen, Hinojosa enlisted:

> That I was influenced by summers there [Arteaga] is easy to see. Easy to see why, too: I was young, had not traveled anywhere outside of the Valley, and I had my first time away from home. I returned to Mercedes that August and, with my parents' signed permission in hand, I enlisted ten days later. The summers in Arteaga had given me my first taste of independence. The experience helped to soften the shock of separation and of being away from my parents and the Valley. (Hinojosa 2000b)

Thus began Hinojosa's wanderings to and from the Valley.

After discharge from the army in 1948, Hinojosa began his undergraduate studies at the University of Texas, Austin. He was recalled in fall 1949, served in the Korean War, and returned in 1951 as a decorated war hero to complete a B.S. degree in Spanish literature in January 1954. He taught at Brownsville High School for two years; other odd jobs followed. In 1962, he again left the valley for graduate studies and earned an M.A. from New Mexico Highlands University in 1963, which was followed by a Ph.D. in Spanish literature at the University of Illinois in 1969.[12]

Hinojosa, like his contemporaries in this study, had developed an interest in writing as a young person. Two of his impressionistic essays on life in Mercedes had won a literary contest conducted by his teachers at Mercedes High School (Saldívar 1985c, 45). However, success in academia came first as professor and administrator. From 1968 to 1970, he taught at Trinity College in San Antonio. From 1970 to 1974, he served as chair of Modern Languages at Texas A&I University in Kingsville; in 1974, he was appointed dean of the College of Arts & Sciences. Hinojosa had begun writing shortly after his arrival at Kingsville. His first paid published piece, "Por esas cosas que pasan," a section of his *Estampas del valle*, appeared in the seminal Mexican American journal *El Grito* in spring 1972.[13] "Por esas cosas" is taken from an account of a homicide that occurred in Mercedes. The narrative of the first book began to take shape from "stories from the older generation, using the military service, people I'd known and grown up with, and so on. The usual with most first novels" (Hinojosa 2001a). While writing his second book, Hinojosa decided on a series, which he named on the cover of his third book. *Estampas del valle* eventually received the third Premio Quinto Sol in 1973. "[I]t was the proper historical moment," acknowledges Hinojosa, "it came along, and I took what had been there for some time, but which I had not been able to see, since I had not fully developed a sense of place; I had left the Valley for the service, for formal university training, and for a series of very odd jobs, only to return to it in my writing" (Hinojosa 1985d, 23–24).

It was a sense of identity formed at an early age that led Hinojosa to conceive of his fictional world. After many years of hesitancy, he began with what he knew best: "I decided to write whatever I had, in Spanish, and I decided to set it on the border, in the Valley" (ibid., 23). The fictional Belken County began to take shape as a clearly defined imaginary geographic region. Invoking Faulkner's relationship to his fictional Yoknapatawpha County, Hinojosa has stated that he is the sole owner and proprietor of Belken County (Hinojosa 1985e, 16). And, like Faulkner before him, Hinojosa drew a schematic map of his invented world which appears in *Estampas del valle*.[14] At the top portion of the map toward the left, hanging in space, Hinojosa situates Kobe, Tokyo, Panmunjon, Fort Sill, and Fort Ord with lines of relation to each other. These are the cities that through the Korean War will affect the Mexican families of Belken County. In the center there is also a list of states in inverted geographic order, with Texas in the north, followed by Arkansas, Missouri, Illinois, Indiana, and Michigan to the south. On either side of the list are arrows pointing down and up. These states are well known to the migrant worker stream that flows back and forth on a seasonal basis from the Valley. These two schematic versions of the real world are juxtaposed against the expanding fictional world of Belken County.

At the bottom of the map, near the international border with the Río Grande flowing north (Hinojosa's conceit), is the fictional Belken County. "The map," Hinojosa informed me, "is fairly accurate, and the position of the river in relation to the town and small cities is realistic" (Hinojosa 2001a). Thus, taking from actual valley border cities, six towns are situated in a line from west to east, from Jonesville-on-the-River, Klail City, Flora, Bascom, and Edgerton to Flads in neighboring Dellis County, with only Relámpago to the north and Ruffing to the south. Jonesville, however, Hinojosa owes to the imagination of Américo Paredes, his relative, who gave Hinojosa permission to use it.[15] In *Estampas del valle*, Hinojosa writes in a parenthetical aside: "(El que sabe mucho más de la gente de Jonesville-on-the-River es don Américo Paredes)" (42). ["The person who really knows a lot more about the people of Jonesville is don Américo Paredes"; 82.] Earlier, Paredes, in his short stories collected in *The Hammon and the*

Beans and in his novel *George Washington Gómez* written during the 1930s, had rendered his border home, Brownsville, as Jonesville-on-the-Grande. Hinojosa's fiction thus extends a Mexican Texas literary tradition begun by Paredes. From Spanish colonization through the seventies in the twentieth century when *Estampas del valle* begins, families have settled, grown, and intermarried so that relatives are scattered throughout Belken County towns (as is the case with Paredes and Hinojosa). Narrative threads in Hinojosa's fiction will eventually yield to memory and a declaration of genealogy. Through the first installments of Hinojosa's ongoing chronicle, the ethnicity and character of each town emerges. Klail City, founded by Rufus T. Klail, is the county seat and also the largest, with about ten thousand inhabitants, and historically divided into two wards, the South for Anglos and the North for Mexicanos. Other towns of decidedly Anglo inhabitants include Bascom, Ruffing, and Edgerton. This is a world of apartheid: Mexican towns, Mexican neighborhoods, Mexican schools, and Mexican cemeteries. As a child, Rafa noticed that in restaurants in Ruffing raza and negritos are refused service (Hinojosa 1973, 169). The newest valley town, Flora (alborotados y mitoteros; "excitable and loud"), and the oldest, Relámpago, as their names indicate, are populated mostly by Mexicans. To the south of Jonesville-on-the-River lies Barrones, Tamaulipas, the fictional rendition of Matamoros.

The Lower Río Grande Valley is composed of some thirty towns a few miles distant from each other. Like other border agricultural areas, the Valley in Hinojosa's fiction is known for its year-round growing season, each town having its own agricultural product. After surviving the war in Korea, twenty-one-year-old Rafa Buenrostro, in *Claro varones de Belken*, will take the Missouri-Pacific train to Belken County, thinking of the Valley's great agricultural wealth and variety: "El Valle, cerca del Golfo y con su río lleno de agua dulce está rodeado por un semi-desierto y por consiguiente lo que aquí se ve parece fuera de lugar: palmas, naranjos, toronjos, plátanos del Valle, algodón en su temporada y verduras de todo tipo el año entero. . . . Caña y sorgo rumbo a Edgerton donde primero antes que nadie, salen los melones y las sandías. En Relámpago, casi siempre, la primera paca de algodón; en Ruffing, la cebolla y la fresa. Cada pueblo tiene su fama y en Klail City las naranjas ombligonas y en verdura, el repollo" (171). ["It's near the Gulf with the Río Grande gently flowing, and surrounded by a semi-desert what one sees seems out of place: palm trees, citrus groves, Valley bananas, cotton, if it's summer, and all kinds of vegetables, all year round. . . . There are sugar cane and sorghum crops toward Edgerton where cantaloupes and watermelons are also a steady crop. Relámpago usually brings the first bale of cotton; in Ruffing, it's onions and strawberries. Each Valley town has some distinction in this regard and Klail City has the sweetest navel oranges and best cabbage anywhere"; 170.] In the year 2000, Hinojosa reflects on land, family, and two hundred years of Mexican culture that have produced an identity with place: "La economía del Valle, en su gran proporción, basada en lo agrícola y eso, la tierra, es lo que ha llegado a cimentar una querencia al Valle. Importante también es que esa larga estancia de más de dos siglos y medio en el mismo sitio, ha establecido la estabilidad que se necesita para identificarse íntimamente con el lugar" (Hinojosa 2000a, 44). ["The economy of the Valley, in great measure, based on agriculture, the land, is what has cemented a love for the Valley. Also important is that the settlement of more than two centuries in the same place, has established the stability that is needed to identify intimately with the place."] Rafe Buenrostro returns from Korea. He will no longer make his living from farming like his forefathers; however, his older brother Israel and younger brother Aarón will continue on the Carmen Ranch. But Rafa *does* return to the Carmen Ranch to recuperate from the devastation and death witnessed many miles from home.

The area had been settled originally by the Four Founding Families, the Vilches, Campoys, Farías, and the Buenrostros. The Buenrostros arrived in the valley accompanying Escandón from Querétaro (Hinojosa 1973, 127). Through these four families the Mexican ranching culture is recalled. The Mexican town of Relámpago, to the south and closest to the Río Grande, is in the area of still-existing Mexicano ranches, the most important of which is el Rancho del Carmen, where the Buenrostro family has lived since Spanish-Mexicano colonial times. To the geographic space imagined for *Estampas del valle*, Hinojosa will provide readers with a historical time line in the opening pages of *Claros varones de Belken*: "Aquí empieza lo nuestro; claven esas estacas" (11) ["Here is where our story begins; brace yourselves"; 10], affirms Andrés Buenrostro Rincón, 1729–1801. The Buenrostro Rancho del Carmen is historically significant; this is also the name of the ranch owned by the Cortina family. Don Juan Nepomuceno Cortina, a member of a wealthy landed family, was one of the first to defend his right with his pistol in his hand. In 1859, according to the well-known account, Cortina shot a Brownsville Anglo marshal in the arm in defense of Cortina's Mexican servant, who was being beaten by the marshal. Following a proclamation outlining grievances against Texas authority, Cortina organized a force of some five hundred men that captured Brownsville. Cortina maintained control of the area and defeated the Brownsville Rifles and Tobin's Rangers. The Rancho del Carmen was the site of battles between Anglos and Cortina's band (Webb 1965, 175–193; Paredes 1958, 134–135; De León 1983, 54; Montejano 1987, 32–33). In *Estampas del valle*, old-timers in a bar recall: "Don Jesús [Buenrostro] tenía unas tierras cerca del Carmen. ¿Donde se echaron a los rinches? Ahí mero" (50). ["Don Jesús owned some land near el Carmen. Where they fought off the Rangers? That's the place"; 89.] In addition, the opening stanza of one of the versions of "El Corrido de Gregorio Cortez" begins with "En el condado del Carmen / miren lo que ha sucedido / murió el Cherife Mayor / quedando Román herido; In the County of El Carmen / Look what has happened; / The Major Sheriff died, / Leaving Román wounded" (Paredes 1958, 158). Gregorio Cortez shot Sheriff Morris in self-defense in Karnes County, but most variants of the corrido changed Karnes to El Carmen, according to Paredes (189).[16] Thus in history, in folklore, and in Hinojosa's fiction, the site of Texas-Mexican resistance maintains its rich symbolism—don Jesus Buenrostro defending his Rancho del Carmen. In *Ask a Policeman*, readers discover that the state of Texas has officially recognized the Spanish/Mexican settlement of the Río Grande Valley. The cemetery of the Old Families by the Carmen Ranch is a state-designated landmark (20).

Against the Buenrostros and the Old Families stand the Anglo new-comers, the Klail-Cooke-Blanchard ranch families, Hinojosa's representation of the King-Kleberg family fortune amassed first by Richard King in the 1850s–1880s and then by his son-in-law Robert Kleberg in the 1920s–1930s. At the death of Richard King in 1885, the King Ranch had 500,000 acres; by the death of Robert Kleberg in 1932, the ranch had grown to 1,250,000 acres south of the Río Nueces in Kleberg County, still controlled today by the Kleberg family.[17] One of the early purchases on record by Richard King is a ranch of 10,770 acres acquired for $200 from seller Pedro Hinojosa in 1854 (Montejano 1987, 65). In Belken County, the Klail-Cooke-Blanchard families dominate the valley economy and banking and medical services through the Cooke Bank of Klail City and the Klail Cooke Hospital. Irony of ironies, in *Ask a Policeman* Rafe Buenrostro will eventually marry Sammie Jo Perkins, a member of the Cooke family who lives in the big house on the Cooke Ranch.

The King Ranch occupies a special place in Anglo-Texan history. It was the largest ranch in Texas, and its cowboys, mainly the Mexican kineños, were part of a brief but storied moment in Texas history—the cattle drives of Spanish longhorns to markets in Kansas and Colorado roughly from 1866 to 1895 (ibid., 55). Hinojosa is not interested in what has become *the* Texas myth turned into literature as well as film. While serving in Korea in 1951, Rafe Buenrostro will be asked if in Texas he is a cowboy, "[N]o, my brother farms," he will correct the common misconception (Hinojosa 1993, 136). Hinojosa concentrates on the lives of an oppressed group, the Texas Mexicanos who, over time, because of market conditions, as the history of the King-Kleberg family indicates, were displaced from the traditional ranching culture described by Américo Paredes in the opening pages of his *"With His Pistol in His Hand"* (7–15). "At mid-century," writes David Montejano, "the rural Mexican population was equally divided in thirds among ranch-farm owners (34%), skilled laborers (29%), and manual laborers (34%). By the turn of the century, the top two tiers had shrunk—ranch farm owners comprised 16 percent of the Texas-Mexican population, skilled laborers 12 percent—and the bottom tier of manual laborers had expanded, comprising 67 percent, or two of every three adult Mexicans" (73).

In Belken County only a few Mexicans possess land. These are divided into groups by Hinojosa in *Estampas del valle*: "la raza que llegó a quedarse con tierra se podía dividir casi en dos partes: en primer lugar, los más viejos que se formaron en contra de los bolillos en trámites de sí-y-no (aunque también corrió la sangre); y en segundo lugar, los otros los ansiosos, o sea la raza que se granjeó con la bolillada para comerse las sobras en forma de tierra que les dejaban los montoneros, los políticos, y los abogados" (122). ["La raza that managed to keep their lands could almost be divided into two categories: first, the older generation who banded together against the Anglos in 'logrolling' deals (although blood was shed); and secondly, the rest, those that were covetous, that is, la raza that sided with the Anglos in order to eat the leftovers in the form of land that rebels, politicians, and lawyers left to them"; 143.] In the first group stand the Old Families, the Campoys, Farías, Vilches, and Buenrostros, all defending their lands. To the second group belongs the Leguizamón family, which arrived in the valley in 1865 and extended itself through Bascom, Flora, and Ruffing through land acquisition and marriage; they allied themselves with the Escobars and the Leyvas and with the Anglos, the Cookes, Blanchards, and Klails. Of the hated and feared Leguizamón only don Javier Leguizamón is alive. Equally despised are the coyotes, the go-betweens, loners like Polín Tapia and Adrián Peralta. These, like the

Leguizamón, are perceived as threats to the community. Loyalty to the immediate family, to the extended family, and eventually to the group is the most important virtue. In *Estampas del valle* and *Generaciones y semblanzas*, Hinojosa will tell the stories of Mexicans displaced from their lands who, in the twentieth century, work the soil on the migrant worker trails in Michigan, Illinois, and Indiana.

Displacement of the Mexican ranching culture by Anglo-Texan ranchers in the nineteenth century and large-scale agriculture in the early decades of the twentieth century was preceded by military conquest, first with the establishment of the Texas Republic in 1836 (in Mexico referred to as la rebelión del '36) followed by the conquest, occupation, and annexation of half of Mexico's territory after the U.S–Mexico war of 1846–1848 (in Mexico known as la Guerra del '47 because of the U.S. invasion of Mexico, including la Ciudad de México, in that year). In 1958, World War II veteran Américo Paredes, in *"With His Pistol in His Hand,"* turned his scholarly attention to the age of armed resistance through his study of the heroic border corrido. And hero Gregorio Cortez served in legend and song as the symbolic embodiment of Mexican ranchers in conflict with Anglo-Texan law enforcement: "Síganme, rinches cobardes, / Yo soy Gregorio Cortez; Follow me, cowardly rangers, / I am Gregorio Cortez" (160). "El Corrido de Gregorio Cortez," argued Paredes, was one in a tradition extending back to Juan Nepomuceno Cortina in the mid-nineteenth century to Aniceto Pizaña and the Seditionists in 1915–1916. Hinojosa does not dwell on the man who defends himself with his pistol in his hand. Even Texas lawman Rafe Buenrostro does not carry a gun. Hinojosa's fiction explores the issue of resistance after conquest. How does one resist in defeat in daily activities side by side with the conquerors? In his second book, *Generaciones y semblanzas*, Hinojosa, in Mexican Spanish, will serve notice to his readers that heroism comes in different forms:

> Aquí no hay héroes de leyenda: esta gente va al escusado, estornuda, se limpia los mocos, cría familias, conoce lo que es morir con el ojo pelón, se cuartea con dificultad y (como madera verde) resiste rajarse. El que busque héroes de la proporción del Cid, pongamos por caso, que se vaya a la laguna de la leche. (1)

> These are no legendary heroes here. These people go to the toilet, they sneeze and blow their noses, they raise families, know how to die with one

eye on guard, and they yield with difficulty like most green wood and thus
do not crack easily. Those seeking heroes of the caliber of El Cid, say, can
very well go to Hell and stay there. (2)

This is Hinojosa's second book, like his first, written in Spanish, offering
his readers a Mexican world existing completely independent of the
dominant group: "A la raza de Belken, la gringada le viene ancha; por su
parte, la gringada, claro es, como está en poder, hace caso a la raza cuando
conviene: elecciones, guerra, susto económico, etc. (Las cosas más vale
decirse como son si no, no)" (1). ["The Chicanos of Belken could do with
or without them; the *bolillos*, on the other hand, being the dominant
group, pay attention to the Chicanos when it's a matter of convenience:
during elections, wartime, economic plight, etc. (Better to speak candidly
about things or else not at all)"; 2.] As an oppressed group, the Mexicans
respond with resilience: "Verdad es que hay distintos modos de ser
heroico. Jalar día tras día y de aguantar a cuanto zonzo le caiga a uno
enfrente no es cosa de risa. Entiéndase bien: el aguante tampoco es cerrar
los ojos y hacerse pendejo. . . . La gente sospecha que el vivir es heroico
en sí" (1). ["It's true that there are several ways of being heroic. It's no
laughing matter to work from day to day, putting up with any damn fool
who shows up along the way. One thing should be clear however: to
endure is not to ignore things or to deceive oneself. . . . People suspect
that living is heroic enough"; 2.]

IV

As he began writing, Hinojosa steered away from traditional Texas fiction,
the great epic scale common to some Westerns. The world of ranching,
horses, and cattle and the south Texas physical landscape are noticeably
absent. Instead, Hinojosa focuses on people, genealogies, and relationships forged through time. The fictional world that emerges from
Hinojosa's first books written in Spanish, *Estampas del valle*, *Generaciones
y semblanzas*, and *Claros varones de Belken*, is based on a Mexican
world—its various classes, cultural expressions, and language—recalled
from the twentieth century by various narrators. With each new chronicle
installment, Hinojosa captured a new experience in a variety of narrative
forms—fragmented sketches, epistolary novel, poetry, detective fiction—
and structural formats—letters, personal journals, audiotapes, interviews,

Spanish-language radio, conversations in bars, baseball games. These are minor moments that reveal in situ a richly nuanced cultural world. As the first books were published, critics, including myself, noted the collective character of Hinojosa's fiction.[18] However, from this collective biography will emerge a central character, Rafa Buenrostro. The entire Cronicón del Condado de Belken/Klail City Death Trip through *Ask a Policeman* of 1998 is the complete life of a Texas Mexicano born in 1930, orphaned by his Mexican parents at a young age, who manages to forge his own identity taking from his two Texas cultures. Certainly, Hinojosa uses other narrator characters, such as Rafa's cousin Jehú Malacara and the writer P. Galindo. These are also masks worn by Hinojosa. But it is Rafa, character, narrator, and listener, whom Hinojosa has selected to maintain the sense of unity to the cronicón of Belken County. In *Claros varones de Belken*, Rafa is, according to old-timer Esteban Echevarría, "muchacho joven que vives entre los viejos y con sus viejos recuerdos" (209) ["a young man who lives among the old who live with their old memories"; 208]. The outlines of future book installments with the Rafa Buenrostro character are already adumbrated in 1973. The last of the estampas y vidas ("sketches and lives") of *Estampas del valle* is titled "Una vida de Rafa Buenrostro," which is narrated by Rafa in thirty very brief fragments, describing events from childhood to his return from Korea to his departure from the valley for the University of Texas at Austin.[19]

While pursuing his Ph.D. at the University of Illinois, Hinojosa came across two fifteenth-century Castilian chronicles, *Generaciones y semblanzas* (ca. 1450–1455) by Fernán Pérez de Guzmán and *Claros varones de Castilla* (ca. 1486) by Fernando del Pulgar. According to Hinojosa, "Llegué a la lectura de *Generaciones y semblanzas* como parte de mi lectura graduada. Lo leí, como casi todo, por interés y no como asignatura. Recuerdo haber leído la obra varias veces así como *Claros varones* . . . y muchas obras del medioevo. Ciertamente no seré el único en el mundo que piensa que la lit. de ese tiempo era una de vigor, de una fuerza, de un estilo limpio y fuerte" (Hinojosa 1984). ["I came to read *Generaciones y semblanzas* as part of graduate reading. I read it, like most of my readings, because of interest and not as an assignment. I recall having read the work several times as well as *Claros varones* . . . and many more works of the medieval period. Certainly I am not the only one in the world who believes that the lit. of that period was one of vigor, strength, of a clean vigorous style."] In his graduate studies, Hinojosa's literary interests had gravitated toward narrative, toward a direct, straightforward

Peninsular literary realism. In 1963, he earned a master's degree in Spanish literature with a thesis on the oral tradition in *Don Quijote*. At the University of Illinois, he completed a dissertation on Spain's most prolific nineteenth-century writer, the realist Benito Pérez Galdós. Given Hinojosa's interests in empirical and realistic narrative, it is not surprising that he would find inspiration in two not-so-well-known Peninsular works.

The cronicón is a form of narrative historiography that developed on the Iberian Peninsula in the transition from the Medieval Age to the Renaissance. The books written by Guzmán and Pulgar are chronicles narrated as a series of biographical sketches of past heroes, virtuous men, who because of their deeds as well as failures needed to be recalled to serve as examples. These two historians wrote after the period of the oral epics in Spain but, of course, before the rise of the novel. In sharp distinction to careless medieval writers, Guzmán demonstrates a realistic impulse when he warns against chroniclers "de poca vergüeña e más les plaze relatar cosas estrañas e maravillosas que verdaderas e çiertas" (1) ["with very little shame who receive more pleasure from recounting strange and marvelous things instead of truthful and real ones"]. These are writers-historians of narrative empiricism, and they stand, as does Hinojosa, against the delusions of romantic writing: "When I first started to write . . . I had to eschew the romanticism and the sentimentalism that tend to blind the unwary, that get in the way of truth. It's no great revelation when I say that romanticism and sentimentalism tend to corrupt clear thinking as well" (Hinojosa 1985d, 19–20). "Serious writing," affirms Hinojosa, "is deliberate as well as a consequence of an arrived-to decision; what one does with it may be of value or not, but I believe that one's fidelity to history is the first step to fixing a sense of place" (ibid., 24).

Through memorial, "personal eyewitness," and registro, "written documents," Guzmán and Pulgar derive their historical characters and events from the recent history of Spanish kingdoms and fiefdoms prior to the unification of the Peninsula under the Catholic Kings. This is an age of seignorial estates and powerful patriarchal families in which la caballería is still important, but it is also a world in transition, contrasting a prior warrior ethic with a more gentlemanly or aristocratic view of manhood based on a virtuous life. When we think of the world of the ranchero society of the Río Grande Valley, the Mexicano patriarchal lineages, the fiefdoms that evolved out of the heroic age of border conflict to life under Anglo-Texan rule, then we can understand the analogy that Hinojosa is pursuing in his cronicón of Belken County. Américo Paredes, before Hinojosa, also pursued the medieval analogy with Texas Mexicano culture in *"With His Pistol in His Hand"*:

> *El Corrido de Gregorio Cortez* has been presented as a prototype of the *corrido* of border conflict, a ballad form that developed on the Lower Border of the Rio Grande. There a ballad community much like those of medieval Europe existed during the nineteenth and early part of the twentieth century. Culture homogeneity, isolation, and a patriarchal traditional way of life made the existence of a native folk balladry possible. (241)

The heroic age of border conflict has given way to an age of coexistence, and it is the cronicón that is called upon to represent the disappearing rural ranching world which Hinojosa knew as a child and which was the home of his father's people.[20]

Readers of *Estampas del valle* and *Generaciones y semblanzas* were hard pressed to find a clearly outlined plot. Instead, plots were given to the reader as a series of brief sketches in a variety of forms outlining characters and their traits, a literary portraiture of people dealing with the everyday problems, the inner history of a people necessary to develop the larger history of Texas. Hinojosa's first works are devoid of the Aristotelian moment in which plot seems to hinge on one single incident that has been developed in linear fashion. Hinojosa clarifies: "For the writer—this writer—a sense of place was not a matter of importance; it became essential. And so much that my stories are not held together by the *peripeteia* or the plot as much as by *what* people who populate the stories say and *how* they say it, how they look at the world out and the world in; and the works, then, become studies of perceptions and values and decisions reached by them because of those perceptions and values which in turn were fashioned and forged by the place and its history" (Hinojosa 1985d, 21). The cronicón, beginning with *Estampas del valle*, thus allows Hinojosa to write his version of Texas history as a series of estampas or semblanzas: "A fin de cuentas, este mundo es como una botica: hay un poco de todo. Altos, bajos, llorones, valientes, gordos, flacos, buenos, malos, listos y pendejos, unos enclenques, otros resonantes de salud. El escritor, sin permiso de nadie, se sale a la calle y escoge de todo un poco" (116). ["In the last analysis, the world is like a drugstore: there's a little bit of everything. All kinds of people: tall, short, cry babies, fat, skinny, good, bad, sharp, dumb, some sickly and others as healthy as can be. The writer, without anyone's leave, goes out into the street and takes a little bit from here and there"; 137.] The flow of time is arrested within a frame in which the perceptible, the observable is the focus of writing. Hinojosa dwells on this form having characters represent themselves through monologues and dialogues, thus capturing the speech of the people according to sociolinguistic strata rather than solely through a narrator's description.

The origins of biographical narrative are in Plutarch, of whom Pulgar and Hinojosa are well aware. The first biographer, the Greek Plutarch, in his *Parallel Lives* aimed at representing character, virtues, and vices, not through glorious deeds, but through trivial actions. Just as a portrait painter, explained Plutarch, attempted to show likeness, resemblance (the Spanish "semblanza") through features, physiognomy ("semblante"), he would represent an individual life in writing, biography, through the outward signs of the psyche (Plutarch 1928, 225). As in Plutarch's accounts of famous men, in Guzmán's narrative the flow of events is secondary to more imaginative, rhetorical, and didactic demands. In each sketch, Guzmán establishes a lineage, describes physical characteristics disclosing temperaments and moral qualities, "senblantes e costunbres . . . façiones e condiçiones" (4) ["physiognomies and manners . . . features and temperaments"]. The same holds true for Pulgar some thirty years later. Writing for Reina Isabela de Castilla y León and inspired by the love for his land, Pulgar will set down in writing the genealogies and deeds of Castilla's notable men: "[E]screviré los linajes e condiciones de cada uno, e algunos notables fechos que fizieron: de los quales se puede bien creer que en autoridad de personas, e en ornamento de virtudes, e en las abilidades que tovieron, así en ciencia, como en armas, no fueron menos excelentes que aquellos griegos e romanos . . . que tanto son loados en sus escripturas" (4). ["I will write of the genealogies and temperaments of each one, and some of their notable deeds; from which it can be understood that in their authority, and in the glory of their virtues, and in the expertise they possessed, in knowledge, as well as in arms, were no less in stature than the Greeks and Romans . . . who are so praised in their writings."] In all cases, men's and women's actions were to be judged by the cardinal virtues of prudence, temperance, fortitude, and justice. In Hinojosa's fiction similar situations will obtain with the added virtues of loyalty to and compassion for the group, most apparent in the Buenrostro family and its symbolic patriarch don Jesús.

Now Plutarch was a Greek who wrote in Greek under Roman rule and his *Parallel Lives* are sketches of both Greeks and Romans. "Being the issue of a Texas Mexican father and his Anglo Texas wife," Hinojosa too has lived, in his own words, his "parallel cultures" from "first-hand experience" (Hinojosa 1985e, 13). Hinojosa is a Mexican writing in Spanish under Anglo-Texan rule and the analogy with Plutarch's *Parallel Lives* is pursued by Hinojosa in his work. In *Generaciones y semblanzas*, don Aureliano Mora lost his son, Ambrosio, a World War II veteran, shot in the back by Deputy Sheriff Van Meers in front of the J. C. Penney store in Flora. Van Meers was found innocent of any wrongdoing. Texas Ranger Choche Markham testified on his behalf. Three years after the death of his son, in a fit of anger, don Aureliano, crowbar in hand, smashed the insulting metal plaque listing Klail's men who had served during the war. To Klail City's Mexican policeman don Manuel Guzmán, don Aureliano declares: "Digo que somos griegos, don Manuel . . . los esclavos en casa de los romanos . . . tenemos que educar a los romanos . . . los bolillos . . . que son lo mismo" (149). ["I said we're like the Greeks, don Manuel . . . slaves in the homes of the Romans . . . We had to educate the Romans . . . the *bolillos* . . . they're one and the same thing"; 150.] In this brief sketch of don Aureliano Mora, Hinojosa strikes a blow against the "often repeated one-sided telling of Texas history" (Hinojosa 1985d, 23). Thus Hinojosa describes the lives of Texas Mexicanos in a difficult period in their history. However, there is a sense of looking back at the turn of the century, and prior to the coming of Anglo settlers, as a classic period with Mexican models to emulate, claros varones, hombres rectos y cabales, "complete gentlemen, just and real men." As in Guzmán and Pulgar, Hinojosa's claros varones are dead.

In the 1993 *Useless Servants*, Rafa Buenrostro records the following in his daily journal entry during the heaviest fighting of the Korean War: "January 27. We started our offensive on Jan 25. (Became an adult, 21-years-old on the 21st.)" (118). Rolando Hinojosa was born on 21 January 1929. *The Useless Servants* is his personal fictional journal of his experience in Korea. Rafa, Hinojosa's contemporary, his alter ego really, is the narrator assigned by Hinojosa to recall what don Jesús Buenrostro called "Texas, our Texas, that slice of hell, heaven, purgatory and land of our Fathers."

Embedded in Hinojosa's first book, *Estampas del valle*, is the beginning of the cronicón of the "land of our Fathers." In the section "Los Revolucionarios ("The Revolutionaries"), Hinojosa pays homage to a disappearing generation born in the nineteenth century: "Se acaban los revolucionarios. En el condado de Belken, en el Valle, quedan pocos, unos libres y otros con menos fortuna, prisioneros en esas *rest homes* de las que nadie se salva. . . . Los otros, los libres, se están acabando también, salvo que ellos saben todavía muy bien quiénes son y qué fueron" (121). ["The Revolutionaries are getting scarce. In Belken County, in the Valley, a few are left, some free and others, less fortunate, are prisoners in those nursing homes from which no one is saved. . . . The rest, those that are free, are also thinning out, except that they still know very well who they are and what they were"; 142.]

Don Víctor Peláez, a tall and thin norteño, worked in his brother's carnival troupe, la Carpa Peláez, that traveled the valley. However, before that he was Lieutenant Colonel Víctor Peláez, born in Arteaga, Coahuila. He experienced the last campaigns of the Mexican Revolution in the Huastecas of San Luis Potosí and Veracruz at the service of Generals Manuel Avila Camacho and Lázaro Cárdenas. He also lived through the assassinations of revolutionary leaders Emiliano Zapata in 1919 and Venustiano Carranza in 1920. Don Víctor was un "hombre derecho y recto en su trato y comportamiento" ("an upright and honest man in his dealings and manners") and a beer drinker. When don Víctor died of renal problems, not many knew of his previous life south of the border.

Don Manuel Guzmán was a U.S. citizen, a cotton farmer, milkman, baker, farmworker, and railroad worker in Texas, as well as a Mexican soldier. He was born in Campacuás, Hidalgo County, Texas, and became the Mexican sheriff of the Mexicano barrio of Klail City. However, as a young man he joined the northern campaign of the Revolution serving under Alvaro Obregón and Francisco Villa, experiencing Villa's defeat at the Battle of Celaya in 1915. Don Manuel outlived the violence of the Revolution. However, short on patience, quick-tempered, and foul-mouthed, he died of a brain hemorrhage while talking to his wife as she took off his boots (Hinojosa 1973, 45).

Like don Manuel Guzmán, Valley elders Braulio Tapia and Evaristo Garrido also fought in the Mexican Revolution because they were born in the United States, just like their ancestors in the eighteenth century. Because of history and proximity to Mexico and families on both sides of the river, these soldiers did not distinguish the river or land as jurisdictional barriers. This disrespect for national boundaries was inherited from fathers, uncles, and grandfathers, the previous nineteenth- and eighteenth-century generations, who were also in their own way revolucionarios, who fought for their rights in their native land, which is now called the United States of America (ibid., 121). Although don

Manuel Guzmán lived most of his life in south Texas, working in a variety of jobs, the lives of Don Manuel, like those of his generation, were lived in a Mexican world: "Leía y escribía lo que se dice bien; el inglés lo chapuceaba pero siendo un hombre discreto no se metía mucho con ese idioma. Las vidas de don Manuel fueron en español" (124). ["He could read well and also write out what was said; he could get along in English but, being a discreet man, he didn't use it much. The lives of don Manuel were in Spanish"; 145.]

In Hinojosa's succeeding Spanish-language installments, *Generaciones y semblanzas* and *Claros varones de Belken*, the fragmented chronicle sketches are bound together by the deaths of father figures for Rafa—don Jesús Buenrostro and Esteban Echevarría. These are men born in the nineteenth century and recall the Mexican ranching world for Rafa's generation. Don Jesús appears only briefly in the second part of *Generaciones y semblanzas*, speaking one line to Rafa (77). Don Jesús died in 1946 while working and defending his Rancho del Carmen. He was murdered by two Mexican nationals hired by Alejandro Leguizamón. However, even in death his presence is felt throughout the community. This is the case with old-timers who recall don Jesus Buenrostro, *el quieto*, hombre recto y cabal: Esteban Echevarría holding court among men in El Oasis bar as ex-G.I. Rafa listens; truck driver Leocadio Gavira, *el rápido de Oklahoma*, talking to P. Galindo while traveling through the Midwest with migrant workers; and don Marcial de Anda sitting on his park bench exchanging greetings with Rafa. As in the Spanish chronicle with its posthumous fame as an ethical force within society, both Anglo and Mexican male behavior will be judged against *el quieto*. For example, against the blustery, opportunistic Texas Ranger George (Choche) Markham, the supposed friend of la raza, stands the Michigan school-teacher Tom Purdy in *Generaciones y semblanzas* who, along with his wife, helped Mexican farmworkers in the early sixties: "Este señor, sin dinero, pero con empeño y decisión y sin que nadie viniera y le soplara en el oído . . . en silencio . . . decidió que ayudaría a una gente—que por ser gente—merecía tratarse como tanto" (113). ["This man, without money, but with dedication and determination, without having anyone come and whisper in his ear . . . in silence . . . decided to help a people—who because they were people—deserved to be treated as such"; 114.][21]

The death of Esteban Echevarría, the last of the Klail City old-timers, the revolucionarios, will close and provide unity for *Claros varones del Belken*. Echevarría dies in 1960 when Rafa is thirty years old, at a time when Rafa takes up his role in the Texas world emerging in the second half of the twentieth century. In the section titled "Con el pie en el estribo" ("Going Home"), Echevarría will recall for Rafa the Valley before the coming of the Anglos. "This conversation," writes José David Saldívar, "fairly describes what historians call the transformation from a precapitalist, agrarian society into a modern commercial order" (Saldívar 1991b, 78). Indeed, Echevarría in his own way describes the transformation of the valley: land fenced by barbed wire; a social order where a handshake is of no legal value; dances where admission is charged; young people who refuse to speak Spanish; the Anglos with their property, banks, and contracts (Hinojosa 1986a, 207, 209). Echevarría ends with the palm trees native to the Río Grande Valley now cut down and in the possession of the Anglos, like the Mexicans: "Y allí están las palmeras. . . . Las palmeras que se daban en el Valle y que crecían como Dios quería hasta que la bolillada vino con sus hachas y las cortaron como si tal cosa. . . . Parece mentira. Ahora ellos mismos venden palmas pa' sembrar. . . . ¡qué bonito, chingao! ¿Quién los entiende? Sí, vendiendo palmas pa' sembrar. . . . Si ellos fueron los que las cortaron . . . palmas que se doblaban pero que no cedían, palmas que perdían hojas y nacían otras hasta que vinieron las hachas . . . así como la gente" (209). ["And what about our palm trees? Palm tress that grew as God wanted them until the Anglos came with those axes o' theirs and then cut them down as if they were nothing. Incredible. Now they're the ones who sell palm trees for planting! Isn't that great? Who can understand these people? Selling palm trees for planting. Ha! It was they who cut them down. Palm trees that would bend but not break, palm trees that lost their fronds and then would grow new ones until the axes came"; 208.]

Echevarría also recalls the wars: "Rafa, y las guerras . . . las guerras de tu padre aquí en el Valle, las de tu hermano en el *oversea*, y la tuya Rafa, y las otras guerras de ellos a las cuales siempre nos inmiscuyen" (209). ["And the wars, Rafe. Those in the Valley, your brother's overseas, and your own, Rafe, and those other wars of theirs in which they always involve us"; 208.] Other valley Mexicanos died, the generations that went off to fight, this time at the service of the United States. Genaro Castañeda, El Maistro, veteran of World War I, was wounded in France. Amadeo Guzmán and Ambrosio Mora fought in World War II. Chano Ortega from Klail City died in 1944 in the D-Day Invasion of France (Hinojosa 1973, 158). And Rafa Buenrostro's Korean War generation, the young men who fought and died ten thousand miles from Belken County—David "el tío," el Riche, Joey "Pepe" Vielma, Chale Villalón, and Tony Balderas (Hinojosa 1977, 71; Hinojosa 1986a, 17). Their parents didn't know exactly where or why they went to fight; however, these soldiers left the valley knowing full well who they were.

In the 1993 *Useless Servants*, Hinojosa will pick up this narrative thread in the life of Rafa Buenrostro. This book is both a continuation of the Belken County chronicle and a remembrance of a U.S. war of a half century ago lived by a young American. This is a chronicle, localized and private—no wider references to political or military strategies between the United States, North and South Korea or China, or personal battles between President Harry Truman and General Douglas MacArthur. It is Sergeant Rafe Buenrostro's daily journal kept amidst the chaos of fighting from July 1950 to September 1951 as a member of the 219th Field Artillery, part of a larger United Nations army in a police action thousands of miles from Texas. Young Buenrostro, away from his home for the first time, was fighting the North Korean People's Army and the Chinese Communist Forces as well as the extreme cold, heat, and disease, witnessing the atrocities of war, the victimization of the innocent, the racism of his fellow Americans, and the segregation of black soldiers. Maneuvering back and forth across rivers and mountains, following orders, Rafe was a useless servant like the Chinese Communists in Korea who "also fought for their masters in a foreign land" (184).

During a restful stay in June 1997 in Rudolfo and Patricia Anaya's Casita in Jémez Springs, New Mexico, Hinojosa recalled a tragic day lived by a young Texas Mexicano in Korea in 1950. In a letter written in gratitude to his hosts, the peaceful Jémez Canyon valley with its acequia and the nearby Upper Río Grande of New Mexico will bring to mind another old, disputed river territory:

> The Río Grande has also witnessed its share of American history, often a one-sided telling of it, but lo que el hombre propone, Dios dispone which finds its corollary in Man proposes and God disposes.
>
> The River Naktong in southwestern Korea is also an old, meandering body. The Monsoon comes to Korea with unfailing fury and regularity in June and July—sometimes during the first two weeks of August. During those times, the river transforms itself into an ominous presence.
>
> Militarily there was an important bridge that spanned the Naktong which, once crossed, would lead, during the first few months of the Korean War, to the beleaguered port of Pusan. It was a high bridge and necessarily

so because of the snow melt which was soon followed by the Monsoon. It was also a sturdy, steel-reinforced bridge.

In the late summer of 1950, when the North Korean People's Army was running roughshod over a still green, inexperienced U.S. Army, the Naktong bridge became strategically—and tactically—important.

By late afternoon, on that bright, sunny day, most but not all of the American forces had crossed and began assembling for the march east. The Battle Police—harried and tired—was doing its best to escort the remaining troops across safely and attempting, not always with any degree of success, to keep the refugees out of the way and off the bridge.

It was not an easy job. Hundreds, perhaps thousands—some estimated three thousand—South Korean refugees were also seeking refuge from the N.K.P.A. and mobbed the roads and the bridge.

The order to destroy the bridge was given and relayed once, twice, and a third time until the order was finally carried out. . . .

It's estimated that a thousand civilians died that afternoon along with the oxen and, yes, camels, used to transport the miserable belongings of those children, their mothers, aunts and sisters, the men and the old men, the elders with their black, shiny top hats (a sign of distinction) who were thrown hundreds of feet in the air in bits and pieces along with parts of the steel-reinforced concrete bridge that bright, sunny day. (Hinojosa 1997, 7–9)[22]

In *Useless Servants*, Rafe writes in his journal: "The Gen (don't have his name yet) gave the order himself. And then the bridge was destroyed. Blown up. Hundreds died on it: kids, families, animals. Joey [Vielma] and I turned our backs to avoid seeing the bodies. The bridge was blown up in all kinds of pieces. A roar, a geyser of water and who knows what else went up in the air. All the time, our vehicles revving the motors, but we could still hear the screaming and the crying. The Engineers had set the charges and were waiting for all units to get across. This was worse than any hand-to-hand fighting we had had in Chuhiwon" (35). The general who gave the order, writes Hinojosa in 1997, was Hobart Gay, "whose military career ended that day." Rafe and Hinojosa, barely out of their teens, survived that Korean "river of blood" to see another year of fighting and "learned, at first hand, the meaning of 'total war'" (Hinojosa 1997, 9).

The hostile weather, a history of conflict, and racism in Texas served Rafe well for enduring the war, the weather in Korea, and the racism of the U.S. Army—"speak English goddamit" (Hinojosa 1993, 80). Born an American, a Mexican to himself as well as to his fellow Texans, Rafe too had lived his life in Spanish, like his predecessors.

Rafa recalls, in *Generaciones y semblanzas*, attending Valley neighborhood schools, "escuelitas," where the old revolucionarios who left Mexico taught children Spanish literacy—reading, writing, and arithmetic—and ended the school day singing the Mexican national anthem: "Cuando se acababa la escuela americana en mayo . . . uno estaba seguro de piscar algodón dos meses y de ir un mes a la escuela mexicana del señor Bazán . . . MEXICANOS AL GRITO DE GUERRA" (73). ["When school was over in the American schools in May . . . one could count on picking cotton for two months and on attending Mr. Bazán's Mexican school for one month . . . MEXICANOS AL GRITO DE GUERRA"; 74.] Thus a sense of identity was fostered by this early childhood neighborhood schooling and later in public schools in Klail City's Mexican North Ward school—"la escuela de la raza."

These early childhood experiences were crucial for surviving in racially divided Klail City. On entering Memorial Junior High, Rafa Buenrostro will refer to the Anglicized Mexicans of the South Ward as those who were dispossessed of culture and who didn't know how to defend themselves: "la raza del South Ward . . . ésos tenían miedo (quizá vergüenza) de hablar español" (71) ["the South Ward Chicanos . . . they were probably afraid [perhaps ashamed] of speaking Spanish"; 70, 72].[23] "Nosotros los del North Ward (como sabíamos quiénes éramos y qué éramos), exigíamos footballs tan buenos como los que les daban a la bolillada" (67). ["Those of us from the North Ward [since we knew who we were and what we were] demanded footballs as good as those the *bolillos* got"; 68.] Indeed, North Ward Mexicanos Rafa Buenrostro and Jehú Malacara felt on entering senior high as if they were entering enemy territory (49). *Generaciones y semblanzas* will end with ex-G.I.'s Rafa Buenrostro and Jehú Malacara looking back on their high school senior class: "En la clase, como en este relato hay mucha separación sin decir palabra y con cierto entendimiento aprendido o adivinado por ambos lados" (177). ["In our class, as in this account, there is a great deal of segregation; it exists without a word, but with an understanding, which has been learned or intuitively grasped, by both sides"; 178.] Separation indeed; at Klail Senior High, teacher Miss Pyle and fifteen-year-old Elsinore Chapman had barred Rafe from entering the library unaware that twenty years later Rafe would be an English teacher there.

The Korean War is an all-informing event for the citizen-soldier-writer Rolando Hinojosa and his narrator-character Rafa Buenrostro. Rafa Buenrostro will return from Korea to contribute to the history of the Río Grande Valley in *Estampas del valle*, *Generaciones y semblanzas*, and *Claros varones de Belken*. The Spanish-speaking, Mexican world of the fictional Belken County will emerge as Rafa wanders between the valley and the University of Texas, Austin, memorializing the valley elders, friends, and las familias mexicanas of the previous generation, many of whom saw him leave for and return from the war. The historically symbolic Buenrostro Rancho del Carmen will serve as a locus of identity, with its direct reference to the nineteenth-century resistance of the Mexican revolucionario don Juan Nepumoceno Cortina. Near the end of the twentieth century, Texas lawman Rafe, of the Rancho del Carmen, is married to Sammie Jo (Perkins) Buenrostro, she of the big house on the Cooke Ranch. Here, then, in *Ask a Policeman* of 1998 is at least one resolution to cultural conflict, that "separación sin decir palabra y con cierto entendimiento aprendido o adivinado por ambos lados."[24] And Rolando Hinojosa-Smith, the Ellen Clayton Garwood Professor of Creative Writing in the English Department at the University of Texas, Austin, like Rafe, will return to Texas and the valley to contribute to the literature and history of Texas through his *Cronicón del condado de Belken*—a fusion of Fernán Pérez de Guzmán's and Fernando del Pulgar's Peninsular classicism, biographical portraiture of small-town America as in Michael Lesy's *Wisconsin Death Trip*, and the culture of Greater Mexico.

"COMO MÉXICO NO HAY DOS"

Sandra Cisneros's Feminist Border Stories

*The stewardess handing out declaration forms has given
me the wrong one assuming I'm Mexican but I am! . . .
I only want to get rid of my underarm hair quick before
the plane touches down in the land of los nopales . . .
into the arms of awaiting Mexican kin on my father's side of
the family where I open my arms wide armpits clean as a
newborn's soul without original sin and embrace them like the
good girl my father would have them believe I am.*

— SANDRA CISNEROS, "ORIGINAL SIN"

I

"Como México no hay dos" is a popu-
lar Mexican saying as well as a mariachi favorite of the same title written
by Pepe Guízar (see Concepción 1972, 83–84). The song lyrics and saying
are expressions of territorial and cultural pride and refer to the border
between the United States and Mexico: a drink of tequila is called for, no
need to cry over lost land because there is only one México. However, the
upshot of recent discussions on political reform and cultural pluralism in
Mexico has forced Mexicans to accept that there is more than one Mexico
within and outside the international border. At the request of progressive
Mexican professors, intellectuals, and artists, the 25th Annual National
Association for Chicana and Chicano Studies (NACCS) Convention was

held in Mexico City in the city's historic center around la Plaza de la Constitución, el Zócalo, and at numerous tradition-rich venues such as la Casa de la Primera Imprenta en América, el Colegio de San Idelfonso, el Museo Nacional de las Culturas, la Antigua Escuela Nacional de Jurisprudencia, el Extemplo de Santa Teresa, and el Museo del Templo Mayor.[1] On 24 June 1998, the conference opened under an overcast sky and ceremonial rain at the heart of Aztec Tenochtitlán, at the archaeological site of the Templo Mayor, the temple to the sun god Huitzilopochtli, the Aztec supreme deity. La buena vibra of the opening reception—food, music, dance, and Aztec ceremony—gave way in the following days to the realities of the conference. There is still a good deal of misunderstanding between Mexicans and Chicanos that was evident in panel discussions. Mexican panelists continually spoke of Chicano culture as if it were a monolithic whole. Language was also a stumbling block to communication: Mexicans spoke Spanish; Chicanos, English. Class bias was also apparent. Mexican intellectual and upper- and middle-class snobbery has always been a negative factor in assessing Mexican American culture, literature, and art, which still are informed by traditional Mexican working-class symbols. However, some panel sessions at the conference dealt with the influences of Mexican and Mexican American cultures on each other. Despite the cultural differences exposed at the conference, the encuentro was an acknowledgment of Mexican diversity beyond the political borders of the nation. The conference was organized around the central theme "dos comunidades y un mismo pueblo." The year of the conference, 1998, also marked the 150th anniversary of the Treaty of Guadalupe Hidalgo, signed in Mexico City.[2]

The U.S.-Mexico border created a cultural diaspora that Mexican intellectuals and government officials have only recently accepted. It is a fact worth noting that a significant portion of Mexico's population will always be outside its national boundaries. During the 2000 Mexican presidential campaign, Vicente Fox of the Partido Acción Nacional and Cuauhtémoc Cárdenas of the Partido de la Revolución Democrática traveled through California, Illinois, and other states in an effort to reach the swing vote: Mexicans in the United States who would influence their counterparts in Mexico. On 8 May 2000, Vicente Fox, in an unprecedented move, addressed the California Senate in English with the following message: "I am here to tell the 18 million Mexicans that live in the United States that your mother country, which you still feel in your hearts and minds, will soon be in good hands" (Sheridan and Stewart

2000, A3). The 18 million (actually more than 20 million) Mexicans in the United States whom politician Fox refers to now constitute a growing diaspora that reaches beyond the traditional West, Southwest, and Midwest borders into the South and Northeast. Atlanta now has a population of some 100,000 recently arrived Mexicans. New York City, with over 300,000, is now the sixth-largest U.S. metropolitan center with respect to population of Mexican origin. According to a recent survey conducted by the Mexican *Reforma* and the *Los Angeles Times*, 34 percent of Mexicans have worked at one time or another in the United States and 45 percent of Mexicans have relatives living in the United States.[3] Most Mexicans living in the United States will return to their communities in less than two years. Thus tremendous migration is one of the fundamental characteristics of Mexico's population at the beginning of the twenty-first century.

With migration comes an infusion of capital and values on both sides of the border. As we look to the future, will Mexicans adopt northern ways of doing things? Will the U.S. mass media, products, and popular traditions change Mexico? "[T]he 'Americanization' process," wrote Carlos Monsiváis in 1995, "in Mexico and Latin America in general will move inexorably forward" (40). A half century earlier, before Fox's address to the California legislature, Octavio Paz, traveling through Los Angeles, had described in *El laberinto de la soledad* a group of young Mexican Americans, pachucos, who had completely rejected their culture—language, religion, customs, and beliefs (14). What the outsider Paz viewed as rejection was in fact cultural resistance and adaptation, the emergence of a bicultural, bilingual Mexican world.[4] What had been a Mexican problem in the fifties is now a Mexican solution in terms of political and economic clout. In 2000, Vicente Fox was campaigning in the United States among a group of Mexicans whose money sent back to Mexico amounts to the third-largest item—estimated between $6 billion and $8 billion—in the Mexican economy (Silva-Herzog 1999, 12). In view of their emerging power, perhaps, now the diverse Mexican and Mexican American communities of the United States that for so long had been misunderstood and ignored by Mexican nationals can become for progressive critics a model for cultural adaptation, for the reconsideration of values where the worthiest ideals, customs, attitudes, and institutions may prevail. "The Chicano experience," Monsiváis asserts, "is . . . an important factor in the reconstitution of Mexican nationalism—which persists despite everything, even if its expression is at times mythological. This new Mexican nationalism will be bilingual. It will incorporate what is useful of the immigrant experience and retain what is most precious of the old ways and customs" (Monsiváis 1995, 41).[5]

The "Bienvenida al Congreso" for the 25th NACCS conference in Mexico City also made note of the factors leading to the acknowledgment of the diverse Mexican communities on the northern side of the border, communities whose combined population now amounts to one-sixth of all Mexicans:

> [E]n los últimos años, los chicanos han venido incrementando su atención e intereses en nuestro país, no sólo por las profundas raíces biológicas y culturales que los vinculan a este territorio, sino por la integración económica cada vez mayor que se ha ido dando de manera acelerada entre ambas naciones, en el contexto de la regionalización y la globalización. Del lado mexicano también se ha incrementado el interés por la cuestion chicana (en parte por la problemática migratoria), no sólo en lo académico sino en los ámbitos político, económico y cultural. (*Programa* 1998, 1)

> In recent years, Chicanos have increased their attention and interests in our country, not only because of the profound biological and cultural roots that link them to this territory, but also because of the greater and greater economic integration that has occurred in an accelerated manner in both nations, in the context of regionalization and globalization. From the Mexican side too, interest in Chicano issues has increased (in part due to the migration problematic), not only in academic but also in political, economic, and cultural spheres.

The stories that I have selected from Sandra Cisneros's 1991 *Woman Hollering Creek and Other Stories* give evidence to a burgeoning binationalism, a porous border where there exists an infusion of labor and values across cultures.[6] What Américo Paredes nearly a half century ago had termed Greater Mexico, Mexico in a cultural sense, has now forged toward to the forefront on both sides of the border.

II

"I felt I was Mexican"

Cisneros's *The House on Mango Street*, first published in 1983, is one of the better-known books in Chicana and Chicano literature and is studied widely in secondary schools and across a variety of departments in the university curriculum. *The House on Mango Street*, conceived originally as a personal writing assignment at the Iowa Writers Workshop, is the product of an emerging American writer showing the U.S. intellectual community her knowledge of European and American literary traditions.[7] Through her young character Esperanza Cordero, Cisneros pursues parallels with the founding male epics of the Western tradition, the New Testament and *The Odyssey*. There are allusions to English-language modernist writers, James Joyce's motif of the epiphany and Virginia Woolf's feminist manifesto, *A Room of One's Own*. There are numerous explicit references to the English version of Grimm's *Fairy Tales*. Though *The House on Mango Street* is, according to Cisneros, the story of a young, poor "American-Mexican" girl growing up in Chicago, it is a transatlantic book (Cisneros 1983, xv).

In a 1982 autobiographical statement for Wolfgang Binder's *Partial Autobiographies: Interviews with Twenty Chicano Poets*, Cisneros confessed that when she began formal training as a writer at Chicago's Loyola University in the midseventies, she did not know she was a Chicana writer, and if someone had labeled her as such, she would have denied it (Cisneros 1985b, 59). Furthermore, she did not know of any Chicano writers in Chicago, nor was she aware of the Chicano Movement in the Southwest. "I felt I was Mexican," Cisneros explains, "and in some ways Puerto Rican because of the neighborhood I grew up in, and I especially felt American because all the literature I had read my whole life was mainstream" (ibid.). However, toward the end of the seventies after her two-year stint at the Iowa Writers Workshop, Cisneros joined the Chicago-based Movimiento Artístico Chicano and worked three years in a progressive Latino Youth Alternative High School as teacher and counselor. "I suppose working with this progressive staff," Cisneros writes, "shaped my political ideology and gave me a sense of direction and roots" (68). The students at the high school, whose lives later found their way into the poems of her first published collection, *Bad Boys* (1980), and stories in *The House on Mango Street*, heightened her sense of identification and social concern. In the Binder autobiographical sketch, Cisneros makes no mention of a feminist consciousness, although she offers: "I do not give readings/workshops for free, unless it is for the Latino or black community, a not-for-profit agency, *a women's cause*, or some political group I believe in" (70; emphasis mine).

In 1984, after the publication of *The House on Mango Street* and with an emerging profile as a Chicana writer, Cisneros embarked on a new direction personally and creatively. She left her birthplace, Chicago, and traveled to San Antonio, Texas, first working as the literature director for the Guadalupe Cultural Arts Center in San Antonio, then as a guest lecturer in creative writing at Texas Lutheran College in Seguin. From 1985 to 1986, she held a Dobie-Paisano Fellowship from the Texas Institute of Letters. A year of uninterrupted writing at J. Frank Dobie's Paisano Ranch produced the first stories that were to become *Woman Hollering Creek*.[8] During this period, Cisneros established a working relationship as an associate editor with Norma Alarcón's feminist *Third Woman* journal and press of the same name. As Cisneros traveled around the country giving lectures and readings, she referred writers to Alarcón and invited Latinas to contribute to *Third Woman*. In 1987, Alarcón's Third Woman Press published Cisneros's book of poetry, *My Wicked Wicked Ways*, the manuscript that she had presented in 1978 for her M.F.A. at the Iowa Writers Workshop.

Early in her stay in Texas, Cisneros produced two notable works of criticism that should be read as her own feminist manifestos. In a 2000 interview with Bridget Kevane and Juanita Heredia, Cisneros credits Norma Alarcón with first making her aware of her feminist consciousness. In a visit to Cisneros's apartment, Alarcón is amazed not to find children's toys or a man's things. Cisneros reconstructs the scene:

> [W]hen she [Alarcón] came to Chicago, she stayed with me at my apartment. I remember the day she arrived. She looked around and did not see any children's toys or a man's things and asked, "You live here by yourself?" I said, "Yeah," matter-of-factly. Then she asked, "How did you do it?" When she said that, that is when my feminism began, right there, because I felt like crying. Because I did not realize how hard it had been to arrive at that apartment of my own and no one had understood how hard it was for me until Norma asked, "How did you do it?" (Cisneros 2000a, 50)

"My Wicked Wicked Ways: The Chicana Writer's Struggle With Good and Evil, or Las Hijas de la Malavida," presented in Chicago at the Modern Language Association convention in December 1985, is the first expression of a young woman's private thoughts and feelings of a hard-fought independence.[9] In this still-unpublished essay, bearing the date and location "12/1985, Paisano Ranch, Austin, TX," Cisneros assumes the first person and breaks with her timid past to speak about her culture, family, and writing as a much more focused public intellectual, as a Chicana feminist:

> Looking back, that tumultuous summer [1975] I had marched off to college, and, with relief, left my father's house, that frying pan, only to leap into the fire of an all-Anglo writers workshop. The move forced me to have to deal with my "otherness" for the first time—my race and class difference, and to develop, at long last, a feminist consciousness. (2–3)

In her essay, Cisneros writes of finding the source for her obsession with sin and guilt, good and evil in her two cultures. As her father said, she had turned out bad, *"echada a perder"* (3). In being the first child, the only female in the family, to leave her father's house unmarried, she had turned out "un-Mexicanized, gringo-ized, deflowered, ruined" (ibid.). In coming to terms with her Mexican past and her present feminist consciousness, Cisneros shifts between her own and other Chicanas' critical and creative discourses, all marshaled against the "goody-two-shoes solution of family and church," a rebellion, invoking Cherríe Moraga's "A Long Line of Vendidas," which is "interpreted as a betrayal, a Malinchenization, a deviation from our heritage" (ibid.). Against her Mexican culture's strict adherence to a feminine code of behavior, Cisneros continues to describe herself in print as nobody's mother and nobody's wife.[10] In addition to Moraga's *Loving in the War Years* (1983), Cisneros strengthens her argument by citing Norma Alarcón's essay "What Kind of Lover Have You Made Me, Mother?" (1983) and poems from Alma Villanueva's *Blood Root* (1977), Lorna Dee Cervantes's *Emplumada* (1981), Ana Castillo's *Women Are Not Roses* (1984), and Naomi Quiñones's *Sueño de Colibrí* (1985). "My Wicked Wicked Ways" is a personal statement as well as an indication of Cisneros's growing awareness of a Chicana intellectual community.

The following year, in Alarcón's *Third Woman* journal, Cisneros published a critique of Texas feminism titled "Cactus Flowers: In Search of Tejana Feminist Poetry."[11] Cisneros begins her essay by acknowledging her move to Texas "two years ago" (Cisneros 1986, 73). What stands out in the article is Cisneros's openness to speaking out against the perceived feminism of Texas writers: "As an outsider I can't pretend to like, understand, or empathize with all of the work of my *compañeras*. Several enjoy a local popularity that frankly baffles me. But precisely because I'm not

Texan, nor anybody's *comadre*, I feel a certain privileged liberty to have my say" (ibid.). Cisneros offers a survey of selected Texas writers who are either promoted by Chicano book publishers as feminists or who define themselves as feminists, among them Angela de Hoyos, Pat Mora, Rosemary Catacalos, Teresa Palomo Acosta, Evangelina Vigil, Mary Sue Galindo, Maria Limon, and Rebecca Gonzales. Cisneros notes the variety of themes and styles, from Tex-Mex bilingual oral to the writerly text, but is brutally honest about the timidity of some of the more-established Texas writers. Staking out her political and literary territory, Cisneros ends with the most forceful statement to that date:

> To admit you are a writer takes a great deal of audacity. To admit you are a feminist takes even greater courage. It is admirable then when Chicana writers elect to redefine and reinvent themselves through their writings. One should be wary of those, however, who purportedly speak for the oppressed while remaining part of a system of sociosexual oppression. Tokens are selected because they are saying what the patriarchy wants to hear, and I believe that what the Tejana writer has to say, needs to say, is much too urgent to seek the approval of oppressors. (79)

Cisneros has taken a stand against the patriarchal politics of the Chicano Movement of the sixties and seventies in favor of radical feminism. The new kid on the block has stated her case— "make room, a new voice has entered the critical conversation on gender."

Woman Hollering Creek developed out of Cisneros's experiences in Texas, her engagement with an emerging Chicana feminism, and her exploration of Mexican culture.[12] The stories of *Woman Hollering Creek* are embedded in the popular cultural traditions—stories, beliefs, music—of Greater Mexico/América Mexicana on both sides of the border. In *The House on Mango Street*, Cisneros, through her young protagonist Esperanza, addressed the plight of urban Mexican and Latina women before the feminist movement. The women on Mango Street live in a Chicago of the late sixties. In *Woman Hollering Creek*, Cisneros confronts the problems faced by Mexicanas and Mexican American women in both urban and rural social environments in the wake of the Chicano and feminist movements. As in *The House on Mango Street*, Cisneros strikes a balance between the individual and the collective. The three sections of *Woman Hollering Creek* can be read as the collective story of Mexican women from childhood to maturity. Cisneros takes the reader from issues of early identity formation to decisions regarding adult relationships. Cisneros asks for the first time in Chicana and Chicano literature, and in a variety of ways, how do women and men relate to each other as lovers after feminism and the Chicana Movement?

And to express her new thematics and locale, Cisneros abandons the sustained poetic childlike quality of her language in *The House on Mango Street* for a more differentiated and situated style. Cisneros does not write in Spanish, but her language, with bilingual patterns, is more attuned to the expressions and nuances of Mexicans on both sides of the border.[13] Indeed, Cisneros's linguistic binationalism in *Woman Hollering Creek* is apparent from the opening dedication to her Mexican American mama, who gave her the "fierce language," and her Mexican papá, who gave her "*el lenguaje de la ternura.*" Elvira Cordero Anguiano bequeathed to her daughter the voice of an urban immigrant child, working-class, anti-Catholic, free thinking, and smart-mouthed. Cisneros acknowledges that she has created very anti-stereotypical Latina characters because of her mother's point of view. Her father, Alfredo Cisneros Del Moral, on the other hand, has given Cisneros the lyrical voice in her writing, sweet, tender, and spiritual (Cisneros 2000a, 55). Cisneros will shuttle back and forth between styles, languages, and cultures.

To set the tone for each of the sections of the book, Cisneros chooses as epigraphs lyrics taken from popular Mexican songs that one would hear on the radio. In the first section, "My Lucy Friend Who Smells Like Corn," Cisneros recalls childhood love and happiness through the lyrics "*También yo te quiero / y te quiero feliz,*" by Francisco Gabilondo Soler, widely known to children on Mexican radio as Cri Crí, El Grillito Cantor, "The Little Singing Cricket."[14] The second section, "One Holy Night," addressing themes of adolescence, begins with the widely popular bolero "Piel Canela," written by Puerto Rican Boby Capó, here interpreted by the sultry siren of the fifties María Victoria. "*Me importas tú y tú y tú/y nadie más que tú.*" "I love you, and you, and you, and no one else but you." The last section on adult love relationships, "There Was a Man, There Was a Woman," opens with the ranchera singer Lola Beltrán's rendition of Tomás Méndez Sosa's "Puñalada Trapera," "*Me estoy muriendo/y tú como si nada.*" Unbearable pain in the face of indifference. The book ends like a mariachi son with a formulaic, ¡tan *TÁN!*

Woman Hollering Creek is therefore in many ways a bold move for a Midwest writer: claiming the border area for her writing, updating the Texas literary tradition, and exploring the doubleness of Mexican

American culture. Though Cisneros was born in Chicago, Mexico is not foreign to her. During her childhood, like other Mexican American families, her family shuttled back and forth between Mexico and the United States. Like the Southwest, the Midwest has had a history of Mexican migration beginning early in the twentieth century. Her family follows a classic pattern of immigration. After the Mexican Revolution, Cisneros's maternal grandfather worked his way through the Midwest on the railroads and after settling in Chicago, sent for her grandmother and family in Guanajuato. Cisneros's Chicago neighborhood was a Mexican neighborhood and her family always identified as Mexican. Perhaps it is a matter of distance, explains Cisneros: "We in Chicago were physically farther, but emotionally closer to Mexico. We had relatives in the interior. We had ties to Mexico in a way we did not have ties to Illinois" (Cisneros 1992, 295). Her decision to relocate to San Antonio grew out of a personal and creative need to live Mexican culture and language on a daily basis: "I made a conscious choice to move to Texas a few years ago precisely because I realized, 'My God! This is what I grew up with in my house, and I hear it everywhere, and I need to live here because this is where I'm going to get the ideas for the things I need to write about.' To me, it's exciting to be living in San Antonio, because it's the closest I can get to living in Mexico and still get paid. To me, San Antonio is where Latin America begins, and I love it" (ibid., 288).

I have chosen stories in which Cisneros crisscrosses the border in a personal and creative way in a critical confrontation with a utopian, folkloric, or legendary Mexican culture to which working-class Mexican Americans have returned over and over again.[15] The sacred space of Tepeyac, Mexico City, the village of Anenecuilco de Zapata in the state of Morelos, the town of Monclova in the northern state of Coahuila, Chicago, the Texas cities of San Antonio, Austin, and Seguin are the physical landscapes to which Cisneros will bring classic and familiar tales and figures for scrutiny—Tonantzín, la Virgen de Guadalupe, Emiliano Zapata and the Mexican Revolution, the legend of La Llorona, the heroines of telenovelas, the sordid tales of ¡Alarma! magazines, and Mexican calendars with their bold, colorful images, the annual renewal of a still-unconquered Aztec world. Cisneros's Mexican origins are clearly evident in her stories not only in detail and nuance but also in the respect with which she treats her characters from both sides of the border.

III

For the first section of *Woman Hollering Creek*, Cisneros draws on her childhood memories of La Capital, not Washington D.C., but Mexico City. Cisneros's family moved back and forth between Mexico and the United States, settling permanently in Chicago when she was eleven years old. The Cisneros family would travel to Mexico City to the section of Tepeyac, near the Basílica to the Virgen de Guadalupe, and stay with the paternal grandparents at La Fortuna number 12. Cisneros explores the child's point of view, revealing a little girl's identity formation in relation to a Spanish-language world. While the young child, later the adult woman, clings to favored elements of Mexican culture, the child is at times linguistically and culturally misunderstood by individuals from her two molding cultures.

"We're Mericans, We're Mericans"

In "Mexican Movies," Cisneros chooses the golden age of Mexican cinema to represent the golden age of childhood. The story is titled "Mexican Movies," but Cisneros turns the camera on the audience: the Mexican family—father, mother, and children. Mexican films serve as a pretext to examine attitudes toward children in Mexican culture. "Niños menores de cinco años entran gratis" is a phrase that may be added to an announcement for a family-oriented event in Mexico and the United States. Cisneros examines through her story the way children are included within the family and how gender roles are assigned in Mexican culture.

The setting is a movie theater on a Saturday night, a theater that most assuredly could be in Mexico because of the tortas and churros sold in the theater. But the theater exists in the United States in a Mexican neighborhood where Mexicans come to see Mexican films. The story, told through a child's wandering point of view in first person, focuses on the rural musical charro genre that gave birth to Mexico's national cinema and a sentimental view of the nation's origins with the 1936 *Allá en el rancho grande* starring actor-singer Tito Guízar. Two great male idols of the forties and fifties, Pedro Armendáriz and Pedro Infante, are recalled. First mentioned is Pedro Armendáriz, most probably in his starring role in Luis Buñuel's 1952 *El bruto*, where, according to the limited but revealing understanding of the narrator, the male lead who "undresses the lady" is also "just plain dumb." The young narrator prefers the happy-ending films of Pedro Infante. For the child, Infante films with the charro—the gay Mexican on horseback singing to ladies on a balcony—are preferable to the more sexual and violent Pedro Armendáriz film in which he is in love with a bad woman, the boss's wife.

To prevent his children from viewing a sex scene, Papa gives the narrator and her younger brother, Kiki, quarters and sends them to the lobby. The children are thus allowed the freedom to be by themselves, create their own fantasies, and play in the lobby. Other children climb onto the stage, others play in the aisles, sooner or later a baby cries. Because of culture and class, children accompany the parents on Saturday night to the theater, even though the films may not be suitable for children. The parents may ignore them: "Papa doesn't move when he's watching a movie and Mama sits with her legs up because she is afraid of rats" (Cisneros 1991, 13). So it is the narrator, who is older, who must see after her little brother, Kiki. The only mention of the narrator's age and sex is that she can read NUTRITIOUS and DELICIOUS on a popcorn box and is able to enter the ladies' bathroom and with a quarter get from the machine a "pink lipstick the color of sugar roses on birthday cakes" (12). For the narrator, freedom to play and enjoy being a child also means responsibility for the younger sibling.

Sooner or later, the children fall asleep, and that is when they are assured of their parents' affection. The parents go out on Saturday night to entertain themselves but also take their children. The best part, the little girl narrates, is the ending, like in the happy and sentimental movies, when the parents pick up the children in their arms and take them home. They are awake but pretend to be asleep. The story reveals a certain sense of understanding and bonding, the parents in their world, the children in theirs, but still a family assured with safety and security. "So when we wake up," says the narrator at the end of the story, "it's Sunday already, and we're in our beds and happy" (13).

In "Mericans," with its linguistically ambiguous title, Cisneros crosses the border to Mexico City and takes up the issues of transnational and gender identity through three Mexican American children. Micaela, Alfredito, and Enrique, who are also Michelle, Junior, and Keeks, must deal with their dual worlds as they wait outside the national shrine of pilgrimage to La Virgen de Guadalupe. Inside the church the awful Spanish-speaking grandmother, as Mexican cultural duty dictates, prays for her family and the three grandchildren. The children cannot go and have fun like other Mexican children in the plaza. There are clear boundaries for behavior; they must wait in the sun by the church entrance until the grandmother returns.

The narrator Michelle/Micaela notices the penitents coming to the Virgin walking on their knees. But that is not important for her. She is not taken by the solemnity and ritual so meaningful to faithful Mexicans. She has her own physical and cultural suffering with which to contend. First, she is waiting outside in the sun with her two brothers. Second and more important, she is undergoing her own rite of passage whereby gender differences are displayed publicly. Because Michelle is a girl, the brothers refuse to play with her: "'*Girl*. We can't play with a *girl*.' *Girl*. It's my brothers' favorite insult now instead of 'sissy'" (18). However, she doesn't allow herself to cry because crying is what *girls* do.

Micaela enters the church to look for the grandmother. The church is a cultural space foreign to Micaela: "Why do churches smell like the inside of an ear? Like incense and the dark and candles in blue glass? And why does holy water smell of tears? The awful grandmother makes me kneel and fold my hands" (19). Micaela is Mexican and understands Spanish when she pays careful attention but she does not conform to proper Mexican behavior. Micaela refuses to sit quietly, then is sent out by the grandmother just in time to see two compatriots, a man in shorts and a woman in pants, U.S. tourists who stand out among the crowd. In exchange for chiclets, the woman asks Junior in incorrect Spanish for ¿*un foto, por favor?* The foreigners are going to take back a stereotypical remembrance of Mexico, of a Mexican child, Junior, squatting against the wall of the church with his eyes shut, who throughout the afternoon ordeal is merely obeying orders and trying to stay out of the sun.

For the Mexican grandmother, the children are not wholly Mexican and are treated with condescension; they were "born in that barbaric country with its barbarian ways" (19). On the other hand, the lady tourist takes these barbarians for her own culturally biased view of Mexican children. They are, after all, physically indistinct from the other Mexican children in the plaza. The children, however, are Mexicans but also Americans. "But you speak English!" exclaims the lady in disbelief. They are a fusion of both cultures and are able to pass between cultural borders. The children speak Spanish and English and enjoy not the religious practices but the popular cultures of both countries, the Lone Ranger, Flash Gordon, La Familia Burrón comics, the flying feather dancers.

When Micaela is banished from the church, she responds to her grandmother's Spanish with an improper and impolite "What?" The grandmother interprets with a quizzical ¿*Güat?* The *güat* and *un foto* stand as signs of cultural and linguistic misunderstanding. Who recognizes and accepts the fusion of both cultures? Repeating Junior's response to the lady tourist, Michelle/Micaela affirms at the end of the story in a linguistically improper but culturally accurate English her dual identities: "We're Mericans, we're Mericans, and inside the awful grandmother prays" (20).

In the ending story of the first section, "Tepeyac," the narrator gathers thoughts from early childhood to adulthood. The story is offered in a stream-of-consciousness technique with only commas within paragraphs to capture continuous segments of thought as they occur in the narrator's mind.

The story is set at nightfall, at the end of the business day, again at the important Mexican site, the shrine of Our Lady of Guadalupe, which the narrator refers to as La Basílica de Nuestra Señora, as is the custom in Mexico. Tepeyac, according to legend, is the hill on which the Virgen de Guadalupe appeared to the Indian Juan Diego in 1531. The anonymous narrator in the first person makes reference to the public gathering of street vendors selling religious articles, balloons, food, and shoeshine and to the importance of the site of pilgrimage, so important that pilgrims will take back with them a Recuerdo de Tepeyac, a photo with a false canvas backdrop of the site. As the story unfolds, the reader realizes that the narrator has taken back to the United States her own recuerdo de Tepeyac and twenty-seven years later returns as a pilgrim to recall not the shrine but the day-to-day activities that were so much more meaningful.

The narrator recalls, with a precise eye for detail and exactness, going to bring the grandfather home from his work at the Tlalpería—the hardware store at the corner of Misterios and Cinco de Mayo. At the end of the day, when all leave the public square, the child is sent by the abuela to bring Abuelito home. The child will hold Abuelito's hand, shaped like a valentine, and recall step by step, the return trip, businesses and residences with their inhabitants, eventually counting the stairs up to the house on La Fortuna number 12. Grandfather and child will eat dinner together and eventually fall asleep through the sound of the television. The grandchild's accurate recall of detail is symbolic of the unspoken love for the grandfather. As the two count together the stairs, readers realize that the story is told from the point of the adult, counting uno, dos, tres, ending at veintisiete—not the steps but now the years. The adult returns at twenty-seven, not to climb the hill of Tepeyac like other pilgrims, but to visit the now changed, smaller and darker, childhood neighborhood. The narrator, like the changed neighborhood and the Basílica that is old and crumbling, has been transformed by time and circumstance but still remembers Tepeyac.[16]

When the grandfather died, he took with him "to [his] stone bed something irretrievable, without a name" (23). "Who would've guessed," thinks the narrator, "it is me who will remember when everything else is forgotten" (ibid.). The child who left for the "borrowed country," "the one he will not remember, the one he is least familiar with," is now the adult grandchild for whom La Fortuna number 12 and its environs are the special places of childhood memory, of home and belonging. "When I visit Mexico [City]," confesses the writer Cisneros in the interview with Kevane and Heredia, "I always go to the Basilica of the Virgen de Guadalupe. I go past the house that was my grandparents'. I always have a picture taken of myself in front of the recuerdo de Tepeyac backdrops" (Cisneros 2000a, 55).

In these three brief stories, unlike later stories offered to the reader with divisions, Cisneros traces the movements of the female child from her smallness in a wide world to an adult whose perspective has been changed by her worlds. Mexican Americans have long been treated with condescension by Mexican nationals as pochos, inauthentic, Anglicized Mexicans. Indeed, Mexican American experience during Cisneros's childhood was characterized as rootless in the 1956 Robles Arenas's play and film *Los desarraigados*.[17] Here in *Woman Hollering Creek* Cisneros dispels this Mexican view by giving expression to the diversity of Mexican and Mexican American culture. Others like Cisneros who have traveled back and forth across the border will find themselves in her fiction, in her physical and emotional proximity to Mexico of the fifties. The elders in these interrelated stories, whether in the United States or in Mexico, have transmitted elements of Mexican culture to their children. The Mexican American female child, however, as Cisneros clearly articulates, has already begun a process of linguistic and cultural doubleness; she is accepting her Mexican culture yet affirming her difference: "We're Mericans." While accepting the Pedro Infante happy-ending films, she finds machismo and its attendant sexual violence "just plain dumb." The grandmother's traditional veneration of the Virgen de Guadalupe does not hold the same significance for the child. Indeed, for the unnamed Cisneros of the three stories, relationship and bonding are revered, not tears, religion, and prayer.

"When I was a little girl," writes Cisneros, "we traveled to Mexico City so much I thought my grandparents' house on La Fortuna, number 12, was home. It was the only constant in our nomadic ramblings from one Chicago flat to another. The house on Destiny Street, number 12, in the colonia Tepeyac would be perhaps the only home I knew, and the nostalgia for a home would be a theme that would obsess me" (Cisneros 1987b, 18). With this early sense of home and belonging as a point of departure, Cisneros will more forcefully and acutely examine the condition of a variety of Mexican women on both sides of the border.[18]

IV

In the stories that I have chosen from the final section, "There Was a Man, There Was a Woman," Cisneros, through a variety of Mexican literary and popular genres, develops a variety of linguistic registers, voices, to tell stories of women's adult desires, of love gained and love lost. The canción ranchera epigraph, *"Me estoy muriendo/y tú como si nada,"* by Lola Beltrán, expresses Mexican women's condition in the face of an unyielding patriarchy. However, these stories, except for one, situated historically between 1985 and 1990, bear the influence of Cisneros's emergence as a Chicana feminist. Hurtful love, which can be both physical and mental, is not the ending tragedy for a woman. A naive mexicana immigrant, an Indian woman born in the nineteenth century, a Texas university student, an artist who has lost her cultural moorings, all find their own identity independent of the male.

Un hecho de la vida real

Although published in 1991, "Woman Hollering Creek" dates in manuscript form from spring 1988.[19] According to Sonia Saldívar-Hull, this story emerged out of Cisneros's commitment to popular feminism. "Surrounded by Chicana community activists, writers and artists," writes Saldívar-Hull, "Cisneros identified with a group of Chicana 'popular feminists' who struggled to change the literary scene as well as the lives of less privileged women around them" (Saldívar-Hull 2000, 105). In an informal interview with Saldívar-Hull, "Cisneros told how these [popular feminists] indeed became 'mujeres de fuerza' as they, in fact, ran an underground railroad for women, both Chicanas and recent Mexican immigrants, victimized by their men and by the economic collusion between the United States and Mexico on both sides of the border" (ibid., 106).[20]

The story of Cleófilas in "Woman Hollering Creek" is drawn from these south Texas real case histories of battered Mexican immigrant women.[21] Into this story of physical and emotional victimization, Cisneros will weave stories from popular culture, from the mass media—television and fotonovelas—together with traditional folk and religious beliefs. "Woman Hollering Creek" is similar in narrative strategy to *The House on Mango Street*, where from a feminist perspective, Grimm's fairy tales were subverted to show the repressive nature of fictitious stories of love too imaginative and too idealized to hold up against the harsh realities of imprisonment, abuse, and poverty. In Cisneros's first book of fiction and in "Woman Hollering Creek," women's characterization is based on the dual allied sexual ideologies of romance and domesticity that socialize women to accept their roles in the economy of the household. Here Cisneros tells a Mexican telenovela, or soap opera story, with the formulaic happy ending but now recontextualized within a feminist perspective.

In "Woman Hollering Creek," we have the familiar story of a Mexican woman, Cleófilas, who waits in her father's house for her future husband, Juan Pedro, who has returned to Monclova, Coahuila, to take her to Seguin in south Texas. As traditional culture dictates, a woman must wait in her father's house to be taken away to the house of her husband, who will then be in the position of the father. It is important to emphasize that Mexican patriarchy is a cultural norm that has been reinforced by law. Unlike the legal code in the United States that is based on English Common Law, the legal code in Latin American countries descends from Roman Law through the Spanish colonial empire. According to the law of patria potestad, the father and husband as father are the legal authorities within the household. Poor, hardworking Cleófilas, Cisneros argues in fairy tale fashion, lives in a world of men—a father and six "good-for-nothing" brothers—without a mother. It is the father Don Serafín who will give Juan Pedro "permission to take Cleófilas . . . across her father's threshold, over several miles of dirt road and several miles of paved, over one border and beyond to a town en *el otro lado*—on the other side" (Cisneros 1991, 43).

To draw parallels between Mexican culture on both sides of the border, Cisneros situates her story in cities almost equidistant from the border. Seguin is on a lonely stretch of Interstate 10 west of San Antonio.

From Eagle Pass and Piedras Negras, on the border, Mexican Highway 57 goes down to Monclova. Both places are, in a sense, like Cleófilas herself in the middle of nowhere. Both cities are described as places of "dust and despair."

In her small town of Monclova, Cleófilas internalizes the models of femininity offered to her by the mass media, books, songs, and telenovelas—stories about passion and love, good and evil. What one finds, especially in Mexican telenovelas, are models of romance inherited from Latin American nineteenth-century romanticism and melodrama in which the central character is a woman. Very seldom in a telenovela will the central character be a man. In 1958, viewers enjoyed the very popular Mexican *Gutierritos* with Rafael Banquells in the starring role. Since then, Mexican telenovelas have been almost the exclusive domain of the female actress-singer. Probably the most well-known novel of nineteenth-century Spanish American Romanticism is the melodramatic *María* (1867) by the Columbian Jorge Isaacs. The title is highly symbolic of the Marian cult of the chaste, demure, suffering, passive woman who gives all for love. Recent telenovelas that recall their nineteenth-century namesake include *Simplemente María* (1969), *María de Nadie* (1985), *María Mercedes* (1992), *Marimar* (1994), *María la del Barrio* (1997), and *María Isabel* (1997), although catchy names like *Cristal*, *Esmeralda*, and *Yesenia* will do. Telenovelas, however, are also slick, modern entertainment, a formulaic genre delivered nightly to viewers wrapped with a romantic ballad. The genre was established by Mexico's media giant Televisa in the fifties and is now distributed by the Univisión chain in the United States.[22] Telenovelas are consumed in Mexico and the United States, mostly by working-class people, both men and women, although the genre's marketing strategies, as Cisneros argues in her story, are aimed at working-class women. But as my mother says, "¿Qué más hay?" "What else is there?" In the Los Angeles area, telenovelas, three of them, occupy nightly Spanish language broadcast time from 7:00 P.M. through 10:00 P.M. on Univisión affiliate KMEX and the U.S. rival, Telemundo KVEA, which offers telenovelas from Argentina, Brazil, Colombia, and Venezuela that have a different format.[23]

The telenovela that Cleófilas enjoys is the 1985 *Tú o Nadie, You or No One*, with Mexican singer-actress Lucía Méndez in the starring role. Like other soaps, *Tú o Nadie* teaches that women must put up with all kinds of hardships of the heart, separation and betrayal, and loving, always loving no matter what, tú o nadie, to suffer for love is good. "The women's narrative," writes Frances L. Restuccia of this story, "conveyed by the telenovela naturalizes the sweetness of pain; Cisneros writes to denaturalize the oxymoron" (Restuccia 1996, 56). While Cisneros refers to one particular well-known telenovela and its star, all telenovelas repeat the same plot. The good woman's sacrifice for the family will be rewarded usually by a change in station in life. The poor, good girl after many trials will eventually marry well or inherit wealth. In *Tú o Nadie*, Lucía Méndez is made to look modern and beautiful: "[O]n the Bayer Aspirin commercials—wasn't she lovely? Does she dye her hair, do you think?" (Cisneros 1991, 44). Méndez with her light hair, eyes, and skin, like other female soap stars who do not resemble a largely mestizo nation, has been hugely popular with working-class Mexicans. But in her telenovela role Méndez is a very traditional woman. However, for Cleófilas, Méndez is an attractive role model; she is a better alternative to her life in Monclova, with her father and her brothers. Cleófilas's solution to her fate in *"Monclova, Coahuila. Ugly"* comes in the form of Juan Pedro, whom she believes will fulfill her telenovela dreams of a better life in the more advanced "El Norte," in *"Seguín, Tejas"* with its "nice sterling ring to it. The tinkle of money" (45).

In Texas, Cleófilas finds herself in the role of the traditional Mexican woman imprisoned within her house, in a Mexican American neighborhood, withstanding the physical abuse and the loneliness and estrangement from her home in Coahuila. Nothing has changed on the other side of the border; she is much like the two elderly women who flank her. Soledad, who calls herself a widow, but was actually abandoned by her husband. Dolores—whose house smells too much of incense and candles—lives grieving for the loss of her sons, killed in war, and her husband who died of grief over the sons. These women are both passive, suffering martyrs, Our Lady of Solitude and Our Lady of Sorrows, images of the Mater Dolorosa, Mary who gave her all for family and son.

These two women, along with Cleófilas, live near Woman Hollering Creek. It once had a Spanish name but is also known now in bilingual Texas as La Gritona. The creek and the suffering women who inhabit the area are references to the Mexican oral tradition. "Is it La Llorona, the weeping woman? La Llorona, who drowned her children. Perhaps La Llorona is the one they named the creek after," wonders Cleófilas, "remembering all the stories she learned as a child" (51). Many children, like Cleófilas as a child, have heard the widespread Mesoamerican legend of La Llorona: the weeping woman, who after killing her children, haunts bodies of water, lamenting her fate of not fulfilling the role of the good mother.[24] Here, Cisneros changes the folk legend of La Llorona. "Lady Soledad" and "señora Dolores" are two Lloronas, weeping for their lost men.

With these women, Cisneros is collapsing the tradition of the sacrificial mother, the suffering mother, the Mexican mujer sufrida, with the folk legend of La Llorona, pointing out the sad fate of these women: "The neighbor ladies, Soledad, Dolores, they might've known once the name of the *arroyo* before it turned English but they did not know now. They were too busy remembering the men who had left through either choice or circumstance and would never come back" (47).

Cleófilas, through her telenovelas, had wanted passion, romantic passion, but what she received instead were crimes of passion. Her life in Seguin has turned into the stories of the *¡Alarma!* magazines that she disliked. These magazines, *¡Casos de Alarma!* or *Valle de Lágrimas*, are scandalous fotonovelas that depict violence and depraved sexuality. These magazines tell of stories that would happen to other women and so are read vicariously. Cleófilas's life has become a *¡Caso de Alarma!*[25] She is the protagonist in a story of a naive, rural young woman who after several years in Texas has become the suffering mother. Her husband beats her black and blue; she is on her second child while he has another woman. Readers do not know much of Juan Pedro because Cleófilas herself is unaware of much of his life outside the home; besides, she does not go out unless it is with her husband. What readers are witnesses to are scenes of domestic violence. Cleófilas is the silent, passive recipient of her husband's frustration and alcoholism, though she must comfort him, "his tears of repentance and shame, this time and each" (48).

The narrative sequence offered in third person in "Woman Hollering Creek" is interrupted by a dialogue, actually a first-person telephone conversation between two women. So here, for the first time, Cleófilas, who has been within the world of men—her father and brothers, her husband and his friends—and the world of traditional women—telenovelas and fotonovelas—now is involved with an alternative world of women. This telenovela turned caso de alarma story will not end with death, as Cleófilas fears. Cleófilas frees herself from Juan Pedro with the assistance of two Mexican American activists: Graciela, who works in a medical clinic and, as her name indicates, is ironically not divine but human intervention, and Felice, who gives the story its favorable resolution for Cleófilas. Through these women, readers become aware of the brutality to which Cleófilas has been subjected. Graciela to Felice: "I was going to do this sonogram on her—she's pregnant, right?—and she just starts crying on me. *Híjole*, Felice! This poor lady's got black and blue marks all over. I'm not kidding. From her husband. Who else? Another one of those brides from across the border" (54).

Pain or rage, Cleófilas had wondered when she first crossed the arroyo as a newlywed with Juan Pedro. Now Cleófilas is once again crossing Woman Hollering Creek, riding with Felice in a pickup truck to San Antonio so that she may make her way back to Mexico. At the end of her story, Cisneros has placed side by side two opposite models of womanhood. With these two women, Cisneros is invoking the widely held Manichaean view of women in Mexican masculinist literature as la buena and la mala. In 1950, in his *El laberinto de la soledad*, Octavio Paz distinguished two conceptions of woman in Mexican culture. La buena is the ideal companion of the male, she is passive, the repository of values as virgin and mother (Paz 1959, 32). For Mexican men, la mala is hard, unmerciful, independent like the macho (ibid., 35). Death may be the price la mala must pay for behaving like a man. Whether in elite literature, popular fiction, historietas (comics), fotonovelas, or telenovelas, these dual images of women have been continually reproduced. The Mexican American feminist Cisneros has taken a critical posture against Mexican literatures of feminine oppression by writing a story based on an eighties telenovela whose central theme, like the rest of its genre, educates Mexican women to be beautiful, find love, get married, and have children.[26] In a counterstory to *Tú o Nadie*, the medical assistant Graciela and Felice are Mexican American women who have joined in solidarity to help the abused housewife Cleófilas free herself from Juan Pedro and possibly death. For Cleófilas, stories in the newspapers seemed to confirm tales told by Juan Pedro and his friends: "This woman found on the side of the interstate. This one pushed from a moving car. This one's cadaver, this one unconscious, this one beaten blue. . . . Always. The same grisly news on the pages of the dailies" (Cisneros 1991, 52).

According to Cisneros's plot, Cleófilas is la buena. She has lived in the shadow of her husband, valuing passion and intimacy over intelligence and self-realization. She has without question loved, obeyed, and served Juan Pedro and provided him with children. Felice should be la mala, the rebellious woman, the equal of the male. Felice, however, is not la mala; she is both the sign for equality and the alternative happy ending, the strong woman of independent means who is going to deliver

Cleófilas to freedom. Cleófilas is amazed at this woman who doesn't have a husband and who drives a man's vehicle, a pickup truck, and yells loud like a man, like a mariachi, when she crosses Woman Hollering Creek. "Did you ever notice," Felice tells Cleófilas in Spanish pocked with English, "how nothing around here is named after a woman? Really. Unless she's the Virgin. I guess you're only famous if you're a virgin" (55). The arroyo, however, is not named after the Virgin. For that reason it "makes you want to holler like Tarzan," laughs Felice to Cleófilas (ibid.). Recrossing that newlywed threshold, Woman Hollering Creek/La Gritona, Cleófilas hears a different reenactment of the Grito de Independencia, the Grito de Dolores, given at the birth of the Mexican patria. The "official" Fiesta del Grito, ¡Viva México! given throughout Mexico and Mexican United States on the evening of 15 September and which had been a rallying cry for the farmworkers and activists in their campaigns for social justice during the first phase of the Chicano Movement, is now uttered by Felice against women's oppression, against the Marian cult of martyrdom.[27]

¡Casos de Alarma! reads the title of the genre, with the subtitle Presenta: Un hecho de la vida real, and the scandalous plot summary "vivía como una reina . . . pero un día amaneció muerta" (see Herner 1979, 242). Following the generic conventions, Cisneros has taken her story from un hecho de la vida real, an event taken from real life, from her own experiences with battered Mexican women in Texas. "Woman Hollering Creek" is the product of Cisneros's social and literary activism; it is the writer's solution to a Mexican problem that crosses borders. Cleófilas, like other Mexican women in the United States, will return to patriarchal Mexico; however, she will return with a new understanding of herself as a woman and as a mother.[28] Woman Hollering Creek had served as a place of refuge for Cleófilas to go with her child away from her husband, away from Dolores and Soledad: "La Llorona calling to her. . . . La Llorona. Wonders if something as quiet as this drives a woman to the darkness of the trees" (Cisneros 1991, 51). The creek, which in summer was only a puddle, in springtime was a "good-size alive thing, a thing with a voice all its own, calling in its high, silver voice" (ibid.). Now heeding La Gritona's call, Cleófilas hears Felice laughing again, "but it wasn't Felice laughing. It was gurgling out of her own throat, a long ribbon of laughter, like water" (56). The naive, silent, suffering Cleófilas returns to Mexico with a voice, a storyteller with a new version of La Llorona.[29]

"The Wars Begin Here in Our Hearts and in Our Beds"

Of the Mexican revolutionary leaders that emerged in the first decade of the twentieth century, Emiliano Zapata is the one whose political ideals continued to have currency long after his death. During the sixties Chicano Movement, artists looked to him as a visible reminder of resistance on behalf of campesinos, land, and culture. Many murals as well as posters, *Tierra o Muerte* (1967) by Emanuel Martinez and *Emiliano Zapata* (1969) by Rupert García, featured Zapata prominently (*Chicano Art* 1991, 239–241). A red poster of a photograph of Zapata with his "¡Tierra y Libertad!" was one of the favorites of young Chicanos. And, of course, the struggle for autonomy in the state of Chiapas that shook Mexico's PRI political foundations in the first days of 1994 was inspired by the mestizo leader from the state of Morelos. The Ejército Zapatista de Liberación Nacional has kept the name of Zapata alive into the twenty-first century.

The title "Eyes of Zapata" would make first-time readers think that Cisneros takes as her central protagonist General Emiliano Zapata, the leader of the southern Mexican Revolution. Cisneros does takes this historical figure as well as "the myth, the legend, the god" that was Emiliano Zapata as her protagonist; however, she invents for him a personal life with a fictional lover, Inés Alfaro, who has been rescued from historical oblivion. The character Inés is the traditional Mexican woman, born in the nineteenth century, who is not just la otra but assumes the role of the heroine possessed with a personal as well as a historical vision. Cisneros's story is not the male-centered epic of war but the Mexican woman's epic of love, of constancy and waiting.

The Mexican Revolution has inspired Mexican writers throughout the twentieth century. Indeed, any history of Mexican literature must list the writers and works of the Mexican Revolution, beginning with Mariano Azuela's *Los de abajo* (1915), Martín Luis Guzmán's *El águila y la serpiente* (1928), Nellie Campobello's *Cartucho* (1931), Francisco L. Urquizo's *Tropa vieja* (1931), Gregorio López y Fuentes's *Tierra* (1933), José Revueltas's *El luto humano* (1943), Agustín Yáñez's *Al filo del Agua* (1947), Juan Rulfo's *El llano en llamas* (1953) and *Pedro Páramo* (1955), Carlos Fuentes's *La muerte de Artemio Cruz* (1962), Elena Poniatowska's *Hasta no verte, Jesús mío* (1969), and Laura Esquivel's *Como agua para chocolate* (1989), to name some of the most prominent as well as most recent. The fiction of the Mexican Revolution has not been the exclusive domain of male writers; however, the topics of revolutionary Mexico, the man on horseback, agrarian reform, and political maneuvering have been addressed mostly by men.

Zapata does not always figure as one of the central protagonists in the novels of the Mexican Revolution. His presence in literature is due mainly to his military campaigns in the early years of the Revolution between 1910 and 1915. Martín Luis Guzmán, who championed Pancho Villa over Zapata, referred to him as "el apóstol de la barbarie hecha idea" (Guzmán 1991, 350) ["the apostle of barbarism converted into an ideal"]. In his *Ulises criollo* (1935), José Vasconcelos, a supporter of Francisco I. Madero, with whom Zapata feuded over agrarian reform, deprives Zapata of any great historical importance:

> Zapata, un guerrillero del Sur, campesino sin letras, se rebeló contra el gobierno provisional. . . . Antiguo caballerango de una finca, Zapata contaba con la adhesión de varios centenares de labriegos. Al principio sólo quería garantías para sus soldados, reconocimiento de su grado y sus servicios. Después se rodeó de leguleyos; se convirtió en el instrumento de los despechados y comenzó a crearse el zapatismo. (457)

> Zapata, a warrior from the South, an illiterate farmer, rebelled against the provisional government. . . . A former hacienda horseman, Zapata relied on the support of several hundred farmhands. At first he only wanted guarantees for his soldiers, recognition of his rank and services. Later he surrounded himself with shyster lawyers; he became the instrument of the vengeful and thus began zapatismo.

It is López y Fuentes in his *Tierra* who first gave Zapata heroic grandeur, the fallen leader who, although assassinated, will live on: "En Cuatula fue exhibido el cadáver y en voz baja comenzó la leyenda:—No es el general [Zapata]. . . .—No, compa, el general tenía una seña muy particular cerca del pómulo. . . .—Y éste no la tiene." (López y Fuentes 1933, 168) ["In Cuatula his body was displayed and in whispers the legend began:—This is not the general (Zapata). . . .—No, friend, the general had a very special mark near his cheek. . . .—And this one does not have it."][30] Fighting under the banners of "¡Tierra y Libertad!" and the Virgen de Guadalupe, Zapata and his zapatistas have long outlived all negative literary portrayals and political infighting to become the symbols of the centuries-old struggle for social justice and agrarian reform. In a bold venture, Sandra Cisneros, a writer from Texas, crosses the Chicano topics border into contested

Mexican literary territory to re-create the hero Zapata and *the event* of Mexican history of the twentieth century.

Like other stories and novels of the Mexican genre, Cisneros's "Eyes of Zapata" is a mixture of history and fiction. The historical frame of reference, Cisneros makes clear, is the failed Revolution of 1910 covering the years between 1910 and 1919, the nine years of fighting for Zapata that ended with his death. Cisneros has acknowledged researching the life of Zapata. John Womack's well-known *Zapata and the Mexican Revolution* (1968), which like the Chicano Movement was a product of the sixties, has served as one of the principal sources for historical information.[31] "What follows is a story," begins the historian Womack in his preface, "not an analysis, of how the experience of the Morelos villagers came to pass—how their longing to lead a settled life in a familiar place developed into a violent struggle. . . . Zapata is most prominent in these pages not because he himself begged attention but because the villagers of Morelos put him in charge and persistently looked to him for guidance, and because other villagers around the Republic took him for a champion" (x). Following Womack's historical documentation, Cisneros also invents a story, not limited to Zapata, the champion of his people. Cisneros's story is the fictional biography of Zapata as the male in the Mexican household. What we find in Womack's biography is the historical character Zapata given life with ideals, thoughts, even dialogue that Cisneros takes as her own. Cisneros imaginatively filters the history of the Revolution through the eyes of Inés Alfaro, who in Womack's book is only a footnote. Inés, not Womack, tells her story of Zapata and the Mexican Revolution.

In the opening night scene of intimacy between lovers, Inés hovers over a sleeping Zapata: "I put my nose to your eyelashes. The skin as soft as the skin of the penis, the collarbone with its fluted wings, the purple knot of the nipple, the dark, blue-black color of your sex, the thin legs and long thin feet. For a moment I don't want to think of your past nor your future" (Cisneros 1991, 85). From this first description, Inés will begin her own personal story of Miliano, the name Zapata went by.

Miliano was born in the village of Anenecuilco, Morelos (now known as Anenecuilco de Zapata).[32] As a young man, he had a reputation for being a horseman who liked good horses and fancy saddles. He would dress as a charro, with silver buttons, and was known to enjoy good Havanas.[33] Zapata began organizing during the race for governor of Morelos in 1909, siding with Patricio Leyva against the government of

Porfirio Díaz.. That same year he was named chief of the pueblo of Anenecuilco. The call for revolution came from San Antonio, Texas, on 20 November 1910 from Francisco I. Madero, in the form of the 5 October "Plan de San Luis Potosí." Zapata answered a few months later. After several years of political and military activity, in March 1911 he was named Jefe Supremo of the southern revolutionary forces. In April of the same year he was commissioned General Emiliano Zapata.

When Zapata was named chief of Anenecuilco in September 1909, according to the historical record, his uncle gave him the communal land titles. According to Womack, "It was no mere bundle of legal claims that Zapata took charge of, but the collected testimony to the honor of all Anenecuilco chiefs before him, the accumulated trust of all past generations in the pueblo. This was his responsibility. And when a year and a half later he decided to commit his village to revolution, he buried the titles in a strongbox under the floor of the church" (371).[34] Through Inés, Cisneros refers to the titles: "And I see the ancient land titles the smoking morning they are drawn up in Náhuatl and recorded on tree-bark pa-per—*conceded to our pueblo the 25th of September of 1607 by the Viceroy of New Spain*—the land grants that prove the land has always been our land" (112).[35] Other Indian pueblos have similar documents that date to the Spanish colonial empire, communal Indian lands recognized by Spain. According to testimony offered by Womack, Zapata, who had a great sense of duty and history, was fighting for what the titles represented. "*Por esto peleo*," Womack quotes Zapata (372). As the war wore on, Zapata entrusted the titles to his secretary, Francisco Franco, stating, according to Womack, "'I'm bound to die some day . . . but my pueblo's papers stand to get guaranteed'" (ibid.), dialogue that Cisneros repeats verbatim (87).[36] Zapata did send Franco to retrieve them. According to the historical record, no one knows where the titles are buried. However, Inés narrates:

> And I see that dappled afternoon in Anenecuilco when the government has begun looking for you. And I see you unearth the strong box under the main altar of the village church, and hand it to Chico Franco—*If you lose this, I'll have you dangling from the tallest tree*, compadre. *Not before they fill me with bullets*, Chico said and laughed.
>
> And the evening, already as an old man, in the Canyon of the wolves, Chico Franco running and running, old wolf, old cunning, the government men Nicolás sent shouting behind him, his sons Vírulo and Julián, young,

crumpled on the cool courtyard tile like bougainvillea blossoms, and how useless it all is, because the deeds are buried under the floorboards of a *pulquería* named La Providencia, and no one knowing where they are after the bullets pierce Chico's body. Nothing better or worse than before, and nothing the same or different. (Cisneros 1991, 112)

In 1947, Franco and his two sons, Vírulo and Julián, were killed by government soldiers in the manner described by Cisneros (Womack 1968, 381–382). Nicolás Zapata, Zapata's son, became the cacique—the strong man, the political boss—of Anenecuilco for the PRI. As Inés narrates, on 10 April 1919, Zapata died at the hands of a traitor, José Guajardo, who gave him a sorrel horse the day before he had Zapata and his guards ambushed.[37]

There is also the personal life of Zapata, which is relegated to a few paragraphs in Womack's biography. Cisneros has taken from these details to invent her intimate portrait. Zapata married Josefa Espejo in 1911, although he already had a child by another woman. Zapata, like other men of his time, assumed that he would have children by other women he cared about; however, the legal marriage, notes Womack, was for establishing family and legitimate heirs (107–108). By his wife he had two children, Felipe and María Asunción, who died in infancy, as Inés asserts. Womack offers sketchy information on the children of Zapata's amorous adventures. Zapata's other children, whose mothers remain unknown, appear in a footnote: Nicolás born in 1906, Eugenio in 1913, María Elena in 1913, Ana María in 1914, Diego in 1916, María Luisa in 1918, and Mateo in 1918 (242n2).

Womack, however, offers the following information about a love affair in a restful little town: "The days Zapata passed in his offices in an old rice mill at the northern edge of town. . . . In the evenings he and his aides relaxed in the plaza, drinking, arguing about plucky cocks and fast and frisky horses, discussing the rains and prices with farmers who joined them for a beer, Zapata always smoking slowly on a good cigar. The nights he spent back at his quarters with a woman from town; he fathered two children with a woman from Tlatizapán" (242). Tlatizapán had become his haven, "the moral capital of his revolution," a place to which he returned (ibid.). This anonymous woman is the basis for Inés Alfaro, whom Cisneros names after one of Zapata's lovers, Inés Aguilar. According to the historical record, Inés Aguilar was the mother of Nicolás and María Elena, or Malena as Inés calls her.[38] In an interesting combination of history and fiction, Inés recalls Zapata's other children: "María Luisa from that Gregoria Zúñiga in Quilamula. . . . Diego born in Tlatizapán of that woman who calls herself *Missus* Jorge Piñeiro. Ana María in Cuautla from that she-goat Petra Torres. Mateo, son of that nobody, Jesusa Pérez of Temilpa. All your children born with those eyes of Zapata" (101).[39]

Judging from photographs, Zapata's eyes were certainly a prominent external feature of his character. In his opening prologue, "A People Chooses a Leader," Womack refers to the Anenecuilcans sensing "a painful independence about him" (6). His fellow villagers retold a story about Zapata that might have accounted for his severe countenance. "Anenecuilcans recalled a story of his childhood," Womack relates, "that once as a child he had seen his father break down and cry in frustration at a local hacienda's enclosure of a village orchard, and that he had promised his father he would get the land back. If the incident occurred, he was nine years old at the time. . . . If the story was apocryphal, still the determination that it chronicled did burn in his glance, though he was tough as nails and no one fooled with him, he did look near tears" (ibid.).[40] The mythical Zapata that Womack narrates is the grief-stricken and lonely warrior with "eyes hard and tender all at once" whom Inés wants to gather up in her arms as if he were a child (87).[41]

These are the historical sources for Cisneros's imaginative re-creation. Cisneros's "Eyes of Zapata" is similar in style, scope, and intent to Juan Rulfo's Mexican classic *Pedro Páramo*; both narrate the events of the period of armed struggle beginning with 1910.[42] Both stories, betraying their titles, are as much about the patriarch, cacique, or revolutionary leader as about the conditions of women under patriarchy. Both authors provide for the voices of women to bear witness, to offer a testimonio against Páramo and Zapata. Dolores Preciado, of the landed aristocracy, Eduviges Dyada, the prostitute, Damiana Cisneros, Páramo's servant, Dorotea, the beggar, and Susana San Juan, the rebel against patriarchy, all speak from the grave about their lives in revolutionary Mexico. In her story, Cisneros has created the character of an Indian woman, a marginal woman taken both from a historical footnote and from a figure possessed of great wisdom, the well-known Mazateca curandera from Oaxaca, María Sabina.[43] Sabina's voice provided Cisneros with the initial inspiration for Inés Alfaro's powerful and poetic narration. "Eyes of Zapata" is the story of Zapata's faithful lover till the end, Inés Alfaro, who speaks Mexicano and Spanish, who prays to both Christian and Indian deities. Like Rulfo's women, Inés, through omens, dreams, and visions, reveals to the reader in a Spanish-like poetic English the harsh conditions of village life during the turmoil of the Revolution.[44] While it is the man who history records, the woman in Cisneros's tale, like Rulfo's Susana San Juan, is the spirit of change, the one who poses the questions about gender relations.

The intertwined lives of Zapata and Inés are retold in one single night when Zapata returns to their home. He is no longer the dashing young man on horseback with whom Inés fell in love but now the tired revolucionario, forty years old. While he sleeps, she expresses her love for him, recalls the past and looks to the future. Inés has been enduring, *aguantando* reads the narrative, nine years of the Mexican Revolution. Given the time frame, Inés will soon lose Zapata; he is destined to die that year, 1919. In the last section of the story, Inés is able to see the past— the death of her mother—and the future—the death of Zapata. When Zapata returns to Inés the night of the story, it will probably be their last time together.

Inés lives the secondary status of a Mexican woman. She recognizes she is not just "la otra" but really one of the many. Zapata never promised to marry her but still established a house for her and their children. Inés knows that she will never be first. She knows he is married to María Josefa from Villa de Ayala and knows firsthand of his love for her. Inés and Zapata have a son, Nicolás, who Zapata recognizes as a Zapata. No harm should come to his son, he tells her. Because of her love for Zapata, she was expelled from her father's house, called a perra. In spite of her love for Zapata, living the life of "la otra" also means abandonment. Through nine years of the Mexican Revolution, through political and economic chaos, she perseveres, survives alone.

The character of Inés is more than a match for the legendary hero. She is a special woman, strong and independent, unafraid of hard work, of dying, of going to jail, unafraid of el gran general Zapata. She is not the shy, rural Mexican girl; she did not turn her eyes when he looked at her the first time they met: "You circled when I tried to cross the *zócalo*, I remember. I pretended not to see you until you rode your horse in my path, and I tried to dodge one way, the other, like a calf in a *jaripeo*. I could hear the laughter of your friends from under the shadows of the arcades. And when there was no avoiding you, I looked up at you and said, *With your permission*. You did not insist, you touched the brim of your hat, and let me go" (108). Francisco Franco tells Zapata, "small but bigger than you, Miliano." The story then is Cisneros's homage to the endurability of this

Mexican woman, able to love no matter what. Inés will always be waiting without questioning, accepting being Zapata's woman in the scornful eyes of the community—wife, witch, lover, whore? (105).

To overcome her hurt, Inés learns forgiveness and elevates herself in spirit and acquires a new perspective. Out of her grief, her heart begins to flutter and leave her body. She takes flight, transformed into a tecolote, a bird of the night. She closes herself to everyone in the day and opens herself up to flight at night, and sees all. She becomes a nagual, a guardian spirit, and keeps vigil so that no harm will come to Zapata while he sleeps, even with his wife: "One night over *milpas* and beyond the *tlacolol*, over *barrancas*. . . I flew. . . . And when I alighted on the branch of a tree outside a window, I saw you asleep next to the woman from Villa de Ayala, that woman who is your wife sleeping beside you" (98). Inés has learned to come out of herself for him: "we never free ourselves completely until we love, when we love we lose ourselves inside each other. Then we see a little of what is called heaven. When we can be that close that we no longer are Inés and Emiliano, but something bigger than our lives. And we can forgive, finally" (89). Libertad, freedom, also comes from within. It is also personal. It is the ability to be charitable with each other, to be bigger than ourselves.

Inés Alfaro is Cisneros's imaginative alternative to the warrior hero: the story of love within the story of war; the personal story to be read against the historical biography. It is through Inés that we see an alternative to male privilege. Of Zapata's love for his firstborn son, Nicolás, Inés recalls: "If anything happens to this child, you said, if anything . . . and started to cry. I didn't say anything, Miliano, but you can't imagine how in that instant, I wanted to be small and fit inside your heart, I wanted to belong to you like the boy, and know you loved me" (106). After nine years of war, of subservience to General Zapata and the Revolution, Inés inquires while Zapata sleeps: "But I swear I've never seen more clearly than these days. Ay, Miliano, don't you see? The wars begin here, in our hearts and in our beds. You have a daughter. How do you want her treated? Like you treated me?" (105). Though the story is titled "Eyes of Zapata," it is Inés who has a sense of duty, who is possessed of moral vision and historical perspective. She sees the futility of the Revolution: Nicolás becomes a cacique and member of the PRI; Francisco Franco and his sons murdered by Nicolás; the land titles, the tierra that Zapata had fought for, according to Womack and others, never respected and hidden in a pulquería. These events occur in one night through the Indian woman's memory and vision while Zapata lies with eyes closed, ignorant of the fact that he will soon die.

The lives of the historical figure Zapata and the fictional character Inés transcend their historical moment in the first decades of the twentieth century. And this is possible not only because of the broad sweep of events that Cisneros captures in a short story but also because Cisneros, like her character Inés, is possessed of great vision. "Eyes of Zapata" reminds readers that broadly based struggles for social justice begin in one's home, with family, with family members, with lovers, in bed.

"Virgencita, What Little Miracle Could I Pin Here?"

Frida Kahlo's blue house in the southern Mexico City suburb of Coyoacán has a room where the owner's ex-votos are displayed completely covering a wall. Ex-votos depict the natural and the supernatural, giving evidence of a miraculous intervention in the real world of the believer. These miracles are not sanctioned offically by the church. The ex-votos are thus a collective portrait of a people and their beliefs. Taking the time to study and read the many examples of this genre of religious folk painting accompanied by a brief narrative, the visitor to Kahlo's home would have a sense not only of the deeply rooted religious convictions of Mexicans but also of the daily tragedies and miracles of a community. "Little Miracles, Kept Promises" is also a gallery of twenty-three miniature slices of life along the greater Texas-Mexico border. From her home in San Antonio, following the conventions of the genre, Cisneros presents her literary portraits, each composed of an invocation to a religious figure, followed by a narrative requesting spiritual assistance or expressing gratitude for a miracle granted, ending with the believer's name and place.

Beginning with the first fragment, dated 1988, Cisneros's portraits cover the physical landscape from Matamoros in the Mexican state of Tamaulipas on the Gulf of Mexico to Dallas in the north, through a variety of rural towns from the Río Grande Valley as well as urban centers like San Antonio, Austin, and Houston. With each monologue, which can comprise a single sentence or a fully developed short story, a religious ritual is enacted. A wide variety of spiritual and human agents are invoked: Christ, the Black Christ of Esquipulas from Guatemala; the Virgen in various guises, Virgen de Guadalupe, Virgen de los Remedios, Nuestra Señora de los Lagos; saints, San Antonio for lovers, Saint Jude for lost causes; local healer, don Pedrito Jaramillo; non-Catholic deities, the Seven African Powers; and humans Pancho Villa, John F. Kennedy, and Pope John Paul.

Male and female characters of different ages make their wishes known concerning material well-being, good fortune, health, and love. Rene and Janie Garza of Hondo give thanks for a healthy baby. Señor Gustavo Corchado B. of Laredo requests for his wife a healthy recovery after surgery. Grandma and Grandfather from Harlingen plead for a drug-free grandson. Victor A. Lozano of Houston is pleased for the return of his home. César Escandón of Pharr would like a job with good pay. Brenda Camacho and Sidronio Tijerina of San Angelo want a stolen truck returned. Thus a cross-section of social classes—Spanish speakers, English speakers, bilinguals, Mexican nationals, Texas-Mexicans, recent immigrants, uneducated and educated—reveals the community's hopes and aspirations in the eighties.

Implicit in "Little Miracles, Kept Promises" is historical change: the diversity in the culture is reflected in the diversity of roles for women and men. Ms. Barbara Ybáñez of San Antonio asks San Antonio de Padua, the patron saint of lovers, for a man, "a man man. I mean someone who is not ashamed to be seen cooking or cleaning or looking after himself. In other words, a man who acts like an adult" (Cisneros 1991, 117). Barbara Ybáñez does not want a spoiled Chicano man; she wants someone who is liberal and progressive, who desires an equal, not afraid of a woman who is strong, intelligent, and sure of herself (118). Until then she will turn the saint's statue upside down. Teresa Galindo from Beeville requests la Santísima Señora de San Juan de los Lagos to deliver her from her boyfriend, the cross she bears, to leave her free as before. She has seen the truth and wants to be free of masculine authority. In the fifteenth portrait, given in code, Benjamín T. from Del Río asks the Milagroso Cristo de Esquipulas to watch over Manny Benavides who is in the army. He does not know what to do with his love for Manny and the shame that he feels. Fito Morales of Rockport also gives thanks in Spanish to the Milagroso Cristo Negro for having finished high school. And Eliberto González from Dallas asks Saint Jude to help him pass English 320, British Restoration Literature.

The twenty-three milagritos, however, are divided into two clear but unequal divisions. The ending portrait, concerning Rosario de León, a university student from Austin, Tejas, is the most radical in its content and the most developed in its plot. Rosario is set aside, foregrounded for readers, because she confronts her religion in a different manner from her fellow supplicants. In the previous twenty-two portraits, although indicating change in the culture, the hierarchy of spiritual over human agency remains the same. The faithful leave their religion unchanged. In the ending story, Cisneros subverts the traditional form of the ex-voto: a young woman confronts her gender's history of oppression through the orthodox Catholic representations of the Virgen. Rosario empowers herself by remaking a religious figure into her own identity.

The story is set in familiar cultural territory, a young Texas-Mexican woman in church invoking the Virgencita. As promised, for a miracle granted, Rosario has cut her braided hair and is pinning it on the statue of the Virgen de Guadalupe. What is viewed by mother and grandmother as a tragedy, shedding one's symbol of femininity since birth, is for Rosario a celebratory moment: "My head light as if I'd raised it from water. My heart buoyant" (125). After prayers to the Virgen, Rosario has been informed that she is not pregnant. Overturning the Marian model of motherhood and family, Rosario will defy cultural expectations: she has decided not to be a mother, to live alone, to be an artist.

According to popular belief, in 1531 on Tepeyac hill north of Mexico City's center, Juan Diego, a newly converted Indian, saw a vision of a dark-haired madonna with bronze skin, eyes cast down and hands in prayer, bathed in a halo. The miracle of Guadalupe refers to the apparition as well as to the image of the Indian virgin imprinted on Juan Diego's cloak. The commemoration of this event, celebrated on 12 December, is as popular throughout Mexico and the United States as Mexican Independence Day. The Virgen de Guadalupe is central to Mexican identity and Mexican Catholicism. When Mexicans celebrate her day with prayer, music, and flowers, they do so with the pride of a chosen people: the Virgen chose to appear to a Mexican Indian. In 1810, the relationship between country and faith was sealed. The Virgen de Guadalupe was chosen by independence leader–priest Miguel Hidalgo for the banner that was carried into war against the Spanish rulers, who fought under the banner of the Virgen de los Remedios. In 1913, when Zapata's revolutionaries entered Mexico City, they carried the Guadalupe banner. The belief in the Virgen de Guadalupe has survived every social and political upheaval in Mexico. She is the link between the present and Mexico's Indian past.

The origins of the devotion to the Indian version of the Spanish Virgen lie shrouded in the mystery of the early years of the conquest and colonization of the Aztec world. Before the conquest, Tepeyac hill served as a religious center to the mother goddess, "Tonantzín, our mother." Salvador Carrasco, in his 1998 Mexican film, *La otra conquista*, has given cinematic life to the origins of the Virgen de Guadalupe. Set in the years between 1521 and 1526, between the destruction of Tenochtitlán and the complete subjugation of Mexico's Indian world, the film's plot centers on a world orphaned by the destruction of its gods. "La otra conquista" is the struggle for the hearts and minds of Indians. In the climatic early scene, Topiltzín, one of Moctezuma's many sons, is once and forever changed when he witnesses the destruction of a statue of Tonantzín as a Spaniard places before him a statue of the beautiful, fair-skinned Virgen. Carrasco's fictional creation of the fusion of Spanish and Aztec religions will lead five years later, viewers are informed at the end of the film, to the cult of the Virgen de Guadalupe.

From the film and history of Mexico, one can conclude that the belief in the Virgen de Guadalupe played well into the hands of Spanish priests eager to win over Indians and mestizos to Catholicism—which in 1521 amounted to the largest mass conversion since the early days of Christianity. Since 1519, with the arrival of Cortés on Mexican shores, the Virgin Mother had assumed a prominent visible role in the conquest. As Cortés conquered tribes, Indians were asked to swear allegiance to the king and accept Christianity and the Virgin Mother. One of the original banners carried by Cortés, now in a historical museum in Mexico City, depicts the figure of the European Virgen with hands held in prayer. The origins of Guadalupe are, obviously, also in Spain. Jacques Lafaye traces the American Guadalupe to the Virgen of Guadalupe in Extremadura, Spain. The Spanish Guadalupe cult based on an apparition to a shepherd was well known in medieval Spain (Lafaye 1977, 311–320). What are now considered elements of the iconic figure of the Virgen de Guadalupe—hands in prayer, the halo of sun rays that surrounds her body, blue cape with stars, and gold gown—are evident in sixteenth-century Spanish representations of the Virgen.[45] Statues of this iconic figure exist in El Convento de las Descalzas Reales, located in the very center of Madrid. This was a convent for Spanish nobility from the time of Charles V, 1516 through 1524, and only recently opened. One can imagine similar images colored in the right hue—like the morena Virgen of Guadalupe, Spain—to represent the newly converted Indians as Christianity spread through the Indian world with the arrival of the first Franciscan missionaries in 1524. In an exceptional decision, a church hierarchy, fearful of miraculous visions among the Indians, gave the Virgen de Guadalupe its blessing (Kandell 1988, 165).

The Virgen de Guadalupe, probably more than any other religious figure, is a constant reminder of Mexican Catholicism in both public and private spaces. In Mexican and Mexican American households, the Virgen, as another representation of Mary, is a constant reminder of traditional values associated with the cult of marianismo: women should be silent, passive, demure, and virginal. Women, like Mary, should be resigned to a fate of doing all for the family, with the attendant restrictions that women should not have a voice, desires, passions, or a history.

For Cisneros, as for other Chicana feminists, this is the European patriarchal view of Mary. Artists before Cisneros have reclaimed the image of the Virgen de Guadalupe. Ester Hernández's 1975 *La Virgen de Guadalupe defendiendo los derechos de los Xicanos* depicts a young woman—the Virgen de Guadalupe—in judo uniform kicking in defense of Chicanos (*Chicano Art* 1991, 324). In 1978, Yolanda M. López represented working women in *Margaret Stewart: Our Lady of Guadalupe* and *Victoria F. Franco: Our Lady of Guadalupe* (ibid., 326), and herself in *Portrait of the Artist as the Virgin of Guadalupe* (ibid., 64), each with their bodies bathed in the iconic halo of light. All of these representations endow women with a sense of dignity and worth accorded to the Virgen de Guadalupe, but López's self-portrait of a smiling, athletic young woman, running with muscular legs exposed, sporting tennis shoes, clutching a serpent in one hand and the traditional Guadalupe cape in the other is an especially powerful representation of the Chicana not denying her cultural traditions but heading toward the future.

Like López, Cisneros's Rosario has redefined Guadalupe in her own image. The traditional image of Guadalupe through the suffering of Rosario's mother and grandmother pervades the de León household: "Couldn't look at you without blaming you for all the pain my mother and her mother and all our mothers' mothers have put up with in the name of God. Couldn't let you in my house. . . . I wasn't going to be my mother or my grandma. All that self-sacrifice, all that silent suffering. Hell no. Not here. Not me" (Cisneros 1991, 127). Instead, Rosario wanted a Guadalupe "bare-breasted, snakes in your hand. I wanted you leaping and somersaulting the backs of bulls. I wanted you swallowing raw hearts and rattling volcanic ash" (ibid.). Rosario desires Guadalupe in a heretical mode: free, strong, immodest.

Rosario de León is a symbolic name endowed with past and future meanings: the rosary, the Catholic instrument of hope is also the agent of change; de León is heart and courage as well as a reference to Spanish

Castilla. But Rosario is also a Guadalupana. The university student now sees Guadalupe as a defender of oppressed women: "That you could have the power to rally a people when a country was born and again during a civil war, and during a farmworkers' strike in California made me think maybe there is power in my mother's patience, strength in my grandmother's endurance. Because those who suffer have a special power, don't they? The power of understanding someone else's pain. And understanding is the beginning of healing" (128). Drawing on new understanding of the conquest and colonization of Mexico, Rosario imagines "no longer Mary the mild, but our mother Tonantzín. Your church at Tepeyac built on the site of her temple. Sacred ground no matter whose goddess claims it" (ibid.).

Rosario, an eighties feminist, sees the multivalency of women through Mexican classical antiquity: Guadalupe-Coatlaxopeuh, as she who has dominion over serpents; as Teteoinnan, our mother; as Toci, our mother; as Xochiquetzal, flower-bird, goddess of flowers and love; as Tlazolteotl, goddess of birth; as Coatlicue, goddess of fertility and creativity; as Chalchiuhtlicue, goddess of rivers and lakes; as Coyolxauhqui, goddess of the moon; as Huixtocihuatl, goddess of salt; as Chicomeocoatl, the grandmother goddess, the goddess of corn; as Cihuacoatl, the snake woman, goddess of wisdom.[46] Tonantzín, our mother, fulfills these natural and creative roles as well as the European "Nuestra Señora de la Soledad, Nuestra Señora de los Remedios, . . . Our Lady of Lourdes, Our Lady of the Rosary, Our Lady of Sorrows" (128).

La otra conquista leaves Our Lady Tonantzín in the early decades of the sixteenth century. This is clearly the case with the goddesses of the Aztec pantheon confined to scholarship but never revived into new forms. Coatlicue, for example, in her representation as the stone monolith, will be forever restricted to the frightening figure of death. Here Cisneros takes Tonantzín, Coatlicue, and other mother or natural goddesses and redefines them in the present as sources of positive identity for Rosario.

Moreover, at the end of her visit with the Virgencita, Rosario sees the Virgen de Guadalupe in all her facets, the equal of male-identified religions, she is all at once the Buddha, the Tao, the true Messiah, Yahweh, Allah. She is the Heart of the Sky, the Heart of the Earth, the Lord of the Near and Far—the sun, moon, and space in Mesoamerican cosmology. Guadalupe in all her guises—nature, fertility, space—is, finally, for the artist Rosario, the patrona of possibility. Guadalupe is "the Spirit, the Light, the Universe," she is all of creation itself. After the twenty-two intimate portraits of tragedies and hope, Cisneros ends with a grand celebratory Mexican mural of creation with woman at the center. "Mighty Guadalupana Coatlaxopeuh Tonantzín," ends Rosario, "When I could see you in all your facets, . . . I could love you, and, finally, learn to love me" (128–129).

On 11 and 12 December, more than at other times, the area surrounding the Basílica to Nuestra Señora María de Guadalupe, Reyna de México, Emperatriz de las Américas y de las Filipinas, is teeming with close to a million faithful celebrants, many of them walking on their bleeding knees up to the Christian temple on top of Tepeyac hill. This is the fusion of Catholic and Indian religions, sacrifice and celebration, commemorating the miracle of 1531 that transformed Mexican culture.

Rosario de León of Austin, Tejas, also extends this tradition. She enters a church to celebrate her own "little miracle" by pinning her braid on the statue of the Virgen de Guadalupe, among many other milagritos and promises kept: several hospital bracelets; a tiny copper arm; a kneeling man in silver; a house; a truck; photographs of a baby in a charro hat; Sylvia Rios, First Holy Communion, age nine years; mean dude in a bandanna and tattoos; sweet boy with new mustache and new soldier uniform; teenager with a little bit of herself on her lap; blurred husband and wife leaning one into the other as if joined at the hip (124–125). Although still a member of her spiritual community, Rosario speaks from outside the traditional Marian cult. This is the meaning of being the last but also the first. Cisneros tells the reader, through the unequal narrative structure, that Rosario is at the vanguard of change carrying a new Guadalupe banner. Rosario is able to envision a different Guadalupe because Rosario herself has been transformed through learning. Cisneros makes a powerful argument for the education of Chicanas, an education that is culturally specific as well as empowering and liberating. Just as there should not be one meaning for Guadalupe, there should not be one single meaning for women. Rosario has discovered the many facets in Guadalupe beyond the meanings given to her by Catholicism. Although at home Rosario has been labeled a traitor to her culture—"heretic, atheist, *hocicona*, acting like a *bolilla*, white girl, *Malinche*"—she has gained much from the study of Mesoamerican antiquity (127–128). She has gained not only knowledge of history but also self-understanding and self-worth—"I'm my history and my future" (126).

Rosario's new fusion of the old with the new, Cisneros's literary exvoto, is both spiritual and intellectual: she has learned humility and compassion while liberating herself. The artist Rosario is much like the writer Sandra Cisneros, who calls herself a Guadalupana, faithful to a goddess of freedom and creativity.

The Artist at Home/La Peregrina en Su Casa

"*Bien* Pretty" is a kitschy, satirical rewriting of the well-known Mexican myth of the star-crossed lovers Ixtaccíhuatl, the White Woman, and Popocatépetl, the Smoking Mountain.[47] According to popular legend, the two lovers were separated because Popocatépetl had gone off to battle. Popocatépetl's enemies deceived Ixtaccíhuatl, claiming the warrior had died in battle. At the news, Ixtaccíhuatl died of a broken heart. The warrior called upon his mighty powers and built the two volcanoes outside Tenochtitlán. Popocatépetl laid Ixta's body on one range, and close by, he stands guard over her. Cisneros is clearly invoking the sexualized Mexican myth and landscape: the male warrior next to his dormant loved one enshrined as the two volcanoes that dominate the southeastern horizon of Mexico City. In the forties, the Chihuahua artist José Enrique Emilio de la Helguera Espinoza began interpreting Aztec mythology in his colorful calendars. Helguera's work became so popular that it has been reproduced continuously. Although trained as a painter in Mexico and Spain, Helguera became known as the master of kitsch Mexican calendar art. His two renditions of the Ixtaccíhuatl/Popocatépetl story, *La leyenda de los volcanes* (1941) and *El flechador del sol* (1945), became iconic representations of Mexico in Mexican households on both sides of the border. Indeed, along with a statue of the Virgen and the Sacred Heart of Jesus, Helguera's two paintings framed in Mexican wood were prominently displayed during my childhood in our dining room in Calexico.

Cisneros's central protagonist, the artist Lupe Arredondo, on a quest for her roots, desires to continue Helguera's artistic tradition of *La leyenda de los volcanes*: "I'd always wanted to do an updated version of the Prince Popocatépetl/Princess Ixtaccíhuatl volcano myth, that tragic love story metamorphosed from classic to kitsch calendar art, like the ones you get at Carnicería Ximénez or Tortillería la Guadalupanita. Prince Popo half-naked warrior built like Johnny Weissmuller, crouched in grief beside his sleeping princess Ixtaccíhuatl, buxom as an Indian Jayne Mansfield. And behind them, echoing their silhouettes, their namesake volcanoes" (Cisneros 1991, 144). In "*Bien* Pretty," life imitates art: two star-crossed lovers from different worlds, a Mexican American searcher, Lupe, and an immigrant from Mexico, Flavio Munguía, are destined to meet and part in San Antonio. Lupe falls in love with Flavio, her Mexican Prince Popo model. However, in Lupe's *El Pipi del Popo*, the new humorous rendition of Helguera's *La leyenda de los volcanes*, it is the Prince who, no longer romantic, sublime, and beautiful, is lying on his back with anatomical adjustments in order to simulate the geographic silhouettes.[48]

"*Bien* Pretty" is also a reframing of Mexican telenovelas. Various well-known stars and their television vehicles are invoked: Verónica Castro in *Rosa Salvaje* (1989), Adela Noriega in *Dulce Desafío* (1989), and Daniela Romo in *Balada por un Amor* (1990). As in "Woman Hollering Creek," Cisneros takes a critical view of the obsessive and repetitive male and female types brought forth nightly from the Mexican-linked U.S. Univisión network: "men powerful and passionate versus women either volatile and evil, or sweet and resigned" (161). As in other tales in *Woman Hollering Creek*, Cisneros is drawing her narrative materials from those Mexican symbols, whether from Mesoamerican antiquity, modern calendar art, or mass media soap operas, that are represented visually within the confines of the Mexican home. In this story, Lupe Arredondo will come to an understanding of herself invoking the title of an alternative Venezuelan soap, *Amar es Vivir*. There is no happy ending in the traditional sense for Lupe. She is left devastated, broken-hearted by Flavio's return to Mexico. However, Lupe learns that loving is living and living is loving, and, above all, learning to love herself as a woman like the women she has known: "Real women.... The ones I've known elsewhere except on TV, in books and magazines. *Las* girlfriends. *Las comadres*. Our mamas and *tías*. Passionate *and* powerful, tender and volatile, brave. And, above all, fierce" (ibid.).

In a first-person, colloquial tone, Lupe introduces the reader to an important phase of her life. The historical background for the story is the aftermath of the activist phase of the Chicano Movement that began in 1965 when students aided the César Chávez–led boycott of table grapes. Lupe and her Bay Area friend Beatriz Soliz go way back, back to the first grape-boycott demonstrations at the Berkeley Safeway stores. The former students are now adults, single or married but childless, which is to say without traditional families. They are college-educated, have become artists, intellectuals, and professionals. In this Mexican American narrative that I have been constructing, it is remarkable how distanced Lupe Arredondo is in 1990 from the children of "Mexican Movies," who were so close to Mexican culture and family.

Lupe is an artist teacher. Eddie, Lupe's former lover, has stopped his activism and is a paralegal. Lupe's friend Beatriz is a criminal lawyer. In San Antonio, Lupe is staying in the house owned by Irasema Izaura Coronado, a famous Texas poet with a Ph.D. from the Sorbonne "who carries herself as if she is directly descended from Ixtaccíhuatl or something" (119). These former activists are living their lives very differently from the sixties. Eddie left Lupe for a blonde who works for Merrill Lynch. Beatriz is an Aztec dance instructor by night. And Irasema married a huichol curandero. Both Irasema and her husband are on a Fulbright in Nayarit, Mexico. We could identify this group as New Age Latinos. Lupe and her San Francisco friends are members of the coffeehouse, museum, art scene—Café Pícaro, Café Bohème, La Galería, Balmy Way.[49] Lupe's house, which she sublets from "Her Highness" Irasema, is full of New Age, bohemian, Southwest funk: a cappuccino maker, Frida Kahlo altar, Santa Fe plate rack, five strings of red chile lights, life-size papier-mâché skeleton signed by the Linares family, and seventeenth-century Spanish retablo are but a few items in the inventory supplied by Lupe. The house is within the boundaries where the Mexican San Antonians live, "the peasantry," but close enough to the mansions of the historic King William district visited by the tourists. The house is close to the Mexican community but, given the inventory items, distanced in terms of class and culture. As Cisneros argues, these are characters who are spiritual searchers, acquiring the trappings of culture but culturally distant from their original communities. They are into collecting things from the Southwest, Mexico, Latin America, and Spain. It is an appropriation of culture; houses are transformed into veritable private museums.

Through Lupe, Cisneros gives the reader pause to think of the social and cultural contradictions in the wake of the Chicano Movement. Lupe travels from San Francisco to San Antonio with her grandmother's molcajete, a stainless steel wok, a pair of flamenco shoes, eleven huipiles, two rebozos de bolita y de seda, crystals and copal, and Latin music—Paco de Lucía, Gipsy Kings, Astor Piazzolla, Mercedes Sosa, Celia Cruz, Agustín Lara, Lola Beltrán, Pedro Infante, Los Lobos, and Dr. Loco and his Original Corrido Boogie Band. Against the larger backdrop of American culture in the late twentieth century, Lupe clings tenaciously yet tenuously to her Mexican and Mexican American past because her education and profession have taught her to cast a wider intellectual net for music that can be characterized in English as Latin.

Latin, after all, is the way Lupe characterizes her musical selections (141).

Lupe Arredondo, who reached maturity in the Bay Area, leaves her home because of a failed love affair with Eddie. She risks the hostility of racist Texas to accept the position as director of a community cultural center in the Mexican town of San Antonio. Austin may be the state capital of Texas, but San Antonio is the cultural capital of Mexican American south Texas. Lupe escapes the West Coast to find herself within her vocation, to begin serious painting once again. In Texas, she is lonely and distanced from what she knows. A month had not passed since unpacking her van, but already she had convinced herself that San Antonio was a mistake. The San Francisco seascape served as an emotional release, a sense of both freedom and belonging: "In the Bay, whenever I got depressed, I always drove out to Ocean Beach. Just to sit. And, I don't know, something about looking at water, how it just goes and goes, something about that I found very soothing. As if somehow I were connected to every ripple that was sending itself out and out until it reached another shore. But I hadn't found anything to replace it in San Antonio" (143). In Texas, she finds herself attracted to the first man who walks into her house, Flavio Munguía Galindo, the cockroach exterminator, who, Lupe thinks, would make a great live model for the perfect Aztec Prince Popo. As a visual artist, Lupe is attracted to Flavio's outward appearance, his masculinity, and, most of all, his Indianness.

Flavio has migrated to San Antonio from his native state of Michoacán. He has held a variety of working-class jobs on his way to his uncle's house in San Antonio. (Flavio's grandmother, Chavela, was from San Antonio.) He is short, even by Mexican standards, but for Lupe he is divine, he is bien pretty with skin like dulce de leche, like Mexican caramel. He is the Prince Charming that she finally corners on a Sunday at Torres Taco Haven while she waits for her laundry to be done at the Kwik Wash. Flavio, according to Lupe, is made by God out of red clay, like the little clay heads they unearth in Teotihuacán (152). At other times he is a Tarascan head that should be made of jade (154). He is also described with the face of a sleeping Olmec, heavy oriental eyes, thick lips, wide nose, carved from onyx (144). These are well-known artifacts of Mexican classical cultures often found vividly and colorfully displayed in expensive coffee-table books. Lupe has elevated the former farmworker, dishwasher, shrimper, now pest exterminator into mythical proportions.

Flavio, in many ways, comes from a world Lupe does not know anymore. Lupe is not Mexican, not Mexican like Flavio. She reads about Indian myths in the *Popol Vuh*; he learns his from his Mexican grandmother Oralia. She has her aura massaged, wears a Lycra mini with a pair of silver cowboy boots, cooks paella with brown rice and tofu, serves sangria, plays music by Astor Piazzolla, and asks Flavio about the Michoacán indigenous tradition of el baile de los viejitos. He talks about 107 FM K-Suave, Johnny Canales, Los Bukis, and Mil Máscaras and wears Reeboks and Izod shirts. However, the clincher for her is when Flavio makes love in Spanish. *"¡Ay!,"* she sighs, "[t]o have your lover sigh *mi vida, mi preciosa, mi chiquita"* (153). To make love in Spanish, muses Lupe, as intricate and devout as the Alhambra; and at the end of love-making, she asks, thinking of a line from one of the love letters of Georgia O'Keefe, "Flavio . . . did you ever feel like flowers?" (154). They have an affair, meaningful only for Lupe. One Sunday while having breakfast at Torres Taco Haven, Flavio informs Lupe that it is time to leave for Mexico because of obligations to his seven sons, four from his first marriage, three from his second.

The breakup painfully reveals that Lupe does not know who she is except through Flavio. He is what she is not. He is centered in his Mexican culture: "'I don't have to dress in a sarape and sombrero to be Mexican, . . . I *know* who I am'" (151). Lupe is behaving like an imperialist. She is the one who pursues Flavio, captures him, objectifies him, forces him into a stereotype, and limits him in his Mexican identity. He is who he is, a poet, an artist like Lupe, with obvious contradictions. She is self-conscious about her identity; she wants to be, he is. Here Cisneros makes a bold move, for it is the female who is the desiring subject, the intellectual forcing the working-class male to conform to her image of an indigenous artifact or a Third World Indian that she wants to serve as a model for her idealized painting of Prince Popo. It is a fetishizing of Mexican culture that will make her feel complete both as female and as artist.

When Flavio leaves, Lupe is left without a center: "Just the void. The days raw and wide as this drought-blue sky. Just this nothingness. That's what hurts" (157). She tries to heal herself with her New Age devices: rose-quartz crystal to visualize healing energy; burning copal and sage to purify the house; centering herself with her seven chakras. All these prove ineffective, the limpia does not work.

Lupe must be responsible for her own salvation in the material and the cultural world that surrounds her. She begins by returning to her childhood, to Mexican women's popular culture. Alone in her home, she is left to watch telenovelas and read *Vanidades*, and thinks (like the writer Cisneros) about remaking women, the portrayal of women, not the usual commodified stereotypes found in Mexican soaps but like the real women she has known, passionate and powerful, tender and brave.

Meeting a Mexican American woman at Centeno's Mexican Supermarket strikes a chord and begins to empower her. The cashier at the market is much like herself, Lupe thinks, blouse not tucked in to hide a big stomach, same age, but looks old and tired from holding back anger. The cashier says, "*Bien* pretty, your shawl. . . . *Que* cute. You look real *mona*" (161–162). These comments are addressed to Lupe, in her shawl, who feels ugly after the breakup with Flavio. The comments should also remind readers of Lupe's saying of Flavio that he was not pretty unless you were in love with him. Here the compliments, cute and mona, and the magazine, *Vanidades*, with Libertad Palomares on the cover lead Lupe in the direction of both looking and feeling good, which is to say, embracing her body and herself. "Libertad Palomares," says the cashier about the Venezuelan telenovela star on the cover of *Vanidades* purchased by Lupe.[50] "*Amar es Vivir*," Lupe responds automatically with the title of the telenovela vehicle for Palomares, "as if it were my motto" (162). Amar es vivir as in Daniela Romo singing: "*Ya no. Es verdad que te adoro, pero más me adoro yo. . . .* We're going to right the world and live. I mean live our lives the way lives were meant to be lived. With the throat and wrists. With rage and desire, and joy and grief, and love till it hurts, maybe. But goddamn, girl. Live" (163).

After finishing her reworked painting of the Mexico City horizon transformed into romantic myth, *La leyenda de los volcanes*, artist and woman, without the model that meant so much, unite to face the reality of San Antonio. Lupe experiences a new solitude and acceptance: "Everywhere I go, it's me and me. Half of me living my life, the other half watching me live it" (163). This comment comes from someone who had earlier offered: "I have always been in love with a man" (160). The oppressive Texas sky that once made her feel "landlocked and dusty. Light so white and dusty it left [her] dizzy, sun bleached like an onion" (143) is now for her "wide as an ocean, shark-belly gray for days at a time, then all at once a blue so tender you can't remember how many months before the heat split you open like a pecan shell, you can't remember anything anymore" (163–164).

Every sunset she rushes home to her brushes and her painting, to the garage roof on top of her studio. The heat of San Antonio, the roaches in her house, her lack of center are replaced by a new sense of identity, by the sky and the migrating grackles, the urracas. Lupe prefers the Spanish, that roll of the *r* making all the difference. The noisy birds are "big as crows, shiny as ravens, swooping and whooping it up like drunks at Fiesta," but also the urracas resting on branches are "dark and distinct as treble clefs, very crisp and noble and clean" (164). Lupe has journeyed through an internal season now here outwardly represented by another seasonal pest, the urracas of San Antonio in January, when the sky is alive with chatter, throbbing with different colors. She is finally feeling at home with herself after Eddie and Flavio, feeling at home in San Antonio, with her new place. And the ground, dirty with bird shit, does not matter in view of her newly found strength and libertad played out against the sky. "Hurray, hurray," Lupe shouts at the end with joy and affirmation.

This then is the allegory of the artist Guadalupe finally finding a home, la peregrina en su patria. The outcome of the cultural confrontation between the Mexican from Michoacán and the Chicana/Mexican American from the Bay Area may not have turned out the way Lupe would have wanted. But the newly found motto, amar es vivir, means that she has learned from her short stay in San Antonio, from summer through winter. For all along, Lupe was becoming a member of the Mexican community of San Antonio; some of this thanks to Flavio. Lupe no longer frequented the cafés, galleries, and art houses of her San Francisco days. Her transformation had begun at the same time she was attracted to Flavio. At story's end, she has shed her bohemian identity for her more bilingual and bicultural working-class surroundings. During Lupe's affair with Flavio, she frequented Woolworth's, Kwik Wash, Mi Tierra Bakery, Torres Taco Haven, El Mirador restaurant, Casa Preciado Religious Articles, Centeno's Mexican Supermarket, dance clubs such as Club Fandango, Salas's Party House, and El Taconazo Lounge.

Readers do not know more about Flavio after the breakup. However, the romantic love poem "Tin Tan Tan" before *"Bien* Pretty" is written by Flavio under the pseudonym Rogelio Velasco. The poem is dedicated to a Lupita who scorned his love. Indications are that he will continue to be the Mexican male. Lupe, who behaved like an imperialist, is a different person because of her cultural confrontation with Mexico and Flavio. She has come away with an understanding of herself as a woman and artist, with feet now firmly planted in Mexican American south Texas.[51]

V

"A Woman Living on the Border of Cultures"

In 1995, four years after *Woman Hollering Creek*, Carlos Fuentes published *La frontera de cristal: Una novela en nueve cuentos* (*The Crystal Frontier: A Novel in Nine Stories*). The novel's title and formal structure illuminate the continuing encounter of two distinctly different nations. Frontera de cristal, the crystal border, refers to the visible but at times impenetrable cultural worlds on either side of the border. Fuentes has a variety of Mexicans encountering Anglo-American culture during the decades of the eighties and nineties: a gay medical student at Cornell during the Reagan years; a world-renowned Mexican chef eating at a mall in San Diego having to do intellectual and emotional battle with a nation that values efficiency and abundance over good taste; a middle-class migrant worker, victim of Mexico's 1995 economic crash, flown to New York City as part of a weekend cleaning crew; a first-generation Mexican American woman in Chicago serving an aging white woman from the Old South; young women who must leave their families in the interior of Mexico to find work at Ciudad Juárez maquila plants built with U.S. capital. Fuentes's novel is in the tradition of Chicano fiction, the novel-as-tales or composite novel, in which the interlocking stories come together in the final chapter.

For Fuentes, it all comes together at the frontera de cristal, at the border. "Río Grande, Río Bravo," the ending cuento, is a series of character sketches bringing together plots and characters from previous stories, all now seen from a historical perspective—the history of northern Mexico from Native American culture through Spanish conquest, Anglo-American invasion to the present. As the old Mexico—blood, marriage, wealth, business—dies on the El Paso/Ciudad Juárez border with the death of powerful norteño industrialist Leonardo Barroso, new Mexican elements forge to the forefront, creating kinship alliances of a different sort on both sides of the border, as in the sketch "José Francisco":

> Soy chicano en todas partes. No tengo que asimilarme a nada. Tengo mi propia historia.
>
> La escribía pero no le bastaba. Su moto iba y venía por el puente sobre el Río Grande, Río Bravo, cargado de manuscritos chicanos a México y manuscritos mexicanos a Texas, la moto servía para llevar rápidamente palabras escritas de un lado a otro, ése era el contrabando de José

Francisco, literatura de los dos lados, para que todos se conocieran mejor, decía, para que todos se quisieran un poquito más, para que hubiera "un nosotros" de los dos lados de la frontera. (Fuentes 1995, 281)

"I'm Chicano everywhere. I don't have to assimilate into anything. I have my own history."

He wrote it but it wasn't enough for him. His motorcycle went back and forth over the bridge across the Río Grande, Río Bravo, loaded with manuscripts. José Francisco brought Chicano manuscripts to Mexico and Mexican manuscripts to Texas. The bike was the means to carry the written word rapidly from one side to the other, that was José Francisco's contraband, literature from both sides so that everyone would get to know one another better, he said, so that everyone would love one another a little more, so there would be a "we" on both sides of the border. (Fuentes 1997, 252)

Border literature, acknowledges Fuentes through his Chicano character José Francisco, will have a role to play in shattering the frontera de cristal.[52] This emergent Mexican identity within diversity goes a long way, on the one hand, to reject the view of Mexican Americans as inauthentic, Anglicized pochos and, on the other, to understand and accept northern Mexican identity, culture, and art forged out of the Chicano Movement. "El cuento de Cisneros," emphasizes Fuentes, among other Mexican American and Mexican writings carried by José Francisco, will lead to a "nosotros" on both sides of the border (Fuentes 1995, 282).

In the interview with Kevane and Heredia, when asked about concerns with her community, Cisneros answered invoking cross-border alliance and commitment: "As I am getting older, I am writing more about global connections. . . . How does one connect the killings of people in Chiapas to a worker here in San Antonio? What is my role as a writer to the citizens of this country? That is what I am concerned about currently. I also take my responsibility seriously of being a woman who lives on the border of cultures, a translator for a time when all these communities are shifting and colliding in history. Chicanos are in that unique perspective" (Cisneros 2000a, 53).[53]

The seven cuentos from *Woman Hollering Creek* express from the northern bank of the Río Grande the possibility of cross-border solidarity bridging two communities of Greater Mexico. Like Fuentes's novel, Cisneros's stories cover the same period of intense globalization, marked on the border by increased migration of capital, labor, and values back and forth across two nations. Taking into account the events and experiences lived by the women characters in *Woman Hollering Creek*, Cisneros too narrates a convulsive and hopeful period no less revolutionary, culturally speaking, than the much-heralded Mexican Revolution. In each of Cisneros's stories there is cause for celebration and un trago de tequila: through the invention of new models for women, Mexican culture (religious, folkoric, and popular beliefs) and patria (Indian Mexico, Independence, and Revolution) emerge reconsidered. The nosotros—the identities forged out of diversity—that Fuentes longs for, the American Mexican writer Cisneros eloquently demands, will be possible only when nosotras—Mexican and Mexican American women—are culturally embraced in the spirit of freedom, equality, and dignity for all.

AMÉRICA MEXICANA 2001

Más Allá de la Frontera

"We have crossed the international border at Calexico-Mexicali," informs Captain Marín of the 7:00 A.M. Mexicana de Aviación Flight 903 from la Ciudad de Nuestra Señora la Reyna de Los Angeles to la Ciudad de México. In a little over three hours we will be arriving at La Capital/La Gran Tenochtitlán, the heart of Greater Mexico. After passing into Mexican airspace around 7:30 A.M., our flight will level off at 27,000 feet above sea level before traveling through Sonora, Chihuahua, and Zacatecas into the valley of Mexico. The flight attendant walks down the aisle distributing the appropriate customs declaration forms to U.S. and Mexican citizens. As usual, I am taken for a Mexican. "¿Mexicano?" "Sí, pero ciudadano estadounidense," I politely answer the bilingual flight attendant.

My fellow passenger on window seat 12F is having difficulty filling out his Mexican citizen form. Eventually, Carlos, in Spanish, asks for my assistance. The form requests a passport number. Carlos tells me he does not have a passport. I am puzzled. "Are you a Mexican citizen?" "Yes," he answers. "If you do not have a passport, do you have identification?" He shows me his Mexican voter registration card. As we continue filling out the form, I realize that he, perhaps, does not read, although he can write his name. The overwhelming majority of passengers on board are Mexican men, many of whom, dressed in blue jeans, sneakers, and baseball caps, had already formed a line at the Mexicana counter at 4:30 A.M. I am reminded of Carlos Fuentes's short story "La frontera de cristal" in *La frontera de cristal* whose plot tells the story of Mexican men from Mexico City flown to New York City to work as weekend window cleaning crews on Manhattan's high-rises.

"You are returning home," I ask. "Yes, for Navidad." He has not seen his Mexican home for some time. After living in fear for a year, he will be very happy to see his wife and children. He has been in California working without documents. He crossed the border looking for work. I do not know if he walked miles through the desert, if he came in someone's car trunk, or if he paid a coyote to take him across. Now, however, U.S. dollars have allowed him to travel home in style. "I am not a bad man. I came to work." Carlos lives just southeast of Mexico City in the state of Puebla on the border of the state of Morelos. "I have a small house in Chiautla de Tapia. I am used to hard work. I worked in construction in California. In my valley farm, I get paid very little for my harvests. So I came to El Norte to work. It is not easy living without papers. I hope new President Fox will find a way for us to work in the U.S. with papers."

I first traveled to Mexico City more than twenty-five years ago via a two-day train ride from Mexicali. I was a wide-eyed Chicano student visiting one of the great fabled cities of las Américas. I have returned many times, on a yearly basis at the end of the twentieth century. Millions of returning pilgrim-workers like Carlos and me will encounter a changing Mexico. Since the Aztecs, who journeyed from Asatlán, founded México-Tenochtitlán on Lake Texcoco in 1325, since the reigns of Charles I of Spain and Moctezuma II in the sixteenth century, Mexico City has experienced dramatic transformations; on 6 December 2000, www.mexicocity.mx is no different. The U.S.-Mexico border, once confined geographically and conceptually to the outer fringes of Mexican identity, has invaded La Capital. The border, where the U.S.-Mexico trade amounts to $250 billion a year, is now home to twelve million people. This border zone is an international phenomenon: globalization. Following a worldwide trend of urbanization in the Third World in the second half of the twentieth century, the population of Mexican cities that hug the border has more than quadrupled. Many come to the border to work in the maquilas, the global factories, or arrive with the hope of someday crossing the border. The border, however, reaches deep into the United States and Mexico. "In Mexico," Mexican cultural critic Carlos Monsiváis wrote in 1995, "the border with the United States is everywhere. . . . [A]ll of us Mexicans live along that border" (Monsiváis 1995, 41). Never before have the economies and cultures of the two North American neighbor nations been so entwined.

The largest city in the world now welcomes new northern invaders from Asatlán, the Ysla de Californias, and beyond Nova Hispania. Almost anywhere in Mexico City, capitalinos and tourists can wander into Denny's, Burger King, McDonald's, KFC, Domino's Pizza, Baskin Robbins, and Dunkin' Donuts to savor North American favorites. Virtually every cinema house is showing recent U.S. blockbusters. If one prefers to stay at home, Blockbuster Video stores are also available. Television, which through Televisa and its U.S. affiliate Univisión played such a dominant role in Mexicanizing American Mexicans, is bringing U.S. culture to Mexico on an hourly basis. The satellite dish and cable television, soon to go digital, offer virtually the same fare available to U.S. viewers—major network channels as well as CNN, ESPN, TNT, MTV FX, E! and the Weather Channel, among others. A few programs are dubbed in Spanish. On 17 December 2000, a U.S. sports ritual, a Sunday football game between Los Empacadores de Green Bay y los Vikingos de Minnesota, is offered in Spanish. After President-elect Fox requested that those interested in joining his administration send him their dossiers, Mexican cultural critics reported that the Americanization process was in full swing.

Like its capital, Mexico is increasingly a multilingual, multicultural country. However, this phenomenon extends beyond Spanish- and English-speaking worlds. There are some fifty-six original Indian languages still alive in Mexico and along its borders that cannot be denied their spoken and written expression. El Movimiento Indígena Nacional along with the more politically visible Ejército Zapatista de Liberación Nacional from the southern border in Chiapas have created a space for a continuing national dialogue on political empowerment, cultural diversity, and linguistic rights. Increasingly voices from the margin such as the new Mexican indigenista literatures in languages like Náhuatl, Maya, Totonaco, Toztzil, Tzeltal, and Zapoteco that since the seventies have been re-emerging through professional associations, bilingual education, and literary publications will contribute to molding a changing Mexican identity in the twenty-first century where cultural and linguistic pluralism will be accepted across borders. The Americanized Carlos on Mexicana Flight 903, capitalinos, the writers in this study, and this author are all valley Mexicans, speaking our valley languages, living out our local Mexican contradictions in private and public ways.

DE ACÁ DE ESTE LADO

"Welcome to Calexico, Gateway to Mexico" reads the sign at the beginning of my old street, la Calle Imperial/Highway 111. On Monday morning, 17 September 2001, on the other side of the continent, a nation trying to overcome a national tragedy is returning to normalcy. New York's Wall Street is up and running, though trading is down. At the same time, as is the custom, Calexico is already awake at 4:00 A.M. with traffic heading out for work on valley farms. However, El Hoyo, where in the fifties and sixties contractors with their large lumbering trucks would gather people for work, no longer exists. Instead, at El Hoyo is located a Farm Workers Association office. Farmworkers still comprise a good portion of valley residents. According to a 1997 *Los Angeles Times* report, Imperial County, of all the fifty-eight counties in California, has the lowest median income, $14,567. Workers from Mexicali and Calexico now gather away from El Hoyo at Third and Fourth Streets: mostly men, about four hundred, in baseball caps and sombreros norteños. Handshakes, coffee, and doughnuts serve as a way to reach work agreements. The contractor buses and trucks have been replaced by autos, pickup trucks, large passenger station wagons, SUVs. By 6:30 all those who wanted or received work have left for the day to return sometime in the afternoon. Even in mid-September, el Valle is hot. An early start guarantees an early ride home to Calexico and Mexicali.

Next to the Farm Workers Association office at El Hoyo the polluted New River still runs uncontrolled underneath the nearby fence, the international border. At 4:00 A.M. huge floodlights are aimed at the fence for several miles to assist Border Patrol agents in their vans as they look for illegal crossings. Overhead, a fleet of Black Hawk helicopters (the ones used in recent U.S. wars) under the U.S. Customs Service carries out surveillance both day and night patrolling the desert skies for suspicious aircraft and land vehicles smuggling drugs or people. On this Monday, Border Patrol agents are still on alert because of "people crossing our borders to do harm to us." Calexico is just one site in a border stretching from San Diego to Brownsville where some nine thousand Border Patrol agents are stationed.

Through the fence, I can see the U.S.-built maquiladora assembly plants across the border. The border here is symbolic of the relationship between these two nations: the Americanized Mexico I have witnessed in my trips to La Capital; the communities of Maya speakers from Yucatán and Zapotec Indians from Oaxaca that live in the heart of urban Los

Angeles and the approximately eighty thousand Indians from southern Mexico who work the fields in California. Though the Hotel De Anza, now a rest home for elders, still stands next to Our Lady of Guadalupe Church as a relic of a bygone era, much has changed since the romantic Charles F. Lummis first set foot in América Mexicana/Greater Mexico in El Pueblo de Nuestra Señora la Reyna de Los Angeles in January 1885. We are seeing the end of the "American" century in the "Spanish" Southwest at the same time that U.S. global imperialism is facing its first major twenty-first-century crises.

As I leave the Imperial Valley on my way back home to the Los Angeles area, my thoughts turn to my fellow travelers on this literary journey, the American Mexican writers in this book—Américo Paredes, Rudolfo A. Anaya, Tomás Rivera, Oscar Zeta Acosta, Cherríe L. Moraga, Rolando Hinojosa-Smith, and Sandra Cisneros. Though once termed minority writers, they were on the vanguard of change, articulating in many ways the multicultural ethnicities, shifting identities, and border realities, and, indeed, the postmodern anxieties and hostilities, that will continue to come to the forefront in the twenty-first century. When I left Caléxico for Los Angeles and UCLA in September 1963, I was from the border, in other words, from nowhere. Given the political and cultural realities around the globe, now very few can deny that borders are central to our way of thinking. U.S. critic Arnold Krupat regards borders and border-crossings "as perhaps the best means of some broadly descriptive account of the way things 'really' work in the material and historical world" (cited in P. Jay 1997, 176). For Mexican Carlos Monsiváis, all Mexicans live along the U.S.-Mexico border. Yes, indeed, the border is everywhere in Mexico and the United States. As I have tried to show in this book with the social, historical, and cultural worlds depicted by my writer friends, it has been there since sixteenth-century América Mexicana.

> Nuu stale neza.
> Biyubi ni riñe galaa bató Xabizende.
> Hay múltiples caminos.
> Escoge el que lleva al corazón de Juchitán.
> There are multiple roads.
> Choose the one that takes you to the heart of Juchitán.

> —PROVERB OF THE ANCIENT ZAPOTECS

NOTES

REDEFINING THE BORDERLANDS

1. This translates as "with long, loose, baggy khaki pants and always well-shined shoes."

2. I grew up impure and lower class in Calexico and Mexicali. I recall afternoons listening to the newscast on XEW, "serving the Mexican community of both valleys." In our home we heard the Afro-Cuban rhythms of the mambo and chachachá, the big band orchestras of Luis Alcaraz and Pérez Prado, the songs of the Puerto Rican Daniel Santos, the German-influenced Banda de Sinaloa, the border ballads and polkas sung by the Alegres de Terán, the Mexican ranchera sung by the national idols Jorge Negrete, Lola Beltrán, José Alfredo Jiménez, Amalia Mendoza, the romantic ballads of Agustín Lara interpreted by Pedro Vargas, Toña la Negra, or Libertad Lamarque. Fridays were reserved for Mexican movies at the Aztec Theater where we cried with the melodramatic films of the Soler brothers, Doña Sara García, Chachita Muñoz, and Pedro Infante or laughed with the comedians Cantinflas, Resortes, or Clavillazo. My readings in Spanish were limited to the photonovels of my hero, the silver-masked wrestler "el Santo," or the comic book series of illustrated classics. To these modern mass-media forms of communication, I should add the beliefs, stories, proverbs, and sayings of the oral tradition stored in my grandmother's memory. For us, a bat was a mouse that from old age had sprouted wings; and every night behind the alley wandered the Wailing Woman.

3. The area had already been settled by the Cucapá Indians of whom, according to a Mexican census, only several hundred survive.

4. In my research on the Southwest genre and Lummis, I have been influenced by the work of Genaro Padilla. See his "Imprisoned Narrative?" (1991).

5. At the same time that Lummis began publishing his own romantic version of New Mexico, native New Mexican Eusebio Chacón published romantic fiction in the form of two short novels, *El hijo de la tempestad* and *Tras la tormenta la calma*, in 1892. Until recently, Chacón, who received a law degree from the University of Notre Dame, was virtually unknown.

6. I am grateful for the work of editor James W. Byrkit (Lummis, *Charles F. Lummis: Letters from the Southwest*) cited in this section. Byrkit confirmed my own feelings expressed on the Lummis personality which were dismissed early on in my research as heretical. An earlier version of the Lummis section of this chapter was presented as "Reinventing the Border: From the Southwest Genre to Chicano Literature" for the conference "Writing on the Border: Chicano Literature and Criticism," Scripps Humanities Institute, 27 October 1989. See also Mike Davis on Lummis in his political role in the promotion of California as the romantic "Land of Sunshine" (Davis 1990, 24–30). On Lummis, see also my earlier "Editors' Introduction" in *Criticism in the Borderlands* (Calderón and Saldívar 1991).

7. Through the efforts of conservative Spanish intellectuals, the Lummis story of "the largest and longest and most marvelous feat of manhood in all history" (Lummis 1893b, 12) found new readership in a Spain still suffering from the loss of its last American colonies to the United States. In 1916, Editorial Araluce of Barcelona published a Spanish translation by Arturo Cuyás under the title *Los exploradores españoles del siglo XVI: Vindicación de la acción colonizadora española en América*. Shortly after Lummis's death, in 1930, Araluce published the eleventh edition of this book from a grateful nation in homage to the memory of Lummis, *Edición Nacional en Homenaje de España agradecida a la memoria de Carlos F. Lummis*.

8. See Genaro Padilla 1991 (46) for a list of some of the most prominent practitioners of New Mexico's Southwest genre.

9. The title page of *Romance of a Little Village Girl* bears the name of the author as Cleo Jaramillo.

10. For more on Otero-Warren and Jaramillo, see my Chapter 2, "Writing the Dreams of la Nueva México."

11. In *The Folklore of Spain in the American Southwest* (1985), editor José Manuel Espinosa offers detailed information on the personal life and professional career of his father, Aurelio.

12. This first quote is from Part One, written by José Manuel Espinosa as an introduction to his father's work. The rest of the citations are from Part Two, an unpublished manuscript completed in the thirties by Aurelio M. Espinosa whose publication was postponed. This Part Two presents in systematic form ten chapters, the major results of Espinosa's research and writing on Spanish folk literature.

13. Espinosa's classic *Romancero nuevomejicano* of 1915 contains a section II, "Romances modernos y vulgares," which includes what in his words "el vulgo" llama "corridos." Number 52 (64) is the corrido "Los Americanos," the corrido with prose translation included in this chapter. Even late in his career, in his 1954 *Romancero de Nuevo Méjico*, Espinosa continued with his unwavering defense of Spain in the Southwest. Although he emphasizes that "los nuevomejicanos dan a los romances españoles el nombre de *corridos*" (16), the majority of examples collected—eighty—belong to the "Spanish" tradition. Only eleven contemporary selections are included in "Parte Quinta: Corridos, cuandos y otras narraciones romanescas de carácter local" (247–268). This Parte Quinta begins with the corrido de "Los Americanos." A corrido is repeatedly referred to by Espinosa, yet not acknowledged as part of a Mexican or Mexican American corrido tradition.

14. Arthur L. Campa, a scholar who preceded Paredes, also rejected the Spanish fantasy. See Mario T. García's *Mexican Americans* (1989), 281–284.

15. Paredes maintained a distance from Chicanos and the Chicano Movement that was not due solely to age. He always identified as a borderer and spoke of the Border people as "my people." José Limón's reading of Paredes and his work notes the insular or self-sufficient representation of the borderers and their cultural productions, most notably the corrido tradition (Limón 1994, 84–94). Indeed, Limón focuses on the transformation of Texas border culture based on the trope of the fall from grace associated with a new emergent outsider mexicano community, in the "*peón/pocho/pachuco/fuereño*" (93). Limón, Paredes's graduate student at Austin, as he identifies himself, was "a *mexicano* working-class native of south Texas born of *fuereño* parents, growing up in the late forties and fifties. . . . I never knew a time of small ranches and country stores. . . . I knew only the asphalt-concrete *pachuco* mean streets of cities. I knew no pastures, only federal housing projects of *pochos*" (94).

16. When I visited Paredes in Austin in 1996, he planned to write one more book, one of sketches of relatives and friends that he had met on the Texas-Mexico border (see Calderón and López-Morín 2000, 221).

17. The biographical information for Paredes was drawn from a personal interview conducted with Paredes at his home on 13 July 1996 and published in *Nepantla* (see Calderón and López-Morín). UCLA graduate student José Rósbel López Morín also participated in the interview.

18. For more on Carbajal and Escandón, see Hill (1926).

19. Had it not been for folklorist Stith Thompson who, after a distinguished career at the University of Indiana, was a visiting professor at Austin, "*With His Pistol in His Hand*" might not have been published. In 1957, Thompson, who had been placed on Paredes's dissertation committee, presented the work for publication to Frank Wardlaw, editor at the University of Texas Press. Paredes was requested to delete derogatory comments related to the racial biases of his Texas

colleague, Walter Prescott Webb, and criticism of the brutality of the Texas Rangers. Paredes refused, and in the end the press relented (see Calderón 1992, 26n9; Calderón and López-Morín 2000, 220–221). Prior to his dissertation, Paredes had already conducted research on the Texas border corrido. His "The Mexico-Texan Corrido" of 1942, when he was twenty-seven, rehearses the central themes of his dissertation: the medieval flavor of the corrido; musical structure, vocalization, and guitar accompaniment; and cultural conflict in "El Corrido de Gregorio Cortés." This is the title for the corrido given by Paredes, not the correct Cortez.

20. In "Folk Base of Chicano Literature," Américo Paredes writes on Aurelio Espinosa's biased and selective judgment: "The renowned scholar Aurelio M. Espinosa, for instance, made admirable discoveries of remnants of Spanish folklore in the Southwestern United States, but in general he was rarely concerned with the purely Mexican elements, which were decidedly in the majority—or if he did collect them, very seldom did he recognize them as Mexican" (5).

21. On the relationship between the heroic border corrido and Chicano narrative, see Ramón Saldívar's "The Folk-Base of Chicano Narrative" (Saldívar 1990, 10–42). In a slightly different artistic direction, José Limón draws a line of influence from the traditional heroic corrido such as "El Corrido de Gregorio Cortez" through Paredes's *"With His Pistol in His Hand"* as a performance of resistance based on the corrido to the emergence of the poetry of social conflict of the Chicano Movement (Limón 1992, 39–41, 76–77, 88–91).

22. Paredes, always keenly aware of the patriarchal formation of Mexican border culture, stressed this aspect in the opening pages of *"With His Pistol in His Hand"* (1958). Women he knew both personally and professionally would later find a place in his work. *A Texas-Mexican "Cancionero"* (1976) is dedicated "To the memory of my mother, who could sing a song or two." In their role within the household, mothers, Paredes writes, taught their children their first folk songs (xix). Although the border corrido tradition was a male-dominated one, it was not so rigid that it did not allow exceptions, referring to the "daring and unusual" singer Doña Petra Longoria de Flores whom he knew as a child (xix).

23. This biographical sketch is taken from Paredes's Chapter III, "The Man," the source for the film *The Ballad of Gregorio Cortez*.

24. Early in their careers, both Espinosa and Paredes received assistance from major figures in folklore studies. In 1909 in Chicago, Espinosa meet Ramón Menéndez Pidal. Under the direction of Menéndez Pidal, four large collections of Spanish folktales were published. On Espinosa's first research trip to Spain in 1930, Menéndez Pidal furnished Espinosa with a detailed folklore map of Spain (Espinosa 1985, 40). Espinosa considered his folklore studies a contribution to the pioneering work by Menéndez Pidal. As already noted, Stith Thompson was placed on Paredes's dissertation committee.

25. *"With His Pistol in His Hand"* has played an important role in Chicano Studies, especially in the field of history. José David Saldívar was the first literary scholar to reread Paredes within the emerging field of cultural studies. In his "Chicano Border Narratives as Cultural Critique (1991)," Saldívar traced the intellectual work of Paredes as a response to Walter Prescott Webb's *The Texas Rangers* (1935). Webb's white supremacist writing, argued Saldívar, informed the emergence of Paredes as a public intellectual. My own work on Paredes has been greatly influenced by Saldívar's earlier essays on institutional history in Texas. In his interview with me, Paredes acknowledged the role that racism played in his scholarly and "collegial" relationship with Webb on the Austin campus (see Calderón and López-Morín 2000, 225–226).

26. Paredes maintained an ambivalent relationship with the government of the United States. He wrote the poem "The Four Freedoms" (Paredes 1991, 58) in 1941 as a skeptical response to the famous speech of the same title by President Franklin D. Roosevelt delivered to Congress on 6 January 1941. In his speech, Roosevelt declared about an imminent invasion: "The first phase of invasion of this Hemisphere would not be the landing of regular troops. The necessary strategic points would be occupied by secret agents and their dupes—and great numbers of them are already here, and in Latin America. . . . That is why the future of all American Republics is today in serious danger" (7). Paredes writes echoing keywords from "The Pledge of Allegiance": "este país de 'Cuatro Libertades' / nada nos puede dar / Justicia . . . ¿acaso existe? / La fuerza es la justicia, / palabras humorísticas: Justicia y Libertad" (58). During the war crimes trials, Paredes met Hideki Tojo, the Japanese military leader whom he had been asked to interview. On 24 December 1948, Paredes wrote an ironic poem, "Westward the Course of Empire," on the occasion of Tojo's death at the hands of the "civilized" U.S. authorities. According to Paredes, "Hideki Tojo and his fellow 'war criminals' were hanged on December 23, 1948, earlier than scheduled, we were told, so that our Christmas holidays would not be spoiled" (Paredes 1991, 11n140).

27. This article appeared in *Folklore Americano* 14 (1966): 146–163. It was subsequently published in somewhat modified form in English translation as "The Folk Base of Chicano Literature" in *Modern Chicano Writers* in 1979. Its most recent English rendition, "The Folklore of Groups of Mexican Origin in the United States," was included in the 1993 *Folklore and Culture on the Texas-Mexican Border*, the collection of Paredes's major essays edited by Richard Bauman.

28. In his *American Encounters: Greater Mexico, the United States, and the Erotics of Culture* (1998), José E. Limón, continuing Paredes's work on cultural struggle, reveals in a wide variety of cultural contexts the complexities of strife between Anglo and Mexican. While not negating the issue of domination, Limón takes his study in a utopian direction by articulating a space where Anglo and

Mexican might encounter each other in the spirit of "equality, openness, and freedom."

29. For recent studies of *George Washington Gómez*, see José David Saldívar 1993; Ramón Saldívar 1993.

30. In 1952, some of the stories later included in *Hammon and the Beans* were sent under the title "Border Country" to a literary contest sponsored by the *Dallas Times Herald*. Paredes was awarded a prize—$500 worth of books (Calderón and López-Morín 2000, 222).

31. For *The Shadow*, Paredes earned prize money of $500 (see Calderón and López-Morín 2000, 217).

32. In retirement in Austin, Paredes finally received well-earned recognition from both sides of the border. In 1989, he was awarded the Charles Frankel Prize from the National Endowment for the Humanities for his contributions in the field of folklore. In 1991, a representative of the Mexican government bestowed on him the Orden del Aguila Azteca, Mexico's highest honor, for his efforts on behalf of human rights and the preservation of Mexican culture. And in 1997, the American Folklore Society recognized him as the leading scholar in the field of Mexican American folklore.

33. The twelve founding families were composed of twenty-three adults and twenty-one children. All, with the exception of a Filipino from Manila and a Spaniard from Cádiz, were from northern Mexico—Sonora, Sinaloa, Chihuahua, and Durango. Besides the aforementioned men, the adults included four Indian women, four Indian men, two black men, six mulatto women, two mulatto men, one mestizo, one coyota, and one Spaniard born in Chihuahua married to an Indian woman, as was the Spaniard from Cádiz. Of the twenty-one children, two were Indian and the rest were racially mixed (Castillo and Ríos Bustamante 1989, 63–64).

34. Paz, who was born in 1914, accompanied his parents to San Antonio and Los Angeles in 1918–1920. The elder Paz was in the service of Emiliano Zapata.

35. The relationship between J. Frank Dobie and Paredes was not collegial. When Paredes was offered an assistant professorship at Austin, Dobie was still on campus and the acknowledged authority on Texas and Mexican culture even though he never mastered the Spanish language. When Paredes attended Brownsville Junior College, he was in the audience for a Dobie lecture (see Calderón and López-Morín 2000, 225). In *George Washington Gómez* (1990), Paredes fictionalizes this event. Dobie appears as K. Hank Harvey the "Historical Oracle of the State" but is exposed as a fraud by the young writer Paredes (270–272). Since this novel, written between 1935 and 1940, was not published until 1990, Dobie never read Paredes's sharp criticism. In 1996, Paredes, perhaps mellowed by age, had a kindlier view of Dobie: "When I met Dobie here at the university I thought he was, as far as Mexicans are concerned, something of a

fraud. But a lovable, nice old fraud. He never tried to talk Spanish to me. We could talk about other things. But he was a very nice person" (Calderón and López-Morín 2000, 225).

36. Another Texas-Mexican writer appeared on the literary scene in 1958. From his adopted home in Los Angeles, John Rechy looked back on his youth in the El Paso–Ciudad Juárez area. His 1958 "El Paso del Norte," published in the *Evergreen Review*, is a sketch essay of life on the border under white supremacy rendered in the spontaneous prose style common to the Beat Generation. Both of Rechy's parents were born in Mexico. His family lived in the Mexican barrio, El Segundo. Rechy, like Paredes, identified as Mexican and supported the Chicano Movement. Rechy, as is well known, is now acknowledged as one of the leading contemporary American writers. In *The Miraculous Day of Amalia Gómez* (1991), Rechy returned to the Mexican world of El Paso to tell the story of the endurability of the Mexican woman. Unfortunately, a full assessment of Rechy's writings lies outside the limits of the present study. John Rechy will, however, be one of the writers included in another project in progress, "Mexican American Fiction of Los Angeles: Literary, Cultural, and Political Landscapes."

WRITING THE DREAMS OF LA NUEVA MÉXICO

1. Peter Gerhard's *The Northern Frontier of New Spain* (1982) offers a richly detailed overview of all of northern New Spain, including the settlements of Alta California, Nuevo México, Texas, and Nuevo Santander.

2. Central Mexico served as a strategic region in the Spanish New World Empire. As well as serving as the staging ground for the northern conquest into the present states of Arizona, California, New Mexico, and Texas, it was from Mexico that the conquest of Las Filipinas (Nueva Castilla) began in 1565. Mexico served as the overland trade link (Acapulco to Veracruz) between Asia and Spain.

3. In 1752, José de Alcíbar, Miguel Cabrera, and José Ventura Amáez were officially requested to paint three direct copies of the original image of the Virgen de Guadalupe displayed in the Basilica at Tepeyac, Mexico City. One of these three copies, sent to the Vatican in 1754, prompted Pope Benedict XIV to confirm "the Virgen de Guadalupe as patroness of New Spain and instituted a mass and office to be celebrated on December 12, the date of the second apparition of the Virgen and the creation of the image" (Burke 1990b, 362).

4. The following citations from *Old Spain in Our Southwest* can stand as examples of the easy parallels drawn between New Mexican and Peninsular Spanish customs. "In the old days the great Spanish families lived in haciendas" (9). "'Be seated,' ordered her mother. This permission was connected with a custom of the Spanish Court. When a woman was to be raised to the title of

grandee, she entered the presence of the queen carrying a cushion and, after telling her reasons for seeking the title, she was ordered by the queen to 'seat yourself.' This meant that thereafter she belonged to the court group and could be seated in the presence of her queen" (14–15). "The Spaniard is interested in politics because it has a dramatic climax" (30). "The Spanish *doñas* always sat with an air of dignity, as of holding Court" (36). "The Spaniard is not greatly disturbed by an unusual occurrence. He continues his work where he left off, or maybe delays until *mañana*" (47).

5. For more on nuevomexicana writers Fabiola Cabeza de Baca, Nina Otero-Warren, and Cleofas M. Jaramillo, see Padilla 1991 and Rebolledo 1995. Both Padilla and Rebolledo offer a different point of view from the one expressed in this chapter. For both Padilla and Rebolledo, these New Mexican writers' work—autobiographies and cookbooks—was an act of resistance against Anglo hegemony.

6. Cited from a 1954 typescript manuscript, "Origin of La Sociedad Folklorica [*sic*] of Santa Fe," by Cleofas Jaramillo obtained from Santa Fe resident Anita G. Thomas, the eldest member of the organization. According to Jaramillo's manuscript, La Sociedad Folklórica owes its name to the Texas Folklore Society, which she had been invited to join by its founder, J. Frank Dobie.

7. Nina Otero-Warren and Aurora Lucero-White were original members of La Sociedad Folklórica.

8. The Territory of New Mexico was divided into the states of Arizona and New Mexico. The state of New Mexico was the last admitted into the Union.

9. For my earlier interpretations of *Bless Me, Ultima*, see "To Read Chicano Narrative" (1983) and "Rudolfo A. Anaya's *Bless Me, Ultima*" (1986).

10. It is interesting to note that the Virgin of Guadalupe who is so ubiquitous in Mexican American culture is not mentioned by the Hispana writers.

11. The influence of Hopkins is felt, as I demonstrate in this chapter, in landscape imagery. See also Anaya's handling of the odyssey motifs and his interpretation of the concept of epiphany. Anaya's specific use of the spiritual wasteland is Eliot's. See also Márquez 1982 (51). There is a moment (60) in *Bless Me, Ultima* inspired by the opening lines of *The Waste Land*.

12. Other influences aside, the similarities between Anaya and Frye are beyond mere coincidence. Márquez (1982) reaches a similar conclusion (46).

13. To clarify this issue, Frye conceives of displacement in two directions. It is the artistic stratagems used by writers to render plausible the presence of mythical structures (Frye 1957, 136). It is also the tendency in realistic literature to conventionalize content in an idealized direction (ibid., 137). Both are romantic tendencies in narrative and are antirepresentational or highly symbolic (Frye 1976, 38).

14. In the Introduction to the 1999 Warner Books edition of *Bless Me, Ultima*, Anaya describes his rural upbringing in Pastura, New Mexico, where curanderas, cuentos, and landscape contributed greatly to his first book (viii–ix).

15. I am much indebted to Fredric Jameson. His interests in narrative not only parallel my own but also confirm my thoughts on the subject. I have followed his formulations on romance in *The Political Unconscious* (1981; p. 148).

16. Harry Levin (1969) discusses the interest in the existence of the Ovidian Golden Age and the biblical Paradise due to European reports of the cultural primitivism of New World inhabitants (58–62). A similar primitive pastoral or Arcadian world, according to Roy Gridley (1979), has been the consistent image of the Great Plains from the narratives of Cabeza de Vaca and Coronado to the poetry of Allen Ginsberg (62, 69–70). Incidentally, the sea metaphor for the plains was first used by Coronado.

17. Anaya has discussed the need for a collective unconscious (Márquez 1982, 45–48).

18. For Joyce's original statement on epiphany, see *Stephen Hero* (1955; pp. 210–211). The bibliography on the topic is extensive, but for two opposing views see Hendry Chayes's "Joyce's Epiphanies" and Scholes's "Joyce and the Epiphany." In the writing of this chapter I have been aided by Morris Beja's *Epiphany in the Modern Novel* (1971; pp. 71–75).

19. Although the term "epiphany" is a twentieth-century phenomenon, Wordsworth, by all accounts, was the first to fix its typically modern version (see Langbaum 1983). What Abrams (1971) calls Wordsworth's theodicy in landscape (97–117) is akin to Anaya's epiphany in landscape.

20. For the historical circumstances that give rise in Romantic literature to the rhetorical distinction between corrupt city life and innocent landscape, and the consequent search for solace in nature, see Williams 1973 (127–134).

21. In my formulations of inscape, I have been aided by Frye 1957 (121) and Hopkins scholars McCarthy 1968 (67) and Cotter 1972 (3). Hopkins (1959) supplies his own sketchy definition (289).

22. See Lévi-Strauss 1966 (9–28) for his interpretation of myths as structures of thought.

23. Throughout this chapter and in this book, I have used the correct Spanish spelling for Alburquerque.

24. After the defeat of the Acoma Indians in 1599, Juan de Oñate ordered his soldiers to cut off the right feet of twenty-four Acoma Pueblo Indians. In 1998, a struggle over a proposed statue to Oñate celebrating the four hundred years since the first Spanish entrada into la Nueva México reignited old feelings. While some New Mexicans who could trace their ancestry to the original settlers supported the statue, the all-Indian Tribal Council of the state of New Mexico opposed it. Earlier in the year, vandals sawed off the right foot of an Oñate statue

in Alcalde, New Mexico, as a protest against using $255,000 of taxpayers' money for the Oñate memorial (see Rowling 1998).

25. Standing among the ruins of the former Convento de San Francisco in la Ciudad de Zacatecas, I marveled at the blue skies, the thin air of seven thousand feet, the mountain terrain, and the mixture of cultures so similar to the Río Arriba area of the Taos–Santa Fe area. "Fue gente de Zacatecas-Sombrerete la que colonizó Nuevo México" ("It was people from Zacatecas-Sombrerete who colonized New Mexico"), la Licenciada María del Socorro Correa-M., la Cronista de la Ciudad de Sombrerete, proudly informed me in 1997.

THE EMERGENCE OF THE CHICANO NOVEL

1. In the inaugural issue, Nick C. Vaca is listed as editor. The following are associate editors: John M. Carrillo, Steve Gonzales, Phillip Jimenez, Rebecca H. Morales, Ramon Rodriguez, Octavio I. Romano, Armando Valdez, and Andres Ybarra.

2. Tomás Rivera, *". . . y no se lo tragó la tierra"/". . . and the earth did not part"* (Berkeley: Quinto Sol Publications, 1971).

3. It was even thought that Juan Rulfo would write the prologue to the collection. Herminio Ríos-C. (1971a) writes: "Creo que Juan Rulfo escribirá el prólogo." In another archive document titled "Germination of Tierra," Rivera cites Américo Paredes and Pío Baroja's Spanish classic, *El árbol de la ciencia*, as influences. In another archive document, "COMMENTARY ABOUT: *And the Earth Did Not Part/. . . y no se lo tragó la tierra*" (n.d.), Rivera recalls Paredes as an early important influence: "I wrote . . . Tierra because I cared about the Chicanos. And I cared, loved Chicanos because I was one and because I, as a migrant worker and a non-migrant worker, had perceived all the complexities, the virtues, the flaws, the joys, the struggles. . . . Documentation would also bring legitimacy to those original elements of life for the Chicano. The first work I read that had this attitude has been with *His Pistol in His Hand* [sic] by Don Americo Paredes. I read this work in 1958 and since that time I had held on to the idea that we (Chicanos) needed to develop our own works from our own point of view" (1–2).

4. After attending the seminar in Guadalajara, Rivera wrote Leal of his interest in studying Spanish American literature under his tutelage at the University of Illinois (see Lattin, Hinojosa, and Keller 1988, 48).

5. Romano's "Minorities, History, and the Cultural Mystique" (1967), "The Intellectual Presence of Mexican Americans" (1967), and "Social Science, Objectivity and the Chicanos" (1970) are early *El Grito* essays indicative of Quinto Sol's scholarly and creative oppositional project.

6. The document titled "TIERRA manuscript: Original Manuscript on Tierra" is available at the Tomás Rivera Archives, Tomás Rivera Library, University of California, Riverside. The typescript manuscript includes these tales in the following order: "El año perdido," "Los niños no se aguantaron," "Un rezo," "Es que duele," "La mano en la bolsa," ". . . y no se lo tragó la tierra," "La noche estaba plateada," "Zoo Island," "Mario Fonseca," "La cosecha," "La noche que se apagaron las luces," "La noche buena," "Debajo de la casa." Four other tales penciled in after the original table of contents were "La primera comunión," "Los quemaditos," "Eva y Daniel," "El retrato." It appears that "Cuando lleguemos . . ." was the last story written after the original manuscript was submitted.

7. Rivera, letter to Octavio I. Romano-V., Editor, Huntsville, Texas, 22 October 1970, Tomás Rivera Archives, Tomás Rivera Library, University of California, Riverside.

8. In a letter from Heriminio Ríos-C. to Rivera dated 22 March 1971, Ríos explains that after working on the twelve best stories, "Eva and Daniel," "Zoo Island," and "Mario Fonseca" had not worked. Ríos would later eliminate "La cosecha" and replace it with the last story written, "Cuando lleguemos . . ." Four cuadros were also eliminated. In a letter to Luis Dávila, Rivera wrote, "El Pete Fonseca, Eva y Daniel, Zoo Island los van a escluir [sic]." These changes were undoubtedly made with the cooperation of Rivera. Julián Olivares ("Los orígenes primitivos" 214) believes that it was Rivera who made these changes. The four stories eliminated from Tierra are available in The Harvest: Short Stories by Tomás Rivera.

9. In two early lists of chapter titles "Cuando lleguemos . . ." does not appear.

10. Herminio Ríos-C., letter to Tomás Rivera, 3 August 1971, Tomás Rivera Archives, Tomás Rivera Library, University of California, Riverside. The story titles were underlined in the letter.

11. I will keep Rivera's Spanish term "cuadro" as an interpolated frame of reference that gives cohesiveness to the total work.

12. Hinojosa also retitled the fourteen tales from the Quinto Sol English version. In the same year, 1987, Arte Público Press reissued Rivera's novel as . . . y no se lo tragó la tierra/ . . . and the earth did not devour him with a new English translation by Evangelina Vigil-Piñón. Citations in English and Spanish are from this edition.

13. Document titled "COMMENTARY ABOUT: And the Earth Did Not Part/ . . . y no se lo tragó la tierra." Tomás Rivera Archives, Tomás Rivera Library, University of California, Riverside.

14. The only markers of nationality in Tierra are the words "Mex" and "Mexican" uttered by an English-speaking student: "—Hey, Mex . . . I don't like Mexicans because they steal. You hear me? . . .—I don't like Mexicans. You hear, Mex?" (21).

15. The idea of a community was central to Rivera as a writer and informs his critique of Richard Rodriguez: "I find underlined throughout the text [*Hunger of Memory*] a negation of what is fundamentally the central element of the human being—the cultural root, the native tongue. As one reads each essay, one progressively recognizes that what is most surprising for Richard Rodriguez is that silence and his basic culture are negative elements, regressive ones. This pattern of negation is softened somewhat when he thinks of his parents and his love for his parents, but he ultimately comes to the thesis that this silence and the consequent inactive community is something regressive or negative" (Rivera 1984, 6).

16. The political concerns of the Chicano poetic consciousness from its emergence in 1965 through the seventies are documented with examples by Tomás Ybarra-Frausto in his "The Chicano Movement and the Emergence of a Chicano Poetic Consciousness" (1979; pp. 81–109).

17. See Valdez and Campesino 1971.

18. See Kanellos 1984, 7–15; Leal 1985a, 2–12; Leal 1979, 32–44; Leal 1985b, 44–62; Leal and Pepe Barrón 1982, 9–32; Lomelí 1980, 45–55, and 1984, 103–119; Meyer 1979, 11–26; Rivera 1971, viii–xi; and Juan Rodríguez 1979, 67–73, and 1980, 25–26.

19. See Padilla 1984, 31–45; Raymund Paredes 1977, 29–41, and 1982, 71–110.

20. Saldívar writes: "Given the strength of the model text, *Pocho*, it should not be surprising that subsequent Chicano novels have looked to it, consciously or not, for inspiration. I am not here making a case for a Chicano 'anxiety of influence,' but I am suggesting that in its isolation of the differential structure of meaning, of the dialectic between history and art, and the roles played by these issues in the protagonist's creation of a new cultural and personal consciousness, *Pocho* is the central Chicano novel. . . . I would like to sketch a brief history of its impact on Tomás Rivera's *y no se lo tragó la tierra*, Oscar Zeta Acosta's *The Revolt of the Cockroach People*, and Ron Arias' *The Road to Tamazunchale*." See his "A Dialectic of Difference: Towards a Theory of the Chicano Novel" (1979), 79.

21. Rivera's Texas childhood experience is documented in a study of Crystal City Mexican migrant workers published in 1941. See Selden C. Menefee, *Mexican Migratory Workers of South Texas* (1974).

22. See Iser 1978, 172–173, 182–183, 225–226.

23. In one table of contents, the Bartolo cuadro precedes "Cuando lleguemos, . . ." situated as No. 6. Both cuadro and story, dealing with the theme of travel between home and group aspirations, were undoubtedly written to be side by side. It was an important decision to relocate "Cuando lleguemos . . ." as the penultimate story followed by the Bartolo cuadro before "Debajo de la casa."

24. The importance of Mexican oral storytelling for the composition of *Tierra*

can be found in Rivera's "Recuerdo, Descubrimiento y Voluntad" (1975), 66–77.

25. In his "Chicanoizing Don Quixote" (2002), Spanish Renaissance scholar William Childers, drawing on Chicano scholarship (including my earlier "The Novel and the Community of Readers" on Rivera), literature, and culture, has produced a provocative reading of the Spanish knight errant Don Quijote as a "rasquachi, vato loco." Childers, following Diana de Armas Wilson's *Cervantes, the Novel, and the New World* (2000), sees the novel after Cervantes developing in two directions, the English novel informed by Protestant individualism and the more inclusive, informed by hybridity, the mixing of cultures and styles, culminating in recent fiction of the Americas, to which the Chicano novel belongs.

26. I have taken the distinction between epistemological and didactic from John Preston's *The Created Self* (1970).

27. In both the *Quijote* and the *Novelas exemplares*, Cervantes states on several occasions that he writes for the amusement and profit of the idle reader as well as for the imagined community of his república. The Prologue to the *Novelas exemplares* can serve as the best example of the relationship between reader and nation: "Mi intento ha sido de poner en la plaça de nuestra republica una mesa de trucos, donde cada uno pueda llegar a entretenerse, sin daño de barras; digo sin daño del alma ni del cuerpo, porque los exercicios honestos y agradables, antes aprouechan que dañan ("My intent has been to place in the plaza of our republic a game of billiards, where each one may come to entertain himself, without fear of imprisonment; I mean without harm to mind or body, for decent and pleasing exercises provide profit rather than harm"; *Novelas exemplares* 1:22). For a brief but interesting analysis of the emergence of nationalism and the novel, see Anderson 1983, 30–40.

28. See Iser 1974, 50.

29. Rivera 1984, 8–10.

30. Seymour Menton, a well-known Mexicanist, was one of the first critics to read Rivera's tales in the light of Rulfo in his 1972 review. Menton was a good friend of Rivera and had been his professor in Mexican literature in summer school in Guadalajara in 1962. In a well-known 1979 essay Joseph Sommers, another scholar of Mexican literature, refers to Rulfo as an apparent influence on Rivera. While I agree in general with Sommers's opinions, it is *El llano en llamas* (*The Burning Plain*) and not *Pedro Páramo* from which Rivera took much in terms of psychological realism. Unlike the mythic landscape of *Pedro Páramo*, Rivera's ideological conceptualization of the novel refuses to admit of the mythical and the supernatural. In addition, Rivera's progressive vision of Chicano culture lies beyond the fatalism of both *El llano en llamas* and *Pedro Páramo*.

31. To Bruce-Novoa's question on the distinctive perspective on life that Chicano literature offers, Rivera responds: "But I don't think Chicano literature necessarily has a different perspective. If it does, it's in the area of looking at the

world through the eyes of the oppressed, something like a Third World type. That would be an element of distinctiveness" (Bruce-Novoa 1980, 156).

32. See Roffé 1973, 64–66; Harss and Dohmann 1966, 265–267.

33. See Almaguer 1974, 27–54.

34. Tradition as it is lived by the characters in the three central tales is also the most evident limit of hegemony: "It [hegemony] is a whole body of practices and expectations, over the whole of living: our senses and assignments of energy, our shaping perceptions of ourselves and our world. It is a lived system of meanings and values—constitutive and constituting—which as they are experienced as practices appear reciprocally confirming. It thus constitutes a sense of reality for most people in the society, a sense of absolute because experienced reality beyond which it is very difficult for most members of the society to move, in most areas of their lives" (see Williams 1977, 110).

35. I have used the 1971 title with the ellipsis.

36. On the opposition between ideology and utopia, I have been aided by the following: Mannheim 1960, 192–263; Jameson 1981, 281–99; José David Saldívar 1985a, 100–114.

37. The historical nature of Rivera's plot can be read in light of Mannheim's utopian mentality: "As long as the clerically and feudally organized medieval order was able to locate its paradise outside of society, in some other-worldly sphere which transcended history and dulled its revolutionary edge, the idea of paradise was still an integral part of medieval society. Not until certain social groups embodied these wish-images into their actual conduct, and tried to realize them, did these ideologies become utopian" (Mannheim 1960, 193).

38. Here it is important to relate this impersonal narrative strategy to Américo Paredes's "With His Pistol in His Hand," a book Rivera had read in 1958, which, according to Rivera, was the first to document and legitimize the Mexican experience—its struggles, complexities. In Chapter II, "The Legend," the individual author Paredes withdraws from the text to allow the voices of the elders to tell and create the legend of Gregorio Cortez, who will serve as the symbol of Mexican culture caught in struggle with Anglo-Texas authority. At the University of Texas, Austin, Paredes taught "Life and Literature of the Southwest: The Mexican Perspective." In my 1996 interview conducted with an ill and aging Paredes, when asked to recall what books he taught in his course, he immediately responded, "Well of course, Tomás, . . . Tomás and others" (Calderón and López-Morín 2000, 223). The admiration was mutual.

"A RECORDER OF EVENTS WITH A SOUR STOMACH"

1. *The Autobiography of a Brown Buffalo* was first published in 1972 by San Fransisco's Straight Arrow Books of Rolling Stone Press. All citations are from the

1989 Vintage Books edition, hereafter cited as *Brown Buffalo*. Acosta's *The Revolt of the Cockroach People*, first published in 1973 by Straight Arrow books (also now available through Vintage Books since 1989), lies outside the thematic limits of this chapter. This novel will be included in my study of the Mexican American fiction of Los Angeles.

2. It is important to note that in 1967, Quinto Sol Publications of Berkeley, California, began publishing *El Grito*, the first scholarly Chicano journal. In the same year Teatro Campesino performed *Los Vendidos*, the first dramatic piece to examine Chicano identity.

3. For more on the Kerouac-Acosta connection in *The Revolt of the Cockroach People*, see Gutiérrez-Jones 1995 (125).

4. Prior to *Fear and Loathing*, Thompson had published "Strange Rumblings in Aztlan" for *Rolling Stone* (29 April 1971) in which he used the byline Raoul Duke. Thompson was asked to cover the Chicano Movement in East Los Angeles and the death of *Los Angeles Times* reporter Rubén Salazar. Thompson's trip to California had led him to Acosta, who occupies a prominent role in the published article as a Chicano activist attorney. During the writing of the Salazar piece, Thompson and Acosta embarked on the now-famous trip to Las Vegas. "Strange Rumblings" was the first article with political content published by *Rolling Stone*.

5. "The Banshee Screams for Buffalo Meat: Fear and Loathing in the Graveyard of the Weird," *Rolling Stone*, 15 December 1977, 48–59. Also in *The Great Shark Hunt*, 579–604. A different version of Acosta's meeting with Thompson from the one presented in the published *Brown Buffalo* appeared earlier with the slightly different title, "The Autobiography of the Brown Buffalo," in *Con Safos* 2.7 (1971): 34–46.

6. Although Thompson was clearly identified as the star character Raoul Duke in the recent Terry Gilliam film, critics and reviewers were almost completely ignorant that the Samoan attorney Doctor Gonzo was a Chicano based on Acosta, even though there were hints in several important scenes. In one scene Doctor Gonzo is sitting in his Los Angeles office with a poster of the United Farm Workers eagle behind him. In two scenes Doctor Gonzo leaves written notes signed with Acosta's Z. And inserted into the film when Duke bids farewell to Doctor Gonzo are Thompson's last lines from his Introduction to the 1989 Vintage edition of *Brown Buffalo*: "[He] was one of God's own prototypes—a high-powered mutant of some kind who was never even considered for mass production. He was too weird to live and too rare to die" (7). The reception of the film repeats the ignorance of the first reviewers of the book *Fear and Loathing* who identified Doctor Gonzo as Thompson's Samoan attorney, never as Acosta.

7. I met Marco Acosta on 5 May 1987 in Palo Alto, California. Unless otherwise noted, the photocopies of personal documents cited in this chapter were obtained from Marco. This page 9 ("Page 9") of a manuscript is only a single

page untitled and undated. The brackets indicate Acosta's handwritten insertions into the typescript.

8. I have two versions of the same letter with different typescripts. One is undated with corrections and is signed Oscar Zeta Acosta; the other seems to be a final version but is unsigned and is dated 15 October 1973. The dated letter signed by Acosta but without the original return address appears as *"Playboy"* (109) in *Oscar "Zeta" Acosta: The Uncollected Works*, edited by Ilan Stavans (hereafter cited as Acosta 1996).

9. In *Brown Buffalo*, the Owl is similar to the inspirational figure in Goya's Capricho No. 43 titled *Los sueños de la razón producen monstruos ("The Dreams of Reason Produce Monsters")*. Ted Casey transformed into the Owl is the darker side of the imagination. Acosta narrates a scene in which the Owl hovers over him on the floor unable to move because of mescaline: "The black owl rises and flutters his wings over my face. His pudgy body disappears. Two huge, round eyes penetrate into my entire being and consume the universe. Dark, deep green covers the earth on the last day of atonement" (55).

10. A handwritten letter from Ann N. Henry dated 29 October 1972 (Henry 1972) to Oscar Zeta Acosta in Mazatlán, Sinaloa, ends on page 2 with "Love, Annie aka Alice."

11. Acosta did complete two books. For years readers have been hearing about Thompson's only recently published novel, *The Rum Diary*.

12. From an undated, typescript manuscript titled "Oscar Acosta" (3). This typescript appears as "Autobiographical Essay" (ca. 1971) in Acosta 1996 (5–15). In the published autobiographical sketch, the edited opening sentence reads "I, Oscar Zeta Acosta" (5). In my typescript manuscript, Acosta began in third person without the "I," plus the Zeta is hand inserted. In my copy, after the brief introductory paragraph, the rest of the mansuscript is written within quotation marks.

13. This correspondence (letter to Evelyn Shifte; letter from Cecil Smith, Macmillan Company; letter from Henry Robbins, Alfred J. Knopf) is available at Oscar Zeta Acota Collection, Department of Special Collections, Davidson Library, University of California, Santa Barbara. "A Cart for My Casket" is most probably chapters from *Brown Buffalo* dealing with Acosta's youth in Riverbank and experiences before 1967. "Perla Is a Pig" was first published in *Con Safos* 2.6 (1970): 29–31.

14. Green death, green soap suds, green pills, guacamole, green-walled toilet, green chair, green hair, green telephone, green car, green room, green monsters, etc.

15. On Acosta's legal maneuvers in relation to the grand jury system, see Gutiérrez-Jones 1995 (126). In 2000, Chicano and Latino participation on the Los Angeles County Grand Jury is still an issue. All candidates for grand jurors must be screened by a panel of twelve judges. For the grand jury for 1999–2000,

the judges failed to nominate a single Latino (see O'Neill 2000).

16. Like Acosta, in 1970 Hunter Thompson declared his candidacy for the office of sheriff of Aspen, Colorado. Again to demonstrate the difference between these two friends, while Acosta campaigned under the banner of the Raza Unida Party, Thompson solicited the support of Aspen's hippies and freaks and received the attention of the national media, the *New York Times* (see Ripley 1970) and the *National Observer* (see Roberts 1970).

17. Press Release of Oscar Zeta Acosta, "Declaration of Candidacy for Office of Sheriff," n.d. This document appears as "Declaration of Candidacy" in Acosta 1996 (299–301).

18. Acosta fictionalizes this event in *The Revolt of the Cockroach People* (1973; 168–175).

19. The 1970 campaign for L.A. County Sheriff was no less bizarre than the heated 1998 campaign in which Lee Baca, with 61 percent of the vote, became the first Mexican American sheriff in the twentieth century. Baca won over the dead incumbent Sherman Block who received some 630,000 votes. Even after his death, Block was supported by a group of powerful L.A. and state leaders in order to keep the deeply entrenched, status quo power politics alive. Had Block won, the L.A. County Board of Supervisors would have had to appoint an interim sheriff who would not have been Baca.

20. The Department of Justice FBI file is available at the Oscar Zeta Acosta Collection, Department of Special Collections, Davidson Library, University of California, Santa Barbara. Many individuals and Chicano groups were under surveillance during the sixties and seventies. José Angel Gutiérrez has offered an overview history of CIA, FBI, and Secret Service surveillance of Chicanos and Mexicans from 1940 to 1980 (see Gutiérrez 1986).

21. U.S. Department of Justice, Federal Bureau of Investigation, Los Angeles, California, 1 June 1970, Southern Christian Leadership Conference, Racial Matters. Oscar Zeta Acosta Collection, Department of Special Collections, Davidson Library, University of California, Santa Barbara.

22. Also in Acosta 1996 as "Willie L. Brown, Jr." (113–115).

23. Appears in Acosta 1996 as "Testament" (305). In the handwritten manuscript, Acosta ends with his signature "Oscar Acosta, Chicano Lawyer," which the published version deletes.

24. Here it is important to point out the music and visuals in the 1972 *Brown Buffalo* as a product of the sixties and *Rolling Stone*'s Straight Arrow books. Acosta scored *Brown Buffalo* as if it were a film with numerous references to the 1967 psychedelic rock anthems: "Whiter Shade of Pale" by Procol Harum lends both an ethnic and a religious motif throughout the book; Jefferson Airplane's "White Rabbit" and "Somebody to Love" were part of the mind-expanding summer of love in Acosta's travels through the United States and Mexico;

Country Joe and the Fish's "The Masked Marauder" is featured at a love-in in Golden Gate Park; and the decade-defining, surrealistic "Sgt. Pepper's Lonely Hearts Club Band," which Acosta refers to as "bullshit, nonsense" is played on the radio (19). Acosta's search for identity is represented on the brown dust jacket through the thirty-five vérité photos by Annie Liebowitz. The snapshots capture Acosta in undershirt in a variety of poses and emotional states. The front cover has Acosta in his militant self; in the center of the back cover is the image-signature of the buffalo that begins each chapter. Also the 1973 *The Revolt of the Cockroach People* has the huge cockroach cover and cockroaches appearing on the printed pages at intervals throughout the book.

25. For a view of Acosta that is different from mine, see Ilan Stavans's *Bandido: Oscar "Zeta" Acosta and the Chicano Experience* (1995; 112). Citing my "To Read Chicano Narrative," Stavans believes I give Acosta too much agency as a writer.

26. In the 12 July 1967 letter to his parents from Aspen, Acosta writes: "I left San Francisco because the fire had begun to consume me. . . . The horrible depression I'd gone through for the past year had literally left me unable to even concentrate about my problems. Neither the doctors or the pills helped one bit. . . . And so I set out to find out what was at the root of things" (Acosta 1967, 1–2).

27. For this chronology of events, I am indebted to Fredric Jameson's "Periodizing the 60s" and his compilation with Anders Stephanson and Cornel West, "A Very Partial Chronology," listing sixties world events from 1957 to 1976. This was indeed a very partial chronology for not a single Chicano figure or event was included by the compilers. As we have arrived at the next century, when demographers tell us that by 2050 the U.S. population will be one-quarter Latino, the Chicano Movement of the sixties will loom ever larger in the history of the United States.

"MAKING FAMILIA FROM SCRATCH"

1. Moraga's 1983 *Loving in the War Years* arrived the year after Richard Rodriguez's *Hunger of Memory*, which received a great deal of attention from critics and was reviewed, unlike other works by writers of Mexican background, in the mainstream press. Rodriguez's book was a product of the right-wing conservativism and indifference of the late seventies and early eighties. In her book, Moraga sought to extend sixties social activism through new versions of the politics of sexuality, feminism, and race. As I was beginning my teaching career at Yale in 1984 and, like others, responding to Rodriguez by including his autobiography in my course, a very bright young woman from Arizona, white and lesbian, asked me if she could write her paper on a just-published autobiography by a Chicana. The autobiography, of course, turned out to be Moraga's book,

which became, since then, one of the necessary titles in my Chicano literature courses. My student eventually left Yale for a college in Vermont more to her liking, but I still have the written exchanges (we actually never spoke to each other) between us—deep, personal expressions of inner growth and transformation. With this note I want to express my gratitude to her for transforming my class into a learning experience for me.

2. The late seventies and the eighties saw the emergence of Latin American Third World feminism. Indeed, three important books of this cross-border movement, Rigoberta Menchú's and Burgos Debray's *Me llamo Rigoberta Menchú y así me nació la conciencia*, Moraga's *Loving in the War Years*, and the anthology *Cuentos: Stories by Latinas*, were all published in 1983. For more on these parallel movements and their similar agendas, see Sonia Saldívar-Hull's "Feminism on the Border" (1991; 44–56) and *Feminism on the Border* (2000, 161–172).

3. See Norma Alarcón's "The Theoretical Subject(s) of *This Bridge Called My Back*" (1991) for an assessment of the impact of Moraga and Anzaldúa's anthology on Anglo-American feminism.

4. For the location of Moraga and Anzaldúa within the history of Chicana and Chicano literary studies, see my "At the Crossroads of History" and Sonia Saldívar-Hull "Chicana Feminisms" and "Mestiza Consciousness" in her *Feminism on the Border* (2000). This chapter, while acknowledging Anzaldúa's contributions to the field of Chicana literature, deals only with Cherríe L. Moraga. I will, however, cite some selected items from the vast bibliography on Anzaldúa's *Borderlands/La Frontera: The New Mestiza* (1999). For *Borderlands* within the dynamics of south Texas history, the cultural struggle between Anglo and Mexican, see my "Literatura tejana fronteriza" and "Texas Border Literature." Saldívar-Hull's Introduction to the second edition of *Borderlands* offers an enlightening interpretive essay on the book's structure and its cross-border contexts. Through Anzaldúa's reconceptualization of language, identity, and history, *Borderlands* is a feminist reclaiming of Aztlán. In his *Contingency Blues: The Search for Foundations in American Criticism* (1997), Paul Jay sees Anzaldúa belonging to a group of revisionary critics whose work, centered on the politics of location, critiques the unquestioned ethnocentric assumptions of American literature's narrow nationalist ideal. Anzaldúa, along with other critics such as José David Saldívar, Arnold Krupat, and Carolyn Porter, shows a way out of the traditional boundaries of American literary studies toward transcultural and transnational literary formations. And, of course, to Moraga's and Anzaldúa's work should be added the publishing and editorial work of Norma Alarcón, founder of *Third Woman* journal and press.

5. In 2000, Moraga published a new expanded edition of *Loving in the War Years* with four new essays. I address this version of her autobiographical writings

in the "Posdata" section of this chapter. Moraga made changes to the original 1983 publication; they mark her turn toward the Spanish language and Mexican culture. These changes are indicated in the endnotes.

6. "Epilogue: La Mujer Saliendo de la Boca" (131) [Moraga 2000].

7. "To speak two tongues, one of privilege, one of oppression. I must" (xiii) [Moraga 2000].

8. For the most complete portrait of Malintzín/Marina/Malinche in Mexican history and literature, see Sandra Messinger Cypess's *La Malinche in Mexican Literature: From History to Myth* (1991).

9. Delgado Gómez offers information on this single name for two people: "Durante toda la conquista la colaboración entre Marina y Cortés fue tan estrecha que los indígenas llamaban también a Cortés Malintzin, transcrito Malinche por los españoles" (Cortés 192n136; "During all of the conquest the collaboration between Marina and Cortés was so intimate that the Indians also called Cortés Malintzin, transcribed as Malinche by the Spaniards").

10. See "Malinche" in Castellanos 1998, 185–186.

11. Bernal's account is considered a fiction, although he certifies his Marina tale as true: "todo esto lo que digo sélo muy certificadamente y lo juro" (92) ["all this is I say I certify and swear"]. However, he also notes the similarities between Marina's and the biblical Joseph's tales of sale into bondage: "y esto me parece que quiere remedar lo que le acaeció con sus hermanos en Egipto a Josef" (92) ["and this seems to me to want to repeat what happened to Joseph and his brothers in Egypt"].

12. For an analysis of the Malinche character in the novel, see Cypess 1991, 42–57. I have benefited greatly from this analysis.

13. Norma Alarcón offers a very useful and revealing analysis of the Malintzín figure in Mexican and Chicana literature after Paz in her "Traddutora, Traditora" (1989).

14. At midcentury, Paz was not alone in linking the histories of Mexico and the United States. Certainly, Juan Rulfo in his short stories in *El llano en llamas* (1953) understood clearly the migration from Mexico's economically and spiritually dead villages into the north. On the north side of the border, World War II veteran Américo Paredes began his studies of Mexican folklore against the backdrop of the war of U.S. aggression against Mexico. It is interesting, indeed, to compare the views of Mexican culture and identity that emerged on both sides of the border around midcentury.

15. "Máscaras mexicanas" was the first of *El laberinto de la soledad* to appear in print. It was published in *Cuadernos Americanos* 49.1 (Paz 1950; 79–92).

16. "The ritual del beso en la mejilla and the sign of the cross with every coming and going from the house" (103) [Moraga 2000].

17. In 2000, Moraga writes: *"I come from a long line of Vendidas.* I am a Chicana lesbian. My being a sexual person and a radical stands in direct contradiction to, and in violation of, the woman I was raised to be" (108).

18. Moraga wrote the Introducción to the first edition of *Loving in the War Years* (1983) at the death of her grandmother.

19. For an eloquent discussion of the varieties of identities in Moraga's lesbian relationships, see Yvonne Yarbro-Bejarano's "Writing the Lesbian Mother" in *The Wounded Heart* (2001; 127–58).

20. I am repeating Moraga's citation of *The Hungry Woman: Myths and Legends of the Aztecs,* ed. John Bierhorst (New York: William Morrow, 1984).

21. For an analysis of Moraga's plays, see Yarbro-Bejarano's *The Wounded Heart* (2001), Part II, "The Plays."

22. A 2002 edition of *This Bridge Called My Back* was published at the completion of my manuscript. Moraga's "From Inside the First World, Foreword, 2001," reframes her 1981 preface and her 1983 foreword, "Refugees of a World on Fire," in light of the events of September 11. Moraga returns to one of her recurring themes to assess the new First World versus Third World relationship. What had been commonplace in the world has reached U.S. shores—invasion, war, death, terrorism, mass emotional suffering, which is to say ultimate vulnerability. The illusion of U.S. borders and U.S. invulnerability now mirrors what the First World has caused in the rest of the world. A son fears for his mother. For many reasons, for the first time Moraga "fears for [her] children and the world they will inhabit after [her] death" (xxix).

"MEXICANOS AL GRITO DE GUERRA"

1. Hinojosa writes novels in English as well as English versions of his own Spanish novels. I note the English version in the text.

2. See R. Paredes 1982 (100) and Ulibarrí and Gerdes 1978 (158).

3. See also J. D. Saldívar's *The Dialectics of Our America* (1991b) on Hinojosa's entire series as a chronicle written within formal generic constraints (74).

4. *Klail City y sus alrededores* was awarded the prestigious Cuban Casa de las Américas prize for novel in 1976.

5. Hinojosa's choice of the arte mayor syllable line displays his fondness for late medieval Spanish writing, which was, according to him, ruined in the following centuries. On the reason he chose *Generaciones y semblanzas* and *Claros varones de Belken* as titles, he answered me: "Ahora, que por qué escogí esos títulos, creo que el párrafo anterior lo dice todo: admiración por un período y una literatura que luego viene a degenerarse en el siglo 18 con toda esa ramplonería desp. del Siglo de Oro y etc" (Hinojosa 1984). ["Now, as to why I chose those titles,

I think the previous paragraph says it all: admiration for a period and a literature that comes to degenerate in the 18th Century with all that commonness after the Golden Age and etc."]

6. For an overview of the Klail City Death Trip Series from *Estampas del valle* to *Partners in Crime*, see José David Saldívar's *The Dialectics of Our America* (1991b; 62–82). With *Klail City y sus alrededores*, Hinojosa had developed the idea of writing a series but did not name it until *Korean Love Songs* (Hinojosa 2001).

7. The 2001 BBC Arena/Cinemax documentary film *Wisconsin Death Trip* is based on Lesy's book. It should be noted that the influence of William Faulkner is undeniable, especially in the creation of the mythical Belken County with its competing cultures. Hinojosa has expressed his admiration for Faulkner in an interview with José David Saldívar: "Eventually, I fell into Faulkner. Anyone who writes is going to have to read Faulkner. . . . But when I read *The Unvanquished*— which in some ways parallels what I am doing with the Mexican Revolution in my work, as well as the coming together of different cultures—I saw what I wanted to do later on" (Saldívar 1985b).

8. I have drawn some of the information for this historical introduction from *Publicaciones del Archivo General de la Nación XIV—Estado General de las Fundaciones Hechas por don José de Escandón en la Colonia del Nuevo Santander, Costa del Seno Mexicano* (1929).

9. This biographical information is available in Hinojosa's "The Sense of Place" (1985d).

10. I am grateful for Hinojosa's very kind gesture in answering my questions via correspondence. This section on Hinojosa's adolescent experiences in Mexico is taken from a letter to the author, 4 December 2000.

11. "The first piece I wrote in Spanish (not English, since I'd written five pieces for Creative Bits, a writing program in Mercedes High) dealt with two campesinos who attempted to evade the military levy which would raid villages to impress males into one side or the other of the Mexican Revolution. I lost it, it was recovered by my mother, and then I lost it again. It ends with the capture of one of the field hands and with the death of the other who falls into an acequia—an irrigation ditch—which is in Arteaga, Coahuila, and whose blood goes all over Mexico. Not bad, from this distance for a fifteen-year-old" (Hinojosa 2001a).

12. See José David Saldívar's "Rolando Hinojosa's *Klail City Death Trip*: A Critical Introduction" (1985c) for a brief biographical sketch of Hinojosa's travels to and from the valley (44–48).

13. Hinojosa was assisted in his first publication by Tomás Rivera, who sent "Por esas cosas que pasan," "Una vida de Rafa," and "Vidas y milagros" to Quinto Sol for publication. All three were included in Hinojosa's 1973 *Estampas del valle y otras obras*.

14. The map of Belken County that appears in *The Valley* (1983), the English version of *Estampas del valle*, was drawn by someone at Bilingual Press/Editorial Bilingüe.

15. "I did not want to feature any of the Valley towns by name since this would restrict creativity; I decided then, to use other names to have more freedom to situate events as they arose. As for Jonesville, when I was in Kingsville, I called my *pariente*, Paredes, and told him what I was doing. Typically, he was kind enough to give me permission to use Jonesville. Our families, according to his research, go back to the 19th C. He collected at least two *corridos* mentioning the marriages between Hinojosas and Paredeses" (Hinojosa 2001a).

16. Though there is a Texas Cameron County on the border with Tamaulipas, I am also persuaded by the symbolic Rancho del Carmen for the transformation of Karnes County to Condado del Carmen.

17. On the King-Kleberg ranch growth and land acquisition from Mexican ranchers, see David Montejano's *Anglos and Mexicans in the Making of Texas, 1836–1986* (1987), 63–74.

18. See my "On the Uses of Chronicle, Biography, and Sketch" (1985), 141.

19. "Una vida de Rafa Buenrostro" was Hinojosa's second literary effort after "Por esas cosas que pasan."

20. It is important to note that the majority of Hinojosa's works had been published prior to the appearance in the nineties of Paredes's works, which had been written from the time he was in high school to the fifties.

21. See my "On the Uses of Chronicle, Biography, and Sketch" (1985) for more on Hinojosa's don Jesús and the Spanish chronicle.

22. In August 2000, I stayed at Rudy and Pat Anaya's Casita in Jémez Springs, which they have established as a summer residence for writers. Though not a writer, I was graciously offered the house and read the statements left by previous tenant-writers in the Casita notebook. Rolando Hinojosa was kind enough to allow me to include this very personal 1997 statement written in gratitude to his New Mexican friends. I had taken earlier versions of this Hinojosa and the Cherríe L. Moraga chapter to New Mexico with me. Moraga had just left the Casita when I arrived. I was indeed privileged and fortunate to share quarters with such gifted writers.

23. Jehú Malacara clarifies, in *Generaciones y semblanzas*, the origin of the dispossessed nickname for the Anglicized Mexicans of Klail City: "Rafa dice que yo les motejé de *desposeídos* pero en realidad, no fui yo, sino él, Rafa Buenrostro" (169). ["Rafa says that I nicknamed them the *dispossessed*, but in reality, it was Rafa Buenrostro himself who did it"; 170.]

24. Here it is interesting to refer to John Sayles's murder mystery film *Lone Star* (1996) and the director's solution to cultural conflict in south Texas. At the end of the film, viewers are left with an open-ended solution. Anglo-Texan

lawman Sam Deeds and Mexicana schoolteacher Pilar, who are in love with each other, discover that they are engaged in an incestuous relationship: both share the same Anglo father. Pilar, who cannot have children, tells Sam, "Forget history, forget the Alamo." See José E. Limón's *American Encounters* (1998) for a reading of *Lone Star* proposing an emergent equality among races (149–160, 213). In *Ask a Policeman* (1998), the marriage of Rafe and Sammie Jo is of less importance than solving murders. As is the case in Mexican mestizo culture, these intercultural unions happen, y se acabó. We must note that the Texas writer Rolando Hinojosa-Smith is a product of the fusion of Anglo and Mexican. Also, in Hinojosa's *Ask a Policeman* the equality between Mexican man and Mexican woman is represented by the two border law officers—Rafa/Rafe who is chief inspector of Klail City and María Luisa Cetina who is directora del orden público of Barrones, Tamaulipas. New worlds, indeed, at the end of the twentieth century on both sides of the border.

"COMO MÉXICO NO HAY DOS"

1. At its inception in 1972, this organization was the National Association for Chicano Studies (NACS).

2. Despite misunderstandings, I am making an argument for the importance of place and time. The symbolism transformed into action was in evidence throughout the conference in the connections being made between Mexican and Mexican Americans in the United States with their brethren south of the border. One session, for example, dealt with the social and cultural archaeology of the Camino Real that linked Mexico City with Santa Fe, New Mexico, during Novohispanic times. Another examined concretely the influence of union organizing on Mexican laborers in the United States who returned to their Mexican communities with a good deal of political know-how and were able to legally force the Mexican government into concessions hitherto inconceivable.

3. Results of the survey are cited in Silva-Herzog Márquez, "Voting at a Distance" (1999).

4. Octavio Paz wrote, of course, well before the Chicano Movement. The events of the sixties changed his view on Mexican identity in the United States. I met Paz on two occasions, both in academic settings, and he was a gracious, generous person. While I was on the Yale faculty, I had him meet with Movimiento Estudiantil Chicano de Aztlán (MEChA) students. In a small informal setting, he discussed his life and writing with them.

5. What Monsiváis predicted in 1995, the bilingualism of the Mexican citizen, has become a factor in Mexican politics. During the 2000 presidential election, one of PRI candidate Francisco Labastida's campaign issues was to teach English in all Mexican public schools. On 2 July 2000, many bilingual, bicultural Mexican

citizens crossed the border into Mexico to vote in the Mexican presidential election.

6. Mary Pat Brady (1999) takes a view similar to mine: "*Woman Hollering Creek and Other Stories* is an extraordinary example of a text that considers the shifting terrains of power and makes explicit some of the terms of contemporary spatiality through both its narrative style and content" (118). However, Brady's article treats only tangentially the Mexican and Mexican American transnational spatial realities that are the focus of this chapter.

7. Cisneros began *The House on Mango Street* in 1977 as an assignment she wrote on her own as a reaction to a seminar, "Memory and the Imagination," at the Iowa Writers Workshop. Cisneros realized that none of the books in the class, or any of her classes in all the years of education, had ever discussed a house like hers. This was the moment that triggered an awareness of difference and the development of her voice. The book continued to develop through Cisneros's experiences as a teacher and counselor at a Latino Youth Alternative High School. The manuscript, published originally in 1983 by Arte Público Press, was completed in 1982. For more on the genesis of *The House on Mango Street*, see Cisneros's Introduction to the 1994 Knopf edition, especially xiii–xv.

8. During Cisneros's second visit to Yale in 1988, she gave me manuscript copies of "Woman Hollering Creek," "Eleven," "Mexican Movies," "Tepeyac," and "One Holy Night" from a collection she had tentatively titled "The Sky Has Little Eyes." These stories had already appeared in print in Mexican ("Tepeyac") and U.S. journals and collections.

9. I am citing the manuscript that Cisneros gave me when she presented it in 1986 at the Latin American Studies Spring Lectures in Chicano and Puerto Rican Studies at Yale University.

10. In "About the Author" in *Woman Hollering Creek* (1991), the reader finds the following personal information on Cisneros: "The daughter of a Mexican father and a Mexican-American mother, and sister to six brothers, she is nobody's mother and nobody's wife. She currently lives in San Antonio, Texas."

11. "Cactus Flowers: In Search of Tejana Feminist Poetry" was first presented in 1986 at the 48th Annual Writers' Conference, Texas Women's University, Denton.

12. Cisneros first traveled to Texas when she was offered a position as literature director of the Guadalupe Arts Center in San Antonio. To survive, Cisneros would travel to other states to teach. When she was finally self-employed, she chose to make San Antonio her permanent home.

13. Harryette Mullen's "A Silence Between Us Like a Language" (1996) is one of the more incisive and revealing studies of Cisneros's language shifts between English and Spanish, between literary and popular discourses.

14. In the late forties as a child in Calexico, I recall, among my earliest of

memories, singing along with Cri Crí and El Ratón Vaquero as I was introduced to the Spanish alphabet.

15. Daniel Cooper Alarcón in his *Aztec Palimpsest: Mexico in the Modern Imagination* (1997) devotes a few pages (140–147) to the presence of Mexico in five stories from *Woman Hollering Creek*. He correctly concludes that "Cisneros deliberately foregrounds issues of culture difference in her work in ways that complicate our understanding of both Mexican and Chicano identity and resist the consolidation of Mexicanness into monolithic terms" (141). Unfortunately, Cooper Alarcón's analysis is the tourist's view, simplistic and distorted. He incorrectly gives Lupita as the name for Cisneros's Lupe Arredondo in *"Bien* Pretty." The culturally inflected Lupita is not what Cisneros had in mind for her character. Arredondo's Mexican lover, Flavio Munguía, a.k.a. Rogelio Velasco in the love poem "Tin Tan Tan" just prior to *"Bien* Pretty," spells Lupita with an acrostic. Now, that is revealing of the encounter between the Mexican Flavio and Lupe.

16. Cisneros refers to the old eighteenth-century Basílica, not the 1976 postmodern church where the image of the Virgen de Guadalupe is now displayed.

17. J. Humberto Robles Arenas was born in Mexico City but lived in the United States. After serving in World War II, he returned to Mexico. The play, which received the Premio "El Nacional" in 1956, was performed for nine months. It continued to be popular during the fifties and was eventually published in 1962 by the Instituto Nacional de Bellas Artes. The play was described in *El Nacional*, 6 September 1956, as the tragic story of a familia pocha of south Texas "que no logra fundirse totalmente a un medio y a un temperamento extraños, ni aquí tratan de encontrar sus auténticas raíces. Son los 'pochos', gente un poco al garete, desorientados, indecisos o indefinidos" (cited in Robles Arenas 1962, 159) ["that is not able to completely assimilate to a foreign environment and temperament, nor here wants to discover its authentic roots. They are the 'pochos,' people somewhat adrift, disoriented, indecisive, or undefined"].

18. After the completion of this manuscript, Cisneros published her long-awaited novel, *Caramelo or Puro Cuento* (Knopf, 2002). Readers will discover thematic links between *Woman Hollering Creek* and Cisneros's novel based on a family's migration between Mexico City, Chicago, and Texas. The U.S. Mexicana Celaya "Lala" Reyes, the central protagonist, narrates the life of the Reyes family from nineteenth-century Mexico through the late twentieth century (the seventies) in Chicago. Characters from the first section of *Woman Hollering Creek* assume a prominent role in *Caramelo*. The Awful Grandmother and Abuelito of "Mericans" and "Tepeyac" reappear as Celaya's grandparents. As in "Mericans" and "Tepeyac," Celaya describes in rich detail a Mexico of the mid-twentieth century as well as the changed Mexico to which she returns many years later. *Caramelo* is the "Merican" Cisneros's novel of Mexico with a culminating mo-

ment when Celaya discovers that the caramelo-colored (burnt sugar candy) servant Candelaria in the Awful Grandmother's house is her father's daughter. The Mexico south of the border is, in a sense, Cisneros's distant relation. This chapter on Cisneros, "Como México No Hay Dos," I hope, reveals a crucial link in Cisneros's development as a Mexicana writer from *The House on Mango Street* to *Caramelo*.

19. I have the story in manuscript that Cisneros read in 1988 at the Spring Lecture Series at Yale University.

20. In an interview with Jussawalla and Dasenbrock (Cisneros 1992), Cisneros speaks about the background for the story: "'Woman Hollering Creek' tells a true story, and that's the one that gripped me when it happened in Texas" (293).

21. It is also interesting to point out that Woman Hollering Creek does exist in Texas.

22. During the sixties and seventies, Emilio Azcárraga, Mexico's powerful media mogul, built a profitable twelve-station Spanish-language network in the United States. In 1961, KMEX of Los Angeles and KWEX of San Antonio were the first Televisa stations in the United States. Azcárraga was forced to sell his network after the U.S. government accused him of illegally controlling the stations, a violation of foreign ownership laws. Since 1992 Televisa and Venevisión of Venezuela jointly own 25 percent of Univisión (for more on the vast Televisa media empire, see Miller and Darling 1996; Rodríguez 1996).

23. Univisión dominates the Spanish-language market and is the fifth-largest network in the United States. Televisa is the world's largest producer and exporter of Spanish-language television programming (see Jensen and Baxter 1999).

24. The origin and function of the La Llorona folktale has been debated in anthropological literature. In her perceptive analysis of "Woman Hollering Creek," Sonia Saldívar-Hull offers a feminist rereading of two male interpretations (see Paredes 1971; Limón 1986) of La Llorona legend. Drawing on the patriarchal history of the conquest in which Doña Marina/La Malinche/Malintzín Tenepal, by aiding Cortés, is blamed for the downfall of Indian Mexico, Saldívar-Hull equates La Llorona's infanticide with the "political act of resistance by mestiza indigenous women" against enslavement during the Spanish conquest (Saldívar-Hull 2000, 120). The version offered by Cisneros is the one I heard as a child in Calexico.

25. Saldívar-Hull reads "Woman Hollering Creek," along with a scandalous fotonovela about an unfaithful husband, ¡El infiel! where, despite the abuse of women, the "narrative unambiguously blames the women for their men's debased character" (Saldívar-Hull 2000, 114).

26. The term "literature of feminine oppression" is taken from Michèle Mattelart's classic study of fotonovelas, *La cultura de la opresión femenina* (1977).

27. We should recall that in 1967, *El Grito*, by Quinto Sol Publications, was the first scholarly journal of Mexican American thought to emerge out of the Chicano Movement.

28. The reader is uncertain whether Cleófilas knows that her future child is female as Graciela explains to Felice: "Thanks, Felice. When her kid's born she'll have to name her after us right?" (55). Drawing on Gloria Anzaldúa's version of a new mestiza consciousness, Jacqueline Doyle (1995–1996) offers the following intriguing conclusion to the story: "Cleófilas's new child embodies an emerging 'hybrid' mestiza language and consciousness, as Graciela, Felice, Cleófilas, and the child yet to be born, yet to be named cross over in the polyglot interzone of the borderlands" (62).

29. It is interesting to note comparisons between Cisneros's "Woman Hollering Creek" and Mexican filmmaker María Novaro's *Danzón*, released the same year (1991) as *Woman Hollering Creek*. Both are examples of late eighties feminist populism; both works focus on working-class women and draw on popular culture, especially on romantic genres. Cisneros, of course, utilizes romantic telenovelas and Novaro (who cowrites her scripts with her sister Beatriz) returns to the Mexican romantic cabaret films of the fifties and the sensual but stylized dance, the danzón. Both Cleófilas and *Danzón*'s heroine, Julia Solórzano (played by María Rojo), undertake a voyage, led by the male partner or in search of the ideal male partner, but at the end return from their voyage transformed, no longer naive, and perhaps ready to assert their newfound identity; the final outcome is left implied. In both works, the world of women and supportive women is crucial to the heroine's change.

30. In Elena Poniatowska's well-known *Hasta no verte, Jesús mío* (1969), Zapata appears through the eyes of Jesusa Palancares as the charitable, heroic leader of the Mexican Revolution (74–78). Jesusa Palancares is a creation based on Josefina Bórquez, Poniatowska's informant, friend, and nana.

31. In the interview with Kevane and Heredia, Cisneros reveals the following: "In the 'Eyes of Zapata' I was obsessed with María Sabina and Emiliano Zapata. So I took my research and tried something new. I usually write about a woman obsessed with a man whom she makes into a God. I did the reverse this time: a legendary figure and made him into a man" (Cisneros 2000a, 52). I would also like to acknowledge discussions on Cisneros, Womack, and Zapata with Bridget Kevane in 1994–1995 when she was my Ph.D. student at UCLA. For the role of María Sabina as a source for Inés Alfaro, see note 43. At the completion of this manuscript, I became aware of Barbara Brinson Curiel's 2001 article ("The General's Pants") on the Mexican historical sources used by Cisneros for Inés Alfaro, sources also cited by Womack. I would like to thank José David Saldívar for the Brinson Curiel reference.

32. The information for this biographical sketch is found in both Womack 1968 and Cisneros 1991.

33. In his *La tormenta* (1937a), Vasconcelos corroborates the character drawn by both Womack and Cisneros: "Y según cumple al ídolo tribal, Zapata se presentaba en público vestido de charro, águila bordada de oro en la espalda, botonadura de plata riquísima y sombreros que se exhibían en los escaparates lujosos de la ciudad, valuados en miles de pesos" (208). ["And as befits the tribal idol, Zapata would present himself in public dressed as a charro, an eagle embroidered with gold on his back, expensive silver buttons and sombreros that would be displayed in the city's expensive shop windows, valued at thousands of pesos."]

34. Sotelo Inclán, in his *Raíz y razón de Zapata* (1943), offers a list of the Anenecuilco chiefs under the Spanish empire beginning in 1587. These local leaders were the continuation of the original Indian tradition, the calpuleque. Francisco Franco, Zapata's friend and confidant, was the source for Sotelo Inclán's intimate details of Zapata's life.

35. See Sotelo Inclán 1943 (38).

36. Words repeated from Sotelo Inclán 1943 (14).

37. For the first literary rendition of Zapata's assassination, see López y Fuentes's *Tierra* (1933; 147–169). Fernando de Fuentes's classic film *El compadre Mendoza* appeared in 1933, the same year as López y Fuentes's novel of Zapata. *El compadre Mendoza* also takes up the theme of zapatismo and, in fact, is an allegory of the assassination of Zapata. In the film, General Felipe Nieto, a zapatista, is betrayed by his compadre Mendoza, the hacendado. In 1936 Fuentes directed *Allá en el rancho grande*, which gave rise to the musical ranchera genre.

38. Mariano Gill's 1952 "Zapata: Su pueblo y sus hijos" is the historical source for Cisneros's Inés (see 307–308, 310–311). Gill names the woman as Inés Aguilar. See also Brinson Curiel 2001 (409).

39. Cisneros is exact on the correspondence between fictional plot and history. For example, in the story, Zapata returns to Inés when Nicolás was three years old, in 1909, during the Leyva campaign for governor.

40. This incident is narrated by Sotelo Inclán 1943 (170).

41. At other moments in the narrative, Inés will refer to the dual nature of Zapata's character: "Your eyes. Your eyes with teeth. Terrible as obsidian. And beneath that fierceness, something as ancient and tender as rain" (101).

42. The influence of Rulfo is unmistakable in "Eyes of Zapata." As *Woman Hollering Creek* was taking shape, Cisneros had this to say of Rulfo: "A whole generation of the Chicano writers were influenced by the Latin American male boom because that's all we got. Borges was an influence, but the ones I really stay with are Manuel Puig and Juan Rulfo. Rulfo obviously for his rhythms and what

he's doing with his voices. And, of course, you know Rulfo influenced that story I wrote last night, very much so" (Cisneros 1992, 303). I suspect the story Cisneros mentions is "Eyes of Zapata."

43. To find a character whose vision and voice would be the equal of General Zapata was a formidable creative challenge. Cisneros found inspiration for Inés Alfaro in the Oaxacan shaman María Sabina, in Sabina's voice, translated into English in Joan Halifax's *Shamanic Voices*: "María Sabina was a Mazatec curandera who died not too long ago—in the '80s I believe. I have always been very impressed with her wisdom, but it's been difficult to find any texts where she is allowed to speak—she didn't speak Spanish, so one wonders whether the translations done by the German anthropologist—Wassan, and by the other authors are legit. However, a book by Joan Halifax on shamans . . . gave me an entire chapter with Sabina speaking, and though this too was translated, I felt it gave me more of an insight to her as a person and woman. I needed to find a character who would be the equal of a general, and for an indígena that's a tall order—the choices were to make her a prostitute or a witch. . . . So I really had to step on the gas and push myself to fly, literally. It was a great challenge, but greatly rewarding, though this story nearly did me in. Up until the present book [*Caramelo*], it was the most difficult task I'd ever approached" (Cisneros 2000b).

44. To Kevane and Heredia, Cisneros offers the following on voice and language in "Eyes of Zapata": "It was a great challenge for me to do that [write about Zapata through Inés] because I had to create a voice that was totally different from any of the other voices that I had created. This voice was set in a different historical time, which, one would understand from the syntax, was speaking Spanish" (Cisneros 2000a, 52). In *El arroyo de la Llorona y otros cuentos*, translated by Liliana Valenzuela, "Ojos de Zapata" reads quite well in Spanish with its intense internal monologue influenced by Juan Rulfo's poetic phrasing: "Era la época de lluvias. Plom. . . plom plom. Toda la noche escuché ese collar de perlas, roto, cuenta tras cuenta tras cuenta rodaba por las hojas de mi corazón" (Cisneros 1996, 107). It is also remarkable how well Cisneros was able to translate her mental Spanish into written English for this story.

45. The images of the Virgen de Guadalupe all adhere to this image of the Virgin Mary, which derives "from the description of the Apocalyptic Woman in Revelation (12:1): 'And there appeared a great wonder in heaven; a woman clothed with the sun, and the moon under her feet, and upon her head a crown of twelve stars.' Specific iconographic features rarely vary. The Virgin always stands on a crescent moon and is encircled by a corona of sunrays, which in turn are surrounded by a scalloped oval of clouds. Other constant elements are the brocade pattern of the Virgin's robe, the specific configuration of stars on her cloak, the lappets of her belt, her tubular cuffs, and the little winged cherub in his buttoned shirt, who supports the Virgin on his head while holding the edge

of her cloak with his right hand and the hem of her robe with his left" (Burke 1990a, 347).

46. Cisneros offers the Indian names for these goddesses but not their meaning.

47. Ixtaccíhuatl is a dormant volcano covered with snow. Thus Ixta is known in the legend as the White Woman, and by extension the Sleeping Woman.

48. According to religious tradition, a young woman will place a statue of San Antonio upside down in hopes of finding a suitor. In a similar but satirical gesture, after ending her affair with Flavio, Lupe inverts the traditional roles of *La leyenda de los volcanes* with Prince Popo lying down. There is a remarkably similar scene in María Novaro's *Danzón* (1991) in which the central protagonist, Julia Solórzano, portrayed by María Rojo, after making love, looks over the exposed dark body of her young male lover with rear to the camera as in classic artistic renditions of women. He lies sleeping while Julia smokes a cigarette. In this affair, it will be the young man who will feel the loss most acutely.

49. Cisneros has stated that the New Age, born-again Chicana Lupe is a parody of Chicana writers including herself: "When I wrote the story I was really making a lot of fun of myself. I was really hard on the Lupe character who was so ridiculous, phony, and silly at first. When I started she was just a New Age, born again Chicana. I like the story a lot. I was also reacting to two portrayals of Chicanas that had just come out, Alma Villanueva's *The Ultraviolet Sky* and Ana Castillo's *Sapogonia*. Who's paying for the rent on that loft? It seemed to me a romanticization and myth-making and overglorification of the Latina artist, not the reality. I knew about paying for an apartment in a scary neighborhood and pretending it was more romantic than poor" (Cisneros 2000a, 53).

50. Unlike the other well-known television stars invoked by Cisneros, Libertad Palomares is Cisneros's creation whose name corresponds to the liberating poetic images at the end of the story.

51. Cisneros told me that she selected *"Bien* Pretty" to end *Woman Hollering Creek*.

52. In the year *Frontera de cristal* was published, Carlos Monsiváis expressed a view similar to Fuentes's concerning the influence of Chicano artists in Mexico: "In the future, will Mexico be a nation of Chicanos, of Mexican Americans? The question is, of course, rhetorical. Nonetheless, it is true that the presence—and the influence—of Chicano culture in Mexico is considerable. This presence is rooted in the strength of a high-profile sector of Mexican-American painters, performance artists, playwrights and filmmakers" (Monsiváis 1995, 41).

53. In 1998, in the *Los Angeles Times*, Cisneros wrote about the Chicana writer's sense of responsibility to a larger family (this is the word she used in the article) on both sides of the border, a heightened sense of responsibility prompted by the death of her father and the massacre of forty-five Mayans in Acteal,

Chiapas, on Christmas Eve 1997: "I know the deaths in Chiapas are linked to me here in the U.S. I know the massacre is connected to removing native people from their land, because although the people are poor, the land is rich, and the government knows this. And the Mexican debt is connected to my high standard of living here, and the military presence is necessary to calm U.S. investors. . . . I have been thinking and thinking about all this like a person with *comezon*, an itching, a hankering, an itch I can't quite scratch. What is my responsibility as a writer in light of these events? As a woman, as a *mestiza*? As a U.S. citizen who lives on several borders? What do I do as the daughter of a Mexican man?" (Cisneros 1998).

WORKS CITED

Abrams, M. H. 1971. *Natural Supernaturalism: Tradition and Revolution in Romantic Literature.* New York: W. W. Norton.

Acosta, Oscar Zeta. 1962. Letter to Evelyn Shifte, Vanguard Press, New York. Oscar Zeta Acosta Collection. Department of Special Collections. Davidson Library. University of California, Santa Barbara.

———. 1967. Letter to Dear Folks. 12 July. Oscar Zeta Acosta Collection. Department of Special Collections. Davidson Library. University of California, Santa Barbara.

———. 1968. Letter to Marco Acosta. March. Unpublished typescript.

———. 1970. "Perla Is a Pig." *Con Safos* 2.5: 5–14.

———. 1971. "The Autobiography of the Brown Buffalo." *Con Safos* 2.7: 34–46.

———. 1972a. *The Autobiography of a Brown Buffalo.* San Francisco: Straight Arrow Books.

———. 1972b. Letter to Alan Rinzler. 12 November. Unpublished typescript.

———. 1973. *The Revolt of the Cockroach People.* San Francisco: Straight Arrow Books.

———. 1974. "Last Will and Testament of Oscar Acosta." 13 January. Handwritten manuscript. Also "Testament." In *Oscar "Zeta" Acosta: The Uncollected Works.* Ed. Ilan Stavans. Houston: Arte Público Press. 304.

———. 1989a. *The Autobiography of a Brown Buffalo.* New York: Vintage Books.

———. 1989b. *The Revolt of the Cockroach People.* New York: Vintage Books.

———. 1996. *Oscar "Zeta" Acosta: The Uncollected Works.* Ed. Ilan Stavans. Houston: Arte Público Press.

———. n.d. "Declaration of Candidacy for Office of Sheriff." Press release. Also "Declaration of Candidacy." In *Oscar "Zeta" Acosta.* 299–301.

————. n.d. Letter to Betty Acosta. Unpublished typescript.

————. n.d. Letter to Helen Brann. Unpublished handwritten manuscript.

————. n.d. Letter to *Playboy* Forum. Also *"Playboy."* In *Oscar "Zeta" Acosta.* 109.

————. n.d. Letter to Willie Brown. Also "Willie L. Brown, Jr." In *Oscar "Zeta" Acosta.* 113–115.

————. n.d. "My Name is Zeta." Unpublished typescript.

————. n.d. "Oscar Acosta." Typescript. Also "Autobiographical Essay." In *Oscar "Zeta" Acosta.* 5–15.

————. n.d. "On Nights Like This". Unpublished handwritten manuscript.

————. n.d. "Page 9." Unpublished typescript.

————. n.d. "The Rise and Fall of General Zeta." Unpublished handwritten manuscript.

Alarcón, Norma. 1983. "Chicana's Feminist Literature: A Re-Vision through Malintzin/or Malintzin: Putting Flesh Back on the Object." In *This Bridge Called My Back: Writings by Radical Women of Color.* Ed. Cherríe Moraga and Gloria Anzaldúa. New York: Kitchen Table: Women of Color Press. 182–190.

————. 1989. "Traddutora, Traditora: A Paradigmatic Figure of Chicana Feminism." In *The Construction of Gender and Modes of Social Division.* Ed. Donna Przybylowicz, Nancy Hartstock, and Pamela McCallum. Special Issue of *Cultural Critique* 13 (Fall): 57–87.

————. 1991. "The Theoretical Subject(s) of *This Bridge Called My Back* and Anglo-American Feminism." In *Criticism in the Borderlands.* Ed. Héctor Calderón and José David Saldívar. Durham, N.C.: Duke University Press. 28–39.

Allá en el rancho grande. 1936. Dir. Fernando de Fuentes. Alfonso Rivas Bustamante, Fernando de Fuentes, and Antonio Díaz Lombardo.

Almaguer, Tomás. 1974. "Historical Notes on Chicano Oppression: The Dialectics of Race and Class Domination in North America." *Aztlán* 5.1–2: 27–54.

American Indian Trickster Tales. 1998. Sel. and ed. Richard Erdoes and Alfonso Ortiz. New York: Viking.

Anaya, Rudolfo A. 1972. *Bless Me, Ultima.* Berkeley: Quinto Sol Publications.

————. 1972, 1999. Introduction. In *Bless Me, Ultima.* New York: Warner Books. viii–xi.

————. 1976a. *Heart of Aztlán.* Berkeley: Editorial Justa Publications.

————. 1976b. "The Writer's Inscape." Paper presented at the Rocky Mountain MLA, Santa Fe, New Mex., 22 October. Abstract in *Rocky Mountain Review of Language and Literature* 30.3 (1976): 161–162.

————. 1977. "The Writer's Landscape: Epiphany in Landscape." *Latin American Literary Review* 5.10: 98–102.

————. 1978. *Tortuga*. Berkeley: Editorial Justa Publications.

————. 1985. *The Adventures of Juan Chicaspatas*. Houston: Arte Público Press.

————. 1990. "Autobiography." In *Rudolfo A. Anaya: Focus on Criticism*. Ed. César A. González-T. La Jolla, Calif.: Lalo Press. 359–388.

————. 1991. *Alburquerque*. Albuquerque: University of New Mexico Press.

————. 1995. *Zia Summer*. New York: Warner Books.

————. 1996. *Rio Grande Fall*. New York: Warner Books.

————. 1999. *Shaman Winter*. New York: Warner Books.

Anderson, Benedict. 1983. *Imagined Communities: Reflections on the Origin and Spread of Nationalism*. London: Verso.

Anzaldúa, Gloria. 1999. *Borderlands/La Frontera: The New Mestiza*. 2d ed. San Francisco: Aunt Lute Books.

Baker, Houston A., Jr. n.d. "LimIts of the Border." Unpublished manuscript.

The Ballad of Gregorio Cortez. 1983. Dir. Robert Young. Films Inc.

Beja, Morris. 1971. *Epiphany in the Modern Novel*. London: Peter Owen.

Borges, Jorge Luis. 1944. *El jardín de senderos que se bifurcan*. In *Ficciones*. Buenos Aires: Ediciones SUR.

————. 1981. "The Gospel According to Mark." In *Borges, a Reader: A Selection from the Writings of Jorge Luis Borges*. Ed. Emir Rodríguez Monegal and Alastair Reid. New York: E. P. Dutton. 308–311.

Brady, Mary Pat. 1999. "The Contrapuntal Geographies of *Woman Hollering Creek and Other Stories*." *American Literature* 71.1 (March): 117–150.

Brinson Curiel, Barbara. 2001. "The General's Pants: A Chicana Feminist (Re)Vision of the Revolution in Sandra Cisneros's 'Eyes of Zapata'." *Western American Literature* 35.4 (Winter): 403–427.

Bruce-Novoa, Juan. 1980. *Chicano Authors: Inquiry by Interview*. Austin: University of Texas Press.

El bruto. 1952. Dir. Luis Buñuel. Internacional Cinematografía.

Burke, Marcus. 1990a. "A Mexican Artistic Consciousness." In *Mexico: Splendors of the Thirty Centuries*. New York: Metropolitan Museum of Art. 321–356.

————. 1990b. "Painting: The Eighteenth-Century Mexican School." In *Mexico: Splendors of the Thirty Centuries*. New York: Metropolitan Museum of Art. 361–363.

Calderón, Héctor. 1983. "To Read Chicano Narrative: Commentary and Metacommentary." *Mester* 11.2: 3–14.

————. 1985. "On the Uses of Chronicle, Biography and Sketch in Rolando Hinojosa's *Generaciones y semblanzas*." In *The Rolando Hinojosa Reader: Essays Historical and Critical*. Ed. José David Saldívar. Houston: Arte Público Press. 133–142.

———. 1986. "Rudolfo A. Anaya's *Bless Me, Ultima*: A Chicano Romance of the Southwest." *Crítica* 1.3: 21–47.

———. 1990. "At the Crossroads of History, on the Borders of Change: Chicano Literary Studies, Past, Present, and Future." In *Left Politics and the Literary Profession*. Ed. Lennard J. Davis and M. Bella Mirabella. New York: Columbia University Press. 211–235.

———. 1991. "The Novel and the Community of Readers: Rereading Tomás Rivera's *Y no se lo tragó la tierra*." In *Criticism in the Borderlands*. Ed. Héctor Calderón and José David Saldívar. Durham, N.C.: Duke University Press. 97–113.

———. 1992. "Texas Border Literature: Cultural Transformation and Historical Reflection in Américo Paredes, Rolando Hinojosa and Gloria Anzaldúa." *Dispositio* 16.41: 13–27.

———. 1993, 1994. "Literatura fronteriza tejana: El compromiso con la historia en Américo Paredes, Rolando Hinojosa y Gloria Anzaldúa." *Mester* 22.2 and 23.1: 41–61.

Calderón, Héctor, and José Rósbel López-Morín. 2000. "Interview with Américo Paredes." *Nepantla* 1.1: 197–228.

Calderón, Héctor, and José David Saldívar. 1991. "Editors' Introduction, Criticism in the Borderlands." In *Criticism in the Borderlands*. Ed. Héctor Calderón and José David Saldívar. Durham, N.C.: Duke University Press. 1–7.

Carpentier, Alejo. 1976. *Los pasos perdidos*. La Habana: Editorial de Arte y Literatura.

Carrasco, David. 1982. "A Perspective for a Study of Religious Dimensions in Chicano Experience: *Bless Me, Ultima* as a Religious Text." *Aztlán* 13.1–2: 195–221.

Castellanos, Rosario. 1998. *Obras II: Poesía, teatro y ensayo*. Compilación y notas de Eduardo Mejía. México, D.F.: Fondo de Cultura Económica.

Castillo, Pedro, and Antonio Ríos Bustamante. 1989. *México en Los Angeles*. Trad. Ana Rosa González Matute. México, D.F.: Alianza Editorial Mexicana.

Cervantes Saavedra, Miguel de. 1922–1925. *Novelas exemplares*. 3 vols. Ed. Rodolfo Schevill y Adolfo Bonilla. Madrid: Gráficas Reunidas.

———. 1947. *El ingenioso hidalgo don Quijote de la Mancha*. 10 vols. Ed. F. Rodríguez Marín. Madrid: Real Academia Española.

Chicano Art: Resistance and Affirmation. 1991. Ed. Richard Griswold del Castillo, Teresa McKenna, and Yvonne Yarbro Bejarano. Los Angeles: Wright Art Gallery, University of California, Los Angeles.

Childers, William. 2002. "Chicanoizing Don Quixote: For Luis Andrés Murillo." *Aztlán* 27.2 (Fall): 87–117.

Chipman, Donald. 1957. "The Oñate-Moctezuma-Zaldívar Families of

Northern New Spain." *New Mexico Historical Review* 52: 297–310.

Cisneros, Sandra. 1980. *Bad Boys*. San Jose: Mango Publications.

———. 1983. *The House on Mango Street*. Houston: Arte Público Press.

———. 1985a. "My Wicked Wicked Ways: The Chicana Writer's Struggle With Good and Evil or Las Hijas de la Malavida." Unpublished essay.

———. 1985b. "Sandra Cisneros." In *Partial Autobiographies: Interviews with Twenty Chicano Poets*. Ed. Wolfgang Binder. Erlangen: Verlag Palm & Enke. 54–74.

———. 1986. "Cactus Flowers: In Search of Tejana Feminist Poetry." *Third Woman* 3.1–2: 73–80.

———. 1987a. *My Wicked Wicked Ways*. Bloomington, Ind.: Third Woman Press.

———. 1987b. "A Writer's Voyages." *Texas Observer*, 25 September: 18–19.

———. 1991. *Woman Hollering Creek and Other Stories*. New York: Random House.

———. 1992. "Sandra Cisneros." In *Interviews with Writers of the Post-Colonial World*. Ed. Feroza Jussawalla and Reed Way Dasenbrock. Oxford: University of Mississippi Press. 286–306.

———. 1994a. Introduction. *The House on Mango Street*. New York: Alfred A. Knopf. xi–xx.

———. 1994b. "Original Sin." In *Loose Woman: Poems by Sandra Cisneros*. New York: Vintage Books. 7–8.

———. 1996. *El arroyo de la Llorona y otros cuentos*. Trad. Liliana Valenzuela. New York: Vintage Español.

———. 1998. "The Genius of Creative Flexibility." *Los Angeles Times*, 22 February: M2, M6.

———. 2000a. "A Home in the Heart: An Interview with Sandra Cisneros." In *Latina Self-Portraits: Interviews with Contemporary Women Writers*." Ed. Bridget Kevane and Juanita Heredia. Albuquerque: University of New Mexico Press. 45–57.

———. 2000b. E-mail to the author. 19 July.

———. 2002. *Caramelo o Puro Cuento*. New York: Alfred A. Knopf.

El compadre Mendoza. 1933. Dir. Fernando de Fuentes. Interamericana Films y Producciones Aguila.

Concepción, María. 1972. *Pepe Guízar: Pintor musical de México*. México, D.F.: Editores Asociados.

"Contempt in Arson Case of Chicanos." 1971. *Herald Examiner*, 11 August: 1.

Cooper Alarcón, Daniel. 1997. *The Aztec Palimpsest: Mexico in the Modern Imagination*. Tucson: University of Arizona Press.

Cortés, Hernán. 1993. *Cartas de relación*. Edición, introducción y notas de Angel

Delgado Gómez. Madrid: Clásicos Castalia.

Cotter, James Finn. 1972. *Inscape: The Christology and Poetry of Gerard Manley Hopkins*. Pittsburgh: University of Pittsburgh Press.

Cypess, Sandra Messinger. 1991. *La Malinche in Mexican Literature: From History to Myth*. Austin: University of Texas Press.

Danzón. 1991. Dir. María Novaro. Macondo Cine Video.

Davis, Mike. 1990. *City of Quartz: Excavating the Future in Los Angeles*. London: Verso.

De Leon, Arnoldo. 1983. *They Called Them Greasers: Anglo Attitudes toward Mexicans in Texas, 1821–1900*. Austin: University of Texas Press.

Díaz del Castillo, Bernal. 1989. *Historia verdadera de la conquista de la Nueva España*. Edición, índices y prólogo de Carmelo Sáenz de Santa María. Madrid: Alianza Editorial.

Doyle, Jacqueline. 1995–1996. "Haunting the Borderlands: La Llorona in Sandra Cisneros's 'Woman Hollering Creek.'" *Frontiers* 16.1: 53–70.

"Editorial." 1967. *Quinto Sol* 1.1: 4.

El Saffar, Ruth S. 1974. *From Novel to Romance: A Study of Cervantes's "Novelas ejemplares."* Baltimore: Johns Hopkins University Press.

Eliot, T. S. 1962. *The Waste Land and Other Poems*. New York: Harcourt Brace Jovanovich.

———. 1975. "Ulysses, Order, and Myth." In *Selected Prose of T. S. Eliot*. Ed. Frank Kermode. New York: Harcourt Brace Jovanovich. 175–178.

Espinel, Luisa. 1946. *Canciones de Mi Padre: Spanish Folksongs from Southern Arizona Collected by Luisa Espinel from Her Father Don Federico Ronstadt y Redondo*. *University of Arizona Bulletin* 17.1.

Espinosa, Aurelio M. 1915. "Romancero nuevomejicano." *Revue Hispanique* 33.

———. 1953. *Romancero de Nuevo Méjico*. Madrid: Consejo Superior de Investigaciones Científicas.

———. 1985. *The Folklore of Spain in the American Southwest: Traditional Spanish Folk Literature in Northern New Mexico and Southern Colorado*. Ed. J. Manuel Espinosa. Norman: University of Oklahoma Press.

"Ex-Attorney Acquitted." 1972. *Los Angeles Times*, 17 February: 115.

Fear and Loathing in Las Vegas. 1998. Dir. Terry Gilliam. Universal.

Feeny, Mark. 1997. "*On the Road* Again." *Boston Globe*, 21 September: N1, N6–7.

"Festive Weekend Marks L.A.'s Birthday." 2000. *Los Angeles Times*, 5 September: B2.

"4 Activists Surrender in Biltmore Fire Case." 1969. *Los Angeles Times*, 10 June: 128.

Frye, Northrop. 1957. *Anatomy of Criticism: Four Essays*. Princeton: Princeton University Press.

———. 1976. *The Secular Scripture: A Study of the Structure of Romance.* Cambridge, Mass.: Harvard University Press.

Fuentes, Carlos. 1962. *La muerte de Artemio Cruz.* México: Fondo de Cultura Económica.

———. 1975. *Terra nostra.* México: Editorial Joaquín Mortiz.

———. 1991. *The Death of Artemio Cruz.* Trans. Alfred MacAdam. New York: Farrar, Straus and Giroux.

———. 1995. *La frontera de cristal: Una novela en nueve cuentos.* México: Alfaguara.

———. 1997. *The Crystal Frontier: A Novel in Nine Stories.* Trans. Alfred MacAdam. New York: Farrar, Straus and Giroux.

García, Mario T. 1989. *Mexican Americans.* New Haven: Yale University Press.

———. 2000. *Luis Leal: An Auto/Biography.* Austin: University of Texas Press.

García Márquez, Gabriel. 1967. *Cien años de soledad.* Buenos Aires: Editorial Sudamericana.

Gerhard, Peter. 1982. *The Northern Frontier of New Spain.* Princeton: Princeton University Press.

Gómez, Alma, Cherríe Moraga, and Mariana Romo-Carmona. 1983. *Cuentos: Stories by Latinas.* New York: Kitchen Table/Women of Color Press.

Gill, Mariano. 1952. "Zapata: Su pueblo y sus hijos." *Historia Mexicana* 11.2 (Octubre–Diciembre): 294–312.

González Prada, Manuel. 1941. "El problema indígena." In *Prosa menuda.* Buenos Aires: Ediciones Imán.

Gridley, Roy E. 1979. "Some Versions of the Primitive and the Pastoral on the Great Plains of America." In *Survivals of Pastoral.* Ed. Richard F. Hardin. Lawrence: University Press of Kansas. 61–85.

Gutiérrez, José Angel. 1986. "Chicanos and Mexicans under Surveillance: 1940–1980." In *Renato Rosaldo Lecture Series Monograph*, vol. 2, series 1984–1985. Ed. Ignacio M. García. Tucson: University of Arizona, Mexican American Studies & Research Center. 29–58.

Gutiérrez, Ramón A. 1991. *When Jesus Came, the Corn Mothers Went Away.* Stanford: Stanford University Press.

Gutiérrez-Jones, Carl. 1995. *Rethinking the Borderlands: Between Chicano Discourse and Legal Discourse.* Berkeley: University of California Press.

Guzmán, Martín Luis. 1991. *El águila y la serpiente.* México, D.F.: Editorial Porrúa.

Halifax, Joan. 1979. *Shamanic Voices: A Survey of Visionary Narratives.* New York: E. P. Dutton.

Harss, Luis, and Barbara Dohmann. 1966. *Into the Mainstream.* New York: Harper & Row.

Hartman, Geoffrey H. 1970. "Romantic Poetry and the Genius Loci." In *Beyond Formalism: Literary Essays, 1958–1970*. New Haven: Yale University Press. 311–336.

Hendry Chayes, Irene. 1946. "Joyce's Epiphanies." *Sewanee Review* 54: 449–467.

Henry, Ann N. 1972. Letter to Oscar Z. Acosta. 29 October. Unpublished handwritten manuscript.

Herner, Irene. 1979. *Mitos y monitos: Historietas y fotonovelas en México*. Colaboración de María Eugenia Chellet. Prólogo de Enrique González Casanova. México: Universidad Nacional Autónoma de México; Editorial Nueva Imagen.

Hill, Lawrence Francis. 1926. *José de Escandón and the Founding of Nuevo Santander*. Columbus: Ohio State University Press.

Hinojosa, Rolando. 1973. *Estampas del valle y otras obras/Sketches of the Valley and Other Works*. English trans. Gustavo Valadez. Berkeley: Editorial Quinto Sol.

———. 1977. *Generaciones y semblanzas*. English trans. Rosaura Sánchez. Berkeley: Editorial Justa Publications.

———. 1978. *Korean Love Songs: From Klail City Death Trip*. Berkeley: Editorial Justa.

———. 1981. *Mi querido Rafa*. Houston: Arte Público Press.

———. 1982. *Rites and Witnesses*. Houston: Arte Público Press.

———. 1983. *The Valley*. Ypsilanti, Mich.: Bilingual Press/Editorial Bilingüe.

———. 1984. Letter to the author. 30 June.

———. 1985a. "Crossing the Line: The Construction of a Poem." In *The Rolando Hinojosa Reader: Essays Historical and Critical*. Ed. José David Saldívar. Houston: Arte Público Press. 25–38.

———. 1985b. *Dear Rafe*. Houston: Arte Público Press.

———. 1985c. *Partners in Crime: A Rafe Buenrostro Mystery*. Houston: Arte Público Press.

———. 1985d. "The Sense of Place." In *The Rolando Hinojosa Reader: Essays Historical and Critical*. Ed. José David Saldívar. Houston: Arte Público Press. 18–24.

———. 1985e. "A Voice of One's Own." In *The Rolando Hinojosa Reader: Essays Historical and Critical*. Ed. José David Saldívar. Houston: Arte Público Press. 11–17.

———. 1986a. *Claros varones de Belken/Fair Gentlemen of Belken County*. English trans. Julia Cruz. Tempe, Ariz.: Bilingual Press/Editorial Bilingüe.

———. 1986b. "River of Blood." *Texas Quarterly: Sesquicentennial Collector's Issue*. January.

————. 1987a. *Klail City*. Houston: Arte Público Press.

————. 1987b. *This Migrant Earth: Rolando Hinojosa's Rendition in English of Tomás Rivera's ". . . y no se lo tragó la tierra."* Houston: Arte Público Press.

————. 1990. *Becky and Her Friends*. Houston: Arte Público Press.

————. 1991. *Los amigos de Becky*. Houston: Arte Público Press.

————. 1993. *The Useless Servants*. Houston: Arte Público Press.

————. 1997. Letter to Rudy and Pat Anaya. 16–26 June.

————. 1998. *Ask a Policeman*. Houston: Arte Público Press.

————. 2000a. "Breve pesquisa del Valle del Río Grande." *Ventana Abierta* 3.9 (Otoño): 43–47.

————. 2000b. Letter to the author. 4 December.

————. 2001a. E-mail to the author. 28 August.

————. 2001b. E-mail to the author. 29 August.

Hopkins, Gerard Manley. 1959. *The Journals and Papers of Gerard Manley Hopkins*. Ed. Humphrey House. London: Oxford University Press.

"Hunter S. Thompson, Commando Journalist." 1973. "On the Scene." *Playboy*. November: 188.

Iser, Wolfgang. 1974. *The Implied Reader: Patterns of Communication in Prose Fiction from Bunyan to Beckett*. Baltimore: Johns Hopkins University Press.

————. 1978. *The Act of Reading: A Theory of Aesthetic Response*. Baltimore: Johns Hopkins University Press.

Jameson, Fredric. 1981. *The Political Unconscious: Narrative as a Socially Symbolic Act*. Ithaca: Cornell University Press.

————. 1984. "Periodizing the 60s." In *The 60s Without Apology*. Ed. Sohnya Sayres, Anders Stephanson, Stanley Aronowitz, and Fredric Jameson. Minneapolis: University of Minnesota Press. 178–209.

Jameson, Fredric, Anders Stephanson, and Cornel West, comps. N.d. "A Very Partial Chronology." In *The 60s Without Apology*. 210–215.

Jaramillo, Cleofas M. 1939. *Cuentos del Hogar/Spanish Fairy Stories*. El Campo, Tex.: Citizen Press.

————. 1941. *Shadows of the Past/Sombras del Pasado*. Santa Fe, New Mex.: Seton Village Press.

————. 1942. *The Genuine New Mexico Tasty Recipes/Potajes Sabrosos*. Santa Fe, New Mex.: Seton Village Press.

————. 1954. "Origin of La Sociedad Folklorica [*sic*] of Santa Fe." Unpublished typewritten manuscript.

————. 1955. *Romance of a Little Village Girl*. San Antonio, Tex.: Naylor.

Jay, Gregory L. 1997. *American Literature and the Culture Wars*. Ithaca: Cornell University Press.

Jay, Paul. 1997. *Contingency Blues: The Search for Foundations in American Criticism*. Madison: University of Wisconsin Press.

Jensen, Elizabeth, and Kevin Baxter. 1999. "Univision: TV Success Story That Will Last?" *Los Angeles Times*, 13 July: A1, A19.

Joyce, James. 1955. *Stephen Hero*. New York: New Directions.

———. 1961. *Ulysses*. New York: Vintage Books.

———. 1964. *A Portrait of the Artist as a Young Man*. New York: Viking Press.

Kandell, Jonathan. 1988. *La Capital: The Biography of Mexico City*. New York: Henry Holt.

Kanellos, Nicolás. 1984. "Introducción." In Daniel Venegas's *Las aventuras de don Chipote o Cuando los pericos mamen*. México, D.F.: Secretaría de Educación Pública, Centro de Estudios del Norte de México. 7–15.

Lafaye, Jacques. 1977. *Quetzalcóatl y Guadalupe: La formación de la conciencia nacional en México*. Trad. Ida Vitale y Fulgencio López Vidarte. México, D.F.: Fondo de Cultura Económica.

Langbaum, Robert. 1983. "The Epiphanic Mode in Wordsworth and Modern Literature." *New Literary History* 14: 335–358.

Lattin, Vernon E., Rolando Hinojosa, and Gary D. Keller, eds. 1988. *Tomás Rivera 1935–1984: The Man and His Work*. Tempe, Ariz.: Bilingual Press/Editorial Bilingüe.

Leal, Luis. 1979. "Mexican American Literature: A Historical Perspective." *Revista Chicano-Riqueña* 1.1 (1973): 32–44. Updated version in *Modern Chicano Writers: A Collection of Critical Essays*. Ed. Joseph Sommers and Tomás Ybarra Frausto. Englewood Cliffs, N.J.: Prentice Hall. 18–30.

———. 1985a. "Cuatro siglos de prosa aztlanense." *La Palabra* 2.1 (1980): 2–12. Reprinted in his *Aztlán y México: Perfiles literarios e históricos*. Binghamton, N.Y.: Bilingual Press/Editorial Bilingüe. 51–62.

———. 1985b. "Periodización de la literatura chicana." In *Aztlán y México: Perfiles literarios e históricos*. Binghamton, N.Y.: Bilingual Press/Editorial Bilingüe. 44–62.

Leal, Luis, and Pepe Barrón. 1982. "Chicano Literature: An Overview." In *Three American Literatures: Essays in Chicano, Native-American, and Asian-American Literature for Teachers of American Literature*. Ed. Houston Baker Jr. New York: Modern Language Association. 9–32.

Lesy, Michael. 1973. *Wisconsin Death Trip*. New York: Pantheon Books.

Lévi-Strauss, Claude. 1966. *The Savage Mind*. Chicago: University of Chicago Press.

Levin, Harry. 1969. *The Myth of the Golden Age in the Renaissance*. New York: Oxford University Press.

Limón, José E. 1986. "La Llorona, the Third Legend of Greater Mexico: Cultural

Symbols, Women, and the Political Unconscious." *Renato Rosaldo Lecture Series Monograph*, vol. 2, series 1984–1985. Ed. Ignacio M. García. Tucson: University of Arizona, Mexican American Studies & Research Center. 59–93.

———. 1992. *Mexican Ballads, Chicano Poems: History and Influence in Mexican-American Social Poetry*. Berkeley: University of California Press.

———. 1994. *Dancing with the Devil: Society and Cultural Politics in Mexican-American South Texas*. Madison: University of Wisconsin Press.

———. 1998. *American Encounters: Greater Mexico, the United States, and the Erotics of Culture*. Boston: Beacon Press.

Lomelí, Francisco. 1980. "Eusebio Chacón: Eslabón temprano de la novela chicana." *La Palabra* 2.1: 45–55.

———. 1984. "An Overview of Chicano Letters: From Origins to Resurgence." In *Chicano Studies: A Multidisciplinary Approach*. Ed. Eugene García, Francisco Lomelí, and Isidro Ortiz. New York: Teachers College Press. 103–119.

Lone Star. 1996. Dir. John Sayles. Castle Rock.

López y Fuentes, Gregorio. 1933. *Tierra: La revolución agraria en México*. México, D.F.: Editorial México.

López-Gastón, José R. 1985. *La tradición hispánica de Nuevo México*. México, D.F.: Editorial Progreso.

Lucero-White, Aurora. 1936. "*Romances* and *Corridos* of New Mexico." Federal Writers Project of New Mexico.

Lummis, Charles F. 1879. *Birch Bark Poems*. Cambridge.

———. 1891. *A New Mexico David and Other Stories and Sketches of the Southwest*. New York: Charles Scribner's Sons.

———. 1892a. *Some Strange Corners of Our Country*. New York: Charles Scribner's Sons.

———. 1892b. *A Tramp Across the Continent*. New York: Charles Scribner's Sons.

———. 1893a. *The Land of Poco Tiempo*. New York: Charles Scribner's Sons.

———. 1893b. *The Spanish Pioneers*. Chicago: Charles McClurg.

———. 1898. *Awakening of a Nation: Mexico of Today*. New York: Charles Scribner's Sons.

———. 1925. *Mesa, Cañon and Pueblo*. New York: Century.

———. 1930. *Los exploradores españoles del siglo XVI: Vindicación de la acción colonizadora de España en América*. Trad. Arturo Cuyás. Barcelona: Editorial Araluce.

———. 1989. *Charles F. Lummis: Letters from the Southwest. Sept. 20, 1884–March 14, 1885*. Ed. James W. Byrkit. Tucson: University of Arizona Press.

Lummis Fiske, Turbesé, and Keith Lummis. 1975. *Charles F. Lummis: The Man and His West*. Norman: University of Oklahoma Press.

McCarthy, Adrian J. 1968. "Toward a Definition of Hopkins' 'Inscape.'" *University of Dayton Review* 4: 55–68.

Mckeen, William. 1991. *Hunter S. Thompson*. Boston: Twayne Publishers.

McWilliams, Carey. 1968. *North from Mexico: The Spanish-speaking People of the United States*. New York: Greenwood Reprint Edition.

Madsen, William. 1964. *The Mexican-Americans of South Texas*. New York: Holt, Rinehart and Winston.

Maldita Vecindad. 1993. *Gira pata de perro 93*. México, D.F.: Maldita Vecindad.

Mannheim, Karl. 1960. "The Utopian Mentality." In *Ideology and Utopia: An Introduction to the Sociology of Knowledge*. Trans. Louis Wirth and Edward Shils. New York: Harcourt Brace Jovanovich. 192–263.

Márquez, Antonio. 1982. "The Achievement of Rudolfo A. Anaya." In *The Magic of Words: Rudolfo A. Anaya and His Writings*. Ed. Paul Vassallo. Albuquerque: University of New Mexico Press. 33–52.

Mattelart, Michèle. 1977. *La cultura de la opresión femenina*. México, D.F.: Ediciones Era.

Menefee, Selden C. 1974. *Mexican Migratory Workers of South Texas*. Washington, D.C.: Government Printing Office, 1941. Reprinted in *Mexican Labor in the United States*. Ed. Carlos Cortes. New York: Arno Press.

Menéndez Pidal, Ramón. 1924. *Poesía juglaresca y juglares*. Madrid: Tipografía de la "Revista de los Archivos."

———. 1929. *La España del Cid*. Madrid: Editorial Plutarco.

Menton, Seymour. 1972. Review of ". . . y no se lo tragó la tierra." *Latin American Literary Review* 1.1: 111–115.

Meyer, Doris. 1979. "Felipe Maximiliano Chacón: A Forgotten Mexican-American Author." In *New Directions in Chicano Scholarship*. Ed. Ricardo Romo and Raymund Paredes. La Jolla: Chicano Studies Monograph Series, Chicano Studies Program, University of California, San Diego. 11–26.

Miller, Marjorie, and Juanita Darling. 1996. "The Eye of the Tiger: Emilio Azcárraga and the Televisa Empire." In *A Culture of Collusion: An Inside Look at the Mexican Press*. Ed. William A. Orme Jr. Miami: North-South Press, University of Miami. 59–70.

Monsiváis, Carlos. 1995. "Dreaming of Utopia." *NACLA, Report on the Americas* 29.3 (November–December): 39–41.

Montejano, David. 1987. *Anglos and Mexicans in the Making of Texas, 1836–1986*. Austin: University of Texas Press.

Moraga, Cherríe (L.). 1983. *Loving in the War Years: Lo que nunca pasó por sus labios*. Boston: South End Press.

———. 1993. *The Last Generation: Prose and Poetry*. Boston: South End Press.

———. 1997. *Waiting in the Wings: Portrait of a Queer Motherhood.* Ithaca, N.Y.: Firebrand Books.

———. 2000. *Loving in the War Years: Lo que nunca pasó por sus labios.* 2d ed. Cambridge, Mass.: South End Press.

Moraga, Cherríe, and Gloria Anzaldúa, eds. 1983. *This Bridge Called My Back: Writings by Radical Women of Color.* 2d ed. New York: Kitchen Table: Women of Color Press.

———. 2002. *This Bridge Called My Back: Writings by Radical Women of Color.* Exp. and rev. 3d ed. Women of Color Series. Berkeley: Third Woman Press.

Moraga, Cherríe, and Ana Castillo, eds. 1988. *Esta puente mi espalda: Voces de mujeres tercermundistas en los Estados Unidos.* Trad. Ana Castillo y Norma Alarcón. San Francisco: Ism Press.

Mullen, Harryette. 1996. "'A Silence Between Us Like a Language': The Untranslatability of Experience in Sandra Cisneros's *Woman Hollering Creek.*" *MELUS* 21.2: 3–20.

Ninth Annual International Desert Cavalcade. 1948. Presented by Calexico Winter Festival Association. Ed. Randall Henderson. Cover Art by Leonard Parker. El Centro, Calif.: Desert Magazine Press.

Olivares, Julián. 1990. "Los índices primitivos de . . . *y no se lo tragó la tierra* y cuatro estampas inéditas." *Crítica* 2.2: 208–222.

O'Neill, Ann W. 2000. "Latinos Are Underrepresented on County Grand Jury." *Los Angeles Times,* 26 March: B1, B7.

Otero-Warren, Nina. 1936. *Old Spain in Our Southwest.* New York: Harcourt, Brace and Company.

———. 1942. *Folk Songs of the Spanish Southwest.* Comp. Education Projects. War Services Program. Work Projects Administration, State of New Mexico.

La otra conquista. 1998. Dir. Salvador Carrasco. 20th Century-Fox México.

Padilla, Genaro. 1984. "A Reassessment of Fray Angélico Chávez's Fiction." *MELUS* 11.4: 31–45.

———. 1991. "Imprisoned Narrative? Lies, Secrets and Silence in New Mexico Women's Autobiography." In *Criticism in the Borderlands: Studies in Chicano Literature, Culture, and Ideology.* Ed. Héctor Calderón and José David Saldívar. Durham, N.C.: Duke University Press. 43–60.

———. 1993. *My History, Not Yours: The Formation of Mexican American Autobiography.* Madison: University of Wisconsin Press.

Paredes, Américo. 1942. "The Mexico-Texan Corrido." *Southwest Review* 27: 470–481.

———. 1958. *"With His Pistol in His Hand": A Border Ballad and Its Hero.* Austin: University of Texas Press.

———. 1966. "El Folklore de los grupos de origen mexicano en Estados Unidos." *Folklore Americano* 14: 146–163.

———. 1971. "Mexican Legendry and the Rise of the Mestizo: A Survey." In *American Folk Legend: A Symposium*. Ed. Wayland D. Hand. Berkeley: University of California Press. 97–107.

———. 1976. *A Texas-Mexican "Cancionero": Folk Songs of the Lower Border*. Urbana: University of Illinois Press.

———. 1979. "The Folk Base of Chicano Literature." In *Modern Chicano Writers*. Ed. Joseph Sommers and Tomás Ybarra-Frausto. Englewood Cliffs, N.J.: Prentice Hall. 4–17.

———. 1990. *George Washington Gómez*. Houston: Arte Público Press.

———. 1991. *Between Two Worlds*. Houston: Arte Público Press.

———. 1993a. *Folklore and Culture on the Texas-Mexican Border*. Ed. with introd. Richard Bauman. Austin: Center for Mexican American Studies, University of Texas, Austin.

———. 1993b. *Uncle Remus con chile*. Houston: Arte Público Press.

———. 1998. *The Shadow*. Houston: Arte Público Press.

Paredes, Raymund. 1977. "The Promise of Chicano Literature." In *Minority Language and Literature: Retrospective and Perspective*. Ed. Dexter Fisher. New York: Modern Language Association. 29–41.

———. 1982. "The Evolution of Chicano Literature." *MELUS* 5.2 (1978): 71–110. Rev. and expanded in *Three American Literatures: Essays in Chicano, Native-American, and Asian-American Literature for Teachers of American Literature*. Ed. Houston Baker Jr. New York: Modern Language Association. 33–79.

Paz, Octavio. 1950. "Máscaras mexicanas." *Cuadernos Americanos* 49.1 (enero–febrero): 79–92.

———. 1959. *El laberinto de la soledad*. México, D.F.: Fondo de Cultura Económica.

———. 1961. *The Labyrinth of Solitude: Life and Thought in Mexico*. Trans. Lysander Kemp. New York: Grove Press.

Pérez de Guzmán, Fernán. 1965. *Generaciones y semblanzas*. Ed. Robert Brian Tate. London: Tamesis Books.

Pérez-Linggi, Sandra M. 2001. "The *Nuevomexicano* Literary Tradition: From the Spanish Conquest to Statehood." Diss. University of California, Los Angeles.

Perry, Paul. 1992. *Fear and Loathing: The Strange and Terrible Saga of Hunter S. Thompson*. New York: Thunder's Mouth Press.

Plutarch. 1928. *Plutarch's Lives*. Trans. Bernadette Perrin. 11 vols. Loeb Classical Library Series. New York: G. P. Putnam's Sons. Vol. 7.

Poniatowska, Elena. 1969. *Hasta no verte, Jesús mío*. México, D.F.: Ediciones Era.

Preston, John. 1970. *The Created Self: The Reader's Role in Eighteenth-Century Fiction*. New York: Barnes & Noble.

Programa. 1998. *XXV Congreso, National Association for Chicana and Chicano Studies*. Centro Histórico de la Ciudad de México, 24–27 de junio.

"Proverbios de los antiguos zapotecos"/"Diidxagola binnigula'sa." 1999. In *Guie' sti' diidxazá/La flor de la palabra*. Estudio Introductorio y Selección de Víctor de la Cruz. México, D.F.: Universidad Autónoma de México, Centro de Investigaciones y Estudios Superiores en Antropología Social. 56–57.

Publicaciones del Archivo General de la Nación XIV—Estado General de las Fundaciones Hechas por Don José de Escandón en la Colonia del Nuevo Santander, Costa del Seno Mexicano. 1929. México, D.F.

Pulgar, Fernando del. 1971. *Claros varones de Castilla*. Ed. Robert Brian Tate. Oxford: Clarendon Press.

Rebolledo, Tey Diana. 1995. *Women Singing in the Snow*. Tucson: University of Arizona Press.

Restuccia, Frances L. 1996. "Literary Representations of Battered Women: Spectacular Domestic Punishment." In *Bodies of Writing, Bodies in Performance*. Ed. Thomas Foster, Carol Siegel, and Ellen E. Berry. *Gender* 23: 42–71.

Ríos-C., Herminio. 1971a. Letter to Tomás Rivera. 22 March. Tomás Rivera Archives. Tomás Rivera Library. University of California, Riverside.

———. 1971b. Letter to Tomás Rivera. 3 August. Tomás Rivera Archives. Tomás Rivera Library. University of California, Riverside.

Ripley, Anthony. 1970. "'Freak Power' Candidate May Be the Next Sheriff in Placid Aspen." *New York Times*, 19 October: 44.

Rivera, Tomás. 1970. Letter to Octavio I. Romano-V. 22 October. Tomás Rivera Archives. Tomás Rivera Library. University of California, Riverside.

———. 1971. "*. . . y no se lo tragó la tierra*"/"*. . . and the Earth Did Not Part*." Berkeley: Quinto Sol Publications.

———. 1975. "Recuerdo, Descubrimiento y Voluntad." Trans. Gustavo Valadez. *Atisbos* 1: 66–77.

———. 1982. "Chicano Literature: The Establishment of a Community." In *A Decade of Chicano Literature (1970–1979): Critical Essays and Bibliography*. Ed. Luis Leal et al. Santa Bárbara, Calif.: Editorial La Causa. 9–17.

———. 1984. "Richard Rodriguez' *Hunger of Memory* as Humanistic Antithesis." *MELUS* 11.4: 8–10.

———. 1987. *. . . y no se lo tragó la tierra/. . . and the earth did not devour him*. Trans. Evangelina Vigil-Piñón. Houston: Arte Público Press.

————. 1989. *The Harvest: Short Stories by Tomás Rivera*. Ed. and trans. Julián Olivares. Houston: Arte Público Press.

————. n.d. "COMMENTARY ABOUT: *And the Earth Did Not Part/. . . y no se lo tragó la tierra.*" Tomás Rivera Archives. Tomás Rivera Library. University of California, Riverside.

————. n.d. "Germination of Tierra." Tomás Rivera Archives. Tomás Rivera Library. University of California, Riverside.

————. n.d. Letter to Luis Dávila. Tomás Rivera Archives. Tomás Rivera Library. University of California, Riverside.

————. n.d. *TIERRA* manuscript. Original manuscript on *Tierra*. Tomás Rivera Archives. Tomás Rivera Library. University of California, Riverside.

Robbins, Henry, Editor, Alfred A. Knopf. 1962. Letter to Oscar Acosta. 1 November. Oscar Zeta Acosta Collection. Department of Special Collections. Davidson Library. University of California, Santa Barbara.

Roberts, Edwin. 1970. "Will Aspen's Hippies Elect a Sheriff?" *National Observer* 2 (November): 6.

Robles Arenas, J. Humberto. 1962. *Los desarraigados*. México, D.F.: Instituto de Bellas Artes, Departamento de Literatura.

Rodríguez, América. 1996. "Televisa North: Spanish Language News in the United States." In *A Culture of Collusion: An Inside Look at the Mexican Press*. Ed. William A. Orme Jr. Miami: North-South Press, University of Miami. 71–87.

Rodríguez, Juan. 1979. "Notes on the Evolution of Chicano Prose Fiction." In *Modern Chicano Writers: A Collection of Critical Essays*. Ed. Joseph Sommers and Tomás Ybarra-Frausto. Englewood Cliffs, N.J.: Prentice-Hall. 67–73.

————. 1980. "Jorge Ulica y Carlo de Medina: Escritores de la Bahía de San Francisco." *La Palabra* 2.1: 25–26.

Roffé, Reina. 1973. *Juan Rulfo: Autobiografía armada*. Buenos Aires: Ediciones Corregidor.

Romano-V., Octavio I. 1967a. "The Historical and Intellectual Presence of Mexican Americans." *Quinto Sol* 2.2: 32–46.

————. 1967b. "Minorities, History, and the Cultural Mystique." *Quinto Sol* 1.1: 5–11.

————. 1970. "Social Science, Objectivity, and the Chicanos." *Quinto Sol* 4.1: 4–16.

Romano-V., Octavio I., and Herminio Ríos-C. 1972. "Quinto Sol and Chicano Publications: The First Five Years (1967–1972)." *El Grito: A Journal of Contemporary Mexican American Thought* 5.4: 3–6.

Roosevelt, Franklin D. 1942. "The Four Freedoms Speech." Annual Message to Congress Delivered by Franklin D. Roosevelt on January 6, 1941. In *Voices of History: Great Speeches and Papers of the Year 1941.* Ed. Franklin Watts. New York: Franklin Watts. 5–13.

Rowling, Rebecca. 1998. "Tribute to Spaniard Renews War." *Los Angeles Times,* 17 May: B11.

Rulfo, Juan. 1953. *El llano en llamas.* México, D.F.: Fondo de Cultura Económica.

———. 1955. *Pedro Páramo.* México, D.F.: Fondo de Cultura Económica.

Saldívar, José David. 1985a. "The Ideological and the Utopian in Tomás Rivera's *y no se lo tragó la tierra* and Ron Arias' *The Road to Tamazunchale.*" *Crítica* 1.2: 100–114.

———. 1985b. "Our Southwest: An Interview with Rolando Hinojosa." In *The Rolando Hinojosa Reader: Essays Historical and Critical.* Ed. José David Saldívar. Houston: Arte Público Press. 180–190.

———. 1985c. "Rolando Hinojosa's *Klail City Death Trip*: A Critical Introduction." In *The Rolando Hinojosa Reader: Essays Historical and Critical.* Ed. José David Saldívar. Houston: Arte Público Press. 44–63.

———. 1991a. "Chicano Border Narratives as Cultural Critique." In *Criticism in the Borderlands: Studies in Chicano Literature, Culture, and Ideology.* Ed. Héctor Calderón and José David Saldívar. Durham, N.C.: Duke University Press. 167–180.

———. 1991b. *The Dialectics of Our America: Genealogy, Cultural Critique, and Literary History.* Durham, N.C.: Duke University Press.

———. 1993. "Américo Paredes and Decolonization." In *Cultures of U.S. Imperialism.* Ed. Amy Kaplan and Donald E. Pease. Durham, N.C.: Duke University Press. 292–311.

Saldívar, Ramón. 1979. "A Dialectic of Difference: Towards a Theory of the Chicano Novel." *MELUS* 6.3: 73–92.

———. 1990. *Chicano Narrative: The Dialectics of Difference.* Madison: University of Wisconsin Press.

———. 1993. "The Borderlands of Culture: Américo Paredes's *George Washington Gómez* and Chicano Literature at the End of the Twentieth Century." *American Literary History* 5.2: 272–293.

Saldívar-Hull, Sonia. 1991. "Feminism on the Border: From Gender Politics to Geopolitics." In *Criticism in the Borderlands: Studies in Chicano Literature, Culture and Ideology.* Ed. Héctor Calderón and José David Saldívar. Durham, N.C.: Duke University Press. 203–220.

———. 1999. Introduction. In *Borderlands/La Frontera: The New Mestiza* by Gloria Anzaldúa. 2d ed. San Francisco: Aunt Lute Books. 1–15.

———. 2000. *Feminism on the Border: Chicana Gender Politics and Literature.* Berkeley: University of California Press.

Sarmiento, Domingo Faustino. 1977. *Vida de Juan Facundo Quiroga, o Civilización y barbarie*. México, D.F.: Porrúa.

Scholes, Robert. 1964. "Joyce and the Epiphany: The Key to the Labyrinth?" *Sewanee Review* 77: 65–77.

Schroeder, Albert H. 1972. "Rio Grande Ethnohistory." In *New Perspectives on the Pueblos*. Ed. Alfonso Ortiz. Albuquerque: University of New Mexico Press. 41–70.

Sheridan, Mary Beth, and Jocelyn Y. Stewart. 2000. "Mexican Candidates' Visits Highlight California Clout." *Los Angeles Times*, 9 May: A3, A30.

Silva-Herzog Márquez, Jesús. 1999. "Voting at a Distance." *Voices of Mexico* 46: 11–12.

Smith, Cecil, Executive Director, Macmillan Company. 1962. Letter to Oscar Acosta. 27 December. Oscar Zeta Acosta Collection. Department of Special Collections. Davidson Library. University of California, Santa Barbara.

Sommers, Joseph. 1979. "From the Critical Premise to the Product: Critical Modes and Their Application to a Chicano Literary Text." In *New Directions in Chicano Scholarship*. Ed. Ricardo Romo and Raymund Paredes. La Jolla: Chicano Studies Monograph Series, Chicano Studies Program, University of California, San Diego. 51–80.

Sotelo Inclán, Jesús. 1943. *Raíz y razón de Zapata*. México, D.F.: Editorial Etnos.

Stavans, Ilan. 1995. *Bandido: Oscar "Zeta" Acosta and the Chicano Experience*. New York: IconEditions, an imprint of HarperCollins Publishers.

Thompson, Hunter S. 1971a. *Fear and Loathing in Las Vegas: A Savage Journey to the Heart of the American Dream*. New York: Popular Library.

———. 1971b. "Strange Rumblings in Aztlan." *Rolling Stone,* 29 April: 30–37.

———. 1977. "The Banshee Screams for Buffalo Meat: Fear and Loathing in the Graveyard of the Weird." *Rolling Stone,* 15 December: 48–59.

———. 1979a. "The Kentucky Derby Is Decadent and Depraved." In *The Great Shark Hunt: Strange Tales from a Strange Time*. New York: Warner Books. 23–40.

———. 1979b. "What Lured Hemingway to Ketchum?" In *The Great Shark Hunt: Strange Tales from a Strange Time*. New York: Warner Books. 429–434.

———. 1979c. "When the Beatniks Were Social Lions." In *The Great Shark Hunt: Strange Tales from a Strange Time*. New York: Warner Books. 460–464.

———. 1998. *The Rum Diary*. New York: Simon and Schuster.

Torri, Julio. 1917. *Ensayos y poemas*. México, D.F.: Porrúa.

———. 1940. *De fusilamientos*. México, D.F.: Casa de España en España.

Ulibarrí, Sabine, and Dick Gerdes. 1978. "Mexican Literature and Chicano Literature: A Comparison." In *Ibero-American Letters in a Comparative Perspective*. Ed. Wolodymyr T. Zyla and Wendell M. Aycock. Proceedings of the Comparative Literature Symposium, vol. 10. 26–28 January. Lubbock: Texas Tech Press. 149–167.

U.S. Department of Justice. 1970. Federal Bureau of Investigation. Southern Christian Leadership Conference. Racial Matters. Los Angeles, California. 1 June. 3 pp. Oscar Zeta Acosta Collection. Department of Special Collections. Davidson Library. University of California, Santa Barbara.

Valdez, Luis, and El Teatro Campesino. 1971. *Actos*. San Juan Bautista, Calif.: Cucaracha Press.

Vasconcelos, José. 1937a. *La tormenta: Segunda Parte de Ulises criollo*. Sexta Edición. México, D.F.: Ediciones Botas.

———. 1937b. *Ulises criollo: Vida del autor escrita por el mismo*. Octava Edición. México: Ediciones Botas.

———. 1948. *La raza cósmica*. México, D.F.: Espasa Calpe.

Webb, Walter Prescott. 1965. *The Texas Rangers: A Century of Frontier Defense*. Austin: University of Texas Press.

Williams, Raymond. 1973. *The Country and the City*. New York: Oxford University Press.

———. 1977. *Marxism and Literature*. Oxford: Oxford University Press.

Wilson, Diana de Armas. 2000. *Cervantes, the Novel, and the New World*. Oxford: Oxford University Press.

Wisconsin Death Trip. 2001. Dir. James Marsh. BBC Arena/Cinemax.

Womack, John. 1968. *Zapata and the Mexican Revolution*. New York: Alfred A. Knopf.

Yarbro-Bejarano, Yvonne. 2001. *The Wounded Heart: Writings on Cherríe Moraga*. Austin: University of Texas Press.

Ybarra-Frausto, Tomás. 1979. "The Chicano Movement and the Emergence of a Chicano Poetic Consciousness." In *New Directions in Chicano Scholarship*. Ed. Ricardo Romo and Raymund Paredes. La Jolla: Chicano Studies Monograph Series, Chicano Studies Program, University of California, San Diego. 81–109.

PERMISSIONS
ACKNOWLEDGMENTS

Grateful acknowledgment is made to the following for use of previously published and unpublished materials:

A portion of Chapter 1 appeared originally as "Reinventing the Border" in *American Mosaic: Multicultural Readings in Context*, 554–563. Ed. Barbara Roche Rico and Sandra Mano. Boston: Houghton Mifflin, 1991. It is reprinted by permission of Houghton Mifflin.

Part of Chapter 2 was previously published as "Rudolfo Anaya's *Bless Me, Ultima*. A Chicano Romance of the Southwest," *Crítica* 1.3 (1986): 21–47, and is reprinted with permission of Rosaura Sánchez for *Crítica*.

Part of Chapter 3 was previously published as "The Novel and the Community of Readers: Rereading Tomás Rivera's *Y no se lo tragó la tierra*" in *Criticism in the Borderlands: Studies in Chicano Literature, Culture, and Ideology*, 97–113. Ed. Héctor Calderón and José David Saldívar. Durham, N.C.: Duke University Press, 1991. It is reprinted with permission of Duke University Press.

Lines from Sandra Cisneros's "Original Sin" from *Loose Woman*. Copyright © 1994 by Sandra Cisneros. Pubished by Vintage Books, a division of Random House, Inc., and originally in hardcover by Alfred A. Knopf, Inc. (1994). Reprinted by permission of Susan Bergholz Literary Services, New York. All rights reserved. "Original Sin" was first published in *Emergency Tacos* by March/ Abrazo Press (1989).

Excerpt from *Gira pata de perro 93* appears by permission of Maldita Vecindad.

Excerpt from "LimIts of the Border," an unpublished manuscript by Houston A. Baker Jr., is printed by permission of the author.

Excerpts from correspondence and e-mail from Rolando Hinojosa-Smith appear by permission of the author.

Excerpts from the unpublished manuscript "My Wicked Wicked Ways: The Chicana Writer's Struggle with Good and Evil or Las Hijas de la Malavida" and e-mail from Sandra Cisneros appear by permission of Susan Bergholz Literary Services on behalf of the author.

Citations from Oscar Zeta Acosta's personal papers and materials from the Oscar Zeta Acosta Collection, Department of Special Collections, Davidson Library, University of California, Santa Barbara, appear by permission of Marco Acosta. Other citations from Acosta's personal papers appear by permission of Marco Acosta.

Citations from manuscripts and correspondence from the Tomás Rivera Archives, Tomás Rivera Libary, University of California, Riverside, appear by permission of Mrs. Concha Rivera.

INDEX

CPSIA information can be obtained
at www.ICGtesting.com
Printed in the USA
FSOW01n2126101117
40917FS